Detaining Time

Also Available From Bloomsbury

Evil: A History in Modern French Literature and Thought, Damian Catani
The New Human in Literature, Mads Rosendahl Thomsen
Philosophy and Literature in Times of Crisis, Michael Mack

Detaining Time

Temporal Resistance in Literature from Shakespeare to McEwan

Eric P. Levy

Bloomsbury Academic
An imprint of Bloomsbury Publishing Plc

BLOOMSBURY
LONDON · OXFORD · NEW YORK · NEW DELHI · SYDNEY

Bloomsbury Academic
An imprint of Bloomsbury Publishing Plc

50 Bedford Square	1385 Broadway
London	New York
WC1B 3DP	NY 10018
UK	USA

www.bloomsbury.com

BLOOMSBURY and the Diana logo are trademarks of Bloomsbury Publishing Plc

First published 2016

© Eric P. Levy, 2016

Eric P. Levy has asserted his right under the Copyright, Designs and Patents Act, 1988, to be identified as Author of this work.

All rights reserved. No part of this publication may be reproduced or transmitted in any form or by any means, electronic or mechanical, including photocopying, recording, or any information storage or retrieval system, without prior permission in writing from the publishers.

No responsibility for loss caused to any individual or organization acting on or refraining from action as a result of the material in this publication can be accepted by Bloomsbury or the author.

British Library Cataloguing-in-Publication Data
A catalogue record for this book is available from the British Library.

ISBN: HB: 978-1-4742-9204-7
ePDF: 978-1-4742-9206-1
ePub: 978-1-4742-9205-4

Library of Congress Cataloging-in-Publication Data
A catalog record for this book is available from the Library of Congress.

Cover design: Eleanor Rose
Cover image © Paul Mellon Collection

Typeset by Newgen Knowledge Works (P) Ltd., Chennai, India
Printed and bound in Great Britain

Dedicated to Ross Labrie.

Contents

Acknowledgments	ix
Introduction	1
1 The Mimesis of Time in *Hamlet*	27
2 Dickens's Pathology of Time in *Hard Times*	51
3 Time and Metempsychosis in *Ulysses*	67
4 "the horror of the moment": Fear and Acceptance of Time in *Mrs. Dalloway*	85
5 The Phenomenology of Temporal Trauma in *To the Lighthouse*	111
6 The Beckettian Mimesis of Post-Temporal Time	135
7 Postlapsarian Will and the Problem of Time in Ian McEwan's *Enduring Love*	153
8 Further Perspectives: Explication of Gilles Deleuze's Temporal Theory	177
9 Further Perspectives: Application of Gilles Deleuze's Temporal Theory	197
Epilogue: Time and Agency	215
Notes	237
Works Cited	247
Index	267

Acknowledgments

I am grateful to two colleagues at the University of British Columbia – Professors Emeriti Ross Labrie and Steven Savitt. The former unstintingly supported my compositional efforts with the patience and perspicuity of a great friend and scholar. The latter, with exceptional generosity and good will, introduced me to and guided my initial steps through McTaggarts's temporal philosophy. I wish also thank Professor Robin Le Poidevin at the University of Leeds, Professor Philip Turetzky at Colorado State University, and Professor Clifford Williams at Wheaton College for their assistance in clarifying, via e-mail, various issues in the philosophy of time which perplexed me. I wish also to thank the anonymous readers, commissioned by Bloomsbury Academic, for many helpful suggestions. Finally, I owe much to the staff at Bloomsbury, and want particularly to mention the three experts there with whom I communicated most frequently: Mr. James Tupper, Senior Production Editor, Mr. Mark Richardson, Assistant Editor, Literary Studies, and Mr. Srikanth Srinivasan, Copy Editor.

Parts of this book were previously published in modified form in the following journals, all of which have graciously granted permission to reprint: "The Mimesis of Time in *Hamlet*," *Philological Quarterly* 86.4 (2007): 365–392; "Dickens' Pathology of Time in *Hard Times*," *Philological Quarterly* 74.2 (1995): 189–207; "The Mimesis of Metempsychosis in Ulysses," *Philological Quarterly* 81.3 (Summer, 2002): 359–77; "The Beckettian Mimesis of Time," *University of Toronto Quarterly* 80.1 (2011): 89–107; Postlapsarian Will and the Problem of Time in Ian McEwan's *Enduring Love*," *Renascence: Essays on Values in Literature* 61.3 (Spring 2009): 167–189.

Introduction

*Man flies from time, and time from man, too soon
In sad divorce this double flight must end.*
                    Edward Young, "Night Thoughts"

Have you not done tormenting me with your accursed time!
                    Samuel Beckett, Waiting for Godot

Time beating away like a meat ax.
                    Henry Miller, Tropic of Cancer

In a dream one night in 1981, I suddenly awoke to find a demonic old man, his face blank and pitiless, poised beside my bed. The next instant, he raised his right hand, wielding a knife, and plunged it toward my chest. Before thought could prompt me, I thrust out my left hand and grasped his wrist, stopping the attack. Then I awoke for real.[1] What did this dream mean? On the one hand, it evokes Shakespeare's observation in Sonnet 12: "And nothing 'gainst Time's scythe can make defence" (1942, 1373). Mortality cannot dispute this truth. Every life—indeed, every current circumstance—must eventually end. But on the other hand, the dream contradicts this truth, for in it the knife of extermination, which would cut off or cut short that which has endured, is arrested and forestalled. Thus the dream represents, almost like an archetype, a fundamental human response to the problem of time: the reflex to obstruct temporal passage, because it is viewed negatively as a menace to life and what is cherished in life.

Literature abounds in depictions of the conviction that the anisotropy or one-way forward movement of time occasions pain. A searingly poignant formulation appears in Aldous Huxley's *Antic Hay* in reference to a night of chaste intimacy enjoyed by two characters, Gumbril and Emily: "For them there were no more minutes. But time passed, time passed flowing in a dark stream, staunchlessly, as though from some profound mysterious wound in the world's side, bleeding,

bleeding for ever" (1923, 146). This metaphor of the passage of time as blood flowing "staunchlessly" from an irremediable wound epitomizes the association of temporal passage with the suffering of loss and depletion. However, the notion of redemption is implicit in this metaphor, since the wound in the world's side, from which issues the blood of time, corresponds to the wound opened in Christ's side by the *longche* or lance of the centurion Longinus during the Crucifixion. This combination of wound and redemption—temporal passage as both the cause of pain and the means by which such suffering, through deepened understanding, is overcome—informs many literary texts, and finds perhaps its most lapidary expression in T. S. Eliot's "Burnt Norton": "Only through time time is conquered" (1963, 192). A trenchant expression of the struggle with time, bereft of such reconciliation, occurs in Herman Melville's *Pierre: or, The Ambiguities*: "Oh, what a quenchless feud is this, that Time hath with the sons of men!" (1852, 8).

The literary representation of time has received extensive scholarly attention, involving manifold approaches.[2] The present investigation is the first to focus on and analyze the project, depicted variously in diverse texts, to reconstitute or reconceptualize time, so that its movement no longer threatens security. The pathos of passage—the notion that temporality entails pain—displays extraordinary diversity of expression and consequence. The nature and ideational content of the pain vary according to the text concerned—and sometimes, in further differentiation, according to the characters concerned. But in each case, the passage of time is construed as a cause of suffering or distress. The perception of temporal passage as a source of pain activates or provokes countervailing strategies, practices, or modes of attention whose purpose is to ward off and protect against the threat posed by temporality. Ironically, the defensive constructions respectively deployed in various texts only aggravate and complicate the temporal distress they seek to alleviate. Yet that very futility enables fructification. For in all these texts, except those comprising the Beckettian oeuvre, a new conceptualization of time eventually emerges, whereby the individual is reconciled to the inescapable impingement of temporality and redeemed from counterproductive—and ultimately self-destructive—attempts to deny, resist, avenge, or alter it. In this regard, the texts concerned achieve perhaps their greatest profundity—each in a different way and with different implications.

Ironically, though time, in the celebrated literary texts to be examined, is an urgent focus of concern, the most important ways of responding to it—and the ones that perhaps most illumine the reader's world—proceed beneath conscious awareness. For example, in *Hamlet* the deeper purpose of the revenge morality to forestall the threat regarding the movement of time toward the future by subjecting the present to the authority or primacy of the past is not recognized in the world of the play. Hence, investigation requires a mode of analysis equipped to penetrate beneath the textual surface in order to uncover and explicate both the nature and the consequences of resistance to the anisotropy or one-way forward movement of time. That method can be described as *tomographic*, as it entails examining selected texts from different angles and at varying depths in order to disclose their temporal orientation more completely. The approach entails three distinct perspectives, sequentially pursued. The first concerns analyzing, in separate chapters, each literary text in terms of its own content, sometimes with the assistance of various philosophies of time. Here I address the *singularity* of each text in order to enable its sui generis or distinctive representation of time—its representation, more precisely, of experience challenged by temporal awareness—to emerge whole and sound, as a difficult birth is aided by the cautious use of forceps and a speculum.

In this section, as elsewhere in the study, the deployment of concepts forged in philosophy facilitates inquiry into the temporal structures of experience respectively represented in selected literary texts, even as the investigation shows how these structures violate and constitute alternatives to the temporal orders propounded in philosophy. The philosophical theories of time applied here include those of Aristotle, Immanuel Kant, Henri Bergson, John McTaggart, C. D. Broad, and Edmund Husserl. My aim is not to proffer what Gregory Currie labels "a literary philosophy of time," but instead to investigate confrontations with time in literature through detailed examination of diverse literary texts, aided, when appropriate, by detailed explication and application of several philosophical theories of time (1999, 61). Philosophy is invoked not to reduce literary texts to demonstrations of extant temporal theories, but to provide analysis with conceptual clarity and precision, enabling the formulation and unfolding of insights inaccessible otherwise. Through what J. N. Findlay terms its "notional diction," philosophy enables "a deepening of our conceptual grasp" by subjecting the concepts with which we think to rigorous testing and evaluation, in order to, as Broad indicates, "determine their precise meanings and their mutual relations" (Findlay 1958, 20, 79; Broad 1952, 16).[3] Hegel encapsulates the link between philosophy and precision: "Philosophising requires, above all, that each thought should be grasped in its full precision and that nothing should remain vague and indeterminate" (1991, 127–28 [§80]).

Consideration of philosophical theory enables clarification of conceptual novelty in literature, beyond the reaches of the theories concerned. Far from construing literary texts as versions of philosophical theory, the study, where appropriate, harnesses theory in order to disclose the unique and original contributions of literary practice. However, the primary modality of inquiry concerns literary analysis conducted through close reading of the texts concerned. Some chapters rely almost exclusively on this modality, without extensive reference to philosophical theory.

The second perspective from which the literary texts are examined concerns the temporal philosophy of Gilles Deleuze—a twentieth-century French philosopher whose work, though influential and increasingly popular, is often misunderstood. In Chapter 8 of this book, I first provide a thorough explication of both his own theory and the Kantian roots from which it springs, illustrating difficult points by means of literary examples and counterexamples. Then, in Chapter 9, I apply Deleuzian principles to the analysis of the texts already investigated in Chapters 1 through 7. The emphasis on Deleuze seeks not to accord his temporal theory primacy over others, but instead to extend, deepen, and enrich my discussion of literary confrontations with time, by highlighting aspects of the literary texts invisible otherwise, whether these elements accord or conflict with Deleuze's constructions.

The third investigative perspective emerges in the Epilogue, where I again examine the literary texts, but this time in terms of the relation between time and agency. Here, complete, alternate, and extremely compact interpretations of the texts concerned focus on further implications of being in time—in this case, at the level of unfolding self-determination. Ordinarily, analyses of agency take time for granted. But, in the literary texts under examination, characterization of time is crucial to agency, and the process of securing proper relation to time, proceeding differently in each text, ultimately frees (except in the Beckettian oeuvre) agency from a crucial factor undermining its own power of self-direction.

Having introduced my method, I turn now to the texts treated. *Hamlet, Hard Times, Ulysses, Mrs. Dalloway, To the Lighthouse*, a wide range of Beckettian texts, and *Enduring Love*. Insofar as literary texts represent experience, they necessarily deal with time or what E. M. Forster refers to as "life in time" (1927, 29). Paul Ricoeur makes a useful distinction between (narrative) texts that entail depiction of time and those that explicitly foreground and examine time. The former category is labeled "tales of time," the latter, "tales about time" (1985, 2.101).[4] My own choice of texts concerns a more narrowly defined category whose taxonomic or classifying principle involves the struggle against and, in most cases, reaffirmation of temporal passage. A further criterion of selection, within this category, concerns *intensity* of involvement with time. In the chosen texts, such involvement is an urgent and vital concern, at the core of personal identity and sense of self (or, in the Beckettian case, flight from self). The texts selected for extended treatment in separate chapters are distinguished by their challenging, relentless, original, and dramatic representation of struggle with temporal passage. Of course, these texts, drawn from British and Irish literature and conforming to my primary areas of literary research, are not the only eligible candidates. But since books, like life, have finite length, I could not adequately discuss all the literary texts, in the regional areas just mentioned, that most fully, vividly, and searchingly explore the confrontation with time. In short, as my study aims to be propaedeutic, not definitive—to beckon readers toward further investigation, not to confine them within a rigid summa—I chose texts whose explication seemed most likely to fulfill my instructional purpose. For this reason, I include two Virginia Woolf novels, as that author displays extraordinary range, power, and depth in her treatment of the agon with time.

As Keith Faulkner notes, "Time faces us like a problem: we do not control it, it controls us" (2006, 1). In the literary texts engaging my study, awareness of time impinges on lived experience, regardless of readiness and capacity to achieve appropriate or authentic accommodation (the technical philosophical term is *adequation*) to it—to come to terms, that is, with an aspect of reality contrary to personal preferences, without distorting either one's own intrinsic nature or one's inalienable predicament as a temporal being. The more time is viewed as a factor to be controlled, the more life is beset by destructive patterns of thought and behavior. Indeed, in *Hamlet* and *Hard Times*, as we shall discover, for example, the content and insistence of dominant social norms (revenge morality in the former, mechanization of both work and calculation in the latter) stem from the unacknowledged but relentless project to control the anisotropy of time, as do prominent psychological fixations (grief, in Hamlet's case, and inability to imagine a future different from the present, in Louisa's).

In both these works, temporal awareness is *tragic*, because attempts to redeem it from inveterate limitation are doomed to failure, even in the achievement of success. In *Hamlet* (probed in Chapter 1), delay ironically provides Hamlet with time to pass through a complex series of steps in the arduous process of reconceptualizing the passage of time, and achieving breakthrough to a different temporal dispensation, wherein the movement of time toward the future, instead of provoking fear and the defensive reflex to perpetuate the past, now unfolds the purpose of the past beyond prior understanding of it. Yet with his death, the world of the play resumes or, more precisely, continues (since only Hamlet participated in this reconceptualizing process) to run on its metalled ways of one-track thinking about time. Central to this analysis of the play is the bipartite structure of time—its passage or movement construed according to two distinct series. In one, time is configured as the dimension of changing tense (future to present to past). In the other, time entails the tenseless dimension of permanent succession, whereby events are arrayed in an inviolable sequence according to whether they are earlier than, simultaneous with, or later than each other. Careful examination of these distinct series (termed, respectively, the *A*-series and *B*-series by the philosopher John McTaggart) discloses a level of meaning in *Hamlet* inaccessible otherwise.

In *Hard Times* (treated in Chapter 2), temporal tragedy is less irremediable. Though some characters never achieve enlightenment, and one character (Stephen Blackpool) dies in the course of enlightening himself and others, by the end of the novel, the community that comes together in the attempt to save Stephen (from his fall to the bottom of a mining shaft) undergoes a revolution in temporal awareness occasioned and symbolized by the mechanics of the rescue attempt. Time is "hard" in the novel because the (unconscious) project to forestall the temporal ills that flesh is heir to (in the mode of senescence and decline), prompts formation of a dystopic regime (Coketown) in which temporal continuity is reduced to repetition compulsion, wherein each new moment, instead of extending the duration constituted by its predecessors, is severed from them, with the result that time both begins and ends in each instant. Through "self-suppression," which ironically includes stifling awareness of the imposed temporal regime, self-interest ultimately engenders self-destruction (Dickens 1969, 195, 303).

In *Ulysses* (analyzed in Chapter 3), the anisotropy of time displays the additional property of *concussion*—"Time shocked rebounds, shock by shock"—such that temporal continuity, as experienced on the individually developmental level, is punctuated by "convulsions of metamorphosis"—a condition that provokes countervailing and self-stifling reactions, respectively, in Stephen and Bloom, by which to forestall transformative entry into the next phase until selfhood has grown strong enough to forswear the security offered by dwelling in the past, and achieve readiness to meet the challenges of a transformed present (1992, 40, 817). The hallmark of Joycean metempsychosis concerns the coexistence of contrary tendencies in the same character: (a) the prior or inveterate self, which resists rupture with the past, and (b) the ensuing or emergent self, which accepts, and even seeks, movement toward a different future. The task of successfully achieving metempsychosis is complicated by what might be termed "specular selfhood": the tendency of character to see that which is experienced as a reflection of its own sense of identity. Perception becomes self-reflection, and the self thus reflected is bound to the inveterate one. To move beyond such fixation, a new relation between time and selfhood must be devised—one entailing acknowledgment of participation in a larger process or continuity than that encompassed by self-reference.

In *Mrs. Dalloway* (discussed in Chapter 4), resistance to the anisotropy of time leads to heterogeneous temporal experience, such that discordant temporalities coexist in the same awareness: isochronal time (characterized by division into equal units whose regular and inviolable succession offers the illusion of security amid temporal flux) and durational time (characterized not only by Bergsonian prolongation of the past into the present, but also more importantly by the vulnerability of any present moment to inundation by temporal flow, through an inability to detach emotionally from the remembered past or to accept elapse of a treasured present). Here, though temporally sensitive characters remain vulnerable to "the horror of the moment," they can ultimately accept temporal passage by recognizing—indeed experiencing—that its consequence is an enriched "power of feeling" (Woolf 1992, 8, 212). Instead of Vitruvian Man, inscribed in a circle, the novel presents what might be termed *Big Ben Man*, contained within the "leaden circles" propagated by Big Ben's bells, that ultimately function as barriers, shielding experience from the "shocks of suffering" (145) occasioned by exposure to unregulated temporality. Extrication from these circles—or, more precisely, from the need to be protected by them—is one aspect of the great temporal challenge in the novel. It entails empowerment to live exposed to temporal flow, in full acceptance of "the process of living" (203).

In *To the Lighthouse* (examined in Chapter 5), the anisotropy of time is ultimately represented as a brutal, leviathan force spreading disaster and chaos through the tragic momentum of its passage—a movement so devastating that, to those enduring its ravages, temporal flux entails not orderly succession, but recurrence of disorder and mayhem. In these circumstances, reconstituting the sense of order in time entails summoning and harnessing the creative use of memory or, more precisely, retrospective perspective to compose recollected fragments into a reformulated whole that the movement of time both enables and inevitably shatters. Like the future, the past is a zone of becoming. Yet whereas the future is a zone of becoming because nothing in it has yet happened, in the novel the past is a zone of becoming because everything in it has already occurred. This is a central paradox in the novel—one whose explication is facilitated by the application of carefully explained concepts derived from Broad and

Husserl: concepts that illumine *To the Lighthouse* even as they entail philosophical assumptions contrary to those prevailing in the novel.

Enduring Love (analyzed in Chapter 7), opens with an extraordinarily vivid account of the anisotropy of time, construed here as the passage of seconds and even nanoseconds in the course of a fatal attempt to rescue a boy stranded in the gondola of an errant touring balloon. Thus foregrounded at the outset of the novel as a source of trauma, the anisotropy of time is sequentially linked with a variety of issues, culminating in interrogating the scope and efficacy of the human will—ultimately its *willingness* to will, aware that action, by precipitating consequences to be encountered in the future, threatens to increase the traumatizing potency of temporal movement. By contrast, the Beckettian mimesis of time (discussed in Chapter 6), deploys a range of tactics to replace the anisotropy of time with what might be called a post-temporal dispensation, where the mutability attendant on temporal flux is replaced by various states of "changelessness," such that the continuity of time sustains "one enormous second" ("Texts for Nothing" 1967a, 118, 82). At bottom, time is demoted to illusion, in order to sustain a mentality or cognitive orientation toward experience that repudiates change and the vicissitudes of transient circumstance.

These brief comments on the literary texts to be treated serve as aids to orientation only, and do *not* constitute chapter summaries. The representation of time in literature concerns the representation not just of awareness *of* time, but also the unfolding of that awareness *in* time. Hence, that which, through critical explication, is cumulatively understood about this representation cannot, without loss or distortion, be detached from the steps leading to and involved in such understanding. Brief summaries cannot capture this intricate process driven by diverse factors, each offering its own contribution and requiring distinct analysis, but instead tends to convert process into product or result.

The commitment informing my approach is to sustain direct and detailed engagement with literary texts, through adjusting exegetical focus and tactics to the intricacy of each text considered. It is a commitment that can be easily misconstrued if the reader approaches my study with expectations conditioned by a prevailing tendency in contemporary criticism to subordinate texts to theory. In prioritizing the individuality of each text, my inquiry does not entail the application of, or quest for, literary theory, whereby individual texts are treated as confirmations of a generalizing thesis about literature. Nor should my references to philosophical theory be construed as an attempt to reduce literary texts to a set of propositions drawn from a different discipline. Though my inquiry into the literary representation of time deploys philosophical theory, it avoids the subordination of literary texts to such theory for reasons that brief elaboration will clarify.

The moment theory enters the scene, what is seen or noted is immediately restricted. As Alfred North Whitehead remarks, theory is "content to understand the complete fact in respect to only some of the essential aspects" (1961a, 146). For example, if we want to formulate a theory of momentum, we must abstract mass and velocity from all the other properties of individual bodies that move. Philosophical theories of temporal awareness proceed by generalization. That is, by abstracting the universal elements of temporal awareness—elements applicable to every experience of time, regardless of its particular content—such theories enable precise delineation of what temporal awareness fundamentally and indispensably entails—at least from the theoretical perspective analyzing it. Pozzo's pronouncement on human life in Beckett's *Waiting for Godot* inadvertently parodies the recourse of temporal theory to generalization:

> [O]ne day we were born, one day we shall die, the same day, the same second.... They give birth astride of a grave, the light gleams an instant, then it's night once more. (1954, 57)

In effect, Pozzo here enunciates a theory of human time through isolating certain features that all lives share in common while omitting everything else. Each life is bracketed by birth and death, as in Thomas Nashe's *The Unfortunate Traveller* (1594): "Whatsoever is born is born to have an end" (1964, 252).[5] With Pozzo, the interval between those markers, filled with *particular* experience and event, is left out of consideration, with the result that time itself—human time as registered by the individual enduring in it—is bereft of significance and even reality: "the same day, the same second."[6] In formulating his view, Pozzo employs the first principle of theory, abstractive generalization, which entails deliberate narrowness of perspective in order to consider particulars in terms of a common factor or form. His tendency to obliterate particulars through recourse to generalization foregrounds, and indeed almost satirizes, the risk of distortion inherent in the application of theory—a risk noted by the celebrated Belgian medievalist Henri Pirenne: "But I have been careful not to resort to theories, lest I should do violence to the facts" (1936, v).[7]

In this context, a vital question arises: how is temporal theory to be applied to the literary mimesis of time without thereby subordinating the particularity of a given text to the generalities that theory propounds? On the one hand, application of philosophical theory to literary texts, if improperly conducted, risks reducing those texts to formulations alien to them. On the other hand, probing the literary representation of time without recourse to precise notions honed in philosophy risks missing the conceptual depth of the texts treated. The solution is twofold: first to ensure compatibility between theory and text, and second to clarify (a) the degree to which the configuration of time in the text diverges from the paradigm propounded by the theory and (b) the consequences of its doing so.

The privileging of theory is just one misleading expectation that some readers might bring to perusal of the current study. Given the topic and the chronological range of texts treated, it might also be assumed that my approach is historical, and that my project is to provide—or devise—a developmental analysis of the literary representation of time, with respect to resistance to temporal passage. At this point, a can of worms snaps open—one that I shall endeavor firmly to close, leaving better fisherman than I to bait their hooks with the contents. Historical analysis of the literary representation of time—the attempt, well formulated by G. J. Whitrow, to put "time itself into temporal perspective" (1988, vii) by generalizing the notion(s) of time expressed in the literature of a given era—is a popular but treacherous enterprise. Though accurate historical generalizations can illumine, inaccurate ones can mislead. For this reason A. L. Rowse, the great historian of Elizabethan England, counsels caution: "It is not merely hazardous to generalize—generalizations are apt to commit one to untruths" (1950, 222).

There are two risks associated with historical generalization. The first concerns invalidity; the second concerns influence. Regarding invalidity, historical generalizations are often vulnerable to refutation by counterexamples. Moreover, to argue that a given attitude toward time begins with a certain era or at a certain date conversely requires that the attitude did *not* exist before the era or date in question. Hence, such arguments unwittingly entail the attempt to prove a negative—a perilous enterprise that, to achieve logical validity, must establish incontrovertibly not just absence of evidence but also evidence of absence (of such evidence). As Chris Wickham, an outstanding historian of the Early Middle Ages, observes: "It is hard to prove negatives, and tempting to talk away ambiguous evidence" (2005, 284). The second risk of historical generalization entails the dissemination of misconceptions that can influence subsequent studies of the period and texts concerned. In *The Culture of Time and Space: 1880–1918*, Stephen Kern acknowledges the need for accuracy in generalization so that misleading claims do not proliferate: "But if one is to make generalizations about the culture of an age, one must be able to show how a wide variety of phenomena have certain common features in their essential nature or function" (2003, 4).

Kern handles generalization adroitly. But not all generalizing investigations of temporal awareness match his standard. Since erroneous generalization can confuse more than it clarifies, I wish next to review influential studies in the history of temporal awareness that succumb to erroneous generalization. At stake here is the need to expose and dispose of inveterate and widespread misconceptions that impede understanding of the literary mimesis of time, and counterproductively prioritize historical method in studies of that mimesis. To rebut these misconceptions, I deploy a wide range of counterexamples drawn from Ancient Greece to the twentieth century. My aim is simply to identify and remove misleading formulations, so that the representation of time in each text considered can be investigated—and appreciated—without distortion by them. Let me not be misconstrued. Historically oriented analyses can serve as invaluable aids in exploring a topic such as the literary representation of time. However, lest ill-founded claims made in some analyses engender misconceptions that might obscure or skew the reader's view of my own investigations, it is appropriate now to address the matter in some detail. There is no need to see through a glass darkly when the means are at hand to clean the lens.

Our review can commence with several studies citing the early nineteenth century as a pivotal point in the history of temporal awareness. There can be no disputing the fact of change during or immediately prior to this period. Indeed, its acknowledgement is a historian's commonplace, though its precise dating remains open to qualification. J. H. Plumb, for instance, locates the pivot point a little earlier: "Between 1760 and 1790 it was crystal clear that there were two worlds, the old and the new" (1950, 78). What remains not so clear, however, is the impact of this change on temporal awareness.

Matei Calinescu claims that awareness of "historical time, linear and irreversible, flowing irresistibly onwards"—the "sense of *unrepeatable time*"—is the hallmark of modernity: a period whose origin he locates in the first half of the nineteenth century, with figures such as Baudelaire (1987, 13 [original emphasis]). Yet this claim succumbs to copious counterexamples, proving that the notion of irreversible time significantly antedates the starting point indicated by Calinescu. These can be selectively indicated here by a short list, arranged chronologically in two sections: the first constructing temporal passage as fluvial flow, the second as succession.[8] The list can be prefaced by the celebrated expression of the one-way forward movement of time in Shakespeare's *Macbeth* (written ca. 1606 and published posthumously in 1623), where life is construed as the purposeless passage of irreversible time—"To-morrow, and to-morrow, and to-morrow"—in which the imminent future ("to-morrow") is continuously converted into the past, until life itself ends: "All our yesterdays have lighted fools / The way to dusty death" (5.5.19, 22–23).

One of the earliest formulations of time in terms of movement "flowing irresistibly onwards," to retrieve Calinescu's phrasing, occurs in Book IV, Section 43 of Marcus Aurelius's *Meditations* (written ca. 170–180 AD): "As a river consisting of all things that come into being, aye, a rushing torrent, is Time. No sooner is a thing sighted than it is carried past, and lo, another is passing, and it too will be carried away" (1961, 91). (Though this temporal image obviously derives from Heraclitus's notion of the river into which one cannot step twice, that pre-Socratic philosopher did not—at least in his extant fragments—pursue the connection between time and flux). A medieval example occurs in *The Romance of the Rose* (ca.1237–1275) by Guillaume de Lorris and Jean de Meun: "This never-lingering Time, who all day long / Is going and never will return, / Resembles water that forever flows / But ne'er a drip comes back" (1962, 2, 163–66). The most celebrated Renaissance fluvial formulation of time appears in the *Notebooks* of Leonardo da Vinci: "In rivers, the water that you touch is the last of what has passed and the first of that which comes: so with time present" (2008, 258). A High Baroque version of the fluvial metaphor of time flowing irreversibly in one direction occurs in Robert Burton's *The Anatomy of Melancholy* (1651): "*Yield to the time: follow the stream*" (1838, 428 [original emphasis]).[9] Perhaps the most religiously stirring rendition of the fluvial metaphor of time appears in Isaac Watts' Late Baroque rendering of a verse in Psalm 90 in 1719: "Time, like an ever rolling stream" (1806, 125). Six years earlier, in 1713, Sir Isaac Newton, in the *General Scholium* appended to his celebrated *Principia*, defined absolute time in terms of irreversible flow: "Absolute, true, and mathematical time, of itself, and from its own name, flows equably without relation to anything external" (quoted in Whitehead 1929, 70). A superb neoclassical fluvial expression of unrepeatable time occurs in Samuel Johnson's *The History of Rasselas, Prince of Abyssinia* (1759): "Distance has the same effect on the mind as on the eye, and *while we glide along the stream of time* whatever we leave behind us is always lessening, and that which we approach increasing in magnitude" (1883, 121 [my emphasis]).

The seventeenth and eighteenth centuries offer splendid British philosophical formulations of irreversible temporal passage in terms of *succession*, not fluvial flow. In 1689, John Locke, in the fourteenth chapter of Book II of *An Essay Concerning Human Understanding*, identified succession as the first idea contributing to the notion of time: "First by examining what passes in our minds, and how are ideas there in train, constantly some vanish and others begin to appear we come by the idea of *succession*" (1996, 82). The first principle of succession is that its terms are ordered in irreversible sequence. Hence, a moment that has passed always remains past, and can never again become present. This is irreversible time par excellence: "[I]t is as impossible for the duration of that flame for an hour last night, to coexist with any motion that now is, or forever shall be, as for any part of duration, that was before the beginning of the world, to coexist with the motion of the sun now" (1996, 82). An earlier philosophical linking of time with irreversible succession appears in Thomas Hobbes's *Leviathan* (1651), where the passage of time is associated with the succession of impressions impinging on awareness, such that any present and current impression is inevitably succeeded by others, causing the original impression, formerly present, to fade progressively in the memory retaining it: "And any object being removed from our eyes, though the impression it made in us remain, yet *other objects more present succeeding and working on us*, the imagination of the past is obscured and made weak" (1958, 28 [my emphasis]). A crystalline eighteenth-century British Empiricist formulation of time as succession occurs in Book I, Section II, of David Hume's *A Treatise of Human Nature* (1739) "'Tis a property inseparable from time, and which in a manner constitutes its essence, that each of its parts succeeds another, and that none of them, however contiguous, can ever be co-existent" (1887, 31).[10]

Thus, on the basis of the counterexamples provided above, it is certain that, in both English literature *and* philosophy, the notion of "unrepeatable time" was well established long before the early nineteenth century. Indeed, 2,250 years before the date that Calinescu assigns to its origin, awareness of unrepeatable time erupts with spectacular force in Xenophon's *Anabasis* (composed around 420 BC), a work that recounts the gruelling and resourceful escape of 10,000 Greek mercenaries, deprived of their leaders by sudden treachery in the midst of hostile Persian territory in 401 BC. On awakening from a dream shortly after the catastrophe, Xenophon interrogates his predicament: "What am I lying here for? The night is passing and at dawn the enemy will probably be here .... Am I waiting until I become a little older? I shall never be any older at all if I hand myself over to the enemy" (1972, III, 1). Here Xenophon realizes that survival depends on recognizing the irreversibility of time: he must act now or never have a chance to act again. This emphasis on timely action entails much more than the familiar Greek *kairos*, defined by Yuasa Yasuo as "[t]he quality of time for the subject to act under a certain situation, for it carries such meanings as 'the proper time to act' and 'the arising of an opportunity'" (2008, 15). For in this case, "the proper time to act" is determined by recognition not just that the opportunity concerned (i.e., acting for the sake of survival) will not come again, but also that continuation of Xenophon's own passage through time (as expressed in the notion of becoming "older") depends on his response.[11]

The correspondence between (a) Xenophon's sense of time and (b) the "irreversible," "unrepeatable" time, always "flowing irresistibly onwards," that Calinescu attributes to modernism emerges more clearly when we consider the context carefully. Immediately prior to interrogating his predicament, Xenophon, exhausted and distressed, falls asleep and dreams that his father's house is suddenly destroyed by a lightning bolt. The dream, of course, suggests that the past and the security it afforded are gone forever. Xenophon must face an entirely new and threatening present. What was is no more. This is irreversible time par excellence. For it not only involves awareness of irreversible change from past to present, but also entails, after Xenophon awakens, as we have seen, acute awareness that the passage of time, from night to dawn, threatens more change. Xenophon's only salvation is to decide to change his orientation to temporal movement from passivity to agency—from "waiting to become a little older" to accepting the necessity of taking responsibility for his fate (by assuming the role of a military officer, in the absence of those treacherously slaughtered).

Xenophon's awareness of irreversible, unrepeatable time (the sense of time that Calinescu finds exclusively in modernism) must be carefully distinguished not only from kairos, as already suggested, but also from *chronos*, as these are the two temporal constructions most often associated with Ancient Greece. As Paul Tillich indicates, chronos ("measured or clock time") is "quantitative," whereas kairos is "qualitative" (1963, 3.369).[12] But the time that passes in Xenophon's description cannot be accounted for by either term, though it obviously displays characteristics of both. It accords with kairos insofar as it emphasizes, to deploy Tillich's phrase, "the time in which something must be done" (1963, 3.369). It accords with chronos insofar as it emphasizes the measurement of time remaining. Yet it accords with neither kairos nor chronos insofar as it concerns Xenophon's registration of his own involvement in the irreversible movement of time—a movement that continues no matter what he does, and that, in his current circumstance, imposes the imperative that he act with efficacy immediately.[13]

Thus Calinesu's claim that the sense of unrepeatable time begins in the early nineteenth century collapses under the weight of the counterexamples just considered. But Reinhart Koselleck's claim that, prior to the beginning of the nineteenth century, "the present and past were enclosed within a common historical plane," such that "[t]emporal difference was not more or less arbitrarily eliminated: it was not, as such, at all apparent," fairs no better (1985, 10). In supporting this claim, Koselleck cites Machiavelli's *The Prince* (1513) as corroboration. Yet in that text, Machiavelli explicitly insists on awareness of temporal difference; for without the ability "to change his method to suit the changing times" no prince can long survive (1977, 121). Indeed, Lawrence V. Ryan praises Machiavelli's historical insight: "No other historian or writer on politics up to Ascham's time, including Comines and Guicciardini, had succeeded so well as Machiavelli in the study of proximate historical causes" (1963, 167). In fact, Machiavelli deepened a development in historical awareness that had already achieved considerable depth *more than a century earlier* in the *Dialogues* (likely written between 1406 and 1408) of the renowned Italian Renaissance humanist Leonardo Bruni—a work that, according to Carol Quillen, displays "sophisticated historical sensibility" (2010, 385). David Quint similarly affirms Bruni's awareness of "historical difference from ancient culture" and interprets the *Dialogues* as "the voice of a peculiarly modern consciousness, of the division of that consciousness against its own condition of modernity" (1985, 443, 445). And are we to ignore Petrarch's "Letter to Posterity," completed between 1371 and 1372, at least 34 years before Bruni's *Dialogues*? In that letter, Petrarch—often hailed as the father of Italian humanism—explicitly refers to historical difference: "In order to forget my own time, I have constantly striven to place myself in spirit in other ages, and consequently I delighted in history" (1898, 64).

Moreover, Koselleck's claim regarding lack of temporal differentiation in the Renaissance contradicts the findings of several scholars (whom I briefly review in Chapter 1), including Erwin Panofsky, who links Renaissance philology with temporal discrimination—the ability to view the past as "historically detached from the contemporary world" (1939/1962, 27).[14] To these I can add Wallace K. Ferguson's resounding pronouncement: "The humanists' reverence for antiquity and contempt for medieval culture ... forced upon them *a realization of the passage of time and of the changes it had wrought, from which they developed a new periodization of history*" (1962, 303 [my emphasis]).

As an English example of this attitude, one can cite John Leland (ca. 1503–1552), a celebrated English antiquary, referred to by Rowse as "a very characteristic scholar of the Renaissance," who, in the course of his astonishingly comprehensive itinerary around England, witnessed the dismantling of monasteries and churches, as well as the defacing of sepulchres, resulting from the religious policies of Henry VIII (1950, 32). In Rowse's phrase, Leland recorded "the end of an age" (1950, 33). Similar awareness of the chasm between present and past appears in the work of John Stow (ca. 1525–1605), another English

Renaissance antiquarian who, according to Rowse, was motivated to write his great *Survey of London* (1598), because "[h]e was early troubled for his sympathies with the old order of things" (1950, 192). A superb Elizabethan formulation of temporal difference appears in Book III of Richard Hooker's magisterial *The Laws of Ecclesiastical Polity* (1593): "And of this we cannot be ignorant, how sometimes that hath done great good, which afterwards *when time hath changed the ancient course of things*, doth grow to be either very hurtful, or not so greatly profitable and necessary" (1888, 205-6 [my emphasis]). Moreover, if we move two centuries earlier and consider the work of Geoffrey Chaucer (ca. 1343–1400) in the Late Middle Ages, we also find, according to Lee Patterson, awareness of temporal difference: "There is, in short, something about subjectivity that persuades people that in dealing with it they have entered into a new time, that they have cut themselves off from the past, that they have become moderns. What is striking about Chaucer's explorations into subjectivity is that he seems to have entertained the same idea—although he also seems never to have fully credited it" (1991, 12).

James Chandler's treatment of the Battle of Waterloo (1815) as a watershed in "awareness of conditions of movement from one historical epoch to the next" encounters the same counterexamples as those confronting Koselleck, and cannot be taken as valid (1998, 24). I can add a few more counterexamples from the many available, beginning with the majestic pronouncement of Edward Gibbon, in *The Decline and Fall of the Roman Empire* (first published between 1776 and 1788), regarding the benefits of historical perspective: "It is thus that the experience of history exalts and enlarges the horizon of our intellectual view" (1910, 2.923). In his discussion of eighteenth-century architecture, John Summerson cites the midpoint of that century as a period involving "the complete reorientation of European man to his historic past," and applies the same horizonal metaphor to the expansion of the sense of historical models and authoritative precedents: "Attachment to classical culture meant attachment to history and attachment to history meant the remorseless widening of horizons in every direction until the uniqueness of Rome [as a standard of excellence] began to dissolve in a more general and immensely more complex vision of the whole European past" (1969, 1986, 75).

As another counterexample to Chandler's claim that "awareness of conditions of movement from one historical epoch to the next" does not antedate the early nineteenth century, I can cite the celebrated pronouncement of Ralph Glaber (985–1047), a Cluniac monk, around the year 1000: "It seemed as though the world shook itself and cast off its horary age, and clad itself everywhere in a white robe of churches" (quoted in Coulton 1938, 8)—weighty words that provoked G. G. Coulton's apt observation: "[H]e is one of the very few medieval writers who seem to believe their own day better, or at least no worse, than the days of their forefathers" (1938, 8).[15] A further counterexample concerns the period shortly after the fall of the Western Roman Empire, when Theodoric, king of the Ostrogoths, assumed rule over Italy (493–526). According to John Moorhead, that era was characterized by robust historical awareness: "Authors of the period took delight in a rhetoric of renewal, renovation and restoration; they displayed a *chronological self-consciousness* that found expression in the widespread use, for the first time, of the Latin adjective for 'very recent', *modernus*" (2001, 46–47 [my emphasis]).[16] Indeed, one could push Chandler's watershed back, and cite Thucydides' *History of the Peloponnesian War* (composed perhaps not long after 413 BC) as a text displaying, to invoke Chandler's phrasing, keen "awareness of conditions of movement from one historical epoch to the next." For example, in discussing the background to the Peloponnesian War (431–404 BC), Thucydides provides a capsule history of preceding epochal developments. "The old form of government was hereditary monarchy with established rights and limitations; but as Hellas became more powerful and as the importance of acquiring money became more and more evident, tyrannies were established in nearly all the cities, revenues increased, shipbuilding flourished, and ambition turned towards sea-power" (1972, 43).

Nevertheless, it is provisionally accurate—and indeed a historian's commonplace—to claim that the historical perspective was not equally developed in all periods. For example, Christian Meier points to the lack of such an outlook during the Roman Republic: "They recognized few differences in the temporal dimension" (1996, 33). Herbert B. Workman indicates the lack of historical discrimination in the early second century: "To the Church, as to her Master, time is but an accident. She sees already of the travail of her soul, and is satisfied. The 'not yet' of the cautious critic (*Heb.* ii.8.9) is more than neutralized by the vision of the triumphant King" (1960, 104). Referring to the early centuries of Christianity in the Hellenistic East, Edwyn Bevan similarly emphasizes the notion of history as movement toward a foregone conclusion: "The man brought into the Christian community was brought into a stream of dynamic life going through time towards a definite consummation, a divine event, in the future" (1923, 105). Scholars also often associate the Middle Ages—and more specifically the Gothic portion (1140–1400) of that period—with a focus on unchanging meaning, not transient fact. Ian Watt points to "the medieval conception of history by which, whatever the period, the wheel of time churns out the same eternally applicable *exempla*" (1965, 23)—a conception epitomized by the treatment of each major incident in the Bible as both, to invoke Lotte Brand Philip's phrasing, "a historical occurrence and a timeless truth" (1971, 82).[17] Of course, in the context of the passage from *The Romance of the Rose* and Patterson's comment on Chaucer quoted earlier, it is apparent that the Gothic phase of the Middle Ages was not as bereft of temporal awareness as scholarly convention might make it seem. Moreover, Gothic architecture—one of the most impressive creations of the Medieval mind—gives physical expression to acute awareness of the distinction between past and present. Without such awareness, new ideas in the development of monumental form would not have evolved as rapidly and profusely as they did. According to Jean Bony, only in "distant peripheral areas," remote from the hubs of "workshop transmission" of new ideas, can we observe that, in the Gothic era, "the perspective of history becomes flattened and time loses its normal depth," because "past and present tended to become intermingled as if there were between them no difference in modernity" (1983, 250, 252). Indeed, Gothic architecture is so characterized by the drive toward development and elaboration or supersession of precedent that T. G. Jackson associates it with "the restless temper of the modern world, its passion for progress, its grasping at new ideas and novel methods" (1915, 1.12).

Richard Terdiman approaches the presumed shift in temporal discrimination at the beginning of the nineteenth century from a different angle from that taken by Chandler, emphasizing not divergence from temporal congruity (from the inability, that is, of one age to perceive itself as distinct from a prior one), but loss of temporal continuity (the rupture of the link between past and present). According to Terdiman, this predicament caused what he terms a "memory crisis: ...modernity's experience of an uncertain and tense relation to the past" (1993, 316). Yet, while Victorian literature, for example, does display symptoms of a memory crisis indicating "an uncertain and tense relation to the past"—Heathcliff and Catherine's adult obsession with their shared childhood in *Wuthering Heights*; the spectacular attempt to reenact the theft of the diamond in *The Moonstone*; Tess's inability to escape the doom caused by her tainted past with Alec in *Tess of the D'Urbervilles*—it also displays conviction in temporal continuity, as in Tennyson's "You Ask Me Why, Though Ill At Ease" (1842): "A land of settled government, / A land of just and old renown, / Where Freedom slowly broadens down / From precedent to precedent" (1959, 27). Temporal continuity between past and present underpins Samuel Butler's *The Way of All Flesh* (1903), where the great challenge for Ernest Pontifex is to extricate himself from the relentless influence of prior generations of parenting practices: "What we call death is only a shock great enough to destroy our power to recognise a past and a present as resembling on another" (1966, 262). Butler's genetic theory of character, among other factors, insists on the relation between past and present: "However it often happens that the grandson of a successful man will be more successful than the son—the spirit that actuated the grandfather having lain fallow in the son and being refreshed by repose so as to be ready for fresh exertion in the grandson" (1966, 51).

Terdiman's argument regarding memory crisis is challenged by more than counterexamples. Does what he terms the "experience of uncertain and tense relation to the past" derive from historical factors specific to the period he addresses or from a predisposition in Western culture to foreground separation from the past? In other words, is this condition historical or generic?[18] The notion of losing the past is a leitmotif of Western civilization, stemming from the Greco-Roman and Judeo-Christian inheritance. The notion of loss of the past informs the notion of the golden age in Hesiod's *Works and Days* and Plato's *Cratylus* (397e)—a motif with a celebrated legacy, perhaps including the philosophy of Plotinus, whose ontology of the procession from and return to the One concerns the need to return to a prior state. Moreover, as Ronald Syme notes, "the theorists of antiquity situated their social and political Utopias in the past, not in the future" (1939, 319). J. Huizinga makes a similar observation regarding medieval legislation: "It looks more towards an ideal past than towards an earthly future" (1954, 38). Behind this emphasis on separation from the past looms the myth of Orpheus and Eurydice—certainly one of most poignant expressions of loss of the past in the Western tradition. In addition, the motif of the *nostos* or return home that motivates Homer's *Odyssey* also prioritizes the need to go back to a former place—ultimately, the past. (This is James Joyce's interpretation in *Ulysses*). Indeed, our word "nostalgia" derives from the Greek nostos. According to various scholars contributing to *The Cambridge History of Classical Literature: Latin Literature*, the motif of nostalgia informs the work of several classical authors. W. V. Clausen finds it in Theocritus: "cultivating a special nostalgia by writing of the Sicilian herdsmen of his youth, a landscape of memory" (1982, 301); Niall Rudd detects it in Horace: "tempered by personal feelings of melancholy and nostalgia" (1982, 382); Georg Luck notes nostalgia in Tibullus: "[h]is nostalgia for a distant Golden Age" (1982, 412); and J. C. Bramble attributes it to Juvenal: "a nostalgia for lost ideals, and a more honest, worthwhile world" (1982, 615).

Furthermore, during the later phase of the Hellenistic period, several centuries after the death of Alexander the Great in 323 BC had led to the division of his empire into rival kingdoms respectively founded by the Diadochi or Successors, loss of the past (in the mode of declension of power) provoked the project of military recuperation. Erich S. Gruen explains, with regard to Ptolemaic Egypt: "As with other Hellenistic kingdoms, the burden of the past inspired recurrent efforts to emulate it" (1984, 2.673). Similarly, loss of the past burns at the centre of the Judaic motive to rebuild the Second Temple (destroyed by the Roman emperor Titus in 70 AD), and also informs the myth of the Fall—fundamental to both Judaism and Christianity.[19] Loss of the past permeates Old English poetry, as Corinne Sauders indicates: "Paradoxically for modern readers, the earliest English poetry is often infused with a keen sense of nostalgia for the past, the loss of great civilisations, the passing of time, and the decline and fall of all things" (2010, 3). Loss of the past similarly informed Martin Luther's prosecution of the Reformation—an effort beginning in 1517—as he strove to reverse what R. H. Tawney terms "the slow poison of commerce and finance" that had developed since the Middle Ages: "*The eyes of Luther were on the past*" (1926, 84 [my emphasis]). Near the end of that same century, fixation on the past prompted Jérome Bollery's (died c. 1600) celebrated drawings of the jousting tournament held at Sandricourt in 1493. Anthony Blunt elaborates: "It is unexpected to find an artist commissioned at the end of the sixteenth century to make drawings of a famous feat of chivalry of a century earlier, but the subject may well have appealed to a certain section of the aristocracy which looked back with nostalgia to the days of feudalism" (1953, 104). A striking example of historical perspective in eighteenth-century France—one that involves projection into a future era looking back at the contemporary one—pertains to a negative review of a painting by Jean Marc Nattier (1685–1766). Michael Levey provides the details: "A witty article in the *Mercure* by Cochin, posing as a future critic in the year 2355, made fun of the extraordinary fashion there much have existed in eighteenth-century France for women to lie about holding pots of water and taming eagles to drink wine out of gold cups" (1972, 126).

Even if we dismiss these antecedents as somehow irrelevant, Terdiman's claim that the turn of the nineteenth century inaugurates the "experience of uncertain and tense relation to the past," seems to forget *Hamlet*—the most famous text in English literature and one permeated by the same troubled relation to the past that Terdiman addresses, as we shall see in Chapter 1. In this context, it is crucial to distinguish between a genuinely new attitude toward loss of the past (as in Terdiman's view) and the extension or transformation of an inveterate one.

The most recent example that I want to treat of troublesome generalization in studies of the sense of time in the nineteenth century was published by Sue

Zemka in 2012. Though no doubt useful, her thesis that Victorian novels, as an expression of Victorian culture, treat or represent "a growing separation between durational time and a sensationalized and punctualist present" tends to obscure more than it clarifies (2012, 13). To begin with, Zemka's claim that the nineteenth century displays "hyperawareness of the momentary" (2012, 2) and conspicuous "investment in figures of suddenness" as a direct result of "more precise time reckoning" and heightened concern with "minutes," overlooks *Hamlet*—a play, written two centuries before the beginning of the period Zemka addresses, which opens with close attention to "minutes" (1.1.30) and whose revenge plot, moreover, is founded on the *sudden* death of the prior king, an event recounted *twice*: once by the Ghost and again in *The Murder of Gonzago* (Zemka 2012, 2, 9). Furthermore, apart from this problem of chronological counterexample, Zemka's thesis regarding "a growing separation between durational time and a sensationalized and punctualist present" is directly contradicted by various Victorian novels, as very brief consideration will show. In these counterexamples, suddenness becomes the means by which awareness of continuity (what Zemka terms "durational time") is heightened and reaffirmed—the direct opposite of the dispensation that Zemka finds. In *Hard Times* (1854), for example, for reasons to be clarified in Chapter 2, time (as measured by Mr. Gradgrind's clock) passes as a series of sudden seconds, each elapsing with no connection to before or after. The challenge in the novel is to reconstitute the continuity of time—a project leading to emphasis not on what Zemka terms "figures of suddenness," but instead on the unfolding of redemptive process (as regarding the effort to rescue to Stephen Blackpool from the Old Hell Shaft). Similarly, in George Eliot's *The Mill on the Floss* (1880), Mr. Tulliver's sudden and catastrophic fall from his horse, an event that causes temporary paralysis of mind and body, is followed by the arduous process of recovery—an enterprise that entails recovering "the threads of the past" (1979, 235), and thus reconstituting and reaffirming his place in temporal continuity. Indeed, the Mill that he owns itself embodies the continuity of time (what Zemka refers to as "durational time"): "The Tullivers had lived on this spot for generations" (1979, 276). Ironically, in a way that Zemka does not recognize, what she terms "the interest-value of the moment" serves to enhance the interest-value of process (2012, 9). In *Time and the Literary*, published ten years before Zemka's study, Karen Newman, Jay Clayton, and Marianne Hirsch also foreground the link, in literature, between the moment and process: "the literary often structures our thinking about time now," by "join[ing] immediacy and the instantaneous with their opposite, duration and critique" (2002, 1).

One problem with Zemka's thesis stems from philosophical fuzziness—the failure to recognize that the relation between "a punctualist present" and "durational time" is underpinned by what Terry Pinkard, in a discussion of Hegel, labels "that uneasy, struggling unity between Discreteness, on the one hand, and Continuity, on the other" (1996, 247). Minutes or moments are discrete—that is, they are particulate. But *as* minutes or moments, they punctuate or measure continuity—ongoing temporal extension. In the counterexamples just cited (*Hard Times* and *The Mill on the Floss*), this relation between discreteness and continuity in the conception of time is portrayed with extraordinary vividness and thought-provoking implication.

This brief consideration of scholarly commentary on the shift in temporal awareness in the early nineteenth century suggests the challenges and disputes that historical generalization can encounter. In their study, *Time from Concept to Narrative Construct: A Reader*, Jan Christoph Meister and Wilhelm Schernus describe "time" as "an existentially omnipresent, but philosophically evasive concept and phenomenon" (2011, ix). Yet from the counterexamples educed above, it is apparent that accurate generalization regarding historical shift in temporal awareness is similarly evasive. Moreover, in jumping from the nineteenth to the twentieth century, we encounter perhaps the most striking instance of generalization vulnerable to puncture by counterexample—namely, Ursula K. Heise's claim that "postmodernism challenges the notion of time as such" (1997, 38). Despite the innumerable postmodern literary texts explicitly exploring temporal awareness (several of them treated either briefly or at length in my book), Heise insists on "the diminished relevance of temporality and historicity to contemporary experience as one of the central features of postmodernist culture" (1997, 33). Moreover, her claim regarding "historicity" is contradicted by Peter Middleton and Tim Woods who, in a monograph published three years after Heise's investigation, note "the growing intensity of late twentieth-century efforts to recover and conserve the past" (2000, 22).

It should be evident by now that, without careful and copious qualification, inquiries into the temporal concerns of the literature of a given era risk falling into a double bind. On the one hand, no one can deny that the era in which an author writes conditions his or her interpretation of time.[20] But on the other hand, if not appropriately circumspect, generalizing about the treatment of time in the literary texts of a given period can promulgate error. Moreover, as far the present study is concerned, historical generalization poses another and perhaps more insidious risk—one that pertains to obscuring the idiosyncratic aspect of experience of time. On the one hand, time is universally fundamental to experience—ordering it into intelligibility by imposing succession or the sense of "one after another" on it. But on the other hand, time is registered by each individual in a unique and distinctive manner. In short, the passage of time is constant, but personal relation to that constant, regardless of the era involved, varies according to the individual concerned.[21]

Before launching an investigation of literary texts, brief summary of some basic distinctions in the philosophical analysis of time will be helpful in preparing the reader for a more thorough treatment of them at various points later in this study. To begin with, "time" is an equivocal, not univocal, term—"a term used in many different ways," according to Cornelius Castoriadis (1991, 38). Garrett J. DeWeese concurs: "We should not assume that every occurrence of the word refers to the same concept" (2004, 8). In fact, this diversity of sense and reference applies even to the *being* or ontological status of time. Is time something in itself, apart from the things that happen? More precisely, is time *substantive* (subsisting independently of the events occurring in it) or *relationist* (constructed from the series of events that happen)? The first theory is termed *substantivalism*, because it treats time as something real and autonomous in its own right. Sir Isaac Newton provides an example: "Absolute, true, and mathematical time, of itself, and from its own name, flows equably without relation to anything external" (quoted in Whitehead 1925, 70). A superb literary example of this construction occurs in *Enduring Love*, as five men try to restrain an errant touring balloon carried aloft by a gust of wind, while they desperately cling to the ropes dangling from it: "Every fraction of a second that passed increased the drop, and the point must come when to let go would be impossible or fatal" (McEwan 1997, 14). Here the insistent pressure of temporal flow seems as immediate, concrete, and independently existent as the wind whose rushing lifts the balloon perilously high. The second theory is termed *relationism*, because it construes time in relation to the sequence of events that occur. Whitehead elaborates: "There is time because there are happenings, and apart from happenings there is nothing" (1961b, 83).[22] The relationist reduction of time to a sequence of happenings informs the apparent acceleration of time in *Hamlet*, for example, as in Gertrude's reaction to Ophelia's drowning: "One woe doth tread upon another's heel, / So fast they follow" (4.7.162–63). An extraordinary version of relationist time appears in *Waiting for Godot* where, since "Nothing happens," "time has stopped" (Beckett 1954, 27, 24). Substantivalist and relationist constructions of time coexist in *To the Lighthouse*, where, as noted earlier, time is imagined as an indifferent leviathan force, but one whose devastatingly destructive potential is unleashed, as we shall see, by a tragic sequence of events.

Similar ontological ambiguity concerns the relation of time to human consciousness. Does time function independently of human awareness or only as registered and constructed by it? In *Time and Narrative*, Ricoeur respectively denominates these alternatives as *cosmological* and *phenomenological* time (1984, 1.6, 115), but nomenclature elsewhere is diverse. Craig Calendar, for example, refers to scientific and experiential time, while DeWeese opposes physical to personal time (2008, 339; 2004, 9–10).[23] In discussing the possibility of a "literary philosophy of time," Gregory Currie insists that it must privilege a "physical philosophy of time" over less objective variants: "Whatever a literary philosophy of time has to say will have to ... accept the domination of the physical philosophy of time" (1999, 61). Yet his stricture imposes a rule that problematizes its own application. There are many physical philosophies of time. In this circumstance, how is the critic to choose among available candidates and, having chosen, how is that critic to determine whether or not the choice is uniformly suitable for application to each literary text selected for analysis? Moreover, even if these questions can be satisfactorily answered, by imposing "the physical philosophy of time" (however that term is defined) on analysis of temporal mimesis in literature, Currie's prescription entails recourse to Procrustean method, which my own investigation carefully avoids.

The distinction between scientific and experiential time (retrieving Calendar's terminology) receives further delineation in the temporal philosophy of Henri Bergson, which opposes spatialized time to durational time. The former constructs time as a sequence of discrete (separated) and juxtaposed instants, while the latter construes it in terms not of parts, but of an unfolding whole, such that any given moment virtually contains all those preceding it. As suggested earlier, Virginia's Woolf's *Mrs. Dalloway* is often cited as a text presenting both temporal dispensations—an observation that is accurate as far as it goes, but we shall go much further. No literary text more opposes its "in-house" construction of time more intransigently to durational time than does *Hard Times*, where each instant, as measured by Mr. Gradgrind's clock, as we shall see in Chapter 2, restarts time, with no connection to any preceding moment.

Another pair of distinctions in the analysis of time will be helpful, especially in the treatment of both *Hamlet* and *Enduring Love*. If the context for consideration of time concerns the relation of a series of moments or events to a perspective outside that series, then, as John McTaggart indicates, "time presents itself as a movement from future to past" (1927, 11, n.2). Here time is *dynamic* and *tensed*. In contrast, if the context for consideration of time is the relation of the moments in a series to each other, then time, according to McTaggart, "presents itself as a movement from earlier to later." Here time is *static* and *tenseless* (1927, 11, n.2). In Chapters 1 and 8, McTaggart's extremely influential temporal theory will be carefully explicated and applied. But for brief introduction right now, consider the sequential acts of opening this book, then, after a period of perusal, reading these very words, and later closing the book to ponder them. Viewed in the context of the present when these words are actually read, the prior act of opening the book pertains to the past, while the eventual act of closing the book pertains to the future. In this dispensation, the moments of time are continually changing their tensed positions. For example, the present act of reading these words moves inexorably into the past, while the act of closing the book approaches inexorably from the future, until that future moment becomes present, and the book is finally closed. However, these same events, considered in relation to each other, do not pass in the sense of changing their respective tensed positions from future to present to past. Instead, they retain what Quentin Smith refers to as their "respective temporal locations" in terms of precedence, simultaneity, and subsequence (1994, 1). For example, a particular reader's act of opening this book, 24 days after his sixtieth birthday, always precedes his act of reading the passage indicated, while the act of closing the book, after the passage has been read, always follows the earlier acts in the series, no matter how much additional time elapses after these events, just as the dates on a calendar retain their fixed order of succession no matter how much time passes. June 10 of a given year always succeeds June 1 of the same year, and never changes its position relative to June 1, regardless how much time thereafter elapses. Yet, in the context of a given moment—say t_1—*experienced as present* on June 1, June 10 is construed as a date that will continually approach from the future, until finally itself becoming present, at which time the formerly present moment, t_1, will have receded nine days into the past. Here the temporal location of moments, with respect to the tenses they occupy, changes continuously. Hence, depending on the context of temporality concerned, time displays a *transitory* aspect (always involving change) and an *extensive* aspect (stretching in a fixed order of succession according to invariable relations of before, simultaneous with, and after).

1

The Mimesis of Time in *Hamlet*

Hamlet opens with intense attention to time as the sentries "watch the minutes of this night" (1.1.30).[1] The emphasis gains thematic depth when Hamlet formulates his predicament in terms of temporal dislocation: "The time is out of joint. O cursed spite, / That ever I was born to set it right" (1.5.196–97). The problem of time is raised to philosophical status in Polonius's rhetoric: "Why day is day, night night, and time is time" (2.2.88). The importance of time in *Hamlet* has provoked numerous studies, yet none but the present one approaches the matter through recourse to the temporal analysis of John McTaggart, whose celebrated article on the unreality of time, published in 1908 and later republished in the second volume of his metaphysical work *The Nature of Existence*, is often regarded as a seminal treatise in the philosophy of time since the first decade of the twentieth century. Though virtually no philosophers have defended McTaggart's claim that time is unreal, legions of them, in thousands of articles and books on the subject, have addressed some aspect of his description of the two temporal series proper to time (or, more precisely, the notion of time). These two series, easily defined, can serve as powerful lenses though which to analyze and illumine the structure of time in *Hamlet*. The result of our inquiry will be a new understanding of the representation of time—or, more precisely, what Gerhard Dohrn-van-Rossum terms "time-consciousness"—in the text (1996, 3 and passim). For the elements that we shall draw from McTaggart are not theoretical (in the sense of imposing ideational constructs on reality or what actually is), but descriptive, in the sense of articulating the actual conceptual content of the notion of time—what E. J. Lowe calls the "indispensable ingredients in our understanding of what time is" (1991, 43) and what L. Nathan Oaklander calls the "two ways in which we ordinarily conceive and talk about time" (1994b, 157). Despite the fact that McTaggart's theory of the nonreality of time turned out historically to be a dead end, his succinct and penetrating analysis of what time is conceptually—what concepts are intrinsic to the very idea of time—has exercised profound and lasting influence on philosophers of time ever since he published his formulations. Ironically, though ultimately concerned with demonstrating that time is not, McTaggart's analysis has become indispensable to many philosophers in defining what time is.

But before proceeding with this investigation, brief recapitulation of earlier approaches to the problem of time in *Hamlet* will contextualize discussion. A convenient introduction to such considerations concerns emphasis on the Renaissance as the period when temporal awareness broke through to a new level. Georges Poulet stresses the upsurge in the sense of transience: "It is indeed true that one felt then as always, and perhaps more keenly then ever before, the precarious and fugitive character of each lived moment" (1956, 10). David Scott Kastan elaborates on this aspect of the temporal awareness of the Renaissance man: "His world is one in which the unidirectional and irreversible flow of time brings an intensified sense of the fragility and precariousness of being" (1982, 6). Ricardo Quinones underscores this temporal insecurity by pointing to the Renaissance concern with the Saturnine quality of time, construed in terms of its "menacing and destructive" activity, analogous to that of the mythological Saturn, the god who consumed his own offspring (1972, 15). Other scholars foreground more positive aspects of Renaissance temporality by focusing on the achievement of historical perspective. Erwin Panofsky, for example, highlights the role of intense philological study of classical texts that enabled the understanding of ancient civilization "as a phenomenon complete in itself, yet belonging to the past and historically detached from the contemporary world" (1939, 27). Dohrn-van-Rossum addresses the role of nascent technology in fostering awareness of the difference between past and present: "From the beginning of the fifteenth century, at the latest, the preoccupation with inventions developed a historical perspective" (1996, 5).

Scholars dealing directly with the treatment of time in *Hamlet* deploy a range of approaches. Wylie Sypher claims to detect in *Hamlet* a notion of "punctiform" time that, supposedly anticipating post-Renaissance temporal notions, is "discontinuous" and "mechanical," thereby privileging the instant, liberated from past and future (1976, 67–68). Paul Yachnin interprets the opening of *Hamlet* in terms of historical déjà vu, wherein the military vigilance regarding possible invasion reenacts that in July and August, 1599, pertaining to false rumours of a return of the dreaded Spanish Armada that England defeated in 1588 (2002). Maurice Hunt explores the prominence of "regression" and "reversion to the past" (2004, 382, 383). Numerous scholars construe the representation of time in the play in terms of binary oppositions. Frank Kermode applies the terms chronos and kairos, defining chronos as "'passing time' or 'waiting time'" and kairos as "the season, a point in time filled with significance, charged with a meaning derived from its relation to the end" (1967, 47). James S. Baumlin revisited these contraries (2002). In contrast, James Calderwood foregrounds synchronic and diachronic polarity (1983, 189). Elsewhere I have investigated the conflict in *Hamlet* between two temporal dispensations: reiterative time versus teleological time (2008, 150–66). Indeed, the range of opinion on time in *Hamlet* does appear to marginalize Bernard Grebanier's claim that "[t]he time element is of no consequence in the play" (1960, 177).

All of these investigations of time in *Hamlet* focus on ways in which time is constructed, interpreted, or experienced in the world of the play. None bases its inquiry on the conceptual complexity of time itself—the nexus of concepts constituting the very notion of time. The present study undertakes such enterprise, with the aim of uncovering thematic implications never before noted or discussed.

With this background, let us turn now to McTaggart's signal contribution to the understanding of time. According to McTaggart, two kinds of temporal fact are essential to the very notion of time. The first of these (termed the *A*-series) pertains to the transition of tenses from future to present to past. The second (termed the *B*-series) involves the unchanging relations of earlier than, simultaneous with, and later than:

> I shall give the name of the *A* series to that series of positions which runs from the far past through the near past to the present, and then from the present through the near future to the far future or conversely. The series of positions which runs from earlier to later, or conversely, I shall call the *B* series. (1927, 11)

In the *A*-series, time is *dynamic*: moments and events continually change position (either nearer or father) in relation to the present, which, in turn, is continually shifting its own position in the temporal stream. In the *B*-series, time is *static*: the relations among events, in terms of precedence or simultaneity, do not change. For example, the fact that the Fall of Second Triumvirate precedes the Fall of the Third Reich and succeeds the Fall of the First Athenian Empire can never change, no matter how many other events occur. Robin Le Poidevin encapsulates the distinction between the *B*-series, which excludes change, and the *A*-series, which presupposes change: "[I]f it is true at one time that event x is earlier than event y, then it is true at all times that x is earlier than y. Positions in the A-series, in contrast, do change; what is now present was once future and will be past" (1991, 14). Oaklander elaborates:

> On the one hand, we think of time and events in time as *moving*, or *passing*, from the far future to the near future, from the near future to the present, and then from the present receding into the more and more distant past. Events in a series of terms which are either past, present, or future are said to be located in an A-series. On the other hand, we speak and think of moments or events as being earlier than, later than, and simultaneous with other events, and we believe that these relations are unchanging, permanent and fixed. (1994b, 157–58)

These two temporal series, fundamental to the notion of time as McTaggart defines it, figure prominently in *Hamlet*, where their role can be introduced through reference to the dual mimetic project in the play: the representation of both nature and art. Hamlet, of course, cites the first of these: "the purpose of playing ... was and is to hold as 'twere the mirror up to nature" (3.2.20–22). He unwittingly intimates the second—the play's portrayal of itself as a play or work of literary art—when describing his entrapment in a drama written by his own adversaries: "Or I could make a prologue to my brains, / They had begun the play" (5.2.30–31). In its representation of "nature"—that is, the world of experience, subject to continuous flux and change—*Hamlet* foregrounds the A-series. In contrast, in its representation of "art"—that is, the notion of drama as a text already written, comprising a fixed sequence of events—*Hamlet* foregrounds the B-series.

Brief explication will clarify this basic distinction. As noted in the first sentence of this discussion, the sentries on the "platform" of Elsinore are acutely aware of the passage of time (1.2.214). More specifically, through fear of "the omen coming on," they are acutely concerned with the approach of future events toward the present and, through concern with the Ghost, with the recession of past events from the present (1.1.126). This predicament epitomizes the A-series—the notion of time as *the flux or passage of tenses*. Yet, construed as a dramatic text whose parts are fixed in a continuum stretching "before and after" (4.4.37), *Hamlet* constitutes a B-series, comprising events and moments ordered according to the two-place predicates: earlier than, simultaneous with, and later than. Considered in this context, all the moments and events in the play are disposed in an inviolable sequence, independent of considerations of future, present, or past. That is, to interpolate an apt formula of Quentin Smith, they coexist *tenselessly*—always sustaining the same unchanging "relations to each other of simultaneity, earlier than, or later than" (1994, 38). In an alternate formulation, *as a dramatic text, the play comprises a series of successive moments and events simultaneously participating in the same totality.* Thus construed, the moments and events comprising *Hamlet* are "spread out in actual juxtaposition," thereby constituting a "permanent order of succession" or "tenseless array," exactly like the moments and events comprising the *B*-series aspect of time (to quote phrases respectively from Philip Turetzky and Delmas Kiernan-Lewis regarding *B*-time).[2]

This distinction between *A*-time and *B*-time (time as formulated as an *A*-series and time formulated as a *B*-series) can be epitomized in the following manner: think of *Hamlet* from within (as experienced by the characters) and without (as a text comprising a fixed and unvarying series of events). In the former (from within), time unfolds as an *A*-series; in the latter (from without), time unfolds as a *B*-series. Probing the implications of the *A*-series and the *B*-series in the play will disclose a heretofore "undiscover'd" dimension of meaning (3.1.79). To this point, we have indicated only its terms of reference. Now our task is to examine how *A*-series and *B*-series constructions of time—with their corresponding tensed and tenseless formulations of reality—illumine *Hamlet* in general and Hamlet's own rectification of the problem of time in particular.

A-series time in *Hamlet*

Time passes on the platform of Elsinore. The sentries watch the minutes of this night, hear the clock striking one, and note the changing position of the stars. The Ghost senses the approach of dawn, and the moment when his allotted time on the platform expires and his allotted time in purgatorial fire resumes. On this level, the crucial event in the play is the passage of time. Indeed, it is the "argument" of the play, just as, as we shall see, it is the argument of *The Murder of Gonzago*—the play within the play (3.2.27). But how is this temporal passage constructed and construed? In McTaggart's paradigm, the passage of time (as an *A*-series) entails the continuous approach of the future toward the present and continuous recession into the past of that which was present. George Schlesinger elaborates: "Temporal points from the future, together with the events that occur at those points, keep approaching the NOW and, after momentarily coinciding with it, recede further and further into the past" (1994, 214). There is no danger, in this paradigm, that time will ever run out. It passes as a continuous flux of succession, without beginning or end. Moreover, though temporal passage, as D. H. Mellor indicates, is defined as "the dimension of changing tense" from future to present to past, passage itself does not occupy a temporal position (1993, 49). Instead, it is tenseless—that is, its unchanging continuity is not susceptible to distinctions of future, present, and past. Consider, for example, Polonius's construction of time as the continuous succession of night and day: "Why day is day, night night, and time is time" (2.2.88). Although, from the standpoint of a given moment, one particular day or one particular night is susceptible to distinction in terms of futurity, presence, or pastness, the continuous passage of night and day does not itself migrate from future to present to past. Rather its tenseless continuity is presupposed by the continuous transition from the future to the present to the past of any given moment (or day or night) it contains.

But for "[t]he single and peculiar life" in *Hamlet*, time is not inexhaustible (3.3.11). Instead, it is limited and finite, for human life is "mortal and unsure"— unsure, that is, of how much more time has been allotted to it (4.4.51). From this point of view, time is understood in terms not of continuity, but of *expiration*. As such, the passage of time is itself a source of threat, apart from whatever events its passage might bring into the present.[3] Regardless of suspected or expected content, the fundamental threat posed by the future to the present concerns elapse. This construction of temporal passage gives rise to a defense mechanism: a countervailing movement from the present toward the past or from the past toward the present. The subtlest "armour of the mind" concerns the conceptualization of time (3.3.12). Time must somehow be thought of or construed in a way that makes its onslaught less threatening or, conversely, existence in time less vulnerable to temporal movement. The future is the tense menacing the present with relegation to the past. The only security for the present is to return to the past where the future cannot happen. But the past is a treacherous haven, for it threatens the present with the image of its own eventual fate. Having formulated the temporal double bind operant in the world of the play, our task now is to verify its accuracy and explore its implications. Then we shall be in a position to examine the steps by which this temporal construction is dismantled and superseded, though only temporarily.

It is convenient to begin with the pervasive emphasis on the expiration or elapse of time remaining. A list of examples will confirm the prominence of this concern: (a) the time left to the Ghost to haunt the platform, before withdrawing to the flames of Purgatory ("My hour is almost come / When I to sulph'rous and tormenting flames/ Must render up myself" [1.5.3–5]); (b) the time left for the passion of youth to last ("The perfume and suppliance of a minute, / No more" [1.3.8]); (c) the time left for Laertes to board ship ("Yet here, Laertes? Aboard, aboard for shame" [1.3.55]); (d) the time left for proper mourning ("and the survivor bound / In filial obligation of some term / To do obsequious sorrow" [1.2.90–92]); (e) the time left to humanity before the Last Judgment ("Then is doomsday near" [2.2.237]); (f) the time left to the child Players to continue their profession before puberty changes their voices ("Will they pursue the quality no longer than they can sing?" [2.2.344]); (g) the time left to the aged Player King to live ("Faith, I must leave thee, love, and shortly too" [3.2.168]); (h) the time left before Hamlet will implement a deadly stratagem against Claudius ("Hazard so near us doth hourly grow / Out of his brows" [(3.3.6–7]); (i) the time left before Hamlet is shipped to England ("The sun no sooner shall the mountains touch / But we will ship him hence" [4.1.29–30]); (j) the time left before the will loses its motivation ("That we would do, / We should do when we would" [4.7.117–18]); (k) the time left to Ophelia to float before drowning ("But long it could not be" [4.7.179]); (l) the time left before a corpse rots ("How long will a man lie i'th'earth ere he rot?" [5.1.158]); (m) the time left before the murder plot of Claudius and Laertes is implemented ("An hour of quiet shortly shall we see; / Till then in patience our proceeding be" [5.1.289–94]); (n) the time left to Rosencrantz and Guildenstern to live, after the ship bearing them reaches England ("He should those bearers put to sudden death, / Not shriving-time allow'd" [5.2.44–47]); (o) the time left for Hamlet to live after the ship bearing him arrives in England ("That on the supervise, no leisure bated, / No, not to stay the grinding of the axe, / My head should be struck off" [5.2.23–25]); (p) the time left to Hamlet to live after being stabbed by Laertes' envenomed foil ("In thee there is not half an hour's life" [5.2.321]).

This conspicuous emphasis on expiration entails, of course, equal emphasis on the anisotropy or one-way forward movement of time, always in the direction of what has not yet occurred. Yet precisely this preoccupation with the relentlessness of temporal movement prompts the project to reverse the irreversible: to divert the current of time such that it flows toward the past, not the future. The central example or consequence of this project is the revenge morality itself, which construes the future as redress of the past. That is, *the most profound motive of the revenge morality concerns not vengeance, but reversal of the flow of time*. On the platform, the watchers are consumed with apprehension of the "precurse of fear'd events" (1.1.124). But when the future event arrives in the form of the Ghost, it is associated with the past, as the spectre wears armor identical to that worn by the dead King, "when he th'ambitious

Norway combated," long ago (1.1.64). The link between the Ghost and the threat posed by the passage of time is further highlighted by its manner of locomotion. That is, the movement of the Ghost is subtly associated with the movement of time; for its stealthy movement ("Why, look you there, look how it *steals away*") mimics the passage of time that causes all things to become older: "But age with his *stealing steps*" (3.4.136, 5.1.70 [my emphasis]). Thus, the Ghost both invokes and combats the threat entailed in the anisotropy of time. While the Ghost's movement is associated with the passage of time into the future whereby everything already in time succumbs to aging and eventual termination, the revenge imperative that he both embodies and delivers initiates a countervailing focus on and movement toward the past.

The intense anxiety about the passage of time underpinning the revenge morality appears also in the circumstances of the death that the Ghost enjoins Hamlet to avenge: "Upon my secure hour thy uncle *stole*" (1.5.61 [my emphasis]). Here the murderer whose act is to be avenged is subtly associated with the passage of time; for his homicidal movement is described in terms of the same stealing stealth as that we have just seen connected with time itself. Moreover, the time chosen for this assassination ("my secure hour") shows that there is no refuge or security in time. A similar anxiety regarding the passage of time appears in the speech of the Player King in *The Murder of Gonzago*—the play that Hamlet commands to be performed, in preparing his response to the revenge imperative: "Faith, I must leave thee, love, and shortly too" (3.2.168). Here the Player King alludes to his own vulnerability to temporal expiration as a result of aging. These examples, respectively involving (a) the Ghost, (b) the sleeping victim assaulted during his "secure hour," and (c) the Player King, cumulatively suggest that *the ultimate injury that the revenge morality seeks to redress concerns the movement of time or, more precisely, the vulnerability of "the single and peculiar life" to this movement* (3.3.11). It accomplishes or, more exactly, simulates this redress by focusing attention toward the past, away from the future. In this context, movement toward the future accomplishes no more than to exact compensation for what happened in the past. The past remains the primary tense.

The project to reverse or, at least, halt the anisotropy (one-way forward movement) of time appears not only in the revenge project per se, but also is subtly suggested by other means and other activities. Consider first the feverish preparation to defend against expected attack by Fortinbras, eager to avenge the loss of territory occasioned by his father's defeat in single combat with Hamlet Sr., deceased king of Denmark: "Why such impress of shipwrights, whose sore task / Does not divide the Sunday from the week. / What might it be toward that this sweaty haste / Doth make the night joint-labourer with the day" (1.1.78–81). On the surface, Marcellus's questions about these preparations merely foreground—and exaggerate—the urgent continuity of work, even during periods normally devoted to rest, such as night and Sunday. But at a deeper level, his observation ironically suggests *an attempt to negate or nullify the successiveness or consecutivity on which the very movement of time depends*. The succession of night and day is replaced by their simultaneity ("Doth make the night joint-labourer with the day"), while the succession of "week" and "Sunday" is nullified by their virtual identity ("Does not divide the Sunday from the week").

A more powerful example of the attempt to alter the movement of time pertains to Hamlet's madness. In fact, his madness functions as a magnifying mirror in which tendencies in the prevailing construction or conceptualization of time can be seen more clearly. Hamlet subjects time to a process of contraction, such that its intervals, its distinct and consecutive events, approach each other and tend to coalesce. Thus time approximates the measure of simultaneity. He contracts the interval between his father's death and his mother's remarriage: "But two months dead—nay, not so much, not two"; "and yet within a month" (1.2.138, 145). He similarly contracts the interval between the present and his father's death: "For look you how cheerfully my mother looks and my father died within's two hours" (3.2.124–25). In the conventional paradigm, as time moves forward the interval between the present and a *future* event, E, continually contracts, until at last E is now, and no longer in the future. But in his melancholy, Hamlet reverses the anisotropy of time. As time moves forward, the interval between the present and a *past* event, E_1, continually contracts. This contraction ultimately suggests that time is moving backward—the past getting closer to the present. When mocking Polonius's age, Hamlet is not just delivering an insult, but also, ironically, foregrounding his own project to reverse the direction of time: "For yourself, sir, shall grow old as I am—if like a crab you could go backward" (2.2.202–4). This emphasis on the backward movement of time is a symptom of the temporal pathology wherein "[t]he time is out of joint"—a condition functioning as a defense mechanism, designed to protect "the single and peculiar life" against the onslaught of time, construed as inexorable expiration (1.5.196, 3.3.11). At bottom, when Hamlet observes, "It is not nor, it cannot come to good," he expresses not just apprehension concerning his domestic situation, but anxiety, universal in the play, regarding the passage of time itself (1.2.158).

The character most closely linked with vulnerability to the passage of time is Ophelia—indeed she incarnates the pathos of such vulnerability.

The stream in which she drowns obviously suggests the flow of time—a circumstance reinforced by emphasis on the inevitable expiration of the brief period during which, "incapable of her distress," she floats upon it: "But long it could not be" (4.7.177, 179). Her insanity is the ultimate—though ultimately futile—defence against the passage of time, for in it she focuses obsessively on the past, by means of grieving memory: "There's rosemary, that's for remembrance—pray you, love, remember" (4.5.173-74).[4] The great paradox of her insanity is that remembrance enables forgetting—forgetting, that is, the constancy of passage. Time is always flowing. Nothing remains buoyed up in the present for long. As a result of passage or temporal succession, everything present eventually sinks into the past. Philip Turetzky, in a discussion of the A-series, reinforces this point: "A-theory conceives of temporal succession as the change of the present and what is present into the past" (1998, 128). Ironically, of course, Ophelia's obliviousness to temporal succession makes her more vulnerable to it—less able, that is, to anticipate or prepare for its consequences. Thus, the obverse of her preoccupation with the past is helplessness regarding the future: "Lord, we know what we are, but know not what we may be" (4.5.43-44). The only response to the future is vague hope, emptied of specific object, and hence not really hope at all: "I hope all will be well. We must be patient" (4.5.68).

Ophelia's madness is symptomatic of temporal malaise in the world of the play. It simply exaggerates—one might almost say *parodies*—the pervasive distortion of temporal awareness. Temporal flow is construed as hazardous; for it removes from presence that which it brings into presence. Like Ophelia, the revenge morality also privileges obsession with the past—but in the mode of vengeance, not grief. In both cases, as we have seen, preoccupation with the past serves the need to ward off the threat of the passage of time. The fundamental distrust of time (construed as transience or flux) renders the present a site of insecurity, always besieged by anxiety regarding loss of that which cannot be retained. This temporal insecurity penetrates into the "inmost part" of character: the power to enact decision and personal choice (3.4.19). Both Claudius and the Player King emphasize the role of time—or more precisely, of the elapse of time—in thwarting the implementation of decision: "That we would do, / We should do when we would: for this 'would' changes / And hath abatements and delays" (Claudius [4.7.117-19]); "But what we determine, oft we break" (Player King [3.2.182]). The locus classicus of this problem concerns, of course, Hamlet's celebrated "delay" (3.1.72)—a period during which Hamlet finds himself "laps'd in time": "Do you not come your tardy son to chide, / That, *laps'd in time* and passion, lets go by / Th'important acting of your dread command?" (3.4.107–9 [my emphasis]).

Hamlet's assessment of his situation rewards analysis. To begin with, as we have just seen, Ophelia in her madness is psychologically "laps'd in time," for she focuses obsessively on memory of the past, forgetting the passage of time in the present. Yet, despite her distraction, that passage inexorably intrudes, carrying her very life into the past and thereby heightening the pathos of her plight: "long it could not be." Hamlet displays similar symptoms of temporal elapse. In his melancholy, he broods on the past and recoils from the present: "That it should come to this!" (1.2.137). In fact, one might even surmise that revulsion from the present compromises his ability—or willingness—to act in it, and thereby reconfirm its reality. But Hamlet's delay implies something much more profound than this. While "laps'd in time," he progressively deepens his engagement with time—transforms, that is, his notion of temporality and ultimately achieves the concept of "happy time" (5.2.201). In this context, the import of Hamlet's earlier linkage of the revenge imperative with what might be called the temporal imperative becomes clearer: "The time is out of joint. O cursed spite, / That ever I was born to set it right" (1.5.196–97). *The time is out of joint, because its forward movement causes consternation and fear that, in turn, prompt the project to move time backward, by making the future confirm the primacy of the past.* Hamlet's delay presupposes the passage of time—and heightens awareness of the passage of time. But during that passage, the meaning of temporality is progressively reconceived. On receiving the revenge imperative, Hamlet wants revenge to follow immediately, with no temporal elapse at all. "Haste me to know't, that I with wings as swift / As meditation or the thoughts of love / May sweep to my revenge" (1.5.29–31). Ironically, his delay becomes the means of overcoming and transcending the sense of time underpinning the revenge morality that he seeks instantly to obey.

The first turning point in the development in Hamlet's conceptualization of time occurs during his visit to Ophelia's closet, shortly *before* the arrival of the Players. Here the struggle between antithetical attitudes toward the anisotropy or one-way movement of time reaches a crisis whose resolution entails moving beyond the reaches of the prevailing conceptualization, which construes time as a destructive agent whose passage must be defended against by modes of thought that attempt to reverse or ward off its menacing momentum. In Ophelia's closet, according to her anguished account, Hamlet relegates Ophelia to the past, gazing intently at her, as if to imprint the memory of this meeting indelibly on his mind: "He falls to such perusal of my face / As a would draw it" (2.1.90–91).

It is an anguished and momentous occasion. At his departure, Hamlet's gestures suggest that he is leaving not just Ophelia and his former attachment to her, but also, and more profoundly, his attachment to the way he used to prioritize the past in dealing with the temporality. By formulating Ophelia as something to be accessed only through memory, and then looking back at her as he departs as if beholding that which he shall never see again, Hamlet moves toward a new way of construing the passage of time.

Yet discussion of the evolution of Hamlet's conceptualization of time itself requires conceptual flexibility in order to address and keep in focus what Peter Brown, in a discussion of late Roman history, terms "the dynamic quality of the relations of change and continuity" (1972, 51). That is, analysis of Hamlet's emergent ideas of time demands what John K. Davies, in treating economic models, terms an "explanatory framework" with the "conceptual space within which to accommodate the ebb and flow" of competing or discrepant tendencies (2005, 132, 133). Regarding any process of alteration, investigators ordinarily tend to foreground either that which emphasizes transformation or that which emphasizes stability. Jean Andreau elaborates: "Some scholars, therefore, stress the serious nature of discontinuities and crises, whereas others are more receptive to the signs of permanence" (2002, 38). The present study attempts to balance these two poles of interpretation.

The most ambiguous phase of the development of Hamlet's conceptualization of time concerns the period between the arrival of the Players or "tragedians" and the performance of *The Murder of Gonzago* (2.2.327). On the one hand, as we have noted, Hamlet here often emphasizes the notion of temporal regress (the present moving closer to the past), as when insulting Polonius's age or claiming, while seated next to Ophelia for the court performance, that his father died just two hours earlier. But on the other hand, Hamlet begins to register the passage of time positively and to affirm the forward movement of temporal succession. He observes that his actor friend has grown a beard since Hamlet last saw him and that a child actor has grown to the brink of puberty: "Pray God your voice, like a piece of uncurrent gold, be not cracked within the ring" (2.2.423–25). Moreover, he generalizes this observation to include the inevitable maturation of all child actors: "Will they pursue the quality no longer than they can sing?" (2.2.344–45). He is further curious about the effect of the passage of time on thespian skill ("Do they grow rusty"), and is aware of the contemporary—and hence transient—preference for child actors: "They are now the fashion" (2.2.335, 339). He even refers to the inevitability of death in humorous terms: "After your death you were better have a bad epitaph than their ill report while you live" (2.2.521–22).

This positive trend of temporal conceptualization contrasts starkly with the negative conceptualization dramatized in the *The Murder of Gonzago*. The fundamental "argument" of that play concerns the destructive effect of the passage of time (3.2.227)—a notion epitomized in Shakespeare's twelfth sonnet: "And nothing 'gainst Time's scythe can make defence" (1942, 1373). The play opens with the Player King variously calculating the elapse of time since his marriage to the Player Queen: "Full thirty times hath Phoebus' cart gone round" (3.2.150). In subsequent speeches, he stresses his mortality and the transience of human commitment—a phenomenon as natural as the falling of ripened fruit from the branches supporting them: "But fall unshaken when they mellow be" (3.2.186). The emphasis on the destructive passage of time is heightened when we remember, as noted earlier, that the murderer of Hamlet Sr., whose crime is reenacted in *The Murder of Gonzago*, is subtly associated with the stealthy movement of time.

Immediately after Claudius halts the theatrical performance, Hamlet displays acute awareness of the measurement of time. Twice he acknowledges the passage of time by affirming imminent compliance with the command to visit his mother: "Then I will come to my mother by and by"; "I will come by and by" (3.3.374, 375–76). Then he notes the precise time of night: "'Tis now the very witching time of night" (3.3.379). Yet the most important aspect of Hamlet's heightened awareness of time, at this stage of the play, concerns not measurement, but attitude. Whereas, as we have seen, the prevailing attitude toward time is distrustful and pessimistic, when en route to Gertrude's closet, Hamlet displays profound trust and optimism in temporal movement, in diametric contrast to the default or conventional opinion regarding the destructive nature of time. Pausing behind the praying Claudius, whom he unexpectedly encounters, Hamlet again displays acute awareness of time, but on this occasion in terms of the fitness of the present moment for the revengeful action that he has long intended: "Now might I do it pat, and now a is a-praying / And now I'll do't" (3.3.72–73). Here, in a flash of reflection that halts the consummation for which he has devoutly wished, Hamlet postpones assassination. Delay is founded on analysis of the consequences of action at this juncture, when Claudius manifests remorse for the very crime that Hamlet seeks to avenge. In planning to achieve revenge later, "when [Claudius] is drunk asleep, or in his rage," or engaged in other morally reprobate behavior, Hamlet displays trust in temporal movement from the present toward the future (3.3.89). Here the forward movement of time is welcomed, not feared or resisted. Hamlet displays similar trust in the forward movement of time in Gertrude's closet, with this difference. Whereas Hamlet associated the passage of time with optimization of the opportunity to ensure his uncle's *damnation*, here he associates the passage of time (in this case, from night to night) with optimization of the opportunity to ensure his mother's *salvation* (or moral improvement): "Refrain tonight, / And that shall lend a kind of easiness / To the next abstinence, the next more easy" (3.4.167–69).

Hamlet's emergent trust in the forward movement of time contrasts sharply with his adversary's increasing anxiety concerning it. In fact, *to Claudius, Hamlet eventually incarnates or localizes the fearsome anisotropy of time prevalent in the world of the play*: "Hazard so near us doth hourly grow / Out of his brows" (3.3.6–7). He sees in Hamlet's thinking "the precurse of fear'd events" (to interpolate Horatio's comment on dire omens, in the first scene of the play [1.1.124]). In this context, to get rid of Hamlet is to overcome fear or distrust of temporality. Look at how Claudius attempts to do this. In dealing with Hamlet, he reveals his way of dealing with the threat of time. He attempts to instigate events designed to preempt what he fears will happen. By this means, he improvises a kind of certainty, as with the plan to ship Hamlet off to England: "The sun no sooner shall the mountains touch / But we will ship him hence" (4.1.29–30). The import of this command emerges when we remember that Polonius defined the passage of time in terms of the regular succession of night and day. Claudius seeks to render the future—or, more precisely, occurrence in the future—as certain as the alternation of dawn and dusk, day and night. To do this, he must construct the future as a fait accompli: "Delay it not—I'll have him hence tonight / Away, for *everything is seal'd and done* / That else leans on th'affair. Pray you make haste" (4.3.58–60 [my emphasis]). Here, as the italicized clauses suggest, Claudius does everything possible to make the future become the past. Yet in doing so, he reveals his profound distrust of temporal movement; for he desperately seeks to reduce the interval between the present and the future, lest during that period some unforeseen impediment or menace intervene: "Till I know 'tis done, / Howe'er my haps, my joys were ne'er begun" (4.3.70–71).

Hamlet's forced voyage to England constitutes the crisis or thematic hinge of the play, as far as the matter of attitudes toward temporality is concerned. It functions as the transition between "before and after" with respect to the paradigm shift in temporal conceptualization (4.4.37). Just before embarking on this journey, Hamlet encounters Fortinbras's army, preparing to cross Danish territory in order to fight "against some part of Poland" (4.4.12). In contemplating this departure, Hamlet emphasizes the notion of advance toward "the invisible event" or, in Harold Jenkins's gloss, "unforeseeable outcome" in the future (4.4.50).[5] Hamlet's own impending embarkation similarly constitutes advance toward an invisible event. On that ship, Hamlet sails not just toward England, but also into the future. The journey is not dramatized, only later recounted, when it becomes material for a story or narration. It is portrayed or referred to in the play in both the future and past tenses, but not the present. In this regard, it is unique. Something very significant is implied here, yet very difficult to substantiate and even more difficult to explain. Dramaturgically, the event of sailing toward England has a past and future tense, but no present tense. The lack of present tense suggests that Hamlet has temporarily gone beyond the reaches of presentness. That is, he has entered futurity as such, and has not simply moved to a time later than the present. Of course, he has in fact moved to a time later than the present—later, that is, than the moment when his embarkation constituted his transient now. But he has also freed himself from temporal anxiety about futurity—the universal anxiety in the play.

Let us look at this matter more closely. In saying that Hamlet has entered futurity, I do not mean that the ship he boards is an anachronistic time machine that bears him toward a future time—a time period, that is, which is posterior to or later than the time period experienced by Hamlet and the other characters of the play, as if, for example, he were to journey to a subsequent century. Instead, by saying that Hamlet has entered futurity, I mean that he is confronting futurity as such—the tense or zone of time whose unforeseeable contingency causes such "discord and dismay" in the world of the play (4.1.45). In mastering that challenge and situation, Hamlet moves beyond confinement in his preoccupation with temporal passage from present to future dominant in the play. Let us see how this happens. According to Hamlet's account of the voyage, his experience begins with almost paralyzing foreboding: "Methought I lay / Worse than the mutines in the bilboes" (5.2.5–6). Here, very clearly, the movement of the ship is associated with the movement of the present into the future. Awareness of that transition imprisons Hamlet inside the nutshell of his own apprehension. This is perhaps the most extreme version of the recurring predicament concerning "the precurse of fear'd events" (1.1.124). How does Hamlet solve this problem? He does so by confronting the present on its own terms—in terms, that is, of its present circumstances and not in relation to foreboding about what comes next: "Up from my cabin, / My sea-gown scarf'd about me, in the dark / Grop'd I to find out them, had my desire" (5.2.12–14). Here, almost literally, Hamlet gropes from the present into the future—the obscure zone of "the invisible event" whose unknown contingency and outcome he cannot in the present yet see.

Then suddenly, after retrieving and opening the diplomatic "packet" that Rosencrantz and Guildenstern are purveying to the English king, Hamlet discovers the future—the fate that Claudius has planned for him: "My head should be struck off" (5.1.24). Having overcome foreboding regarding the future, Hamlet is enabled to exercise more control over its unfolding, and thereby thwart, at least in this particular instance, Claudius's plot against his life and devise his own plot against the lives of Rosencrantz and Guildenstern: "He should the bearers put to sudden death" (5.1.46). Yet control of the future is obviously impossible. For when Claudius learns that this particular plot against Hamlet has been foiled, he simply devises another, with more insurance against failure: "Therefore this project / Should have a back or second that might hold / If this did blast in proof" (4.7.151–53). Closer investigation of Hamlet's account of his shipboard experience shows that control of the future is not the central issue engaging Hamlet, and a fortiori not the solution to anxiety about the future. Chance and pluck ultimately save Hamlet, not fortuitous forging of Claudius's communication to the English king, as we see in the ensuing "sea-fight" (5.2.54). Even had he not discovered and altered Claudius's lethal instructions, Hamlet still would have escaped his doom. For the boat on which he sails is intercepted unexpectedly by pirates whose ship Hamlet boldly boards to fight them off only to find himself taken "prisoner" when the pirates suddenly disengage from his vessel, and sail away (4.6.18).

The sea-fight entrains an extremely famous archetype in the history of the philosophy of time whose explication can advance our discussion of the status of the future in *Hamlet*. In *On Interpretation* (*De Interpretatione*), Aristotle cites the example of a sea-fight to illustrate the question of whether or not statements about the future are true or false—the question, that is, whether the future is determined (necessary) or indeterminate (contingent): "A sea-fight must either take place to-morrow or not, but it is not necessary that it should take place to-morrow, neither is it necessary that it should not take place, yet it is necessary that it either should or should not take place to-morrow" (9, 19a, 30–34).[6] As Turetzky indicates, the implications of Aristotle's example of the sea-fight have spawned contentious debate that spans centuries: "The problem has been subjected to intense scrutiny" (1998, 29). Basically, the celebrated matter of the sea-fight concerns the question of whether truth-values attach to statements about the future—that is, whether statements about the future are either true or false. Aristotle's solution to this conundrum is that, as Turetzky indicates, "[f]uture alternatives ... must be indeterminate," because, unlike the present and the past, "[t]he future exists only potentially; it has no actual existence" (1998, 28, 29). Statements or claims about the future are neither true nor false, because truth and falsity apply only to that which is or was, not to that which has not yet come to be and which therefore has not been realized or determined. If statements about the future were either true or false, then future events would be already determinate and certain to happen or not to happen, with the result that there would be, as Turetzky indicates, "no real alternatives" (1998, 28). But if there were no real alternatives in the future, then the future would be closed, not open, with respect to possibilities, and there would therefore be no scope for free will. There would be, that is, no alternatives between or among that the will would have freedom to choose. Wittgenstein elaborates: "The freedom of the will consists in the fact that future actions cannot be known" (1967, 32).

It has never before been noted that the issues involved in Aristotle's sea-fight are central to those involved in Hamlet's sea-fight and his sea voyage before and after it. In the play, both the voyage and the sea-fight foreground the utter unpredictability of the future and the corresponding freedom of the will to improvise actions in response to that indeterminacy. Yet repeated encounters with unpredictability do not lead Hamlet to prioritize free will, no matter how resourcefully he responds to emergent circumstance. Instead, he prioritizes providence—the administration of divine plan: "There's a divinity that shapes our ends, / Rough-hew them how we will" (5.2.10). Paradoxically, in Hamlet's view, the openness of the future—and the freedom to respond it—is predicated on predetermination. That is, to interpolate Peter Brown's formulation from a different context, "the individual act of free self-determination—the *liberum arbitrium*—is not denied; but it is mysteriously incorporated in an order which lies outside the range of such self-determination" (1972, 269). Closer examination of Hamlet's courageously achieved insight into temporality will clarify his incorporation of self-determination "in an order which lies outside the range of such self-determination."

Explication can begin with opponent views of futurity. In one, the future is open because, until they happen, future events "are merely unrealized possibilities that can only be specified conditionally" (to interpolate Turetzky's phrasing from a different context) (1998, 153). In the other, the future is closed, because every event and every action is predetermined by providence, as when Hamlet attributes the fortuitous presence of his "father's signet" in his "purse" to divine plan: "Why, even in that was Heaven ordinant" (5.2.49, 48). Ironically, Hamlet reaches the second view (regarding the primacy of providence) only by first achieving, at least by implication, the first view (regarding the openness of the future). Let us see how this happens. The first view entails acceptance of the passage of time: the future is not to be feared and the past is not to be clung to: "Now or whensoever" (5.2.199). This acceptance of the forward movement of time is indispensable to Hamlet's recognition of the agency of providence in shaping the eventual purpose of ends whose original purpose is chosen by the individual will. Through such acceptance, time is seen as the medium in which the ultimate purpose of a prior purpose is disclosed. Immediate purposes are chosen by or given to individual agents, but the ultimate or providential ends of those purposes are revealed only by the unfolding of events in time. For example, the higher or providential purpose of Hamlet's having years earlier learned calligraphy appears only when he must draw on that "learning" to forge a false version of Claudius's instructions to the English king (5.2.35).

As shown earlier, acceptance of the forward movement of time is problematized in the play by expiration anxiety: the future is construed as the tense when allotted time will expire, and therefore the anisotropy of time is feared or resisted. *The ultimate threat of the future is that there will be no more time in it*. In *Hamlet*, the essence of the tragic predicament is the running out or elapsing of time, such that there is no time left to avoid or forestall devastating inevitability—a condition epitomized earlier by the circumstances of Ophelia's temporary buoyancy before drowning: "But long it could not be" (4.7.179). But in the final scene of the play, the site of expiration shifts from the future to the present, for here the threat of expiration is consciously registered as immediate. Examining the contrary responses of Hamlet and Claudius to the imminence of expiration will clarify Hamlet's achievement in resetting the joints of time. For *in the world of the play, death is the ultimate instance of temporal expiration*: "In thee there is not half an hour's life" (5.2.321). On seeing Gertrude drink from the poisoned cup, Claudius expresses *despair* at expiration: "It is too late" (5.2.196). In contrast, on sensing his own imminent death, Hamlet expresses *acceptance* of expiration: "Had I but time—as this fell sergeant, Death, / Is strict in his arrest— O, I could tell you—/ But let it be" (5.2.341–43). For Hamlet, *readiness conquers expiration anxiety*: "If it be now, 'tis not to / come; if it be not to come, it will be now; if it be not / now, yet it will come. The readiness is all" (5.2.216–18). Instead of what might be termed expiration time (the dominant temporal mode in the world of the play), Hamlet affirms "happy time" whose flow from the present to eventual expiration in the future is administered by providence (5.2.201).

The ironic tragedy in *Hamlet* is that the eponymous hero's strenuously achieved anagnorisis or recognition concerning "happy time" soon succumbs to a process of deconstruction with the result that, by the end of the play, expiration anxiety regains its former sovereignty. Hamlet himself begins this process. Though accepting the expiration of his own life, he does not accept the debasement of his reputation during the time that will follow his death. With his dying strength, Hamlet wrenches the poisoned cup from Horatio's grasp, and enjoins him to postpone suicide at least until he has rehabilitated Hamlet's "wounded name" by explaining publicly the factors leading to the deaths that the court "audience" has just witnessed: "Absent thee from felicity awhile, / And in this harsh world draw thy breath in pain / To tell my story" (5.2.349, 340, 352–54). Thus Hamlet ends his life with renewed anxiety regarding the movement of time toward the future. Horatio widens the scope of this temporal anxiety to concern not just the fate of Hamlet's posthumous name but also the mayhem that threatens to follow his death as a result of public confusion regarding its circumstances: "But let this same be presently perform'd / Even while men's minds are wild, lest more mischance / On plots and errors happen" (5.2.398–99). Once again, expiration anxiety prompts the urgency to act before the movement of time brings the next calamity, recalling Claudius' recourse to "desperate appliance" to preempt the fearsome anisotropy or one-way forward movement of time (4.3.10).

The play closes with Fortinbras well positioned (and supported by Hamlet's "dying voice") to assume kingship (5.2.361). Yet Fortinbras is conspicuously associated with the dominant temporal attitude in the world of the play—the attitude that Hamlet temporarily transcended. For he founds movement toward the future on the primacy of the past—a tactic ultimately based, as we established earlier, on the project to reverse—or at least render less intractable—the anisotropy of time: "I have some rights of memory in this kingdom, / Which now to claim my vantage doth invite me" (5.2.394–95). Moreover, Fortinbras is associated with Claudius—the figure who, as also noted earlier, epitomizes expiration anxiety. In anticipating election to kingship, Fortinbras mingles joy with grief ("For me, with sorrow I embrace my fortune"), just as did Claudius with regard to "mirth in funeral and with dirge in marriage, / In equal scale weighing delight and dole" (5.2.393; 1.2.12–13). Fortinbras also shares the same link with martial artillery, as his final command, "Go, bid the soldiers shoot," echoes Claudius's penchant for concussive salvo at the time of his "wassail" (5.2.408; 1.4.9).

Thus *Hamlet* dramatizes a world doomed to perpetuate the same tormented sense of time. Yet the play does adumbrate an alternate temporal conception, where the passage of time is construed in terms of unification, not elapsation. The basis for this construction is established by Hamlet, during his meditation in the graveyard. There, amid the bones and decomposing corpses, he achieves detachment from the past. So much time has passed that its influence on the present has receded from relevance. The past never expires: it just becomes increasingly remote. But through this remoteness, the past becomes the site of transformation: "Imperious Caesar, dead and turned to clay, / Might stop a hole to keep the wind away" (5.1.206–7). That is, in regard to the past, *the notion of continuous transformation replaces the notion of expiration.* "Why, may not imagination trace the noble dust of Alexander till a find it stopping a bunghole?" (5.1.196–98). Of course, the revenge morality adamantly opposes the notion of transformation. Its way of combating expiration is to insist on rememoration, in order to keep the past as vividly present as possible: "Such was the very armour he had on / When he th'ambitious Norway combated" (1.1.63–64). *The revenge morality demands fixation in the present on the memory of the past in order to enable the imperatives of the past to determine movement toward the future.* Here the project is to render the anisotropy of time less threatening and unpredictable by forcing it to obey the authority or "commandment" of the past (1.5.102–3). The ultimate outrage that the past seeks to avenge is elapse: "Cut off even in the blossom of my sin" (1.5.76). This connection becomes more evident when we remember, as shown earlier, that the murderer whose crime Hamlet must avenge is himself associated with the stealthy movement of time. But the more time advances toward the future, the less time remains to do what must be done. The attempt to avenge expiration heightens awareness of it. Ultimately, *the extreme sense of haste pervading the play derives from anxiety regarding the movement of time away from the past.* As temporal passage entrains the recession or increasing remoteness of the past, the past risks losing control over the anisotropy of time.

The breakthrough to a different temporal dispensation, where the movement of time toward the future no longer submits to control by the past, informs Hamlet's remarks in the graveyard, first regarding his tale of escape from the boat bound for England, and then regarding his meditation on the remains of the dead. Aboard the boat, as we have seen, Hamlet becomes aware that movement toward the future is no longer under the control of the past—here in the mode of the nefarious scheme of Claudius: "I sat me down, / Devis'd a new commission, wrote it fair" (5.2.31–32). While contemplating in the graveyard, as we have also seen, Hamlet considers the passage of time in terms of the transformation of the past, not the abiding dominion of the past over the present: "Alexander dies, Alexander was buried, Alexander returneth to dust, the dust is earth, of earth we make loam, and why not of that loam whereto he was converted might they not stop a beer-barrel?" (5.1.202–5). As this quotation suggests, *the most profound transformation that the past undergoes in Hamlet's conception is change from authority over the present to subservience to it.* But if the function of the past is not to control the present but instead to empower it (as, for example, when calligraphic skill learned in the past helps Hamlet deal with present predicament on the ship), then the import of the anisotropy of time changes. For in this context, *instead of intensifying the threat of expiration, movement toward the future enables fructification of prior potential*: "The inward service of the mind and soul / Grows wide withal" (1.3.13–14). Time is out of joint when anxiety regarding the anisotropy of time prompts the project to subject the future to the primacy of the past. Time is set right when the one-way forward flow of time toward the future fructifies or actualizes the potential of the past "beyond the reaches" of its prior conception (1.4.56).

B-series time in *Hamlet*

Yet, by its very nature, the sense of time as an *A*-series, entailing the continuous approach of the future toward the present and the inevitable recession toward the past of that which is momentarily present, is founded on the principle of transience, and therefore tends inevitably to foreground instability. In this dispensation, the present remains an intractably unstable perspective. As a necessary condition of actual experience, the present is *constant*; for experience is always registered in the present, no matter where on the historical timescale the subject undergoing the experience is located. When Alexander the Great lived, his experience occurred in the present tense, just as, centuries later, Hamlet's meditation on him also occurs in the present tense. But in terms of content, the present is *perpetually changing*, for new content continually approaches from the direction of the future as current content continually departs toward the past. As a result, the present is notoriously prone to foreboding and grief, as the play abundantly shows. In this context, the only satisfactory escape from the perils of temporality is somehow to shift from *A*-time to *B*-time: to construe time, that is, in terms not of transition of tense, but of invariable and tenseless order of succession. Here (to interpolate Turetzky's formulations) the notion of "fixed temporal positions" is paramount instead of the notion of "flowing time" (1998, 179).

Of course, each character in *Hamlet* simultaneously occupies two temporal dimensions: the dimension of changing tense (*A*-time) and the dimension of permanent succession (*B*-time). If we read the text or watch a performance, following the action from moment to moment, we encounter characters in the midst of *tensed* awareness—aware, that is, of his or her own experience in terms of the transition from one tense to another. More precisely, in most cases, the awareness of a given character of his or her immediate present is qualified or tinged by awareness of temporal movement toward the future and away from the past. But in addition to inhabiting the dimension of changing tense, each character also inhabits the dimension of *tenseless* succession, wherein each moment of his or her dramatization occupies its place in the fixed and invariable series of moments, stretching before and after, that constitute the content of the play. But the characters are not aware of their status as characters in a dramatic text entitled *Hamlet*. That awareness pertains only to the world outside the text. Nevertheless, careful analysis can disclose a concerted—and increasingly desperate—attempt to achieve, in the world of the play, a conceptual shift from *A*-time to *B*-time.

Precisely this kind of conceptual shift is suggested to Hamlet by Claudius, with respect to the problem of grief management: "But you must know your father lost a father, / That father lost, lost his—and the survivor bound / In filial obligation of some term / To do obsequious sorrow" (1.2.89–92). Here the passage of time is formulated in terms of succession—in terms, that is, not of the transition from future to present to past, but of a series or sequence of moments linked to each other by the relations of earlier than, simultaneous with, and later than. Here, to interpolate Turetzky's phrasing, "time is thought of as a way things and events stand in relations of succession," and not in terms of the relation of events to the moving present (1998, 152). Further examination of the play reveals a relentless effort to convert *A*-time to *B*-time—to construe time, that is, in terms of manifold events disposed in fixed and unalterable series, instead of in terms of the harrowing movement of the future toward the present and the agonizing recession of the past from the present.

In this context, the persistent recourse in the play to event summary—what might be termed the recapitulative compulsion—can be clarified. A short list of summaries and recapitulations provided in *Hamlet* will introduce the topic: (a) Horatio's summary of the events constituting "[t]he main motive" of the military preparations progressing beneath the platform of Elsinore (1.1.108); (b) the Ghost's summary of the circumstances of his own murder; (c) Polonius's summary of Hamlet's descent into madness; (d) Ophelia's summary of Hamlet's visit to her closet; (e) Gertrude's summary of the events attending Ophelia's death; (f) Hamlet's summary of his exploits on the ship, including the subsequent encounter with pirates; and (g) Horatio's impending summary of the events leading to the carnage witnessed by the audience in the play. Collectively, these instances of summary and recapitulation constitute a prominent motif in the play—one that rewards analysis. Preliminary investigation suggests that the function of summary is to overcome the hazard of A-time, whereby the present continually advances into an unknown future. For by demonstrating the derivation of the present from the past, and thereby maintaining the influence of the past on the present, summary counteracts the risk of movement into "the undiscover'd country" of the future (3.1.79). But deeper consideration of the matter suggests that the ultimate function of summary is not merely to neutralize A-time, but to convert it into B-time, by configuring time in terms of immutable succession, not constantly changing transience, and therefore to prioritize temporal position, not temporal flux. Turetzky's comment on the notion of B-time clarifies: "What is correct in the notion that time passes is that events occur in sequence" (1998, 130).

As the play ends, there is feverish preparation to summarize the events leading to the disastrous climax that heaped four corpses on the floor: "But let this same be presently perform'd / Even while men's minds are wild, lest more mischance / On plots and errors happen" (5.2.397–99). Hearing that account is considered crucial to ending the murderous mayhem that it concerns. Hence the play approaches closure with announcement of selective reiteration of its own content. On the surface, the purpose of this recapitulation is to free the future from recurrence of the mayhem in the past. But more profoundly, the impending terminal summary constitutes the hinge from A-time to B-time. First the play unfolds in A-time—as the lived experience of the characters it concerns, each immersed in his or her own awareness of temporal passage in terms of the ceaseless movement of the present away from the past and toward the future. Yet near the end, through reference to imminent summary of its own content, the preceding portion of the play is to be reconfigured in B-time—as a totality whose constituent events comprise a permanent sequence or succession. Yet it is a futile project. No quantity of summary can redeem the world of *Hamlet* from its predicament regarding the passage of time—the apprehension that the future cannot be forestalled and that concerning it the present can never be adequately forewarned. What might happen always threatens to undermine or destabilize what is happening now or to render more remote what happened in the past. Perhaps the ultimate tragedy in *Hamlet* concerns the irremediable disconformity between A-time and B-time: the impossibility of converting the transience of A-time experience into the fixity of B-time succession. This is perhaps the most fundamental level at which time is out of joint.

2

Dickens's Pathology of Time in *Hard Times*

Most criticism of *Hard Times* probes the historical accuracy of the novel—investigating, as Nicholas Coles observes, "those correspondences between Dickens' fictional world and the world he lived in" (1986, 147).[1] Inevitably, this tendency to evaluate the fiction as a medium of fact deflects attention from its deeper implications. Some critics attempt to overcome this limitation through alternate modes of analysis. These include, among many others, broadening the intellectual context to include not merely Utilitarianism but an emerging mentality involving thinkers as diverse as Malthus and Newton (Beauchamp 1989), examining the expressive properties of physiognomy (Hollington 1992) or names (Allingham 1991), and applying the heuristic models of such theorists as Dolezel and Bakhtin to resolve ideological ambiguities (Weber 1989, Fowler 1989). Typological exegesis has been employed to explicate the text as a fairy tale (Mills 1991), an approach deriving ultimately from F. R. Leavis's treatment of the novel as a "moral fable" (1960, 227).

Yet, regardless of particular emphasis or method, almost every study of *Hard Times* seeks to clarify the mimetic import of the novel—to explicate, if only tangentially, the significance of the dystopic condition it concerns. But no prior critic has discovered that the text, while depicting the wretched environment of Coketown and elaborating the doctrine of self-interest on which it depends, provides a profound analysis of the unconscious motive for sustaining such a society. As we shall find, the formative principle of Coketown is the need to create an artificial time that repudiates the natural temporal tendency toward change and decay. In his study of narrative, Peter Brooks relates the universal convention of plot to "the problem of temporality: man's time-boundedness, his consciousness of existence within the limits of mortality" (1984, xi). But, as we shall demonstrate, the fundamental purpose of Coketown is to deny or overcome this very predicament.

A review of some basic points will help initiate our inquiry. The novel begins in a Coketown classroom where Mr. Gradgrind inculcates the first "principle" of a new mentality or way of thinking: "Now, what I want is, Facts."² The purpose of this education is to permit each graduate to enter adulthood equipped for success, which is here defined as the promotion of "self-interest" (303). To this end, the subjective faculties of "imagination" (57) and feeling—especially the ability to feel pity—must be sacrificed in order to develop the one faculty most capable of manipulating the objective world: practical (as opposed to speculative) reason. The perfect product of this education is Bitzer: "His mind was so exactly regulated, that he had no affections or passions. All his proceedings were the result of the nicest and coldest calculation" (150). Yet the ruthless "self-suppression" (195) demanded by this pedagogy ultimately thwarts the "self-interest" (303) it intends to advance. Far from benefitting its adherents by training them to treat every human interaction as "a bargain across a counter" (304) whose sole purpose is personal gain, the predatory mentality encouraged by the Gradgrind system inevitably worsens the condition of everyone under its influence, reducing each to some mode of helplessness. As victims of exploitation, the Hands or workers obviously suffer helplessness, but so do characters of higher station who profit from their plight. The acute distress, experienced in vividly different ways, that afflicts Coketown residents regardless of status (or perhaps it would be more precise to say *according* to status) contradicts the very notion of personal gain on which their society is founded.

The best way to explicate this paradox is to return to the first page where Mr. Gradgrind describes the "way of thinking" (the actual phrase is introduced later by Mr. Harthouse) required by his pedagogy (159). Here the description of Mr. Gradgrind's "square wall of a forehead" (47) is extremely revealing. For the way of thinking that he inculcates does indeed establish a mental wall separating the subject from that which he or she refuses to recognize. As such, this mentality is epitomized more by what it excludes or ignores than by what it admits and retains. In fact, another image frequently associated with this way of thinking involves the barrier. For example, Louisa, Mr. Gradgrind's beloved daughter and vaunted pupil, is described in terms of "the barrier behind which she lived" (207). The barrier image recurs in reference to Mr. Gradgrind's inability to perceive Louisa's "pent-up" emotional need as they discuss the possibility of her engagement to Mr. Bounderby: "But, to see it, he must have overleaped at a bound the artificial barriers he had for many years been erecting, between himself and all those subtle essences of humanity" (135).

Though the passage does not identify the "subtle essences of humanity" that Mr. Gradgrind walls off from consideration, Louisa's ensuing lament regarding "that part of [her] nature" ignored by her upbringing provides a clue: "What do *I* know father ... of tastes and fancies; of aspirations and affections?" (136). The fullest definition of the "subtle essences" neglected by Mr. Gradgrind occurs in a description of the vast area of experience that he prefers to ignore: "human passions, human hopes and fears, the struggles, triumphs and defeats, the cares and joys and sorrows ... of ... men and women" (90). Hence, during this conversation about a decision whose consequences will eventually devastate their lives, both father and daughter are positioned behind invisible barriers obscuring from each not only the other's deepest emotional needs and responses, but also his or her own. Ironically, the driving purpose of Mr. Gradgrind's pedagogy is to maintain such barriers, lest sensitivity to feelings inhibit the exploitative self-interest they facilitate. But in this case his failure to help Louisa cannot be attributed to self-interest alone, for her emotional peril is too obvious and he is not an uncaring man: "He was an affectionate father" (55). Some factor more fundamental than self-interest prevents Mr. Gradgrind from surmounting his "artificial barriers" (135) and understanding the feelings perceived on the other side.

To uncover this factor, we must turn to the second scene in the novel where the struggle to overcome the barrier first occurs. Here Mr. Gradgrind berates his two children, Tom and Louisa, for "peeping ... through a hole in a deal board" (56) in order to glimpse the equestrian show at Sleary's Horse-riding. The full significance of both his outrage and their curiosity begins to emerge when we observe that this fence, through its connection with the later series of barrier references, ultimately symbolizes the partition separating not merely two different social worlds, but a repressive mentality from those aspects of human reality that it dares not recognize. Up to now, we have noted these barriers only in reference to Mr. Gradgrind and his closest pupil, Louisa. But he has no monopoly on the psychological barriers in Coketown. As school owner and exemplary pedagogue, his function is to reinforce and disseminate the way of thinking that creates them, for on it Coketown's industrial prosperity depends. Indeed, as will soon become evident, at bottom Coketown itself is not so much a place as the *localization* of a mentality epitomized by the barrier—or the tendency to exclude certain truths by insisting obsessively on others. Conversely the Horse-riding, separated from Coketown by the fence, is not just an itinerant circus, but a manifestation of the very truths and feelings that the mentality controlling Coketown wishes to obscure.

Unlike Coketown, the Horse-riding society is based neither on oppression of others nor self-suppression. In place of the "eminently practical" (55) morality that divides Coketown residents into two classes, exploiters and victims, the members of the Horse-riding are united by consideration and compassion: "Yet there was a remarkable gentleness and childishness about these people... and an untiring readiness to help and pity one another" (77).[3] Nevertheless Mr. Jupe, the aging "clown" (99) who is no longer able to perform his tricks properly because "[h]is joints are turning stiff" (74), decides to send his daughter, Sissy, from this sympathetic environment to Mr. Gradgrind's harsh school in Coketown. As Sissy explains, her father believes that the Gradgrind pedagogy will somehow protect her from eventually succumbing to the same helplessness from which he now suffers: "he grew so scared and trembling... he felt himself to be a poor, weak, ignorant, helpless man ... he wanted me so much to know a great deal and be different from him" (99). On the surface, Mr. Jupe seems motivated here by the conviction that an education will equip Sissy to pursue employment that puts demands on the mind and not on the body, whose strength is much less durable.

But when we remember that the specific weakness from which Mr. Jupe wishes to protect Sissy concerns susceptibility to aging, the more profound reason for his decision appears. At bottom, Mr. Jupe believes that Coketown will render Sissy invulnerable to *time* and the inevitable deterioration that it entails. His hope, though futile, is not ill founded. For, as we shall see, the formative principle of Coketown *is* the desire to escape vulnerability to time. In fact, when accompanying Mr. Gradgrind to the Horse-riding early in the novel, Mr. Bounderby himself suggests that the attitude to time is what separates the two societies: "[W]e are the kind of people who know the value of time, and you are the kind of people who don't know the value of time" (72). He is thinking, of course, that time is money (to interpolate anachronistically an adage from our own era). But his remark has a much deeper implication.

At the most profound level, time has value in Coketown only through its monotony. For during the unvarying succession of its units, one after another, the illusion is created that nothing can happen but more of the same. This is the time monitored in Mr. Gradgrind's Observatory: "a stern room, with a deadly statistical clock in it, which measured every second and with a beat like a rap upon a coffin-lid" (132). As the quotation suggests, time has one purpose in Coketown: to negate its own movement. Though time itself cannot be stopped, its very passage can be made to signify stasis, for here time is merely the measure of mechanical repetition involving addition and subtraction that cancel each other out: "Time went on in Coketown like its own machinery: so much material wrought up, so much fuel consumed" (126). There is no possibility of change—genuinely organic change, the very process from which Mr. Jupe suffers. Hence monotony is not merely the obvious condition, but also the hidden telos or goal of Coketown, where "the piston of the steam-engine [works] monotonously up and down" (65) and "monotonous smoke" (135) lingers in the air; for the ultimate purpose of this monotony is to perpetuate the need to "kill time" (155). Only through the tedium of such innumerably renewed redundancy can time itself or, more precisely, the cumulative changes it entails, be provisionally overcome.[4]

This attitude toward time reveals its pathological nature more clearly when contrasted with its closest philosophical counterpart: St. Augustine's interpretation of time in the eleventh book of the *Confessions*. There, the same paradox of time persisting only through self-destruction is considered, but with very different results. Ernst Cassirer elaborates: "If, Augustine argues, the present becomes a determination of time, a temporal present, only by flowing into the past, how we can speak of a being that subsists only by destroying itself?" (1957, 3.166). Robert Jordan compresses this paradox: "[W]e cannot maintain that time is, unless it tends not to be" (1972, 262). Augustine solves this conundrum by treating time not as a substance divided into three incompatible parts—past, present, and future—but as a function of the mind's awareness of reality. Cassirer paraphrases Augustine's conclusion: "There is a present of past things, a present of present things, and a present of future things. The present of past things is called memory, the present of present things is called intuition, that of future things is called expectation" (1957, 3.166). Thus, Augustine reaches the celebrated notion of the *distentio* by which consciousness extends its own "now" over all the tenses of time: "time is nothing else than protraction ... of the mind itself" (1951, 323).

By this means, he turns the movement of time toward self-destruction into a source of preservation. For in founding the extensiveness of time on the transience of the present moment, he "unites," to invoke Paul Tillich's phrasing, "an element of abstract unlimitedness with an element of concrete limitedness" (1963, 3.317). More precisely, Augustine views the momentary present as the means by which the mind establishes temporal diversity. This solution, however, is unavailable in Coketown where the present, instead of sustaining awareness of different tenses, knows itself only as a repetition of the same monotony.

But ideal monotony requires sameness in both time *and* space. Hence Coketown is described as an assemblage of homologous parts such that sameness in space assures sameness of time: "It contained several large streets all very like one another, and many small streets still more like one another, inhabited by people equally like one another, who all went in and out at the same hours, with the same sound upon the same pavements, to do the same work, and to whom every day was the same as yesterday and tomorrow, and every year the counterpart of the last and the next" (65). Yet the monotony of Coketown is itself founded on impatience, for the ubiquitous sameness defining the city derives not from conscious planning, but importunate impulse: "the labyrinth of narrow courts upon courts, and close streets upon streets, which had come into existence piecemeal, *every piece in a violent hurry for some man's purpose*, and the whole an unnatural family, shouldering, and trampling, and pressing one another to death" (102 [my emphasis]).

Understanding how, in Coketown, impatience is the cause of monotony and not merely its effect will tighten our grasp of *Hard Times*. Considered in the most general terms, impatience is the refusal to wait for satisfaction (in the case of desire) or relief (in the case of suffering). It is the need to nullify or at least contract the time intervening between project and fulfillment. But more fundamental than the impatience that concerns particular satisfactions or reliefs is the impatience with time itself. This metaphysical impatience demands the eradication of all waiting—but not through the fantasy of instant gratification. Instead, it seeks the eradication of time itself. Louisa's despair provides an excellent example, for here she views her life in terms of its imminent mortality: "[L]ooking at the red sparks dropping out of the fire, and whitening and dying. It made me think, after all, how short my life would be, and how little I could hope to do in it" (94). But as she herself later reveals, the deepest motive of this despair is an impatience for her life to be over, so that she will be excused from struggle during it: "[M]y dismal resource has been to think that life would soon go by, and that nothing in it could be worth the pain and trouble of a contest" (241).

Her strategy deepens the significance of an object already noted: the "statistical clock" that "measured every second and with a beat like a rap upon a coffin-lid" (132). As we have seen, the reflex to dispose of the present, moment after moment, is the essence of the monotony whose aim is to forestall change by turning time into mere repetition compulsion. But this very repetitiveness is driven by an impatience with time as acute as that inside Louisa's despair. The only difference is the time frame concerned. Whereas the impatience sustaining Louisa's despair seeks to accelerate the elapsing of her entire lifetime, the impatience expressed through the monotonous clock is confined to each new moment that is "measured" by "a rap upon a coffin-lid," as if the only purpose of time were to be over and done with. Since the impatient wish to be done with time, to be past or beyond the struggles that time entails, cannot be fulfilled all at once as in Louisa's fantasy, it must be accomplished moment by moment. If time has no end, its very endlessness can be made to signify termination, for time now goes no further than an ever repeating present.

The pathology of this project to abbreviate time can be highlighted through reference to its philosophical contrary: Bergson's notion of duration through which, as explicated by Jacques Maritain, "we are aware of advancing through time and enduring through change indivisibly, yet that we are growing richer in quality and triumphing over the inertia of matter" (1939, 47). Bergson himself defines duration as "the continuous progress of the past which gnaws into the future and which swells as it advances" (1944, 7). In place of this *cumulative* time, Coketown establishes a *momentaneous* time that resumes with each successive instant.

In this context, the primacy of Mr. Bounderby becomes more significant. On the literal level, his dominance in Coketown derives from his position as factory owner. But the more profound meaning of his authority emerges through his description as an incarnation of *impatience*: the very principle that, as we have just seen, is the prime mover of Coketown. Mr. Bounderby seems always at the point of "bursting" (211), as if the emotion in question, vanity or "indignation" (262), were too importunate to control. Two examples will vividly illustrate: "So he left Mr. Bounderby swelling at his own portrait on the wall as if he were going to explode himself into it" (114); "The blustrous Bounderby crimsoned and swelled to such an extent on hearing these words, that he seemed to be, and probably was, on the brink of a fit" (262).[5] As some critics have noted, this swelling tendency has unavoidable phallic implications, especially in the following passage where Mr. Bounderby resembles a giant erection: "A man with a great puffed head and forehead, swelled veins in his temples, and such a strained skin to his face .... A man with a pervading appearance on him of being inflated like a balloon, and ready to start" (58).[6] Yet, though Mr. Bounderby can be interpreted in Freudian terms, the phallic lust that he seems to embody is more important as an index of impatience than as a symbol of repressed sexuality. Indeed, in his own account of it, Mr. Bounderby's willful impatience assumes orgasmic urgency: "I always come to a decision ... and whatever I do, I do at once" (265).

His haste corresponds exactly to the impetuous purposiveness, noted earlier, responsible for the "piecemeal" construction of Coketown: "every piece in a violent hurry for some man's purpose" (102). But the full meaning of Mr. Bounderby's impatient tumescence emerges through the weightless floating associated with it, as when he is compared to a "soap-bubble" (292) or "balloon"

(58). By this self-inflation, he counters a pernicious gravity in the novel—an irresistible force that drags its victims down toward an utterly isolated helplessness.

The chief moments in which characters become victim to this gravity include: (a) Louisa descending Mrs. Sparsit's imaginary staircase, "like a weight in deep water," toward the shame of adultery "at the bottom" (230); (b) Louisa falling helplessly at her father's feet after fleeing from this temptation at the last moment (242); (c) Stephen plummeting down the Old Hell Shaft; (d) Mrs. Gradgrind near death when "the sound of another voice addressing her seemed to take such a long time in getting down to her ears, that she might have been lying at the bottom of a well" (224); (e) Mrs. Sparsit falling at Bounderby's feet after telling him of Louisa's disappearance (258). Against this background of sinking or falling figures, Mr. Bounderby's extraordinary levity (to use the word in its original sense of lightness or buoyancy) can be more profoundly understood.

To begin with, there is an obvious opposition between the *impatience* connected with Mr. Bounderby's levity ("like a balloon, and ready to start" [58]) and the apparent *slowing* of time that is always associated with the contrasting experience of reaching the bottom. A brief review of the evidence will illustrate: as noted, when Mrs. Gradgrind lies dying, as if "at the bottom of a well," sounds seem "to take such a *long time*" to reach her (224 [my emphasis]). Similarly, after falling in despair at her father's feet, Louisa goes through a period of delayed response: "A curious passive inattention had such possession of her, that the presence of her little sister in the room did not attract her notice *for some time*" (243 [my emphasis]). But as the case of Mrs. Gradgrind shows, this languor is the last bastion of self-interest, for it defends against exposure to *other* people's needs: "Upon my word and honour I seem to be fated, and destined, and ordained, to live in the midst of things that I am never to hear the last of" (102). After saying this, Mrs. Gradgrind becomes "torpid again" (102).

The levity of Mr. Bounderby and the languor of Louisa and Mrs. Gradgrind have further implications. In one case, self-interest is expressed through impulsive attention to one's own needs, in the other, through "passive *in*attention" (243 [my emphasis]) to the needs—and even the presence—of others. Hence, in the first, time seems rapid; for the governing principle is impatience for one's own satisfaction. In the second, time seems stagnant, for the dominant principle is obliviousness to what happens to others. Though these responses appear as opposites, they are in fact reciprocal expressions of the same mentality of self-interest. The obverse of importunate selfishness *is* unconcern for others, as demonstrated by the example of Mr. Bounderby whose impatient preoccupation with his own needs leads him to ignore or misconstrue the needs of others, with the result that any Hand "not entirely satisfied" with his situation is accused of expecting "to be set up in a coach and six, and to be fed on turtle soup and venison, with a gold spoon" (109).

The opposition between fast and slow time is even more obvious in Stephen's case. Just before tumbling into the Old Hell Shaft, he is consumed with impatience: "When I fell, I were in anger wi' her [Louisa], and hurryin on t' be as onjust t' her as oothers was t'me" (290). But at the bottom of the pit, time seems hardly to move at all, for there Stephen suffers "dreadful, dree, and long" (289). In fact, at the deepest level, he *is* suffering from time or, more precisely, from the moral insularity that slow time in the novel symbolizes. Indeed, his pain disappears ("'tis ower now") once he learns compassionate patience: "But in our judgments, like as in our doins, we mun bear and forbear" (290–91). Thus, after recognizing how impatient and self-preoccupied anger plunged him into disastrous isolation, Stephen acknowledges sympathetic understanding as the higher principle by which human life can be guided: "my dyin prayer that aw th' world may on'y coom toogether more, and get a better unnerstan'in o' one another" (291). Significantly, when he is raised from the pit by collective effort, those witnessing the rescue are united in "a low murmur of pity" (289). Hence, just as the gravity that pulled Stephen down is associated in the novel with the tendency of self-interest to deepen isolation, so rescue from this gravity is enabled by compassionate community.

Moreover, the overcoming in this scene of the isolating mentality of self-interest is foreshadowed by the circumstances immediately preceding the discovery of Stephen at the bottom of the shaft. While walking with Louisa in the countryside outside Coketown, Sissy suddenly notices "rotten fragments of fence upon the ground" and realizes that the barrier "has not been broken very long" (284). This detail gains its full force when we remember that the self-interest mentality has earlier been associated with the imagery of barriers, suggesting the need to exclude everything not pertinent to self-concern. With Stephen's rescue, this mental barrier is finally broken. Hence the falls in *Hard Times* are not uniformly negative, for, like the felix culpa in the Garden of Eden, they have the potential to confer a knowledge of good and evil by revealing both the destructiveness of the attitude of self-interest *and* the need for some alternative to it. We see this clearly in Louisa's fall at her father's feet: "[Y]our philosophy and your teaching ... have brought me to this. Save me by some other means!" (242). In contrast, through his self-inflating egotism, Mr. Bounderby protects himself against the fall, but at the same time remains obstinately enclosed in his own mentality: "'I don't see it at all, sir,' returned the obstinate Bounderby" (261); "'I don't understand you, yet,' said Bounderby, with determined obstinacy" (261).

Further analysis will clarify the opposition between fast and slow time or impatience and languor central to the novel. Impatience results from the conviction that nothing has importance but immediate satisfaction of one's own needs. But the tyrannical imperative of this impatience reduces everything else to the servile status of mere means by which the end, satisfaction, can be achieved. Self-interest thus involves a paradox. If nothing has importance except as the means for satisfaction, then satisfaction ultimately becomes meaningless, for it can be realized only through that which its own importunity has debased. The only thing holding self-interest up is its insistence on bringing everything else down. Self-interest seeks to found *affirmation* of its own intrinsic value on *negation* of the intrinsic value of that which it exploits. Paradoxically, therefore, self-interest bases its own value on lack of value. Hence, impatience and languor tend to reinforce each other. By regarding the world as a collection of means with no intrinsic value, impatience for satisfaction tends inevitably toward the condition of languor where the quest for satisfaction offers no more than a modulation of boredom. But boredom, in turn, tends eventually to increase impatience for satisfaction.

A striking victim of this vicious circle is Mr. James Harthouse, the man with whom Louisa almost commits adultery. He is introduced to the reader as an incarnation of languor, whose search for satisfaction has led him to be "bored everywhere" (158). In his initial conversation with Mrs. Sparsit, Mr. Harthouse displays languor with a gesture that subtly suggests his servitude to time: "It seemed scarcely worthwhile to finish the sentence, so he *played with his watch-chain wearily*" (154 [my emphasis]). A little later he "*languidly* wave[s] his hand" (155 [my emphasis]). Moreover, in his first conversation with Louisa, Mr. Harthouse mentions "the varieties of boredom" that he has "undergone" (162). Yet much later in their relationship, after Louisa fails to show up for their assignation, Mr. Harthouse's relation to time changes. Languor is replaced by frantic impatience as he waits for "a whole night and a day in a state of so much hurry" (249) for some sign from Louisa. No longer encouraging frivolity, boredom becomes intolerable torment: "[H]e was so horribly bored by existing circumstances" (249).

On the surface, his impatience results from the frustrated desire to renew communication with Louisa. But at the deepest, his impatience simply abbreviates his habitual languor. For in both impatience and languor, his one goal is to "g[e]t through the *intervening time* as well he could" (250 [my emphasis]). The only difference is the amount of time involved. In the state of impatience, that "intervening time" concerns the delay between a specific desire and its anticipated satisfaction. But in the state of languor, the time intervening between desire and ultimate satisfaction expands indefinitely with the result that the passage of time, instead of intensifying expectation of fulfillment, makes expectation seem increasingly pointless. Harthouse languid expects no satisfaction other than "varieties of boredom" (162). Harthouse impatient suffers the boredom of awaiting satisfaction. His love values Louisa not so much as an end in herself (to borrow for a moment from the Kantian notion of morality), but as a means of accelerating his own habitual languor by restoring, at least temporarily, the conviction that time can move him closer to genuine fulfillment (Kant 1959, 56).

Just as consideration of Mr. Harthouse, Louisa's thwarted seducer, elucidates the two poles of languor and impatience sustained by the self-interest mentality, so the related opposition between "self-suppression" (195) and recklessness can be clarified through an examination of Louisa's brother, Tom, the feckless "whelp" (169) whose gambling compulsion forces him to solicit funds from his sister and eventually to steal from Mr. Bounderby's bank, while framing Stephen for the crime. By these actions, Tom is revealed as "incapable of governing himself" (165). At first glance, his immature recklessness in early adulthood appears to be a reaction against the stringent Gradgrind discipline preceding it, for as a child, Tom was "brought up under *one continuous system of unnatural restraint*" that ensured that he "had *never been left to his own guidance for five consecutive minutes*" (165 [my emphasis]). But closer inspection reveals that, far from rebelling against his upbringing, Tom is actually fulfilling it.

As the passage just quoted shows, parental discipline in Tom's childhood was virtually as "continuous" as time itself, since he was never without its direction "for five consecutive minutes." In fact, as we shall soon establish, the effect of the self-interest regime is to make time itself a parental principle of regulation—to put time, that is, in loco parentis so that the individual can never fully assert his or her own independence. The great paradox of Mr. Gradgrind's pedagogy is that, while seeming though sheer strictness to drive its pupils "clean out of the regions of childhood" (48), what this system actually does is to render them incapable of achieving the mature individuality proper to adulthood, for under its tutelage, pupils are trained to have time for nothing but self-interest, with the result that they are molded into identical and "exactly regulated" (150) mechanisms, performing the "calculation" (150) of self-interest again and again with a methodical regularity analogous to that of Mr. Gradgrind's clock that "measured every second and with a beat like a rap upon a coffin-lid" (132). Indeed, when snoring, Bitzer, the prize male product of this system, emits "sounds of a nature similar to what may be sometimes heard in *Dutch clocks*" (209 [my emphasis]).

Perfect devotion to self-interest compromises Bitzer's adult independence. For the rigid self-discipline by which he sacrifices all "affections or passions" (150) to considerations of personal gain simply internalizes in adulthood the same regime of control that dominated his childhood. Hence, though Bitzer and Tom appear as contraries, they share the same immaturity, but simply express it in opposite ways. In one case, that immaturity is perpetuated through severe self-restraint, in the other, through irresponsible recklessness.

The motif of immaturity or, more precisely, refusal of the temporal process of maturation, recurs in the figure of Mr. Bounderby, who is preoccupied with asserting his adult "independence" (160) by repudiating his mother, a woman later identified as Mrs. Pegler. To this end, he retails the myth of her abandonment of him in childhood and his resultant exposure to abuse and homelessness: "I am a bit of dirty riff-raff, and a genuine scrap of tag, rag, and bobtail" (160). But the deeper motive for this unfilial fabrication is suggested by a description of Mrs. Pegler before her identity as Mr. Bounderby's mother is revealed: "It was an old woman, tall and shapely still, though *withered by Time*" (115 [my emphasis]). His repudiation of her is fundamentally a repudiation of the process of aging to which she obviously succumbs. The connection between this repudiation and aging is reinforced when we remember the other case of parental desertion in the novel: Mr. Jupe's abandonment of Sissy. There, as discussed earlier, the reason for abandonment was the father's wish both to escape the "shame and disgrace" of his own aging and to protect his daughter against the same vulnerability, by sending her to Coketown—a place whose monotonous repetition simulates the stasis of time (100).

Ironically, though designed to avoid the shame of aging, the mentality of self-interest increases vulnerability to shame of another kind, but some analysis will be needed to explain it. In a society founded on the principle that "every man is selfish in everything he does" (205), self-interest is not only the sole appropriate motive of action, but also the moral standard by which the worth of an individual is judged, for in this context, self-interest signifies much more than preoccupation with personal gain. At the deepest level, it demands from the individual an unfaltering "independence" (160) that is "self-reliant" (161), "logical" (303), and impervious to the need for pity, either in him/herself or another: "Nobody was ever on any account to give anybody anything, or render anybody help without purchase" (304). The cash nexus must replace both compassion and the "gratitude" (304) that it usually evokes.

In such a society, the need for pity is a shameful anomaly. Hence Mrs. Sparsit can wreak no more humiliating revenge on Mr. Bounderby for marrying Louisa than to feign "compassion on him, as a Victim" (141) for doing so. Later, after fleeing both her marriage and the adulterously inclined Mr. Harthouse, Louisa resents the exposure of her plight to Sissy, the great purveyor of compassion in the novel: "A dull anger that she should be seen in her distress ... smouldered within her like an unwholesome fire (246–47). In fact, the intense need to avoid or at least abbreviate the shame of having weakness exposed deepens the significance of the impatience that we have found central to the novel. For example, after the spuriousness of his story about abandonment in childhood is exposed, Mr. Bounderby paces "up and down" in *"impatient mortification"* until the "spectators" of his predicament finally disperse (279 [my emphasis]).

The shaming gaze that here discomfits Mr. Bounderby is not a local phenomenon. It is ubiquitous in Coketown, and cannot be dismissed as long as self-interest remains the dominant point of view; for vulnerability to shame is simply the reciprocal of self-interest. In a world where personal gain alone matters, and hence where each sees others only as instruments for his or her own advantage, any weakness perceived in another becomes the means of enhancing oneself. But conversely, the mere failure to achieve personal gain, even the need to depend on another's help in order to achieve it (as with Mr. Bounderby and his mother), risks exposure to disgrace, since in this context the very notion of esteem is predicated on the triumph of unassisted selfishness. Moreover, for those unable to satisfy their own self-interest, and who instead are either victims of someone else's selfish exploitation (as are the Hands) or dependent on someone else's patronage (as is Mrs. Sparsit), the best protection against the shaming gaze is to focus it on another. Hence, at the instigation of Slackbridge, the blameless Stephen Blackpool quickly becomes "an object for the undying finger of scorn to point at, and for the avenging fire of every free and thinking mind, to scorch and sear" (268). Hence also, Mrs. Sparsit stares fixedly at the approaching shame of her rival, Louisa: "[S]he kept her black eyes wide open, with no touch of pity, with no touch of compunction, all absorbed in interest" (229–30).

Thus, self-interest posits a world without compassion, where all are vulnerable to a collective and condemning gaze—exactly as depicted in Stephen's nightmare: "[T]here was not one pitying or friendly eye among the millions that were fastened on his face" (123). If this gaze cannot be deflected onto another, as in the examples just cited, then the sole remaining recourse is to sink ever lower into ignominy, until the gaze itself is shamed by what it perceives.[7] This is precisely the tactic adopted by Stephen's dissolute wife: "A creature so foul to look at ... that it was a shameful thing even to see her" (106). It appears also to be Stephen's own unconscious or unwitting strategy, for by a series of actions, such as seeking Mr. Bounderby's advice concerning divorce, refusing to join the workers' combination, and waiting on successive evenings (at Tom's request) in front of the very bank that Tom later robs, Stephen draws increasing suspicion and obloquy upon himself. Indeed, just as his wife through moral dereliction is a "self-made outcast" (121), so too, through his unfortunate decisions, is Stephen—until his dramatic rescue from the Old Hell Shaft. Moreover, the wife's role as a vivid correlative of Stephen's own plight is reinforced by another connection. Rachel refers to her as "wandering and lost .... Wounded too, and bruised" (120)—a condition corresponding to Stephen's when he, "the lost man" (288), lies "mangled" (288) at the bottom of the Shaft.

Once he is brought back to the surface through the perseverance of those committed to his rescue, Stephen changes from an object of "scorn" (268) to an object of pity: "A low murmur of pity went round the throng" (289). Weakness and vulnerability are no longer sources of isolating shame, but elicitors of a collective compassion by which all are united through the act of selfless giving—the exact opposite of the "bargain across a counter" mentality fostered by self-interest (304). This extraordinary shift in attitude toward a fellow "human creature" is enabled by an even more extraordinary shift in the experiencing of time (289). During the course of the rescue, before Stephen finally emerges, time is accorded tremendous narrative emphasis. The two poles of impatience and languor are replaced by the will to help.

Instead of selfish impatience there is now a sense of compassionate urgency, as Sissy's remark to Rachel shows: "You wouldn't leave him lying maimed at the bottom of this dreadful place, a moment, if you could bring help to him!" (285). The haste then manifested concerns, not the imperious and self-interested demand for satisfaction, but the determination to reduce the duration of another's suffering. Similarly, indifferent languor is transformed into the "wrapt suspense" (288) felt by those waiting for Stephen to be raised to the surface. Accordingly, the time "elapsed" (287) is measured, not by Mr. Gradgrind's "statistical clock" (132), which asserts the futility of time "with a beat like a rap upon a coffin-lid" (132), but by the surgeon's "watch" (287). Moreover, the transition from the isolation caused by self-interest to the community of compassion is reinforced by the synchronization of human efforts with the declension of the sun, the archetypal timepiece that illumines all equally: "The sun was four hours lower than when Sissy and Rachel had first sat down upon the grass" (287); "The sun was setting now; and the red light in the evening sky *touched every face there*" (288 [my emphasis]). Thus, through acceptance of the natural movement of time, the isolating gravity associated with the shaming gaze is finally overcome.

In the context of this opposition between two types of time, the natural and the "statistical," the closing of the novel can be better understood. There, the narrator suddenly projects his story "into futurity" (311) and considers the respective fates of the major characters. All except Mr. Bounderby are depicted as having undergone psychological development or change to the limits of their capacity for it. Mr. Gradgrind, for example, is described as "making his facts and figures subservient to Faith, Hope, and Charity" (312), while Sissy blossoms into a wife and mother. But Mr. Bounderby, who dies of a "fit" (312) in the street, remains the same to the very end. In fact, his culminating project is to perpetuate his unchanging identity through endowing in his will 25 representatives of himself. The passage enumerating their duties and circumstances repeats the word "for ever" six times: "each ... should for ever dine in Bounderby Hall, for ever lodge in Bounderby Buildings, for ever attend a Bounderby chapel, for ever go to sleep under a Bounderby chaplain, for ever be supported out of a Bounderby estate, and for ever nauseate all healthy stomachs with a vast amount of Bounderby balderdash and bluster" (312). This artificial perpetuity epitomizes the time dominant in Coketown, for it is nothing more than an extension of the present—and one undertaken in order to deny that change (and ultimately death) have happened. As we remember, it was precisely this desperate need to find protection against change that led Mr. Jupe to send Sissy to Coketown.[8]

3

Time and Metempsychosis in *Ulysses*

Time in *Ulysses* acquires almost physical force, capable of violent destructiveness that terminates an ongoing condition or trend, forcing either painful reconstruction or threatening ultimate cataclysm. Regarding the first alternative, time is the measure of collision and impact: "Time shocked rebounds, shock by shock. Jousts, slush, and uproar of battles, the frozen deathspew of the slain, a shout of spear spikes baited with men's bloodied guts."[1] Regarding the second, time advances toward the end of time itself: "Time's livid final flame leaps" (683); "I hear the ruin of all space, shattered glass and toppling masonry, and time one livid final flame" (28). Linking these alternatives is the notion of time as that which converts the openness of the future to possibility into the closure of the past, where possibility has been replaced by unalterable fact: "Time has branded them and fettered they are lodged in the room of the infinite possibilities they have ousted" (30). This formulation of time in terms of collision and conflagration unfolds its implications in the context of metempsychosis or "convulsions of metamorphosis" (817)—a central principle in the developmental transformations of character in the novel, and one that we shall approach with caution and care.

Like Keats's Grecian Urn, *Ulysses* is a work of art that does "tease us out of thought / As doth eternity." Indeed, the novel boldly foregrounds the "difficulties of interpretation" (790): "Let some meinherr from Almany grope his life for deephid meanings in the depth of the buckbasket" (263). At the level to be investigated in the present study, the challenge of interpretation posed or invited by *Ulysses* concerns not just the meaning of the text and what Richard Kain terms its "richness of reference," but also the meaning of life or, to adopt the formulation in the "Ithaca" chapter, "the solution of difficult problems in imaginary or real life" (*Ulysses* 791; Kain 1966, 87). In this context, A. E. Russell's *mot* in the "Scylla and Charybdis" chapter gains significance: "The supreme question about a work of art is out of how deep a life does it spring" (236). Here art is valued in terms of its profundity—a quality construed to vary according to the depth of the life or, more precisely, of the *understanding* of life proper to its author. In the novel, this view is both challenged and expanded. On the one hand, life can never rival the perfection of art: "University of life. Bad art" (585). But on the other hand, "life is a great teacher" (43), whose lessons can provide the content or inspiration for great art, as in Stephen's account of Shakespeare: "A man of genius makes no mistakes. His errors are volitional and are the portals of discovery" (243). S. L. Goldberg has commented on this idea in *Ulysses*: "The development of the soul is thus the sequence of the epiphanies it discovers" (1969, 74). Here instead of art for art's sake, there is life for art's sake. Conversely, as Stephen indicates, the art thus produced is for humanity's sake: "the eternal affirmation of the spirit of man in literature" (777).

Fundamentally, considered as a mimetic project, the task of *Ulysses* is not just to represent "human life" (642, 819), or to provide "an epitome of the course of life" (546), or "to make up a miniature cameo of the world we live in" (750), but more importantly to illumine "the basis of human mentality" (817). Of course, when addressing the issue of "human mentality" in *Ulysses*, critical tradition is accustomed to draw—often with extremely illuminating results—on the theories of established psychological theoreticians, among whom the most celebrated is Freud.[2] But our own approach will follow cues in the text itself. As the quotation containing the phrase "the basis of human mentality" indicates, the novel posits *fear* as the factor underpinning human mentality: "catastrophic cataclysms which make terror the basis of human mentality" (817). Yet the "cataclysms" occasioning this terror are not uniformly external but pertain also to the inner process of "vital growth" through which life passes in its transit from birth to death: "the fact of vital growth, through *convulsions* of metamorphosis from infancy through maturity to decay" (817 [my emphasis]). This conception, of course, entrains the doctrine of metempsychosis or "transmigration of souls" (77), reinterpreted in the novel to signify the sequential changes of circumstance, perspective, and condition undergone by the individual in the course of a lifetime—changes so extreme that their only adequate metaphor is the transition of the same soul from incarnation in one body to another. Many critics, however, consider Joycean metempsychosis primarily in terms of an Ovidian metamorphosis of classical figures. For example, to Suzette Henke, "Molly is the seductive Calypso and 'Big Mamma' to Ulysses—Bloom" (1978, 83). To Patrick McCarthy, the notion of metempsychosis relates "the world of *Ulysses* to ancient Greece" (1990, 104).

Our own approach to the implications of the Joycean notion of metempsychosis or "convulsions of metamorphosis from infancy through maturity to decay" can be most efficiently introduced by brief reference to the notion of "soul" formulated in the Aristotelian-Thomist synthesis, which Stephen invokes: "it is a simple substance and therefore incorruptible" (732). In its widest definition, the term "soul" signifies the act or principle of operation and function of an organized body. That is, the soul not only animates the body, but is also the singular and abiding principle whereby a body has individual form as *this* body, with its own life and modes of operation. Aquinas elaborates:

> the first thing by which the body lives is the soul. And as life appears through various operations in different degrees of living things, that whereby we primarily perform each of these vital actions is the soul. For the soul is the primary principle of our nourishment, sensation, and local movement; and likewise of our understanding. Therefore this principle by which we primarily understand, whether it be called the intellect or the intellectual soul, is the form of the body. (1952, I, Q. 76, A. 1, resp.)

In this dispensation, not only is there no life without the soul; there is also *no body without the soul*. For in the Aristotelian-Thomist schema, unlike the Cartesian one, the body comes into being *as* a body only through the soul, which is construed as its formative and animating principle. Etienne Gilson clarifies:

> We must not regard a living being as a machine inert in itself but with a soul as its motor. This is what Descartes wanted to substitute for Aristotle's notion of a living being. For St. Thomas, following Aristotle, the soul does not first make a body move, it first makes a body. A corpse is not a body. The soul is what makes it exist as a body. It is the soul which assembles and organizes what we call today the bio-chemical elements ... in order to make a living body from them. (1988, 187)

Unlike the body, which has being only through the soul, the soul itself *is* a principle of being, and therefore, once created, cannot not be. In other words, as Stephen notes, the soul is *incorruptible*, and never ceases to be what it already is. Yet, thus considered, in ontological terms, as a principle or form that, as Gilson indicates, is "indestructible by definition," the soul is immune to alteration or change (1956, 188). As such, the soul (as defined in the Aristotelian-Thomist system) concerns a principle antithetical to the Joycean view of life as sequential "convulsions of metamorphosis." If the soul is the principle of life, then life cannot change—or, more precisely, change in life cannot be made intelligible. Alfred

North Whitehead provides a superb formulation of the opposition between the notion of the soul, just explicated, and the reality of change or novelty in life: "The doctrine of the enduring soul with its permanent characteristics is exactly the irrelevant answer to the problem which life presents. That problem is, How can there be originality?" (1929, 104).

The enduring self-identity characteristic of the Aristotelian-Thomist soul is epitomized by "the gentleman off Sandymount Green that Cissey Caffrey called *the man that was so like himself*" (461 [my emphasis]). But such self-identity does not pertain to the Joycean notion of self, as depicted through Stephen and Bloom in *Ulysses*. The ruptures and dislocations imposed by metempsychosis create a fissured self, not a self-identical one—a condition epitomized by Stephen's reflection in Buck Mulligan's "cracked looking-glass" (6): "Stephen bent forward and peered at the mirror held out to him, *cleft by a crooked crack*, hair on end. As he and others see me" (5 [my emphasis]). The image in the mirror is "cleft" corresponding to the split in identity registered by both Stephen and Bloom, accompanying the passage through metempsychosis—the "convulsions of metamorphosis" that separate the present self from its past instantiations: "I am another now and yet the same" (12). For Stephen, the crack in the mirror—the factor separating him from the past and holding him back from moving freely toward his future—is guilt regarding an action (or refusal of action) in the past, which then seemed necessary for his freedom to become what he could be in the future: "You wouldn't kneel down to pray for your mother on her deathbed when she asked you. Why?" (8). For Bloom, the fissure separating two identities of himself, past and present, is grief concerning the death of his son, Rudy, at the age of 11: "I was happier then. Or was that I? Or am I now I?" (213).

The irony of metempsychosis is that the fissure that it creates between past and present selves inhibits movement toward the next transformation. Regarding Bloom and Stephen, respectively, the present self yearns vainly to return to the time before the most recent change ("Would you go back to then?" [213]; "looking for something lost in a past life" [57]), and broods obsessively on the pain suffered during the aftermath: "Are you not happy in your home your poor little naughty boy?" (95, 213); "Pain, that was not yet the pain of love, fretted his heart" (4). The introspective pull of the past—of "memories which are hidden away by man in the darkest places of the heart" (552)—tends to encourage self-absorbed inwardness, epitomized by the "image of Narcissus" (834) and formulated explicitly in "Ithaca": "He reflected that the field of individual development and experience was regressively accompanied by a restriction of the converse domain of interindividual relations" (778). That is, in the course of "individual development and experience" entailed and enabled by metempsychosis, the self risks progressive isolation from others—a condition epitomized in "Circe" by Stephen's violent hallucination of his spectral mother ("Repent, Stephen" [682]) and Bloom's enrapt vision of the posthumous Rudy as "a fairy boy of eleven" (702). Yet, as the ambiguity of Bloom's vision suggests, metempsychosis also activates the pull of the future, and opens the individual to deeper communication or communion with another. For at that moment, Rudy is both a reification of memory and an adumbration of the imminent bonding between Stephen and Bloom, in the mode of spiritual father and son, evidenced in their respective perceptions of each other in terms of "the accumulation of the past" (807) and "the predestination of a future" (808).

The ambiguous effect of metempsychosis on "individual development and experience" (778), entailing contrary pulls toward past and future, as well as toward isolation and communication, can be clarified through further consideration of the mirror motif. In discussing "the cracked looking-glass" (6), we related the fissured reflection in it to the "convulsions of metamorphosis," when the unity of selfhood splits into two parts, past and present. Bloom's most concise formula for this predicament is "Me. And me now" (224). But on a deeper level, the looking glass is *itself* a reflection of the self looking into it. That is, whereas according to Hamlet (and requoted by Lynch in "Circe"), art holds "the mirror up to nature" (*Hamlet* 3.2.22; *Ulysses* 671), in the novel selfhood is itself a mirror, and the remembered past self is "a mirror within a mirror" (540), as when Bloom recalls his own adolescence:

> He is young Leopold, as in a retrospective arrangement, *a mirror within a mirror* (hey, presto!), he beholdeth himself. That young figure of then is seen, precociously manly, walking on a nipping morning from the old house in Clambrassil street to the high school, his booksatchel on him bandolierwise, and in it a goodly chunk of wheaten loaf, a mother's thought. (540 [my emphasis])

Explication of the Joycean notion of the self as a mirror, and the relation of this notion to the interpretation of metempsychosis, must proceed in stages.

The simplest way to introduce this notion of specular selfhood is through reference to Stephen and Bloom's respective accounts of it. According to their formulations, what the self encounters are reflections of its own sense of identity. "Every life is many days, day after day. We walk through ourselves, meeting robbers, ghosts, giants, old men, young men, wives, widows, brothers-in-love.

But always meeting ourselves" (272 [my emphasis]); *"Think you're escaping and run into yourself"* (492 [my emphasis]). On this level, consciousness is confined within the nutshell of its own preoccupations: outer experience (awareness of external reality) mirrors inner concerns—a condition ironically epitomized in "Scylla and Charybdis" by Mr. Best's citation of Mallarmé's mot on Hamlet: "*il se promène, lisant au livre de lui-même ... reading the book of himself*" (239). In *Ulysses*, to be conscious is to perceive in reality reflections of one's own perspective: "thought through my eyes" (45)—and ultimately to move beyond the limitations of that perspective. This progression, as we shall see, is at the root of metempsychosis. Before continuing with this explication, we should note that one well-established critical view, exemplified by David Hayman, attributes a version of self-reflection through perception to Stephen, but explicitly denies its applicability to Bloom: "Throughout his day Stephen behaves as though everything is an aspect of his self ... Bloom, on the other hand, sees himself in relation to the world" (1970, 35). Stephen's self-perception is construed by one critical school as involving the notion that, as Margaret McBride states, "Stephen produces *Ulysses*"—not as Joyce the author, but as "a purely literary construct, the central character of a surfiction" (a term invented by Raymond Federman, in reference to metafiction or fiction that concerns the world of fiction or act of creating it) (1981, 7; 2001, 29).

The present study will approach self-reflection from a different angle. In order to avoid misconception, it is important to distinguish the specular notion of selfhood from the subjectivist view in philosophy, which, according to Whitehead, maintains that "the nature of our immediate experience is the outcome of the perceptive peculiarities of the subject enjoying that experience" (1925, 84). Obviously, the subjectivist principle applies to character in *Ulysses*. The same object can be invested with different attributes and meaning, according to the mood and circumstances of the perceiver at a given moment, as when Bloom alternately views the nocturnal sky in terms first of "[t]he heaventree of stars hung with humid nightblue fruit" (819), when in Stephen's company, and later in terms of "[t]he cold of interstellar space" (827), when he is once again alone. Yet the Joycean notion of specular selfhood entails both more and less than the subjectivism just defined. It entails *less*, because character recognizes the distorting effect of its own condition on that which it sees, as when Bloom compensates for his sudden vision of "[d]esolation": "Morning mouth bad images. Got up wrong side of the bed. Must begin those Sandow's exercises" (73). Stephen too acknowledges that his perception is conditioned by his own obsessions: "History, Stephen said, is a nightmare from which I am trying to awake" (42). The Joycean notion of specular selfhood also entails *more* than subjectivism. For in this schema, to retrieve Whitehead's phrases, "immediate experience" is not merely "the *outcome* of the perceptive peculiarities of the subject enjoying that experience" (my emphasis), but also the *reflection* of those perceptive peculiarities, in certain cases.

Consider Stephen first. His immediate experience recurrently reflects his own sense of identity. In "Telemachus," for example, his perception of Mulligan and Haines becomes a reflection of his own sense of inadequacy: "In the bright silent instant Stephen saw his own image in cheap dusty mourning between their gay attires" (21). The tendency to see others as mirrors reflecting his own deficiency also informs Stephen's perception of the student Cyril Sergent in "Nestor": "Like him I was, these sloping shoulders, this gracelessness. My childhood bends before me" (34). Here, to see the reflection of his childhood is to aggravate his guilt about rejecting his other's dying wish: "She had saved him from being trampled under foot and had gone, scarcely having been" (33). Similarly, in "Wandering Rocks" Stephen sees his own sister, Dilly, as a reflection of himself: "My eyes they say she has. Do others see me so? Quick, far and daring. Shadow of my mind" (312). At first the reflection seems positive, but it soon entails the image of himself as a drowning man, overwhelmed by remorse of conscience: "She will drown me with her, eyes and hair. Lank coils of seaweed hair around me, my heart, my soul. Salt green death. We. Agenbite of inwit" (313). In immediate context, Stephen's remorse concerns inability to help his impoverished sister. But more profoundly, his helpless immersion in moral "misery" (313) pertains to guilt about his mother—an obsession already, in "Telemachus," associated in his mind with the sea, whose "mirror of water" (9) suddenly reflects his mother's appalling death agony, when he obstinately refused to kneel in prayer by her bed: "The ring of bay and skyline held a dull green mass of liquid. A bowl of white china had stood beside her deathbed holding the green sluggish bile which she had torn up from her rotting liver by fits of loud groaning vomiting" (4).

This is perhaps the most spectacular example, in *Ulysses*, of the specular self, whose immediate experience is the reflection of its own perceptive peculiarities. Ironically, the death agony of Stephen's mother, here so violently recollected, functions as an analogue of the "convulsions of metamorphosis" (817) by which he himself will progress to the next stage of his own "vital growth" (817), and leave behind the welter of remorse in which he is now floundering. In Stephen's case, in order for metempsychosis to achieve a new self, the old one must suffer agonizingly convulsive demise: "A drowning man. His human eyes scream out to me out of horror of his death. I...With him together down... I could not save her. Waters: bitter death: lost" (57). Yet later, in "Proteus," Stephen progresses from this image of himself as the drown*ing* man to the image of the drown*ed* man that, in turn, is associated with the notion of effortlessly sequential transformation and "seachange":

> God becomes man becomes fish becomes barnacle goose becomes featherbed mountain. Dead breaths I living breathe, tread dead dust, devour ruinous offal from all dead. Hauled stark over the gunwale he breathes upward the stench of his green grave, his leprous nosehole snoring to the sun. (63)

The drowning man and the drowned man epitomize the contrary perspectives on metempsychosis presented in the novel—the same object (in this case, metempsychosis) perceived "from two different points of observation" (777), entailing perhaps the most profound version of parallax in *Ulysses*. The drowning man foregrounds the desperate struggle of the prior or inveterate self to survive and maintain its mode of awareness. In contrast, the drowned man symbolizes the supersession of the "perceptive peculiarities" (Whitehead's term) of the inveterate self by the new perceptive orientation of the ensuing or metamorphosed self for whom the past is a reflection, not of its own anguish regarding what was lost or cannot be undone, but of its willingness to accept the "[i]neluctable modality" of change (45). At bottom, the engulfing guilt, symbolized by the drowning man, concerns not remorse per se, but the need to perpetuate emotional identification with the past. That is, the deepest motive for Stephen's guilt concerns responsibility not for what he did, but for what he is going to do, in terms of guiding his "soul," his sense of identity, beyond the reaches of past preconceptions: "Now where the blue hell am I bringing her beyond the veil?" (61). Doubt about his ability to navigate the incertitude of the future is expressed through obsessive guilt regarding the consequences of action in the past. In effect, that guilt about his mother itself becomes a surrogate mother, protecting him from the unknown responsibilities entrained by metempsychosis into manhood. Indeed, in "Scylla and Charybdis," Stephen opposes the certainty of maternal love to the "incertitude" of "the world, macro- and microcosm": "*Amor matris*, subjective and objective genitive may be the only true thing in life" (266). Nevertheless, in "Ithaca," Stephen's potential successfully to resolve his quandary is unambiguously affirmed: "Confidence in himself, an equal and opposite power of abandonment and recuperation" (786).

The hallmark of Joycean metempsychosis concerns the coexistence of contrary tendencies in the same character: (a) the prior or inveterate self, which resists rupture with the past, and (b) the ensuing or emergent self, which accepts, and even seeks, movement toward a different future. The *convulsive* nature of Joycean metempsychosis ("convulsions of metamorphosis" [817]) stems from the desperate refusal of the prior or inveterate self to accept the change or rupture that renders its own "perceptive peculiarities" (Whitehead's term) extinct. From the perspective of that self, change is deadly and, in order to deny change, time must be made to run toward the past, not the future, as exemplified in Stephen's formulation: "Hold to the now, the here, through which all future plunges to the past" (238). This perspective is the contrary of that which (in the "Dead breaths I living breathe" passage, quoted above) views the past as the precondition for transformation in the future. The great pathos of Joycean metempsychosis concerns the agonized refusal of the inveterate self to accept the loss of the past in which its own identity is grounded. Instead of acceptance, there is resistance, expressed through excruciating modes of attachment to the past: for Stephen, in terms of guilt; for Bloom, in terms of grief. Yet, despite the agonies of resistance attending it, the process of metempsychosis does ineluctably unfold. Though Bloom, like Stephen, is currently stranded in a period of painful transition, he has successfully passed through another that corresponds to that in which Stephen now writhes. In a moment of calm reflection, Bloom recalls his own adolescent rebellion against parental religious custom, with a mature understanding that Stephen, regarding his own recent adolescent rebellion against religion, cannot yet achieve: "Because in immature impatience he had treated with disrespect certain beliefs and practices" (853).

The coexistence of opposed tendencies, respectively pertaining to the inveterate and the emergent selves (as we have provisionally termed the nexuses of perspectives and concerns that they reify), applies vividly to Bloom. On the one hand, he obsessively rememorates the past before Rudy's death ("Happier then" [196]), regrets the loss of sexual intimacy with Molly ("Could never like it again after Rudy" [213]), and models his present on the pattern of the past, through the inertia of "habit" (655). But on the other hand, he yearns for novelty ("The new I want" [491]), muses about the possibility of fathering another child ("Too late now. Or if not? If not? If still?" [367]), and acknowledges the forward movement of "irreversible time" (858): "Can't bring back time. Like holding water in your hand" (213); "What now is will then tomorrow as now was be past yester" (631). Yet even here Bloom is ambivalent, for to him the irreversible movement of time can also provoke resistance to dreaded inevitability, as with respect to his daughter's impending loss of virginity ("Will happen, yes. Prevent. Useless: can't move") and Molly's adultery: "Woman. As easy to stop the sea. Yes: all is lost" (81, 351).

Bloom's particular mode of perseverating the past and resisting the forward movement of time can be clarified by returning to the drowning man image. With Stephen, as we have seen, the drowning man represents the desperate conflict between needing to repudiate the past and needing to remain engulfed by the past in order thereby to postpone responsibility for forging a future. With Bloom, the *drowning* man is replaced by the *buoyant* man, unable to drown: "Where was the chap I saw in that picture somewhere? Ah, in the dead sea, floating on his back, reading a book with a parasol open. Couldn't sink if you tried: so thick with salt" (87). Bloom's immunity to drowning is his *preference* for the past. His buoyancy is his sameness of habit: "O Poldy, Poldy, you are a poor old stick in the mud!" (571); "I suppose there isn't in all creation another man with the habits he has" (917). Whereas Stephen struggles with the conflict of having repudiated his past, without yet knowing how to find his future, Bloom clings longingly to the past, even though he knows that renewal of happiness can come only in the future: "Something new to hope for not like the past she wanted back, waiting. It never comes" (128). For this reason, his totem is Rip van Winkle: "Then I did Rip van Winkle coming back" (492). On the one hand, he recognizes that fulfillment can found only by awakening to the future: "The new I want" (491). But on the other hand, he lingers in the past, because he fears the challenge of facing the transformed present: "All changed. Forgotten. The young are old" (492). To return from preoccupation with the past is to risk the dislocation and disorientation caused by the progression of time: "And the coming back was the worst thing you ever did because it went without saying you would feel out of place as things moved with the times" (757).

In this phase of his life, Bloom does not want the future to happen. He is as frightened of the future as Stephen, in his hallucination of his mother's ghost, is terrified of the past. Bloom's deepest "wounds that wanted healing" (466) concern not grief for the past, but fear of the future—and especially aging: "Nadir of misery: the aged impotent disfranchised ratesupported moribund lunatic pauper" (855). Without a son "for an heir," Bloom is unarmed against time: "Leopold that had of his body no manchild for an heir looked upon him his friend's son and was shut up in sorrow for his forepassed happiness" (510). In this condition, death for Bloom means not just personal, but dynastic, extinction: "I too last of my race" (367). Ironically, Bloom's anguish regarding Molly's adultery reinforces this fear of the future and the futile wish to stop the advance of time—a condition symbolized by the fortuitous stopping of his watch at the very moment when Blazes and Molly presumably consummated their afternoon tryst: "Funny my watch stopped at half past four .... Was that just when he, she? O, he did.

Into her. She did. Done" (482). In this context, the deepest motive for Bloom's agonized tolerance of Molly's adultery concerns the opportunities it gives him to heighten his resistance to the movement of time. Indeed, his own resistance to the movement of time is highlighted by the eagerness of his adulterous rival, Blazes Boylan, for its advance: "Boylan with impatience" (343). As Bello suggests in "Circe," the threat of Boylan makes Bloom a Rip van Winkle who resists awakening to the present situation lest he be forced to confront its adulterous changes: "No, Leopold Bloom, all is changed by woman's will since you slept horizontal in Sleepy Hollow your night of twenty years. Return and see" (653).

Bloom's fear of the future can be clarified through investigation of the moment when, in response to the covering of the sun, "slowly, wholly," by a cloud, he suddenly succumbs to "[d]esolation":

> Grey. Far. No, not like that. A barren land, bare waste. Vulcanic lake, the dead sea: no fish, weedless, sunk deep in the earth.... *A dead sea in a dead land, dead and old*.... Desolation, Grey horror seared his flesh.... Cold oils slid along his veins, chilling his blood: *age crusting him with a salt cloak*. (73 [my emphasis])

Just as Stephen, on looking at Dublin Bay, suddenly reflected the bowl holding the bile vomited from his mother's rotting liver, here Bloom, in the shadow of a cloud, suddenly reflects the image of "A dead sea in a dead land, dead and old." Whereas for Stephen, the present is haunted by excruciating guilt, for Bloom the present is menaced by fear of aging: "age crusting him with a salt cloak." Indeed, this "salt cloak" of age corresponds to the "Salt green death" (313) associated with Stephen's drowning man image, discussed earlier. Bloom's drowning man is the ultimate consequence—or, more precisely, the nemesis—of his reliance on habit: "Always the same year after year" (72–73). On the one hand, as we have seen with the image of the buoyant man, floating under a parasol in the Dead Sea, habit secures Bloom's connection with the past, and defers the need to deal with subsequent change. But on the other hand, to cling to the past is to do no more than age in the future. For to cling to the past is to identify with memories that have become "dead and old."

In this context, the supreme irony of Bloom's voyeuristic tryst with Gerty MacDowell, in "Nausicaa," emerges. She incarnates, or is, at least, closely associated with, the fantasy of the idealized past: "Art thou real, my ideal?" (474). More precisely, she is obsessed with the fantasy of "the love that might have been" (453)—a fantasy with which Bloom himself is much engaged, as with respect to Rudy: "I could have helped him on in life. I could. Make him independent" (110).

Though she seeks, through romantic attraction, to "make [Bloom] forget the memory of the past" (466), she herself is consumed with regret for the past—the sense that "the years were slipping by for her," as a result of "an accident coming down Dalkey hill" that lamed her (474). A significant development appears to unfold in Bloom after the masturbatory consummation of his voyeuristic connection with Gerty. He achieves a higher awareness, coordinated with the flittering of the bat, "hither, thither, with a tiny lost cry" (473). In *A Portrait of the Artist as a Young Man*, the bat is associated with the awakening of self-awareness: "a batlike soul waking to the consciousness of itself in darkness and secrecy" (1992, 239). In "Nausicaa," this awakening into "consciousness of itself" is connected with the advent of metempsychosis, whereby the ensuing self supersedes the inveterate one. This suggestion is reinforced by many factors. To begin with, on noticing the bat ("Bat probably"), Bloom immediately reflects on "[m]etempsychosis." (492), and then thinks of the bat in terms that suggest a winged infant, just embarked on rebirth: "Like a little man in a cloak he is with tiny hands. Weeny bones" (493).

The notion of "waking to the consciousness of itself" applies to Bloom's self-contemplation, near the end of the chapter, in the "dark mirror" of a tidal pool (498). Here he concludes that his experience with Gerty will never happen again ("It never comes the same" [498]), nor would he want it to: "Returning not the same" (491). Yet, despite this recognition of the futility of clinging to the past, Bloom remains defined by and under the influence of long established habit. After giving up the attempt to write in the sand, Bloom flings away the stick he had been using: "The stick fell in the silted sand, *stuck*" (498 [my emphasis]). Bloom notes the instance of "[c]hance" ("Now if you were trying to do that for a week on end you couldn't"), but of course he does not note the deeper irony. He himself, in virtue of unchanging habit, is the stuck stick: "O Poldy, Poldy, you are a poor old stick in the mud!" (571). Moreover, in "Sirens," as he focuses longingly on the memory of the first consummation with Molly, he is stuck in present regret for an unattainable past, just as the flies, on the pane of an adjacent window, are stuck in the vain effort to reach the other side: "Me. And me now. Stuck, the flies buzzed" (224). In virtue of this inability to move beyond regret for the past, Bloom's inveterate self is as lame psychologically as Gerty is lame physically. Indeed, lameness or claudication in Bloom is implied by the "slow boot" with which he erases the words written earlier in the sand (498).

The "convulsions of metamorphosis" that characterize Joycean metempsychosis combine gradual emergence of new forms with long-term continuities of old ones. There is no decisive moment when the transformation is complete. But there is, in *Ulysses*, a moment when Stephen and Bloom jointly achieve a new self-perception, through which each now sees himself, not in terms of the isolation imposed by his respective wound, but in terms of that which links each to the other, and, through that bond, to others. The moment, of course, occurs when Bloom and Stephen look at each other in the garden behind Bloom's house at No. 7 Eccles Street, just before Stephen's departure:

> Silent, each contemplating the other in both mirrors of the reciprocal flesh of theirhisnothis fellowfaces. (824)

Here, through seeing the other, each sees himself as a "fellowface"—one defined in terms of likeness and relatedness, not difference and estrangement. This reciprocal perception encourages the opposite of the shrinking reflex earlier displayed by both Stephen and Bloom, as when Stephen worried about spectators when depositing "dry snot" on a rock ledge ("Behind. Perhaps there is someone"), and when Bloom scurried away from the iterant Boylan: "Not see. Not see. Get on" (64, 234). But the deepest implications of the self-perception that Stephen and Bloom achieve through perception of each other emerge through examination of their function as "mirrors."

As noted at a prior stage of our investigation, in *Ulysses* selfhood displays a specular dimension, in virtue of the tendency to turn perception into a reflection of the perceiving self: *percipi* (that which is perceived) reflects *percipere* (the perceptive peculiarities of the perceiving agent). But during the moment of reciprocal reflection in Bloom's garden, the relation between percipi and percipere (that which is perceived and that which perceives) is reversed. For here, that which is perceived (the "fellowface" of the other) reflects and enables a new sense of identity for the perceiver, instead of simply reflecting and confirming the sense of identity already there. Whereas the dominant principle of the inveterate sense of identity was exclusion or isolation, the dominant principle of the emergent one is inclusion or togetherness. These antithetical principles—exclusion and inclusion or isolation and relatedness—constitute the core of the Joycean image of man, and achieve precise formulation when Bloom, after Stephen's departure, again contemplates his own reflection—this time "[i]n the mirror of the giltbordered pierglass," in the front room of his home:

> What composite asymmetrical image in the mirror then attracted his attention?
> The image of a solitary (ipsorelative) mutable (aliorelative) man. (831)

But, according to the notion of specular selfhood that we have explored, the mirror in this instance not only reflects an image of man, but is also *itself* an image of man—an image or objective correlative, that is, of the predisposition to convert perception into self-reflection: a tendency epitomized by "the statue of Narcissus" in Bloom's home (859).

Further examination will clarify the emphasis on self-reflection in *Ulysses*. The ultimate consequence of self-reflection and ipsorelation is insular self-containment—a condition with polar extremes, one positive, the other negative. In the negative mode, the insular self-containment of self-reflection (wherein that which is perceived is contained within the perceiver) is epitomized by Stephen's terrifying hallucination of his mother in "Circe": "Her face drawing nearer and nearer, sending out an ashen breath" (682). The positive mode of the insular self-containment of self-reflection is epitomized in the passage mentioning the statue of Narcissus: "the statue of Narcissus, sound without echo, desired desire" (859). Here awareness is a closed system, where the object of desire is the subject desiring it—or contained within the desiring subject. On the one hand, this condition epitomizes internal harmony, as typified, for example, in Paul Frankl's celebrated account of late Gothic architecture: "a harmony of movement within itself, a living vibration from within, a current which always returns to its own beginning" (1962, 187). But on the other hand, though such harmony might apply to a building or to God, it cannot, for more than a moment, apply to a human being. Bloom approaches this ideal of self-contained harmony when entering the bed, warmed by Molly: "The anticipation of warmth (human) tempered with coolness (linen), obviating desire and rendering desirable" (859). But he knows that his own entry is but one term in an unfolding process: "To reflect that each one who enters imagines himself to be the first to enter whereas he is always the last term of a preceding series even if the first term of a succeeding one" (863).

This is a critical recognition or anagnorisis in *Ulysses*—one that involves matters far more profound than the issue of Molly's adultery. For Bloom here acknowledges that he participates in a larger process or continuity than that encompassed by his own awareness. In "Circe," the greatest threat to Bloom's manhood is the temptation to follow the Nymph "in nun's white habit," and enter a world free from sexual desire: "No more desire .... Only the ethereal" (661). But a greater threat is the narcissistic temptation to be self-contained and self-reflecting, as epitomized in the bath fantasy concluding "Lotus Eaters": "He foresaw his pale body reclined in it at full, naked, in a womb of warmth, oiled by scented melting soap, softly laved" (107). Here the "womb of warmth" ultimately concerns the fantasy of the closed system, where the subject is wholly enclosed by the object of desire—a state of self-contained harmony analogous to that involving Bloom's entry into bed, discussed above. A related womb image occurs near the end of "Ithaca," when Bloom falls asleep: "the manchild in the womb" (870). Yet here the womb image of self-containment is pregnant with implication, regarding the final "convulsions of metamorphosis" (817) that enable rebirth into the next stage of "individual development and experience" (778), where the contraries of ipsorelation and aliorelation will be realigned.

Fundamentally, this realignment concerns relation to time. In contrast to ordinary or parturitional birth, which occurs at a definite point in time ("Child born every minute somewhere"), the metempsychosis in which Bloom and Stephen are respectively involved itself concerns awareness of time (302). Indeed, this is a deeper meaning of the *nostos* or return home, which the link between *Ulysses* and *The Odyssey* implies. For Odysseus, nostos concerns the return to his island kingdom of Ithaca and reunion with his wife, Penelope, after an absence of 20 years. On the immediate level of plot, nostos in *Ulysses* traditionally concerns the return of Leopold Bloom to proper conjugal intimacy with his wife, Molly. Yet, at a deeper level, nostos in the novel concerns return to the present—recovery, that is, of the ability to feel at home or centered in the present. Neither Stephen nor Bloom feels at home in the present—a condition symbolized by the exclusion from home applying to each on the day (June 16, 1904) that the novel concerns. Stephen decides not to return to the Martello Tower ("I will not sleep here tonight"), and Bloom absents himself from home until after midnight, to avoid intruding on Molly's assignation with Boylan (28). A consequence of the inability to feel centered in the present concerns their tendency to view the present in terms of desiring its expiration, so that the discomfort it causes might thereby elapse. Stephen does this, for example, during his disputation in the library in "Scylla and Charybdis": "Life is many days. This will end" (275). Earlier, he had similarly foregrounded the notion of desired expiration in "Proteus": "Tuesday will be the longest day" (63). Likewise, Bloom focuses on the desired expiration of a present moment, during the carriage ride to Glasnevin cemetery, when suddenly examining his fingernails after spotting Blazes Boylan near "the door of the Red Bank": "Mr Bloom reviewed the nails of his left hand, then those of his right hand" (115).

As we have amply reviewed, the fundamental reason for Bloom and Stephen's discomfort with the present concerns obsession with the past—the tendency to live "rere regardant" (64). But discomfort with the present not only results from preoccupation with the past, but also serves the need for attachment to the past. The desire to have the present elapse is ultimately the wish to be in the past, for when the present ends, it will be the past. In this context, the concern is not what future will succeed the elapsed present, but that nothing will succeed the present but more past. The notion of the present as the field through which everything fades into the past, and nothing grows into the future, is epitomized by Bloom's view of the sand, near the end of "Nausicaa": "Hopeless thing sand. Nothing grows in it. All fades" (498). Bloom, of course, cannot see how his remark constitutes a "dark mirror" (498) of his own inveterate mentality. Nor can he see, as we have, the indications of his own emergent change.

These can be further clarified by closer consideration of the notion of fading. On the one hand, as just explained, fading expresses the futility of the present, through which everything succumbs to transience and disappears into the past. But on the other hand, with respect to the spectacular fireworks display, synchronized, in "Nausicaa," with Bloom's voyeurism and Gerty's exhibitionism, fading is associated with revivification of the present, after the climax or conclusion of a prolonged and absorbing experience: "Then all melted away dewily in the grey air: all was silent" (477). That is, fading is here linked with the sense of an ending that entails not only disappearance into the past, but also—and more importantly—refreshment and renewal in the present. The deeper implications of this moment emerge in connection with the reference to dew ("dewily"). For just a little later, Bloom associates "dew" with the awakening of Rip van Winkle from his long slumber and his realization of extended lapse of time between the past and the present: "His gun rusty from the dew" (492). The fireworks episode, coordinated with the interlude with Gerty, involves this second kind of fading, when the present is filled with awareness of the ending of that which is now in the past. It must, of course, be repeated that, in *Ulysses*, the indications of metempsychosis—the ending of one stage of "vital growth" (817) and the initiation of another—are cumulative, without a decisive instant when the transition is complete.

An analogous combination of accumulating change and persisting habit is superbly formulated in Whitehead's account of process or becoming: "There is the aspect of permanence in which a given type of attainment is endlessly repeated for its own sake; and there is the aspect of transition to other things" (1961a, 105). In other words, to interpolate additional phrases from Whitehead, metempsychosis for Stephen and Bloom concerns an unfolding process that entails both conservation and novelty—both "inheritance of aspects from their own past" and "continuous transition" to the future (1925, 100, 125). But, though, in the Joycean schema, "vital growth" is indeed continuous "from infancy through maturity to decay" (817), it nevertheless entails convulsive transitional phases ("convulsions of metamorphosis"), involving psychologically turbulent oppositions between that which was and that which is coming to be. Bloomsday—June 16, 1904—concerns precisely such transitional phases.

4

"the horror of the moment": Fear and Acceptance of Time in *Mrs. Dalloway*

Penetrating toward the thematic core of *Mrs. Dalloway* is an exacting enterprise, challenged by hazard and difficulty. The "astonishing sensibility" (153)[1] of the primary characters (Clarissa Dalloway, Peter Walsh, and Septimus Warren Smith), the exquisite complexity of narrative style and structure, the "great cornucopias" (62) of image and insight, the multiple contexts in which experience is rendered combine, with other factors, to enrich and complicate a text that has entranced and perplexed generations of readers. Gratitude and reverence restrain the critic who does not wish analysis of the text to obscure its surpassing value as a literary work of art comprising "myriads of things merged in one thing"—itself (63).

In the course of her experience on the celebrated day in June 1923 that *Mrs. Dalloway* portrays, the eponymous heroine unwittingly cites a primary concern of the novel concerning her—the communication of feeling: "the enormous resources of the English language, the power it bestows, after all, of communicating feelings" (195). Feelings are the living tissue of the novel—feelings imbued with thought or, more precisely, feelings that derive from or provoke thought, and that therefore seek expression through articulation. This overwhelming immediacy of emotion corresponds to Whitehead's dictum: "The basis of experience is emotional. Stated more generally, the basic fact is the rise of an affective tone originating from things whose relevance is given" (Whitehead 1933, 226). But in the world of *Mrs. Dalloway,* emotion is not merely the "basis of experience," as Whitehead indicates, but also its supreme risk and reward. The relevance of risk and reward applies, for example, to Clarissa's impassioned response, at age 18, to Sally Seton's proximity, more than 30 years earlier, at Bourton. First their intimacy consummates emotional beatitude: "as they walked (up and down, up and down), she uncovered, or the radiance burnt through, the revelation, the religious feeling!" (39). Then the sudden intrusion of Peter Walsh converts this ecstasy to agony: "It was like running one's face against a granite wall in the darkness! It was shocking; it was horrible!" (39). Oscillation between emotional extremes such as plenitude and desolation, "terror" and "ecstasy" recurs throughout the novel, affecting all three primary characters, and widening the reference of Clarissa's "feeling that it was very, very dangerous to live even one day" (213, 9).

A superficial interpretation might claim that the conspicuous fluctuation of feeling in *Mrs. Dalloway* indicates bipolar disorder, especially since the most extreme example of this condition is Septimus Warren Smith—the shell-shocked World War I veteran whose insanity, disastrous search for medical treatment, and eventual suicide occupy part of the novel. Yet such explanation would veil the deeper implication of the condition it examines. Septimus, of course, obviously suffers from an acute psychological disorder, but one that takes to an extreme the normal or default condition of the other two primary characters, Clarissa and Peter. His desperate psychological predicament constitutes a grotesquely magnified and hence distorted version of their own mode of mental operation.

At bottom, Septimus's plight, though pathologically severe, is not anomalous, but *redemptive*. On this fundamental level of signification, Septimus emerges as a Christ figure, "the Lord who had come to renew society" (27), in an "atheist" novel ("not for a moment did she believe in God" [31]), wherein Clarissa adopts her own "atheist's religion" (62, 85). Of course, Sir William Bradshaw, the novel's distinguished psychiatrist, cites the "common delusion" among psychotic patients regarding special status as "Christ" (108). Ironically, in the case of Septimus, that which the distinguished physician dismisses as delusion becomes thematically apt (200). For, to interpose John M. Najemy's phrase from a different context, Septimus is indeed a "sacral presence and salvific power" whose suffering unto death (by defenestration, as he jumps out of a window to escape medical intervention by Dr. Holmes), foregrounds the notion of salvation, not as construed in Christianity, but as formulated in the novel (Najemy 2006, 2008, 341). Here salvation of the soul means not qualification for posthumous entry into heaven, but preservation of "the power of feeling" (212) in life, remaining faithful to "what one felt" (210), protecting the integrity and "privacy of the soul" (139), refusing to submit to the kind of emotional compulsion and duress that Clarissa attributes to Septimus's would-be doctor, Sir William Bradshaw: "Sir William Bradshaw, a great doctor yet to her obscurely evil, without sex or lust, extremely polite to women, but capable of some indescribable outrage—*forcing your soul*, that was it ... Life is made intolerable; they make life intolerable, men like that" (202 [my emphasis]). She explicitly recognizes Septimus's death as an act of redemption, saving the "thing there was that mattered" (202)—the purity and immediacy of one's own feeling—from inevitable contamination by "the process of living" (203). But, as we shall find, the redemption enabled by Septimus's suicide goes far beyond the preservation of a meaningful moment ("This he had preserved") that otherwise would succumb to debasement by "corruption, lies, chatter," as a result of supervening intrusions and distractions (202). At bottom, Clarissa's response to Septimus's death consummates and advances extended reflection on the passage of time, undertaken by various characters and by the narrator. This reflection constitutes a tapestry of interwoven strands of thought regarding the relation of human life to time. Through this complex conceptualization, two opponent formulations of redemption emerge: salvation *from* time and salvation *through* time. The first formulation seeks to escape, by various tactics, confronting the reality of temporality. The second seeks to recognize the benefits that the experience of temporal passage can confer. At the center of this polarity is Big Ben—the great tower-clock whose regulated striking diffuses "leaden circles" of measured time throughout the world of the novel. Explication of these matters will entail multiple steps of analysis. Some of them concern surmounting prior interpretations of the novel whose preconceptions tend to obscure or distort the understanding of time delicately unfolded in the text.

Freeing time from the Freudian developmental paradigm

We can begin with consideration of Elizabeth Abel's Freudian interpretation of the novel.[2] The crux of Abel's argument concerns Clarissa's purported surmounting of a "developmental impasse" that, until her hearing of Septimus's death, impeded her ability to move beyond "the power of her past" and "to embrace the imperfect pleasures of adulthood more completely" (1989, 40). According to Abel, meditation on Septimus's death becomes the means by which Clarissa "recasts the developmental impasse as a choice between development or death"—preserving "the intensity of passion through death or accept[ing] the changing offerings of life" (ibid.). Well presented and indisputably valuable, Abel's inquiry views the novel in terms of Freud's Oedipal narrative, and is thus primed to look for evidence of developmental stages and the dynamics of passing through or balking at them. Yet such an approach conspicuously overlooks what it is not prepared to notice, and imposes an alien construct that contradicts and conceals the relation between time and character unfolded in the text. Brief consideration of this problem, on the factual and thematic levels, will orient our own explication.

On the factual level, there is no evidence that Clarissa's meditation on Septimus's death constitutes a developmental watershed such that she is happier after than before it. She does indeed note her happiness after emerging from the small room in which she reflected on his death: "[S]he had never been so happy" (203). But she does so in a way that obviously refers to an ongoing feeling, day after day, not to a sudden enhancement of joy: "No pleasure could equal, she thought, straightening the chairs, pushing in one book on the shelf, this having done with the triumphs of youth, lost herself in the process of living, to find it, with a shock of delight, *as the sun rose, as the day sank*" (203 [my emphasis]). Moreover, that same morning, hours before hearing of Septimus's death, Clarissa acknowledges, with profound gratitude, the happiness of her life: "It was her life, and, bending her head over the hall table, she bowed beneath the influence, felt blessed and purified, saying to herself, as she took the pad with the telephone message on it, how moments like this are buds on the tree of life ... one must pay back from this secret deposit of exquisite moments, she thought" (31).

On the thematic level, as we shall see, the notion of development that Abel imports from Freud, wherein psychological functioning is postulated to pass through developmental stages according to a chronological schedule of steps or phases, presupposes a relation between time and selfhood counter to that unfolded in the novel. We can begin explication with the notion of individuality. Freudian developmental theory acknowledges diversity of character or individual psychological configuration, but only in terms of degree of aberration from or consonance with a psychological model deemed to apply *universally* to all individuals. As a result, individual difference is construed not as *uniqueness* (that which is itself in its own way) but as an *aberration from sameness*. In contrast, Clarissa construes individual difference as uniqueness, and not in terms of departure from a norm: "And the supreme mystery which Kilman might say she had solved, or Peter might say he had solved, but Clarissa didn't believe either of them had the ghost of an idea of solving, was simply this: here was one room; there another. Did religion solve that, or love"—or, we might add, Freudian developmental psychology? (140). Whereas the Freudian developmental psychology imported by Abel defines the individual in terms of relation to a conceptual construct of its own devising, Clarissa allows each individual to be the source and determination of his or her own identity: "She would not say of any one in the world now that they were this or were that" (8).

Septimus commits suicide in order to prevent falling into the clutches of Dr. Holmes, a figure whom, along with Sir William Bradshaw, he identifies with human nature: "Once you fall, Septimus repeated to himself, human nature is on you. Holmes and Bradshaw are on you" (107). He might have added: Freud is upon you. Once you fall, you are not functioning the same as everyone else, according to the relevant paradigm or template of human nature; you are not submitting to the universal decree of "divine proportion, Sir William's goddess" (109). Self-expression contrary to that deemed consonant with the paradigm is subject to the pressure of curative treatment, otherwise known as conformity: "made it impossible for the unfit to propagate their views until they, too, shared his sense of proportion—his, if they were men, Lady Bradshaw's if they were women" (109). The demand for conformity entails insistence on "conversion"—the requirement that each individual be stamped by the same template, construed in terms of the same norm: "Conversion is her name and she feasts on the wills of the weakly, loving to impress, to impose, adoring her own features stamped in the face of the populace" (109).

Sir William Bradshaw and his psychotherapeutic ilk are just one version of the force of conversion in the world of the novel. Religion and its counterpart, the doctrine of Love (i.e., social love, whereby each individual is enjoined to act in accordance with a universal dictum) is another: "Love and religion! thought Clarissa, going back into the drawing-room, tingling all over. How detestable, how detestable they are!" (138). But the most insidious manifestation of conversion and the imposition of conformist authority concerns the regimen of time, promulgated by the ubiquitous clocks that strike, chime, ring, and boom throughout the day depicted. The narrator explicitly connects Sir William Bradshaw's insistence on conformity and "proportion" with the imposition of clock-measured time:

> Shredding and slicing, dividing and subdividing, the clocks of Harley Street nibbled at the June day, counseled submission, upheld authority, and pointed out in chorus the supreme advantages of a sense of proportion, until the mound of time was so far diminished that a commercial clock, suspended above a shop in Oxford Street, announced, genially and fraternally, as if it were a pleasure to Messrs. Rigby and Lowndes to give the information gratis, that it was half-past one. (112)

In this context, Abel's interpretation of Clarissa Dalloway through reference to Freudian developmental theory becomes unwittingly ironic. For the demand that character be interpreted in relation to a regimen of time, ordering development according to a schedule of stages, duplicates the insistent "clocks of Harley Street" that "pointed out in chorus the supreme advantages of a sense of proportion."

Of course, the novel conspicuously emphasizes the notion of character development through time. The process of maturation, evidenced in the distinction between youth and maturity, is frequently invoked: "When one was young, said Peter, one was too much excited to know people. Now that one was old, fifty-two to be precise (Sally was fifty-five, in body, she said, but her heart was like a girl's of twenty); now that one was mature then, said Peter, one could watch, one could understand, and one did not lose the power of feeling, he said" (212). Indeed, Elizabeth, Clarissa's daughter, is often described in terms of embarkation upon the next stage of development of the power of feeling: "There's Elizabeth, he said, she feels not half what we feel, not yet" (212). But this is not the same notion of development through time as that which Abel imports from Freud. In the Freudian construct, time is the measure of movement between developmental stages. More precisely, it is the means of formulating the notion of development as the progress or regression from stage to stage, for without continuity of time, there can be no succession of stages. But in the Woolfian construct, as encountered in *Mrs. Dalloway*, time is not just the measure of development, but itself a constituent component of that development. That is, time is not merely a measure, but part of that which is measured.

Clarification of this claim can begin with the notion of selfhood. The Freudian paradigm deployed by Abel construes the subject as a temporally unified entity whose development can be measured in terms of degree of success or failure in completing temporally distinct stages of maturation. Yet such construction does not apply to the Woolfian self, as depicted in *Mrs. Dalloway* (through Clarissa, Peter, and Septimus), for here selfhood is not local but diffuse—not integral at one particular point in time, but distended across both interpersonal and temporal boundaries. Consider Clarissa's formulation of her own identity as quasi-ubiquitous and indefinable in terms of simple or exclusive location: "But she said, sitting on the bus going up Shaftesbury Avenue, she felt herself everywhere; not 'here, here, here'; and she tapped the back of the seat; but everywhere" (167). That which applies to location in space applies equally to location in time. Character does not occupy only one point in time at a given moment of time. To be in the present is to be present to the past and future. There is a simultaneity of times in the present moment: "She felt very young; at the same time unspeakably aged" (8). Similarly, selfhood is not limited to the self to which it applies. Instead, it is completed by others with whom it comes in contact: "So that to know her, or any one, one must seek out the people who completed them; even the places" (167).

Superseding the Bergsonian temporal paradigm

A conventional interpretation of the temporally distended self in *Mrs. Dalloway*—the representation of personal awareness as occupying or including several different moments of time simultaneously—invokes the temporal philosophy of Henri Bergson, with its notion of duration or *durée* wherein time is construed as a cumulative and accumulating totality, all of whose content coexists. Durée is the integral unfolding of an indivisible fluency—what Alan Robert Lacey terms "a continuous whole [with] no parts" (1989, 51) and what Philip Turetzky terms an "enduring becoming" that "contains neither intervals nor juxtaposed equivalencies" (1998, 210, 199). In this construction, the past is construed not as a dead or former present, but as that which sustains and enables emergence of the present. For here, the present is the furthest advance of the past, and would have no basis for being without the past. Jay Lampert elaborates: "One might say that time is defined as the increase of what has happened, so the present is the cutting edge of the past" (2006, 50). For Bergson (in *Creative Evolution*), duration entails "the prolongation of the past into the present," with the result that "the whole of the past goes into the making of the living being's present moment" (Bergson 1944, 20, 25). Hence, as he states in *Duration and Simultaneity*, "duration is essentially a continuation of what no longer exists into what does exist" (Bergson 1965, 49).

Bergson (in *Time and Free Will*) opposes the notion of time as duration (durée) to the notion of time as space (*l'étendue*)—the notion of time, that is, as spatialized and hence divisible into discrete, juxtaposed parts, such as moments or instants: "[W]e project time into space, we express duration in terms of extensity, and succession takes the form of a continuous line or chain the parts of which touch without penetrating one another" (1910, 101). This is time as constructed through the analytical function of the intellect, which, as I. M. Bochenski indicates, "can dissect things and recompose them according to some law or system" (1965, 104). It is the time measured by clocks, like those that, in *Mrs. Dalloway*, are engaged in "[s]hredding and slicing, dividing and subdividing" (112). Here the integral fluency of time is reformulated as the sequence of static elements. Turetzky clarifies: "Measurable time, then, reduces time to intervals and simultaneities—abstract time unifying immobile sections" (1998,

199). To interpolate Lacey's very helpful phrases, like objects in space, the parts of measurable time—seconds, minutes, hours, etcetera—"exist separate from and alongside each other," whereas in durée "they interpenetrate and are never completely independent. An experience, for example, is always influenced by all previous experiences" (1989, 22).

This reference to the penetration of the present by the past—Bergson's notion that, to import Gilles Deleuze's phrasing in *Difference and Repetition*, "each present present is only the entire past in its most contracted state"—foregrounds the role of memory in constituting durée (1994, 82). For since the present present is here construed as the "contraction" or gathering together of the manifold content of the past, all of that past is virtually present in the present. Yet the memory thus involved is not personal, but impersonal. It is the principle enabling continuity to continue as the same ongoing whole, without suffering the loss or forgetting of its content. Levi R. Bryant elaborates: "[D]uration is itself memory (insofar as a duration is a continuity and not an existence at a point, and thereby must maintain itself in the expanse of its duration)" (2008, 186). However, the necessity of memory operates not just on the global level, involving the totality of duration, but on the micro-level as well—the level of transition from one moment to the next. Without memory, there could be no transition from one moment to the next, because without memory there would be no means of connecting moments with each other and hence no means of constituting succession. Instead, there would simply be immersion in an isolated moment, whichever it might be. Bergson explains in *Duration and Simultaneity*: "Without an elementary memory that connects the two moments, there will only be the one or the other, consequently a single instant, no before, no after, no succession, no time" (1965, 48). Thus impersonal memory is such stuff as durée is made of.

As many critics have noted, the Bergsonian notion of durée corresponds in some respects with the representation of experience in *Mrs. Dalloway*. For example, the idea, cited above, of duration as "the prolongation of the past into the present" and the converse notion of the present as the contraction of the past appears vividly in Clarissa's registration of "the moment of this June morning on which was the pressure of all the other mornings" (40). It appears too in the simultaneity of times implicit in the present moment: "She felt very young; at the same time unspeakably aged" (8). Indeed, the past abides in the present almost as a physical medium filtering awareness, as evident when Clarissa looks at Peter during their reunion after many years apart: "She looked at Peter Walsh; her look, *passing through all that time* and that emotion, reached him doubtfully; settled on him tearfully; and rose and fluttered away, as a bird touches a branch and rises and flutters away" (47 [my emphasis]). This notion of the past as an airy medium—a kind of aether—through which present awareness passes appears spectacularly on the first page, when, in the midst of the current morning in June 1923, Clarissa simultaneously reinhabits a past morning, more than 30 years earlier at Bourton. The two mornings are copresent in the air that Clarissa on both occasions senses: "How fresh, how calm, stiller than this of course, the air was in the early morning" (3). Here the past is literally the breath of life—that which vivifies the present.

But remembrance of the past is not always so breezy in *Mrs. Dalloway*. That is, the prolongation of the past into the present does not always proceed with the continuity characteristic of Bergsonian durée, where the present is the expanding boundary (what Lampert, as noted earlier, terms "the cutting edge") of the swelling advance of the past. Instead of such seamless continuity, the novel often portrays the risk of discontinuity, when the present suffers excruciating separation from the past that no ensuing temporal passage can bridge and from which no elapse of time can offer relief. Clarissa, for example, suffered traumatic grief on watching her sister "killed by a falling tree," with the result that her only escape from turning "bitter" and blaming "Gods" was to adopt "this atheist's religion of doing good for the sake of goodness" (85). Peter, of course, bears the open wound of Clarissa's rejection of him in favor of Richard Dalloway. The rejection scene remains a moment of permanent agony: "It was awful, he cried, awful, awful!" (71). Yet just as Clarissa overcame the pain of her sister's death, Peter too finds a way of surmounting loss and reestablishing connection with the continuity of time: "Still the sun was hot. Still, one got over things. Still, life had a way of adding day to day" (71). For Peter and Clarissa, the suffering of loss in the present is registered as a sudden collision with an impenetrable wall that blocks forward movement. When Peter interrupts the incipient lesbian intimacy of Clarissa and Sally Seton after their first (and only) kiss, Clarissa feels that "[i]t was like running one's face against a granite wall in the darkness! It was shocking; it was horrible!" (39). When Clarissa later rejects Peter in favor of Richard, Peter feels "that he was grinding against something physically hard" (70).

Though both Peter and Clarissa regain integration with the forward movement of time, Septimus is not as fortunate. Unlike Peter and Clarissa, he cannot reengage with the continuity of time after the traumatic grief occasioned by the death, "just before the Armistice" ending World War I, of "his officer" (94) and friend, Evans. Instead, Septimus falls into a gap or hiatus in the continuity of time—the continuity on which the distinction between past and present is founded: "falling down, down, he cried, into the flames" (73). During the breakup with Clarissa, Peter also suffers "infernally" from loss: "He almost cried out that he couldn't attend because he was in Hell!" (68). Yet Peter's loss remains part of the continuity of time. Years later, he affirms the passage of time beyond the past, even while painfully remembering that past: "she kept coming back at him like a sleeper jolting against him in a railway carriage" (83). In contrast, for Septimus there is no distinction between remembering and reexperiencing. The past is present and the dead return: "Evans was speaking. The dead were with him" (102). Here the relation between past and present becomes the relation between death and life. Yet the terms of this relation are interchangeable; no abiding distinction between them obtains: "I have been dead, and yet am now alive" (75).

According to Mary Ann Gillies, "Septimus is overcome by his memories and loses his grip on the present moment," whereas Peter manages "to keep memories in their place" (1996, 119). This is a misleading distinction. While it is indeed correct to state that Peter keeps memories in their place, it is incorrect to claim that Septimus is overcome by memory. A little analysis will clarify the matter. Memory presupposes the temporal movement whereby the present advances beyond the past. Without this movement, there would be nothing to remember—nothing, that is, not still in the present and therefore available to immediate awareness, without need of memory. In his madness, Septimus experiences time divested of anisotropy. For him, time exists as a preexistent pattern, whose parts or moments coexist in static constancy, in the positions respectively assigned to each. To grasp this paradoxical formulation, consider first his delusional revelation regarding time: "The word 'time' split its husk; poured its riches over him; and from his lips fell like shells, like shavings from a plane, without his making them, hard, white, imperishable, words, and flew to attach themselves to their places in an ode to Time" (76). Here the words of the ode to Time instantly assume their preestablished positions. Once there, they abide unchangingly, each contributing to the totality that they collectively comprise. With Bergson, as we noted, time is duration, and duration is "enduring becoming" (to retrieve Turetzky's phrase)—the continuous prolongation of the past into the present, which in turn is always moving beyond where it was. In contrast, for Septimus, time is a continuity that does not endure, in Bergson's sense, because it is continuity without becoming (without the unfolding of change). When change does occur, it confirms only that there has been no change. This dispensation achieves dramatic expression near the end of the Ode to Time passage, when Septimus and Evans (whom Septimus delusionally believes is hidden behind a tree), sing a duet, until Evans (whom Septimus at this point confuses with Peter Walsh who, by coincidence, is in the vicinity) approaches Septimus, who sees that Evans, marked by neither battle "mud" nor "wounds," has not changed: "he was not changed" (76).

The motif of changelessness extends into the concluding section of the Ode to Time passage, when Septimus construes himself as a "giant mourner," a "colossal figure who has lamented the fate of man for ages" unchangingly, "with his hands pressed to his forehead, furrows of despair on his cheeks," until achieving this revelation regarding Evans and the unreality of death (76). At this point, the motif of changelessness undergoes a modulation. For in his delusion, Septimus hesitates to turn around and make, "to the legions of men prostrate behind him," "the millions [who] for ages ... had sorrowed," the proclamation that will change "despair" to "joy": "He would turn round, *he would tell them in a few moments, only a few moments more*, of this relief, of this joy, of this astonishing revelation" (77 [my emphasis]). Here Septimus prefers to prolong the current changeless state (mourning "for ages"), before a new state, despite its redemptive promise, is inaugurated.

At the root of Septimus's delusions regarding Evans's survival of death is the need to overcome the link between temporality and change. Having been traumatized by changes suffered during the passage of time, Septimus needs to dwell inside the delusion that time is under his control, and that change cannot occur unless and until he permits it. Indeed, the trauma of time casts its shadow across the novel. Clarissa provides one formulation near the beginning of the novel: "[S]he always had the feeling that it was very, very dangerous to live even one day" (9). Septimus knows this in spades. The greatest danger threatened by time is loss—the disappearance into the past of that which was formerly present. Driven mad by loss, *Septimus inhabits a time that passes without anything passing away during it*. On the first page of the novel, when thinking about her memory of Peter, Clarissa refers to the connection between temporal passage and loss: "[I]t was his sayings one remembered ... *when millions of things had utterly vanished*—how strange it was!—a few sayings like this about cabbages" (3 [my emphasis]).

Foreground and background time in *Mrs. Dalloway*

The treatment of time in *Mrs. Dalloway* is deepened and complicated by paradox. On the one hand, there is scission and loss. On the other hand, there is a durée-like retention and continuity: "the drip, drip, of one impression after another down into that cellar where they stood, deep, dark, and no one would ever know" (166). The first is frequently associated with fear of expiration: "But she feared time itself, and read on Lady Bruton's face, as if it had been a dial cut in impassive stone, the dwindling of life; how year by year her share was sliced, how little the margin that remained was capable any longer of stretching, of absorbing, as in the youthful years" (32–33). The second is linked with preference for perpetuation: "he liked continuity; and the sense of handing on the traditions of the past" (128). Yet a deeper paradox than this informs the treatment of time in the novel. Though the time frame of the plot occupies only a few hours of one day in June 1923, time in *Mrs. Dalloway* extends indefinitely backward and forward from that point, encompassing not merely the respective pasts of key characters, and not merely two millennia of British history beginning when the country assumed "its ancient shape, as the Romans saw it, lying cloudy, when they landed," but also the entire span of prior and subsequent human experience, as the current period is simply "[t]his late age of the world's experience"—the latest installment of "this interminable life," sustained by "the passing generations" (26, 10, 178, 90) whose succession continues interminably. Hence, in contrast to the conventional novel where each character is construed as an integral unit of identity, distinct from other characters, in *Mrs. Dalloway* each primary character is construed as a local expression of ongoing human experience.

In "Odysseus' Scar," the celebrated first chapter of *Mimesis: The Representation of Reality in Western Literature*, Eric Auerbach refers to "subjectivisitic-perspectivistic procedure, creating a foreground and background, resulting in the present lying open to the depths of the past" (1953, 5). We can fruitfully apply this notion to *Mrs. Dalloway*, where the foreground/background distinction operates on distinct planes. In one, the foreground concerns the objective present in which a given character is involved—doing, saying, feeling, or thinking something on that day in June. The corresponding background concerns the depth of the personal past with which the present awareness of that character is engaged, as when Clarissa or Peter link a present thought or sensation with a past one, 30 years ago at Bourton. But on a deeper plane, the entire foreground/background just described, informing a character's awareness, is itself subsumed in the limitless expanse of human experience, protracted across "the passage of ages" (90).

The narrator is the primary source of this deep temporal background. As Paul Ricoeur notes, the narrator, endowed "with the ability *to move* from one stream of consciousness to another," sequentially enters or inhabits the respective awareness of various characters (1985, 2.104 [original emphasis]). Yet, as Ricoeur does *not* note, sometimes the narrator withdraws completely from involvement in any character, thereby becoming, like the aeroplane "that turned and raced and swooped exactly where it liked, swiftly, freely, like a skater," a remote perspective on the continuity of human experience, "this thing called life," registered in terms of essential feelings: "this gradual drawing of everything into one center" (22, 133, 16). Significantly, the definitive act of the aeroplane corresponds to that of the narrator—writing: "what word was it writing?" (23). A superb example of the perspective of the narrator, when withdrawn from involvement with any particular character, concerns the passing of "[t]he motor car with its blinds drawn," as it proceeds "down Bond Street," bearing its unidentified cargo of majesty, "whether ... Queen, Prince, or Prime Minister nobody knew" (17). Here the narrator construes the transit of the motor car in the context of the passage of time—what elsewhere is termed the "infinite ages" (89)—when London will have succumbed to "the ruins of time and all those hurrying along the pavement this Wednesday morning are but bones with a few wedding rings mixed up in their dust and the gold stoppings of innumerable decayed teeth" (17–18). In this example, the narrator projects the present moment against the background of the remote future. But in a later passage, concerning the aged, battered beggar-woman "opposite Regent's Park Tube Station" who sings a love song, "remembering how once in some primeval May she had walked with her lover" (89), the narrator projects the present moment against the background of the remote past. For like "the voice of an ancient spring spouting from the earth," the beggar-woman's singing expresses not just one love in one lifetime, but the emotion of love renewed and suffered "[t]hrough all ages": "love which has lasted a million years, she sang, love which prevails" (89). In *Mrs. Dalloway*, the present is open to the expanse of time, on both personal and species-specific levels. The present experience of a given character opens onto the more remote past of that character, as we have seen. But more profoundly, the experience of a given character—the character's transit through his or her own life—is cast against the background of the vast succession of individuals and their respective generations comprising the "pageant" of human experience, across the centuries, before and after (89).

The implications of Big Ben's "leaden circles" of time

In this context of expanded temporality, "the leaden circles" propagated by Big Ben as it strikes the "hour, irrevocable" (4) reveal their deepest implications. But brief review of relevant concepts in the history of ideas must introduce such analysis. In a passage quoted earlier, the narrator associates the chiming of the neighboring "clocks of Harley Street" with "proportion" and the arithmetic processes of "dividing and subdividing" (112). In a slightly earlier passage, Sir William Bradshaw, one of the physicians of Harley Street, is identified as a worshipper of "divine proportion" (109). Moreover, when first mentioned by the narrator, the sound of Big Ben is described as "musical": "Out it boomed. First a warning, musical; then the hour, irrevocable. The leaden circles dissolved in the air" (4). These clustered references to music, divine proportion, mathematical division, and emanating circles entrain profound associations whose explication will deepen our understanding of time in *Mrs. Dalloway*. Though this discussion will be compact, its unfolding must proceed through a series of steps. The notion of time will not emerge again until the third step, but the first two will prepare a different conceptual context for that notion, and the fourth step will unfold the idea of Big Ben Man, inscribed within the leaden circles of isochronal time. The fifth step will explore Mrs. Dalloway's reconciliation with "the horror of the moment"—her fear of being in time (8).

Step 1: Theology of the circle

It is convenient to begin with "the leaden circles" emanating from Big Ben—the great tower-clock "with his majesty laying down the law, so solemn, so just": the supreme source of temporal "authority" in the world of the novel (140, 112). The motif of concentric circles enjoys spectacular prestige in the history of philosophy, beginning with Plato's *Timaeus* (c. 350 BC, date much disputed), where the Demiurge orders the seven stars (sun, moon, and five planets) in concentric orbits around the earth, so that their unvaryingly uniform movement constitutes "a moving image of eternity" (*Timaeus* 37d). The motif recurs in Aristotle's *De Caelo* (*On the Heaven*, c. 332 BC, date much disputed) where, as Sir David Ross indicates, "the universe consists of a series of concentric spheres," each endowed with its own rotary movement (1949, 96). Whereas the concentric circles or spheres in the Platonic and Aristotelian cosmologies are fixed in position around the earth, those involved in the *Enneads* by Plotinus (c. 204–270 AD), the founder of neo-Platonism (a philosophical school or disposition that Chester G. Starr terms "the last and greatest answer to the problems of the world which ancient philosophy erected") are construed as having emanated from a divine center—the One or *En*, which is beyond all intelligibility, since any act of knowing entails distinction between knower and known, hence converting unity into multiplicity (1965, 347). The first emanation from the One is the sphere of *Nous* or Divine Mind. From it proceeds the World Soul, from which in turn emanate human souls. The final stage of the emanative process produces matter, conceived as the privation of light, just as the One is conceived as the source of light, whose brightness diminishes in proportion to the distance from it.

The concentric topographies just summarized privilege the circle and its three-dimensional counterpart, the sphere. As Rudolf Wittkower indicates, "The geometrical definition of God [or more generally, divine order] through the symbol of the circle or sphere has a pedigree reaching back to the Orphic poets"—that is, as early as the sixth century BC (1971, 28). A highly influential and much recycled example, cited by Etienne Gilson, occurs in *Maxims of Theology* by Alan of Lille (c. 1128–1202): "God is an intelligible sphere, whose center is everywhere and the circumference nowhere" (qtd. in Gilson 1955, 174). In what constitutes a superb gloss on this theologico-geometric image, Marsilio Ficino (1433–1499) regards God (in Wittkower's paraphrase) "as the true center of the universe, the inner core of everything, but at the same time as the circumference of the universe, surpassing everything immeasurably" (1971, 28). The inner core of that which it surpasses immeasurably—here the circle represents both the immanence and transcendence of God. More specifically, as we shall now consider, the circle or sphere is identified with divinity, because its shape is associated with such attributes as perfection, symmetry, harmonic proportion, uniformity, infinite continuity, and unity. For this reason, Renaissance church builders considered circular or centrally planned structure as the ideal architectural form for the House of God. A celebrated formulation of these attributes appears in *I Quattro libri dell'architecttura*, the famous architectural treatise by Andrea Palladio, published in 1570 in Venice: "it is enclosed by one circumference only, in which is to be found neither beginning nor end, and the one is indistinguishable from the other; its parts correspond to each other and all of them participate in the shape of the whole; and moreover every part being equally distant from the centre such a building demonstrates extremely well the unity, the infinite essence, the uniformity and the justice of God'" (qtd. in Wittkower, 1971, 23).

Step 2: Proportion and Vitruvian Man inscribed in a circle

All the Godly attributes addressed so far in relation to the circle or sphere—the immanent core ordering everything that it transcends—are implicit in the figure of the man inside or circumscribed by the circle: one of the most famous images reproduced in the Renaissance, most notably in the version created by Leonardo da Vinci. The image derives from what Peter Murray terms "the only technical treatise on the arts to have come down to us from classical antiquity"— Vitruvius's *Ten books on Architecture* (*De architectura libri decem*), written around 23 BC and dedicated to Augustus: "If a man lie on his back with hands and feet outspread, and the center of a circle is located in his navel, then his hands and feet will touch the circumference" (Murray 1969, 53; *De Arch.*, III, I, 1–3, qtd. in Murray, 11). The Vitruvian figure of the man inscribed in a circle— what we can call Vitruvian Man—is freighted with implications whose explication will provide a new point of view from which to consider "the leaden circles" propagated by Big Ben in the world of the novel. In its immediate architectural context, the Vitruvian figure demonstrates a doctrine of proportion, inherited from prior tradition, wherein the parts of the human body display a complex series of interrelated ratios, based on a module or fixed measure: "The face, for example, is the length of the palm, and both are a tenth of the height of the whole body, while the foot is a sixth of the same overall height" (Vitruvius, III, 1, 3, qtd. in Onians 1988, 34). As James S. Ackerman indicates, this system of proportions subjects the human body to a process of division, reducing the whole to "a complex of numerically or geometrically related parts" and construing the whole as "a harmony among discrete members" (1986, 41).

For Vitruvius, the human body provides a paradigm for architectural construction conducted according to proportionality: "In the same way the members of temples should have an appropriate response of commmensurability between the whole structure and the individual parts" (*Ten Books on Architecture*, III, 1, 3, qtd in Onians, 1988, 34). John Onians elaborates: "It is essential that a temple should have a numerical relationship among its parts so that it may have the same perfection of layout as the human body" (1988, 34). Vitruvius's insistence on proportionality in architectural construction derives from ancient Greek architectural practice, whose proportional schemata are succinctly formulated by J. J. Coulton: "Rules of proportion were formulated so that the appropriate size for each element could be derived from a dimension already decided" (1977, 64). Ordinarily, the module or dimensional unit determining the relative sizes of all elements in a single edifice was the half-diameter of the column.[3] All parts of the building were derived from this unit through what Rudolf Wittkower terms "methods of subtraction, addition, multiplication and division of ratios"— methods that correspond strikingly to the "[s]hredding and slicing, dividing and subdividing," undertaken by "the clocks of Harley Street," in pointing "out in chorus the supreme advantages of a sense of proportion" (Wittkower 1971, 138; *Mrs. Dalloway*, 112).

In the Renaissance, the Vitruvian figure inscribed in a circle epitomized "divine proportion"—a term employed, as we have seen, by the narrator of *Mrs. Dalloway* in reference to "Sir William's goddess" (109). Indeed, Luca Pacioli (1446/47–1517), a Renaissance mathematician friendly with Leonardo da Vinci, used the term as the title of his treatise, *De Divina Proportione* (composed in 1496–98): "from the human body derive all measures and their demonstrations and in it is to be found all and every ratio and proportion by which God reveals the innermost secrets of nature" (qtd. in Wittkower 1971, 15). For Pacioli and other Renaissance theorists, as Wittkower explains, "the Vitruvian figure inscribed in a square and a circle became a symbol of the mathematical sympathy between microcosm and macrocosm" (1971, 16).

This correspondence of microcosm and macrocosm is founded on proportionality—a principle discovered by Pythagoras in the sixth century BC, elaborated by Plato in the *Timaeus*, embellished by Plotinus, transmitted via St. Augustine to the Christian Middle Ages, and thence to the Renaissance. Studying musical tones produced by vibrating strings, Pythagoras observed that pitch varied according to measurable ratios of length. Wittkower elaborates: "What he had found was that musical consonances were determined by the ratios of small whole numbers. If two strings are made to vibrate under the same conditions, one being half the length of the other, the pitch of the shorter string will be one octave (diapason) above that of the longer one" (1971, 103). In the Pythagorean tradition and all schools of thought influenced by it, proportion is the fundamental structural principle of the microcosm and the macrocosm—the soul and the cosmos. Hence, as Otto von Simpson indicates, "Without the principate of number, as Augustine calls it, the cosmos would return to chaos" (1988, 22). In the Pythagorean system, music is the sound of proportion, and proportion is the result of numerical ratios, produced by a process of "dividing and subdividing" analogous to that enabling Big Ben and the other public clocks of *Mrs. Dalloway* to produce their "musical" chiming at appropriate intervals (112, 4). John of Salisbury (1176–78), cited by von Simpson, epitomizes the Pythagorean function of musical proportion: "Music, he observes, embraces the universe, reconciling the dissident and dissonant multitude of beings by the law of proportion: 'by this law the heavenly spheres are harmonized, the cosmos as well as man governed'" (1988, 191). Sir William Bradshaw himself could not have put the matter better—he whose function, in a different way, is to reconcile "the dissident and dissonant multitude of beings by the law of proportion"!

Step 3: Reformulating proportion in *Mrs. Dalloway*

Whereas Pythagorean proportion concerns measurement of space (in this case, various lengths of vibrating string), proportion in *Mrs. Dalloway* concerns measurement of time. Sir William Bradshaw can help to advance our analysis, as he founds his psychiatric diagnoses on temporal proportion, dividing and subdividing time into appropriate intervals. Mental health depends on not allowing inward pain to continue beyond its proper duration: "'We all have our *moments* of depression,' said Sir William" (107 [my emphasis]). Introspection too must not continue beyond its proportional limit: "'Try to think as little about yourself as possible,' said Sir William kindly" (108). Just as temporal proportion dictates Sir William's therapeutic regime, so it determines his professional schedule, preventing appointments from continuing beyond their allotted duration: "'Yes?' Sir William encouraged him. (But it was growing late)" (107). This is precisely the point where Sir William's dedication to proportion reveals its venality, for to him, time is money: "To his patients he gave three-quarters of an hour" (108). The more time spent with one patient, the less time remains for remuneration from others: "the wall of gold, mounting minute by minute" (103). But the wall of gold mounting minute by minute, as Lady Bradshaw waits in the her husband's expensive car while he conducts a house call, has implications much deeper than Sir William's monetary greed, as analysis of the continued quotation will show: "the wall of gold that was mounting between them and all shifts and anxieties (she had borne them bravely; they had had their struggles) until she felt wedged on a calm ocean, where only spice winds blow; respected, admired, envied, with scarcely anything left to wish for, though she regretted her stoutness" (103–4).

Here the function of the wall of gold is to separate the Bradshaws from "all shifts and anxieties" and to install their lives "on a calm ocean, where only spice winds blow." Yet, at bottom, it is not money that confers this sense of security, but configuration of time: "minute by minute." Just as Big Ben and the other public clocks reduce the passage of time to the sequence of equal intervals (portions of an hour), so here the passage of time is reduced to a series of equal minutes. This is *isochronal* time par excellence—time formulated in terms of equal intervals or segments, establishing what Henri Focillon, in another context, terms "stable chronological environments" (1989, 139). Isochronal time in the novel simply elapses, ticks on, its passage punctuated by the periodic chiming or booming of clocks. Its contrary is the version of durée threatening the temporal experience of Clarissa, Peter, and Septimus—time formulated as a becoming that, unlike Bergsonian duration, is susceptible not just to memory of the past, but also to the risk of traumatic loss of the past: a duration that, as we have seen, is characterized as much by continuity as by the threat of discontinuity. Perhaps the greatest—and heretofore unnoticed—irony in the novel concerns the consonance between the attitudes toward time pertaining respectively to Septimus (the patient) and Sir William (the doctor). Each in his own way (one through madness, the other through psychiatry) attempts to overcome the hazard of temporality—the inevitable intrusion of destabilizing change: Septimus through the delusion of continuity without change and Sir William though the reduction of time to the unvarying passage of identical minutes.

Closer examination of the wall metaphor in the novel will clarify the distinction between isochronal time and Woolfian durée. Whereas the Bradshaws find security behind the wall, protected by the predictable constancy of isochronal time, "minute by minute," the temporal experience of Peter and Clarissa is vulnerable to painful collision with walls that impede their progress from the present to the future, as when Clarissa, on Peter's interruption of her incipient intimacy with Sally, feels that she has run her "face against a granite wall in the darkness" (39), or when Peter, on suffering Clarissa's later rejection of him, feels "that he was grinding against something physically hard" (70). Whereas recourse to isochronal time shelters fear, openness to Woolfian durée—what we shall call Woolfian time—enables adventure, for here, time, predicated on "the downfall of habit" (57), is new in every moment ("creating it every moment afresh" (4), yet for this reason porous to "trouble and suspense" (26), the very factors walled off by isochronal time. With isochronal time, as majestically propagated by Big Ben, suspense is reduced to confirmation of the inevitable: "an indescribable pause; a suspense ... before Big Ben strikes" (4)—a condition contrary to the "astonishing sensibility" (153) of characters open to Woolfian time, who are repeatedly "taken by surprise" (62) by feelings provoked by moments recalled, currently encountered, or anticipated.

As Ernst Cassirer, in a discussion of Nicolus Cusanus, declares, "Man is completely enclosed in time: indeed, he is completely entrapped in the particularity of any given moment; and yet, despite all this, man proves to be a *deus occasionatus*" [an occasioned or circumstanced god] (1963, 43)—a being capable of discovering and expressing its supreme creativity through engagement with the temporality that constrains it. The leaden circles emanated by Big Ben enclose London in their circumferences. But though Big Ben imposes its *measurement* of time, it does not exhaust or determine the implications of living in time. Instead, the isochronal time that Big Ben imposes, with the "authority" (112) of a god whose commands must not be disobeyed, binds experience inside a pattern of metrical regularity contrary to the intrinsic mutability of temporal experience—its susceptibility to change, its perpetual flux, its intractable surpassing of the security of familiarity: "feeling that it was very, very dangerous to live even one day" (9). At bottom, Big Ben serves the function of Big Nanny, for the concentric circles of isochronal time shield temporal experience against exposure to the tumult of becoming, "all this fever of living" (63), where feeling fluctuates unpredictably, like leaves "as the breeze stirs them ... flinging themselves suddenly aloft" (62).

Step 4: The interpenetration of isochronal and fluid time

Yet there is no stable separation of antithetical temporalities in *Mrs. Dalloway*: isochronal time and fluid time. Instead, temporal experience remains heterogeneous, intermingling these unlikely or contrary elements, in shifting proportions. The temporal awareness of Peter Walsh, for example, though preeminently associated with fluid time or Woolfian durée, is nevertheless deeply interfused with consciousness of the isochronal time disseminated by Big Ben: "Remember my party, remember my party, said Peter Walsh as he stepped down the street, speaking to himself rhythmically, in time with the flow of sound, the direct downright sound of Big Ben striking the half-hour" (52). The peremptory influence of Big Ben is witnessed by Clarissa as she gazes though a window at the old woman who is her neighbor and realizes that what she sees ultimately concerns herself:

> Big Ben struck the half-hour. How extraordinary it was, strange, yes touching to see the old lady (they had been neighbours ever so many years) move away from the window, *as if she were attached to that sound, that string.* Gigantic as it was, it had something to do with her. Down, down, into the midst of ordinary things, the finger fell making the moment solemn. *She was forced, so Clarissa imagined, by that sound, to move, to go*—but where?" (139 [my emphasis])

As the passage shows, isochronal time descends to the level of the will: "She was forced by that sound, to move, to go—but where?" (139). Yet obedience is involuntary: there is no question of resistance, nor even awareness of duress. This is not merely the importunity of schedule, in a life controlled or dominated by the demands of appointment and routine. More profoundly, it concerns the need for temporal order and regularity, because without them life is too vulnerable to upheaval and tumult. This notion is corroborated by the description a few lines later of Big Ben's sound: "that solemn stroke which lay flat like a bar of gold on the sea" (140). Here we find the same references to gold and to barrier that occurred in the passage regarding the Bradshaws' reliance on isochronic time to build "minute by minute" a "wall of gold" between them and the disruptions of change (103). The connection between these passages is further tightened by the reference to the placid sea in each—in one, "a calm ocean," in the other, a "flat" sea. The unvarying placidity of both these seas is distinguished from the intractable agitation of "the troubled sea" (63) that, for Peter Walsh, is a symbol of life with its emotional instability and upheavals. Placid waters are also contrary to the sea of pain in which Septimus psychologically drowns: "I went under the sea. I have been dead, and yet am now alive" (75).

Isochronal time is instituted to regularize life—to render it predictable. But this is achieved at great cost. For the price of security is intrusion upon "the privacy of the soul"—the supreme value in Clarissa's morality (139). We can see this suggested in the response of the old woman to Big Ben: "She was forced, so Clarissa imagined, by that sound, to move, to go—but where?" The old woman represents, for Clarissa, the privacy of the soul that must not be violated: "[H]ere was one room; there another. Did religion solve that, or love?" (140). The worst crime entails forcing the soul—the crime of which both Dr. Holmes and Sir William Bradshaw are guilty: "forcing your soul, that was it ... Life is made intolerable; they make life intolerable, men like that" (202). Yet Big Ben forces the soul, through the imposition of temporal compulsion. Again, we can quote: "She was *forced*, so Clarissa imagined, by that sound, to move, to go—but where?" (139 [my emphasis]).

In *Mrs. Dalloway*, experience is centered on time. However, as the organizing center of experience, time is bipolar, not unitary, and therefore operates in antithetical ways. True proportion concerns the ratio of one temporal framework to another: isochronal and fluid (or Woolfian). Septimus represents total immersion in fluid time—the time of inner awareness. Big Ben represents the imposition of isochronal time—the time of metrical uniformity. The temporal experience of Peter and Clarissa blends both poles, in varying proportion. With these notions of proportion and bipolar temporality, we can return to the Vitruvian image of the man inscribed inside a circle, for the purpose of discovering deeper implications of "the leaden circles" emanated by Big Ben. As we have seen, Vitruvian Man is a paragon of proportion: all his parts are commensurate with each other, such that the size of each can be measured or determined by reference to any other, for all are ordered according to a harmonious correlation of ratios. This schema of commensurability is a microcosm of the proportionality displayed by the macrocosm, ordered according to eternal principles linked to divinity. The circle circumscribing Vitruvian Man is a symbol of that divine order, and represents, to retrieve Palladio's phrase, "the unity, the infinite essence, the uniformity and the justice of God." In *Mrs. Dalloway*, the notion of "divine proportion" is also associated with circumscribing circles. But in this case, the circles are the "leaden" ones emanating from Big Ben, and proportion pertains to the measurement of time, not space. Thus instead of Vitruvian Man, the novel presents what might be termed *Big Ben Man*. Here, as we have seen, the circles ultimately function as barriers, shielding experience from the "shocks of suffering" (145) occasioned by exposure to unregulated temporality. The isochronal time associated with Big Ben reduces temporality to an orderly passage, "minute by minute" (103), ostensibly impervious to unwanted change. But insulation against change leads to complacency—a flaw whose supreme embodiment is the well nourished and "unspeakably pompous" Hugh Whitbread, "with his little job at Court" (125, 6). Ironically, Hugh is described in terms of the same perfect adjustment between microcosm and macrocosm as that displayed in the Vitruvian diagram of a man inscribed in a circle: "Hugh Whitbread, feeling at peace with the entire universe and at the same time completely sure of his standing, said, resting his fork" (114–15). Indeed, men connected to "the upper classes" (176), who have not lost their "sense of proportion" (106, 112, 119), enjoy this advantage over women: "Lady Bruton often suspended judgement [*sic*] upon men in deference to the mysterious accord in which they, but no woman, stood to the laws of the universe" (120).

But there is more to be said here—a different aspect of the matter to be considered. Whereas isochronal time is, as the case of the Bradshaws suggests, associated with the project to live according to a pattern of regularity that precludes "all shifts and anxieties" (103), the temporality linked with public clocks like Big Ben has implications deeper than this. In the world of the novel, the deepest anxiety regarding temporality concerns mortality. It strikes Peter when he thinks of Clarissa while St. Margaret's clock tolls the time: "It was her heart, he remembered; and the sudden loudness of the final stroke tolled for death that surprised in the midst of life, Clarissa falling where she stood, in her drawing room. No! No! he cried" (54). It strikes Clarissa when she thinks of Lady Bruton's face as a chronometric "dial," measuring "the dwindling of life; how year by year her share was sliced" (32). Ironically, though clocks are linked with elapse of life and fear of death, the primacy of clocks in the world of the novel expresses the project to circumvent mortality. As Focillon indicates, the function of isochronal time is "to mold historical life into distinct segments" (1989, 139). In *Mrs. Dalloway*, the passage of time is distributed according to the sequence of days, and the function of the public clocks populating London is to measure the passage of each day, half-hour by half-hour: "the clocks of Harley Street nibbled at the June day" (112). But once the clocks have finished nibbling at that particular June day, the next will follow, and the process of "[s]hredding and slicing, dividing and subdividing" will start all over again (112). In this isochronal schema, instead of elapsing, time is endlessly chewed and renewed.

Yet the signification of clocks remains ambiguous in the world of the novel. On the one hand, they are associated with "submission" to the "authority" of "proportion" (112). In this regard, as we have seen, the administration of isochronal time confers (a) benefits (such as predictable regularity and recurrent renewal) and (b) obligations (the imperatives of schedule and predetermined arrangements). But on the other hand, civilized life, at the level of complexity depicted in the novel, requires clocks and the isochronal measurement of time they entail, in order to achieve the precise synchronization necessary to coordinate social interaction and implement decisions regarding when to do what must be done. This ambiguity is not the nub of the problem, however. For that we must return to the notion of proportion. In the world of the novel, the most fundamental stratum of proportion pertains to the ratio between time given respectively to outer and inner awareness—between connection with the shared, public world and connection with private introspection. Sir William Bradshaw, as we have seen, recommends a minimum of introspection ("Try to think as little about yourself as possible"), whereas his patient, Septimus, engages in the maximum. The climactic example of due proportion between outer and inner concerns Clarissa's response to the news of Septimus's suicide. First, she darts into a small room—a movement connected with withdrawal into solitary contemplation. There, her thoughts probe deeply into the meaning of Septimus's death. In this scene, Clarissa achieves a new relation with the passage of time. It is a bridge or transitional moment, crossing from one attitude toward time to another. Her initial reaction is to interpret his suicide as an act intended to keep a moment or a value forever protected from contamination and erosion by time: "A thing there was that mattered; a thing, wreathed about with chatter, defaced, obscured in her own life, let drop every day in corruption, lies chatter. This he had preserved" (202). This is the same attitude displayed in her youth, when "in white" she descended the staircase at Bourton, aware of supreme happiness and of the need somehow to keep it forever. But the only way to keep that moment alive would be to die in the midst of it: "If it were now to die, 'twere now to be most happy" (202). This attitude profoundly distrusts temporal passage as that which will inevitably take away what Clarissa desperately wants to preserve. Yet in the course of her meditation on Septimus's death, Clarissa achieves provisional reconciliation with temporal passage, construed now as "the process of living" that continues day after day, "as the sun rose, as the day sank" (203).

Step 5: Reconciliation with temporal passage

To understand this transition, analysis of Clarissa's references to darkness/blackness, in the course of her meditation on Septimus's death, is indispensable. First, blackness is linked with the sudden experience of death itself, as a result of suicidal defenestration: "There he lay with a thud, thud, thud in his brain, and then a suffocation of darkness" (202). Yet here the dead Septimus occupies, in some respects, a better position than those who survive. For "death was defiance" (102). That is, death was the only way to defy the irresistible tendency of time to obscure, in the course of its passage, moments that matter—ultimately the period of youth. In death, Septimus is beyond temporality, but such is not the case for Clarissa, Peter, and Sally: "they would grow old" (202). Clarissa's awareness of vulnerability to the passage of time culminates in her reference to "this profound darkness" that envelops or surrounds human life, always threatening to claim more victims, as they succumb to "disaster" or "disgrace" (203), unable, because of "the overwhelming incapacity," intrinsic to the human condition, to maintain buoyancy in "this life, to be lived to the end," and so inevitably "sink and disappear," as would have been Clarissa's fate "if Richard had not been there" (203). From this point of view, time is neither a sustaining nor illumining element. Instead, it is an encroaching darkness that obscures or extinguishes moments that are cherished, so that even the most exquisite can shine no longer than "a match burning in a crocus" (35).

The great transition in temporal attitude follows Clarissa's contemplation of the night sky—another form of gathering darkness: "It held, foolish as the idea was, something of her own in it, this country sky, this sky above Westminster" (203). The sky stretches over the city, just as the life of one person stretches across time: "No pleasure could equal ... this having done with the triumphs of youth" (203). In this context, no moment, however precious and exquisite, is a treasure worth ending life to preserve: "But this young man who had killed himself—had he plunged holding his treasure?" (202). Right after identifying with the sky,

Clarissa notices the old woman who lives nearby: "In the room opposite the old lady stared straight at her! She was going to bed" (203). Here the darkness/blackness motif recurs, as the old woman, in preparation for sleep, suddenly darkens her home: "She pulled the blind now" (204). This action occurs in the midst of an extraordinarily dense passage, occupying just a few lines of text but deploying several key motifs, in addition to darkness. At the center of this complexity is a fundamental opposition: (a) the boisterous conviviality of Clarissa's party, "with people still laughing and shouting in the drawing-room," and (b) the silent solitude of the old woman, "quite quietly, going to bed alone" (204). The link between these contraries is "the clock striking the hour, one, two, three"—an action whose initiation is perfectly synchronized with the old woman's pulling down of the blind: "She pulled the blind now. The clock began striking" (204). On the one hand, Big Ben's striking and the old woman's simultaneous darkening of her house, in preparation for sleep, are associated with the expiration of life, as invocation of the dirge from Shakespeare's *Cymbaline* confirms: "There! The old lady had put out her light! the whole house was dark now with this going on, she repeated, and the words came to her, Fear no more the heat of the sun" (104). Fear of life—or, more precisely, of what time might bring into life—troubles Clarissa, as evident, for example, at the beginning of the meditation in the room: "Then (she had felt it only this morning) there was the terror ... this life, to be lived to the end, to be walked with serenely; there was in the depths of her heart an awful fear" (203). In this context, the booming of Big Ben, near the end of Clarissa's meditation in the room, evokes her latent wish for the expiration of life and the security of death—a wish evident also in Peter's slumberous musing in Regent's Park: "Let me blow to nothingness with the rest" (63). But on the other hand, the insistent booming of Big Ben is now linked with the liveliness and appeal of the party ("all this going on"), so that Clarissa moves beyond her initial compassion for the dead Septimus, and feels drawn instead back to the festivity: "The young man had killed himself; but she did not pity him; with the clock striking the hour, one, two, three, she did not pity him, with all this going on" (204). Here Big Ben contributes to—one might almost say participates in—the uproar of the living, whereas, just a moment earlier, its striking invoked the silence of death.

What are we to make of this ambiguity? Perhaps it is best to begin with what we should not make of it. There is no justification for claiming that Clarissa has achieved a definitive change in her attitude toward time: that her dread of time ("she feared time itself") is finally (to interpolate Sally's words from a subsequent context) "a thing of the past—all over now" (32, 206). For Clarissa's fear of time is so deep ("there was in the depths of her heart an awful fear") that such recuperation would involve not just a change of heart in the idiomatic sense, but a metaphorical heart-transplant, a completely different emotional orientation to life—and that in just a few seconds! Yet, though her inveterate attitude toward time is not a thing of the past, she has achieved a different view of the past—a different view, more precisely, of the movement of time that precipitates the past, the tense designating events that occurred prior to the present. Consider the circumstances of Septimus's death—the "thud, thud, thud" that she imagines when mentally recreating his suicidal fall from the window onto the "rusty spikes" below. The excruciating collision of his plummeting body with an immovable object repeats a familiar motif: the sudden collision with a hard surface that impedes forward movement.

We noted it in reference to (a) Peter's interruption of Clarissa's kiss with Sally ("It was like running one's face against a granite wall in the darkness!") and (b) Clarissa's rejection of Peter: "he was grinding against something physically hard" (39, 70). As earlier explained, the collision motif arises when the suffering of loss in the present impedes acceptance of the forward movement of time, because such progression sunders the present from a cherished moment that now has become the past. Clarissa, as we have seen, attributes the cause of Septimus's suicide to the need to save a cherished moment: "had he plunged holding his treasure?" (202). But at the end of her meditation on his death, she no longer pities him for it ("she did not pity him"), and no longer identifies with the wish to die in order to preserve what the continuation of time will take away. Instead, she embraces this continuity ("all this going on"), and wishes to rejoin it (202). Her fear of time remains, but her response to that fear has changed. Time moves the present into the past. The present can respond by either refusing to accept that movement or embracing it. To refuse that movement is to wish that death might forever protect the cherished present from supersession. To embrace that movement is to remain open to the benefits of temporal passage—gaining through that passage, as Clarissa, Peter, and Sally recognize, a deepening sensibility or "power of feeling": "it went on increasing in his experience" (212).

5

The Phenomenology of Temporal Trauma in *To the Lighthouse*

To the Lighthouse aims at profundity. It confronts "the vast, the general question": "What is the meaning of life?"; "What does it mean? How do you explain it all?"; "What does one live for?"; "why was it so short, why was it so inexplicable" (Woolf 1927, 175, 203, 97, 105).[1] The question is posed in response to the "pathos" (167) of transience ("nothing stays; all changes" [195]) and, more poignantly, the shock of "tragedy" (144, 162), when life is experienced as the encounter with "strife, ruin, chaos" (164). In this context, the great challenge of human experience is the maintenance of proportion and balance, in the midst of "anguish" (100, 96), "anxiety" (68, 87, 101, 117), "desolation (83, 167), "despair" (162), "misery" (50, 203), and "sorrow(s)" (7, 108, 130, 142, 143, 166, 181, 183)—in short, "the weakness and suffering of mankind" (225), in the face of the intractable "complexity of things" (111). Yet, in the novel, the mind is notoriously susceptible to destabilization, by event or emotion, and must repeatedly seek to restore its equilibrium: "The disproportion there seemed to upset some harmony in her own mind" (209); "He upset the proportions of one's world" (213). Under these conditions, the meaning of life is found not through any fixed answer or permanent truth, which abides independent of the mind conceiving it, but in the ever-renewed struggle—one might more properly say, commitment—to configure one's own awareness as a "perspective" (187) or "point of view" (12, 79), capable of seeing the essential "pattern" (145), "coherence" (114), or "unity of the whole" (60) in the flux of "experience" (69, 173) whose content is as fleeting as the movement of time itself: "In the midst of chaos there was shape; this eternal passing and flowing (she looked at the clouds going and the leaves shaking) was struck into stability" (176).

Though "the shock of the event" (122)—the suffering of particular loss or heartache—underpins the tragic "vision" (197, 226) achieved respectively by each of the three principal characters (Mrs. Ramsay, Lily Briscoe, and Mr. Ramsay), at the deepest level the source of tragedy in the novel concerns not what happens in time, but the movement of time itself. This is preliminarily evident, for example, in Mrs. Ramsay's dread of transience—the recognition that "[n]o happiness lasted" (71):

> *it was all ephemeral as a rainbow*—this sound which had been obscured and concealed under the other sounds suddenly thundered hollow in her ears and made her look up with *an impulse of terror*. (20 [my emphasis])

The link between time and tragedy emerges most clearly in the middle section entitled "Time Passes," where the central tragic events in the novel (the deaths of Mrs. Ramsay, Andrew, and Prue) occur parenthetically (that is, as notations enclosed by parenthesis), indicating that these particulars are mere qualifications or adjectives of the substantive source of tragedy—the sheer passage of time. In the *Physics*, Aristotle posits time as essentially destructive, because it entails passage or movement, and movement removes from presence: "For time is by its nature the cause rather of decay, since it is the number of change, and change removes what is" (1941, 221^b1–2). Any structure, any equilibrium of forces, is destroyed by time. In *To the Lighthouse*, the passage of time leaves, in its wake, what Lily Briscoe terms, "strife, ruin, chaos." Even the stars succumb: "the waste of the years and the perishing of stars" (41). Prior security, no matter how long continued, means nothing after time eventually sweeps it away, as with the rent rock in the mountains or the loosened fold of Mrs. Ramsay's shawl, hanging in the nursery: "once in the middle of the night with a roar, with a rupture, as after centuries of quiescence, a rock rends itself from the mountain and hurtles crashing into the valley, one fold of the shawl loosened and swung to and fro" (142).

Of course, any analysis of time in *To the Lighthouse* encounters the problem of distinguishing, in the novel, between (a) representations of the nature of time as it is in itself, objectively, and (b) representations of the nature of time as it is for human experience, subjectively.[2] Indeed, the intellectual work of Mr. Ramsay, the resident philosopher in the novel, foregrounds the relation between subject and object, in the understanding of reality: "Subject and object and the nature of reality" (28). According to his son, Andrew, Mr. Ramsay seeks to know the object of his inquiry objectively, uncontaminated by subjective distortion: "'Think of a kitchen table then,' he told her, 'when you're not there'" (28). The same requirement for objective inquiry, involving independence from any particular point of view, is formulated, outside the novel, by Michael Dummett: "The description of what is really there, as it really is, must be independent of any particular point of view" (1960, 503). Remarkably, in the middle section, "Time Passes," the act of thinking of an object "when you're not there" (in this case, the unoccupied Ramsay vacation home) is prolonged for ten years, with the result that the passage of time is itself the ultimate object of observation, with only the Lighthouse beam as witness:

> The place was gone to rack and ruin. Only the Lighthouse beam entered the rooms for a moment, sent its sudden stare over the bed and wall in the darkness of winter, looked with equanimity at the thistle and the swallow, the rat and the straw. Nothing now withstood them. (150)

Here time itself is construed as a destructive force, which inevitably overwhelms all that endures in it, unless external human agency intervenes: "Mrs. McNab, Mrs. Bast stayed the corruption and the rot; rescued from the pool of Time that was fast closing over them now a basin, now a cupboard" (151–52).[3]

In contemporary philosophy, a distinction is made between the mere passage of time and the change that occurs to things and processes during that passage. In itself, time is neither destructive nor constructive. It is simply, as Aristotle notes (in a passage that seems to contradict his own citation of time as intrinsically destructive), the measure or "number of 'motion' in respect of 'before' and 'after'": "Hence time is not movement, but only movement in so far as it admits of enumeration" (*Physics* 219b2–4). Richard Taylor epitomizes this view: "We presuppose that time is not by itself 'efficacious'; that is, that the mere passage of time does not augment or diminish the capacities of anything and, in particular, that it does not enhance or decrease an agent's powers or abilities" (1978, 224). Donald C. Williams elaborates: "There is passage, but it is nothing extra. It is the mere happening of things, their existence strung along the manifold" (1978, 105). However, in *To the Lighthouse*, the very measure of time is itself destructive or associated with destruction. That is, in "Time Passes," the unit or measure regarding the passage of time, is night, and the movement of time, from unit to unit, is construed in terms of the succession of destructive nights, one after another: "Night, however, succeeds to night. Winter holds a pack a them" (139). Moreover, the notion of time as an intrinsically destructive force or agent is extended to entail the destruction by time of the distinctions proper to it and by which its own duration is measured: "(for night and day, month and year ran shapelessly together . . .) until it seemed as if the universe were battling and tumbling, in brute confusion and wanton lust aimlessly by itself" (147). Here, through destroying the boundaries between the units by which its own duration is measured, time destroys the very principle by which things are said to be in time. As Aristotle notes, "things are in time as they are in number"—that is, to be in time is to be numerable (*Physics* 221ª16). But in "Time Passes," the number by which time is measured is itself destroyed. In this context, all that remains is "the chaos and tumult of the night" (147).[4]

Yet this dispensation is obviously contradicted by the fact that the period narrated in "Time Passes" lasts ten years. That is, though the section concerns the running "shapelessly together" of the units by which time is measured, the duration of the aggregate period is precisely measurable. Moreover, the periodicity of the Lighthouse beam, "coming regularly across the waves first two quick strokes and then one long steady stroke" (68), is itself measurable and invariable—as long as the keepers of the Lighthouse do their job as required. These contradictions, regarding the nature of time, can be resolved, once it is recognized that "Time Passes," at the deepest level, is not about the passage of time in itself, objectively. Instead, in essence, the section concerns the passage of time as it is experienced *subjectively*, by the victims of tragedy and traumatic loss. The succession of destructive nights that ultimately fuse, as we have seen, into one chaotic and tumultuous night constitutes perhaps the most spectacular depiction in literature of the long dark night of the soul. Indeed, the section makes explicit reference to the passage of time in terms of the desperation of the soul, when "[t]he nights are now full of wind and destruction," and the "sleeper" arises "to find on the beach an answer to his doubts," as the means of "bringing the night to order and making the world reflect the compass of the soul" (140).

Perhaps the most poignant reference to the long dark night of the soul concerns the agony of Mr. Ramsay, after the sudden death of his wife:

> Almost it would appear that it is useless in such confusion to ask the night those questions as to what, and why, and wherefore, which tempt the sleeper from his bed to seek an answer.
>
> [Mr. Ramsay stumbling along a passage stretched his arms out one dark morning, but, Mrs. Ramsay having died rather suddenly the night before, he stretched his arms out. They remained empty.] (140)

The passage along which Mr. Ramsay here stumbles is not spatial, but temporal. It concerns time passing during an excruciating decade of his life. The agony of this dark passage is the contrary of the exuberance displayed by his youngest children on vacation, before the long period of tragedy and trauma began: "They were happier now than they would ever be again ... They came bustling along the passage" (65). The bewildering agony of the long dark night of the soul in *To the Lighthouse* emerges more forcefully when we recognize that the entire novel, as suggested at the outset of this chapter, is formulated in terms of the question regarding the meaning of life. Characters are recurrently beset by "human worries" (66), which in normal circumstances can be managed or deferred. But in periods of overwhelming desperation, the question imposes itself relentlessly: "the old question which traversed the sky of the soul perpetually, the vast, the general question which was apt to particularize itself at such moments as these .... What is the meaning of life?" (175). To live without an answer when one is desperately sought and needed is to endure the long dark night of the soul, suffering the most excruciating form of "the dark of human ignorance" (50).

The demand for meaning in life is fundamental to character in *To the Lighthouse*. But meaning, in turn, is fundamentally construed in relation to time. Indeed, the question of meaning in life, quoted at the beginning of this chapter, is posed in terms of time: "why was it so short, why was it so inexplicable" (195). Moreover, on the first page of the novel, the very principle by which character is classified or divided into types concerns attitude toward time: "Since he belonged, even at the age of six, to that great clan which cannot keep this feeling separate from that, but *must let future prospects, with their joys and sorrows, cloud what is actually at hand*" (7 [my emphasis]). The question of meaning in life interrogates the nature of time itself—at least as available to human experience. In the novel, time is problematic and disruptive because of the vulnerability of the present to both the future and the past. The future is a source of worry and anxious uncertainty, while the past is a source of grief and regret. The future brings what cannot be foreseen: "Well, we must wait for the future to show" (143). The past removes what can never return: "it had become, she knew, giving one last look at it over her shoulder, already the past" (121). The challenge is to construct a perspective on the passage of time that perceives both future and past as enriching and stabilizing the present, instead of threatening, undermining, or disorienting it. This is not simply a matter of replacing a "pessimistic" attitude with "positiveness" (66, 211).[5] Ultimately, it entails securing the vulnerable "little strip of time" constituting life through expanding the interval occupied by the present, and reformulating its relation to the adjacent tenses, past and future (66). Explication of this complex enterprise can begin by contrasting the conventional and Woolfian notions of the passage of time in terms of the transition of tenses (future, present, and past), and then focusing attention on the status of the present in each of these two temporal dispensations.

In the conventional construction of the passage of time, superbly enunciated in McTaggart's description of the *A*-series and the *B*-series, discussed in Chapter 1 with regard to *Hamlet*, two notions of temporal succession are entailed. The first, labelled the *A*-series, involves "that series of positions which runs from the far past through the near past to the present, and then from the present through the near future to the far future or conversely" (McTaggart 1927, 2.11). As time passes, an event changes its temporal position, and moves from the far future to the near future, to the present, to the near past, to the far past. In this dispensation, each tense designates a temporal position. That which was an event in the future eventually becomes an event in the past, and in so doing merely changes position in the *A*-series designations of past, present, and future. The second notion of temporal succession, labelled the *B*-series, concerns the movement not from tense to tense, but from earlier to later. Though an event necessarily changes its position in the *A*-series, it cannot change its position in the *B*-series. Once one event occurs before or after another, its position in relation to that other event will always remain either earlier or later.

A remarkable variant of this conventional view of the passage of time is provided by C. D. Broad, in his celebrated work, *Scientific Thought*. Here he formulates temporal passage as a succession of events, extending from earlier to later, sequentially illuminated by a spotlight beam traversing its length, such that whatever is illuminated at a given moment constitutes the present, while the sections illumined earlier or still awaiting illumination respectively constitute past and future:

> We are naturally tempted to regard the history of the world as existing eternally in a certain order of events. Along this, and in a fixed direction, we imagine the characteristic of presentness as moving, somewhat like the spot of light from a policeman's bull's-eye traversing the fronts of the houses in a street. What is illuminated is the present, what has been illuminated is the past, and what has not yet been illuminated is the future. (1952, 59)

A literary version of the spotlight view of time occurs in Flann O'Brien's *The Third Policeman*: "Humanity is an ever-widening spiral and life is the beam that plays on each successive ring. All humanity from its beginning to its end is already present but the beam has not yet played beyond you" (1967, 119).

The spotlight view of time has very curious implications, whose explication will advance our analysis. Everything that happens, happens in time. But in the conventional or spotlight view of time, nothing really happens in time. Nothing happens, because events exist irrespective of the tense in which they appear or are considered. Time is merely an accident or qualification of their own untensed substantiality. For example, the event *e* is construed as already existing in the future before it occurs in the present. Thus, paradoxically, though in this view time is construed as passing, the things of time (i.e., events) subsist unchanged by its movement, such that future, present, and past merely designate modes of being what each event already and always is. In an alternate formulation, events change only their temporal properties, not their degree of reality or what might be termed their purchase on being. To interpolate Dean W. Zimmerman's phrasing, the spotlight theory of time does not draw "the metaphysical line between past, present, and future in terms of what exists" (2005, 403). In fact, to invoke Michael J. Loux's observation, proponents of this view (namely, that time is construed in terms of the ordering of the events or moments according to the *B*-series positions of earlier than, simultaneous with, and later than) "take time to be just another dimension along with the three spatial dimensions, and they hold that all times and their contents are equally real" (2006, 242).

An analogue of this dispensation occurs in *To the Lighthouse* when Lily compares her vivid sense of novelty in the present to that of a passenger in a train who "knows, looking out of the train window, that he must look now, for he will never see that town, or that mule-cart, or that woman at work in the fields, again" (210). The sequence of objects outside the window—some already behind the train, others directly opposite, still more not yet reached—corresponds exactly to the order of events—past, present, and future—invoked in the spotlight view of time. Lily connects this awareness of novelty with the "sense that everything this morning was happening for the first time" (210). But to happen, in this context, means to manifest in the present that which was awaiting disclosure while it was in the future and which, after being experienced in the present, will quickly recede into the past, like the objects viewed through the window of a moving train. Paradoxically, in this schema, the present holds nothing new, for what appears in it was already there in the future. Here, the present is simply the delayed registration of the future, which precedes it, and the anticipation of the past, which will follow.

In the novel, the spotlight view of time (or the railroad view, to invoke Lily's metaphor) is opposed to what might be called the Lighthouse view of time. To clarify this opposition and investigate its implications, discussion can best begin with the defining feature of the spotlight view of time: what Broad terms "the characteristic of presentness" construed as moving along an "eternally" ordered series of events, momentarily illumining each in its passage. In this paradigm, the movement of time leaves the things of time undisturbed by its passage.

Events simply acquire and then immediately shed the characteristic of presentness, without thereby undergoing further change. Moreover, the moving present is itself unaltered by the events to which its passage momentarily accords presentness. This temporal model differs radically from that associated with the Lighthouse. In the spotlight model, the moving present, symbolized by the passing beam, sequentially confers the property of presentness on each successive event that it traverses. But in the Lighthouse model, the Lighthouse beam illumines transience itself. That is, it illumines the moving present as such, not the events that momentarily acquire the property of presentness as the present moves toward the future. For example, the Lighthouse beam illumines transience during Mrs. Ramsay's meditation: "It will end. It will end, she said" (70).[6] Similarly, in the "Time Passes" section, the Lighthouse beam "lingered stealthily" on the carpet of the vacant bedroom of the Ramsay vacation home on the Isle of Skye, illumining "the chaos and tumult" entailed by the passage of time in which, as a result of transience, "nothing stays; all changes" (145, 147, 195). Unlike the spotlight model, where the moving present glides over the succession of events without disrupting the stability of their temporal order, the Lighthouse model undermines stability of succession, for in the tragic world of *To the Lighthouse* the passing of the present—the reality of transience—leaves "strife, ruin, chaos" in its wake (164). Moreover, when the moving present repeatedly removes from presence attachments on which emotional security depends, the passage of time is measured by the hammer strokes of fate: "like the measured blows of hammers ... with their repeated shocks" (145). In these circumstances, the sequence of events no longer matters—only their devastating consequences. Events merge into one continuous ordeal in which "night and day, month and year ran shapelessly together" (147), as transience reduces life to one continuous darkness. To formulate this predicament in McTaggart's terms, in *To the Lighthouse* the transience characteristic of the A-series transition of tenses (due to the moving present) ultimately destabilizes the B-series succession of events ordered according to the relations of before, simultaneous with, and after.

The disintegration of temporal order caused by transience in *To the Lighthouse* can be clarified by reference to Aristotle's notion, in the *Physics*, of the present as the link of time—the node, that is, by which past and future are connected to each other: "The 'now' is the link of time ... for it connects past and future time, and it is a limit of time (for it is the beginning of the one and the end of the other)" (1941b, 222^{a}10). In the novel, instead of functioning as the *link* of time, the present, as the agent of transience, *severs* the coherence of time. On her return to the Ramsay summer home, after a ten-year interval, Lily explicitly registers this severance of the link between past and future. Without that link, the present succumbs to a commotion of memories and perplexities respectively concerning the past and the future:

> She had no attachment here, she felt, no relations with it, anything might happen, and whatever did happen ... was a question, *as if the link that usually bound things together had been cut*, and they floated up here, down there, off any how. How aimless it was, how chaotic, how unreal it was, she thought, looking at her empty coffee cup. Mrs. Ramsay dead; Andrew killed; Prue dead too. (160 [my emphasis])

In this predicament, the only way to reconstitute the coherence of time is to strengthen the present as the link of time, and the only way to do that is to make more time present to the present—to include, that is, more time in present awareness than that which immediately presents itself to awareness. Explication of this matter will deepen our understanding of the Woolfian moment: "there is a coherence in things, a stability; something, she meant, is immune from change, and shines out ... in the face of the flowing, the fleeting, the spectral, like a ruby" (114).

Like the Woolfian moment, the Lighthouse beam also "shines out ... in the face of the flowing, the fleeting," as we have seen. Paradoxically, in illumining transience, the Lighthouse beam also illumines a way of transcending it. In contrast to the sequence of instantaneously consecutive nows viewed from the train, the Lighthouse enables and represents a perspective disclosing the continuity of one experience, unfolding in the unity of an expanded present, where successive impressions constitute an ongoing copresence. The construction of copresence is suggested by the Lighthouse beam's mode of manifestation, such that its separate "strokes" or pulsations are united in one rhythmic "stroking," as when Mrs. Ramsay awakens to see the beam rhythmically "stroking the floor" (172). Here the momentaneous present, lasting but an instant, widens into an expanded present, with many separate, consecutive strokes *copresent* in the awareness of one continuous stroking. The implications of the expanded present are far-reaching, but their investigation requires application of certain philosophical terms and concepts, which must first be clarified.[7]

The first of these concerns the "specious present"—a term referring to the expanded present whereby, to invoke Barry Dainton's phrasing, "a single momentary awareness takes in a temporal spread of phenomena" (2000, 143). Broad formulates this notion technically: "We can say that at any moment t an instantaneous act of prehension grasps a total object which is not instantaneous but stretches back for a short period *T* from the date *t* at which the instantaneous act of prehension takes place" (1933, 2.321). Consider the example of a ticking clock. I hear a tick now, but the act of hearing this tick includes hearing the tick preceding it. The act of hearing the ticking clock unfolds in what is termed the specious present, because the act includes as copresent not just the instantaneously present tick, but also a finite series of ticks preceding it. The hearing of all those ticks occurs during the same specious present. Broad elaborates: "The two ticks of the clock in my example are co-presented; i.e., when the latter is being prehended the earlier is *still being prehended though with diminished degree of presentedness*" (1933, 2.302 [my emphasis]). This notion of diminishing degrees of presentedness is central to the specious present. An auditory version of it appears at the end of Kinglsey Amis's *Lucky Jim* when the sound of the noisy starter of a superannuated car progressively loses presentedness, as its two auditors, Christine and Jim, walk away: "The whinnying and clanging of Welch's self-starter began behind them, growing fainter and fainter as they walked on until it was altogether overlaid by the other noises of the town and by their own voices" (1953, 256). Perhaps the most vivid description in literature of diminishing presentedness in temporal terms occurs in *To the Lighthouse* when Mrs. Ramsay pauses on the threshold of the dining room, waiting "a moment longer in a scene which was vanishing even as she looked," and which, as she leaves, has become "already the past" (121).

But what happens when a specious present ends and becomes the past, as in the example just cited? In Broad's theory, once one specious present ends, another begins, and so on. Each specious present constitutes what Dainton terms "a temporally extended whole" comprising varying degrees of presentedness, but lacking "awareness of [its] neighbours" (2000, 138, 153). That is, although Broad accounts for the continuity of content in each specious present, he does not account for the continuity of awareness itself, from one specious present to another. In other words, Broad's theory unifies the *content* of each specious present (according to the principle of diminishing presentedness), but does not unify the separate *acts* of awareness by which these specious presents are respectively sustained. Yet without such unification, awareness lacks coherence, and disintegrates into separate acts of attention, each concerned with the specious present pertaining to it. If there is "a coherence in things," as Mrs. Ramsay affirms—a coherence that "shines out ... in the face of the flowing the fleeting"—it cannot be explained by Broad's theory of the specious present. However, it can be illumined by Edmond Husserl's phenomenology of time, for, as Dainton indicates, "Husserl does recognize the need to unify consciousness at the level of both contents and acts" (2000, 153). Our task now is to summarize succinctly a relevant portion of Husserl's complex theory of time consciousness and then apply it *To the Lighthouse*. Ultimately, Husserl's phenomenology of time will provide a background against which the very different notion of time developed in *To the Lighthouse* can be seen more clearly.

As Philip Turetzky indicates, "Phenomenological analysis examines time only as it appears immanent in experience" (1998, 157). In other words, such inquiry concerns time as it is given in consciousness, not as it is in itself, as a transcendent reality—something, that is, existing outside of or apart from awareness of it. The problem of transcendence—for example, Andrew Ramsay's invitation to "think of a kitchen table ... when you're not there"—is not one that preoccupies phenomenology (28). Instead, phenomenology deals with phenomena—objects as they appear in consciousness, according to the structuring activity intrinsic to consciousness. I. M. Bochenski elaborates: "it fixes its gaze directly upon whatever is presented to consciousness, that is, its object" (1965, 136). The distinction between immanence and transcendence—between an object as it is presented to consciousness and an object as it is independently—is hilariously illustrated in Samuel Beckett's novel *Watt*: "For Watt's concern, deep as it appeared, was not after all with what the figure was, in reality, but with what the figure appeared to be, in reality" (1959, 227). Through this concern with that which appears in consciousness in the act of perception, Watt unwittingly demonstrates a phenomenological focus on immanence—what Rudolf Bernet, Iso Kern, and Eduard Marbach term "the domain of presuppositionless givenness" (1993, 54).

In accordance with its focus on immanence (what appears in awareness) and its bracketing or suspension of judgment (*epoché*) regarding transcendence (what exists outside the mind's awareness), phenomenology rejects epistemological realism. That is, according to phenomenology, as Joseph J. Kockelmans indicates, "things are not there first and subsequently impress 'pictures' of themselves on our consciousness" (1994, 156). Instead, consciousness *constitutes* or synthesizes its objects, through its own means of knowing them. At the root of consciousness is *intentionality*, the principle that consciousness is always a consciousness of something, just as, to invoke Husserl's expression in *Cartesian Meditations*, a cogito or act of thinking always bears "within itself its *cogitatum*" or that which the act of thinking thinks (1960, 33). Through intentionality, as Husserl states in *Ideas*, consciousness is enabled to weave the data of sequential perceptions "into unitary manifolds, into continuous syntheses and so bring into being the consciousness of something" (1931, §86). Since consciousness entails *ongoing* synthesis or gathering together into unity of diverse data, the basic mode of synthesis—and the one that all others presuppose—is time. Husserl clarifies: "The fundamental form of this universal synthesis, the form that makes all other syntheses of consciousness possible, is the all-embracing consciousness of time" (1960, 43). Through synthesis, consciousness of time confers continuity on experience. More precisely, to invoke Turetzky's phrasing, "time functions to unify experience and its objects," so that "not merely a sequence of static durations, but a unified continuous flow appears" (1998, 174, 171). In virtue of this experiential continuity, to adopt Dainton's formulation, "we are aware not only of the flow of content through our awareness, but we are also aware that our awareness is itself continuous"—that is, "we are aware at any given instant of not only our present perspective on a sensory object, but of our past perspectives on it as well" (2000, 153, 154).

Husserl's analysis of time consciousness demonstrates how this continuity is constituted. In *On the Phenomenology of the Consciousness of Internal Time*, Husserl describes consciousness as a stream comprising "a continuum of continua"—a ceaseless flow of now-points of awareness or what Dainton terms "a compact succession of momentary experiences," each of which constitutes a continuum because it includes retentions and protentions respectively concerning what has just passed and what is about to come (1991, 341; 2000, 151). In this triadic schema, as Bernet et al. explain, the present encompasses a temporal field that "consists in a 'now' with a 'temporal fringe,' that is, with a living horizon of the no-longer (the just-past) and the not-yet (the now approaching) in various gradations" (1993, 103). Kockelmans elaborates: "[T]he *now* does not exist by itself but is always accompanied by the modes of past and future with which it forms the temporal horizon in which every temporal object is given" (1994, 274). Let us examine this dispensation more closely.

In perception, objects are given to consciousness through the now-phase, which is, as Kockelmans notes, "a mode of appearance for an object, not the object itself" (1994, 274). Since the now-phase—what Dainton terms "the present in the strictest sense" (1991, 274)—is instantaneous and without "temporal extension" (Turetzky 1998, 180), it is therefore, as Bernet et al. point out, "constantly passing over into a new phase," with the result that "perception is under constant change; it is in constant flux" (1993, 103). Husserl calls the content of the now-phase a "primal impression": "Each new now is the content of a new primal impression. Ever new primal impressions continuously flash forth with ever new matter" (1991, 70). Since the now-phase of consciousness is the originary site of primal impressions (which, in turn, as Husserl states, are "[t]he 'source-point' with which the 'production' of the enduring object begins"), the now-phase is also referred to as *impressional consciousness* (1991, 30). Each primal impression, being momentary, immediately elapses, and yields its place to a new primal impression, which then occupies the now-phase for an instant until elapsing like its predecessor, and so on. Yet, as Turetzky notes, although each "primal impressional phase changes continuously into something that has been" (1998, 163), it does not thereby vanish or depart from consciousness, but is retained in consciousness in the mode of "just past," instead of "now." When perception of an object in the now phase ceases, consciousness of the object continues, but the consciousness concerned in this phase is *retentional*, not impressional. Husserl provides an example regarding perception of a prolonged tone: "The tone begins and 'it' steadily continues. The tone-now changes into a tone-having-been; the *impressional* consciousness, constantly flowing, passes over into ever-new *retentional* consciousness" (1991, 31). Retention is not recollection. It does not reproduce something no longer given to consciousness in the present. Instead, as Turetzky explains, retention and its counterpart, protention, are "different modes of givenness from being given now" (1998, 172). Lanei Rodemeyer clarifies: "The activity of retention extends the presencing activity of the living present by 'holding on' to what is immediately passing" (2006, 82). Unlike recollection, retention is what Rodemeyer terms "originary experience," not reproduced or retrieved experience, even though "its *content* is no longer present itself" (2006, 78). Turetzky expands: "Retention is a genuine intuiting of the past tone itself, not a construct from sense contents and memorial apprehensions" (1998, 163). As Nicholas de Warren suggests, in virtue of this transition whereby "an original impression *necessarily* succumbs to, or becomes, its own retentional modification," consciousness is characterized by "the entwinement of absence and presence" (2009, 171).

In impressional consciousness, objects are perceived as present. In retentional consciousness, as Dan Zahavi indicates, they "are *perceived* as *past*" (2003, 82 [original emphasis]). Since, to borrow Turetzky phrase, "givenness extends beyond the present instant," the only change that content undergoes in the shift from impressional to retentional consciousness concerns temporal position: "it [retentional consciousness] retains or holds on to exactly what arises in primal impression, positioning it as being past" (1998, 73, 173). In explicating this notion, as we have seen, Husserl cites musical examples, as regarding the hearing of a melody or the sequentially struck tones of a chord. Hearing a melody or the triad of a chord as a sequence of tones requires awareness of temporal duration, and that, in turn, requires some operation by which the tone heard in the present is linked with the one(s) heard before it. Through retentional consciousness, as Zahavi notes, we are able to "experience the triad in its temporal duration, rather than simply as isolated tones that replace each other abruptly" (2003, 82). A ribald parody of this illustration of retentional consciousness occurs in the Addenda to Samuel Beckett's *Watt*, written between 1941 and 1945, a few years after Beckett's tour of Germany from September 1936 to April 1937, and a few more years after publication of the German edition of Husserl's *The Phenomenology of Internal Time Consciousness* in 1928. The parody (which has never before been recognized as such) concerns the description of a picture "representing gentleman seated at piano," who "[w]ith his right hand" sustains a C-chord, "while with other he prolongs pavilion of left ear," and displays the strained facial "expression of man about to be delivered, after many days, of particularly hard stool," as he concentrates on the "dying accord" of the notes just played (1959, 250–51). Here the notion of retentional consciousness is hilariously shifted from the phenomenological to the anal context, as the Beckettian figure focuses his attention on what Husserl refers to as the "dying-away, the fading, and so on, of the contents of sensation when perception proper passes over into retention" (1991, 33).

Retentional consciousness continually acquires new content, as each new now pushes its predecessor into the past. In retaining each moment that has just passed, retentional consciousness also re-retains the moment that it had already just retained, shifting it further back into the past in so doing. Hence, as Bernet et al. explicate, retentional consciousness entails "a continuity of iterated modification": "[t]he primordial impression is modified into a retention of the primordial impression; the retention is modified into a retention of the retention; this retention of second degree is modified into a retention of third degree, and so on" (1993, 104). In this schema, the now-phase is never isolated, but is apprehended with the trailing content of retentional consciousness—what Turetzky terms the "continuous retentional apprehensions of the past and their further retentional modifications" (1998, 165). Hence, in Husserl's phrasing, the "now-apprehension [i.e., the primal impression] is, as it were, the head attached to the comet's tail of retentions, relating to the earlier now-points" (1991, 32). But this "comet's tail of retentions" is not uniformly distinct. Instead, its content becomes increasingly indistinct the farther it recedes from the current now-point, a process that Husserl refers to as a "sinking back into emptiness" (1991, 371). But different metaphors are employed to describe this process. In later manuscripts, Husserl refers to this sinking process as *sedimentation*. Rodemeyer elaborates: "These sedimented experiences are no longer 'on the surface,' as it were, but instead are compacted down underneath it, acting as an inevitable foundation of the present" (2006, 87). As sedimentation progressively overlays older content with more recent matter, the earlier layers become increasingly inaccessible to retentional consciousness, and eventually constitute a necessary but imperceptible substratum. An earlier metaphor for the process of retentional prolongation concerns the notions of temporal perspective and horizon. Here, spatial distance corresponds to temporal distance (from the present), with the result that the further a prior moment is positioned from the present, the more blurred it appears, until, as Turetzky superbly articulates, "[a]t the horizon, retention of elapsed phases recedes into empty retentional consciousness, pushed back continuously until it finally disappears" (1998, 164).[8]

The fundamental condition in *To the Lighthouse* is that "nothing stays; all changes" (195). The same condition obtains in Husserl's phenomenology of internal time consciousness, but without wrenching or tragic effect. For there, ceaseless change also entails ceaseless retention. The regular displacement, in impressional consciousness, of each now-moment by its successor triggers the retention, in retentional consciousness, of the displaced moment just passed, and further entails the re-retention of the moments before that. Hence, in Husserl's schema, it is as true to say "nothing stays; all changes" as to say "all changes, yet all stays" (though in different modes of givenness). Retentional consciousness operates in *To the Lighthouse* too, but with less efficacy than in Husserl's phenomenology. It is convenient to consider the correspondences, and then move to the differences. There are several references in the novel to the sedimentation of the past, in terms that correspond closely to Husserl's description of the same process: "the deposit of each day's living" (58); "He began to search among the infinite series of impressions which time had lain down, leaf upon leaf, fold upon fold, incessantly upon his brain" (184); "turning back among the many leaves which the past had folded in him" (200).[9] Indeed, the correspondence is so close that these passages could serve as illustrations of Husserl's formulation of retentional consciousness, as Herbert Spiegelberg describes it: "the consciousness of the present sinks off steadily below the surface and becomes sedimented in such a way that it is accessible only to acts of recollection" (1994, 131).

Though retentional consciousness functions robustly in *To the Lighthouse*, its operation paradoxically increases separation from the past, instead of establishing connection with it. This paradox can be clarified by considering the repeated references in the novel to temporal passage: "the flowing, the fleeting," "this eternal passing and flowing" (114, 176). Here we find explicit awareness of what Turetzky, in a different context, terms "the flow of immanent time" (1998, 180). In phenomenological terms, such awareness derives from retentional consciousness, which enables awareness of succession—something that impressional consciousness, with its focus on the isolated current instant, cannot achieve. Dainton elaborates: "However, whatever direct awareness we have of phenomenal duration and continuity is located in the retentional matrix, rather than at the level of primal impression. Since primal impressions are momentary, there can be no awareness of change or continuity here, for the familiar reason that a succession of impressions is distinct from an impression of succession" (2000, 155). Whereas, in Husserl's schema, the awareness of continuity enabled by retentional consciousness *sustains* the link between present and past, by attaching each momentary now-phase to what Husserl terms "a retentional tale" (1991, 40), in *To the Lighthouse* awareness of continuity ("the flowing, the fleeting") *undermines* that link, and exposes the present to apprehensions of "rupture" (142), when that which is now will "perish and disappear" (138) into the past: "Just now (but this cannot last, she thought)" (113). The equanimity of the phenomenologist, dispassionately reflecting on the passage of time, from just-now to just-past and all the ensuing iterations of re-retention, cannot relieve anxiety about transience in *To the Lighthouse*, nor assuage the "anguish" (196) caused by temporal loss. This discrepancy in attitude relates to the difference between detachment and engagement. Through phenomenological epoché, Husserl begins analysis with a "disconnexion" [*sic*] that entails "the suspending of the natural world, physical and psychological" (1931, §56), so that "the whole concrete surrounding life-world is for me, from now on, *only a phenomenon of being, instead of something that is*" (1960, 19 [my emphasis]). No such detachment obtains in *To the Lighthouse* where the passage of time is not, to retrieve Husserl's phrase, "only a phenomenon" to be analyzed, but instead appears as the agent of "disintegration" (122) and "annihilation" (196), always threatening life with emotional devastation and physical termination. For this reason, Mrs. Ramsay registers temporal passage as a "ghostly roll of drums [that] remorselessly beat the measure of life," while Mr. Ramsay also construes it in negatively metronymic terms, when pacing "up and down the terrace," fretting about the prospect of diminished fame in the future (20, 21).

Nothing stays; all changes: this is the first principle of *To the Lighthouse*, where the fundamental change concerns the transition of the present into the past—a movement vividly registered by Mrs. Ramsay at the conclusion of the dinner party: "With her foot on the threshold she waited a moment longer in a scene that was vanishing even as she looked, and then, as she moved and took Minta's arm, and left the room, it changed, it shaped itself differently; *it had become, she knew, giving one last look at it over her shoulder, already the past*

(121 [my emphasis]). This is perhaps the most eloquent expression in literature of the transition from a now-moment in impressional consciousness to a just-past moment in retentional consciousness. To uncover the implications of this transition, we must first detach it from the implications entrained by its principal predecessors. The gesture of looking back at a chamber from which one has just departed is a celebrated symbol for attachment to a past that cannot be retrieved. Its locus classicus in Greek myth concerns Orpheus's rearward glance at Eurydice—a reflex that, by violating his vow not to look back while leading her out of Hades, causes her to be drawn again into the Underworld, domain of death, leaving him looking at what will never again live in his present. The supreme analogue of this predicament in English literature entails Hamlet's gesture, on exiting Ophelia's closet, of looking back, "with his head over his shoulder turn'd," at the room from which he is distractedly departing (Shakespeare 1982, 2.1.97). In Hamlet's case, the act of looking back is vividly associated with attachment to the past. Indeed, during his surprise visit to her closet, Hamlet's intention seems to entail an attempt to infuse awareness of the moment indelibly on his mind, so that, when the moment elapses, he will recall it as vividly as a memory of the past as he perceived it as an event in the present: "He falls to such perusal of my face / As a would draw it" (1982, 2.1.90–91). Here the present is experienced as a means of facilitating remembrance of things past—because the past is now precisely what Hamlet is severed from, with "a father kill'd, a mother stain'd," and a sweetheart lost (1982, 4.4.57).[10]

In contrast, in the scene involving Mrs. Ramsay, the act of looking back is associated not with intense attachment to a past that can never return, but with deepened awareness of the movement of time in the present. Through reflection on this scene, the reader has the opportunity for deepened awareness of the movement of time in the novel as well. The "threshold" on which Mrs. Ramsay stands, looking at the emergence of the past, is not merely physical, but also "symbolical" (80, 183). As such, it signifies or epitomizes the temporal position of the present as the threshold of the past. But, of course, the present is equally the threshold of the future. As the threshold of both past and future, the present is the point where what is becomes what was, and where what is will be changed by what is to come. More profoundly, in *To the Lighthouse* the present is construed as the boundary between two zones of becoming: the future and the past. There is no more fixity to the past than there is to the future, which, of course, is notoriously indeterminate. The future is the zone of becoming from which what is not yet eventually emerges as that which is, regardless of prior expectations—a dispensation epitomized by the eponymous project to sail to the Lighthouse, since its execution depends on unpredictable weather: "Yes, of course, if it's fine to-morrow" (7). The past is also a zone of becoming, but for reasons different from those applying to the future. Whereas the future is a zone of becoming because nothing in it has yet happened, in the novel the past is a zone of becoming because everything in it has already occurred.

This is the central paradox in *To the Lighthouse*—one whose explication will entail examining what might be termed Woolfian memory or reconstructive rememoration. But before addressing that task, we must first distinguish Woolfian memory from its two counterparts: retentional consciousness and conventional memory. As already remarked, retentional consciousness is the pre-reflective or involuntary apprehension, in present awareness, of the moment just past, which, in turn, involves the re-retention of the moments preceding it. As a pre-reflective and involuntary operation of the mind, retentional consciousness entails passive synthesis—the gathering together of elements without any conscious or deliberate effort to do so. In contrast, conventional memory involves not retention, in the sense just defined, but reproduction. Whereas retention entails immediate awareness, in the present, of something now past, memory entails retrieval, in the present, of something no longer given to current awareness. Dainton formulates the distinction compactly: "Retentions *present* the past, memory *represents* it" (2000, 155 [original emphasis]). Rodemeyer elaborates: "The difference between retention and recollection remains the difference between what remains present for me and what must be reproduced thought a specific act of consciousness" (2006, 84). But without the prior operation of retentional consciousness, memory would have nothing to recall. Dainton confirms: "Retention generates the original experience of contents occurring and sinking into the past that later memories provide representations of" (2000, 155).

Memory poses no risk in Husserl's phenomenology. It simply accesses content provided by retentional consciousness. In *To the Lighthouse*, however, memory is a dangerous function that threatens to plunge the mind into unbearable grief, as when Lily, while painting on the terrace, suddenly succumbs to the sense of loss that her memory of the deceased Mrs. Ramsay has revived: "No one had seen her step off her strip of board into the waters of annihilation" (196). Moreover, by entailing, as de Warren notes, "consciousness of the difference between the present in which I remember and the past that is remembered," memory foregrounds temporal change (2009, 168). When the difference between remembering present and remembered past is tragic, the act of memory undermines the present with awareness of depletion, as Mr. Ramsay's plight suggests: "You find us much changed" (162). In these circumstances, character encounters a double bind. To remember is to suffer, but to avoid memory is to inhabit a temporality of ceaseless flux ("the flowing, the fleeting") with neither coherence nor abiding meaning. The only recourse is to reconfigure memory, so that it entails not only *reproduction* of the past, but also *conduction* of the present. More precisely, the task is to deploy memory not just to revisit the past for its own sake, but more importantly *to enable awareness of temporal flow in the present to achieve a unifying perspective on the temporal movement of life itself, unfolding through its continuity of phases*. As it happens, Husserl's phenomenology does account for a similar type of temporally unifying awareness, naming it *absolute time consciousness*. But brief analysis will disclose the crucial difference between that notion and the one that it obtains in *To the Lighthouse*. As Dainton explains, Husserl posits absolute time consciousness as "awareness of the continuity of awareness" (2000, 159). It is the factor positioning each moment of experience in the same "steady continuum" of temporal awareness, stretching before and after (Husserl 1991, 249). Turetzky amplifies: "There must be an awareness, simultaneous with the actually present now point, of the whole of time consciousness as a temporally extended continuity of phases" (1998, 181). But this factor is a source of anguish in *To the Lighthouse*, where awareness of the continuity of awareness (to retrieve Dainton's phrase) simply aggravates awareness of the *discontinuity* and rupture occasioned by tragic loss: "Mrs. Ramsay dead; Andrew killed; Prue dead too" (160).

The opposition between continuity and discontinuity is resolved through the Woolfian moment, whose chief attributes, as exemplified by the dinner party, are "coherence," "stability," immutability, and "eternity": "There it was, all round them. It partook, she felt ... of eternity ... there is a coherence in things, a stability; something, she meant, is immune from change, and shines out ... in the face of the flowing, the fleeting, the spectral, like a ruby; so that again tonight she had the feeling she had had once today already, of peace, of rest" (114). The dinner party moment fuses two pairs of opposites: (a) transience and permanence, and (b) dispersion and coherence. With respect to the first pair, the moment is in and out of time. It is in time insofar as it must elapse, and succumb to the flux of time. It is out of time insofar as it is immutable. But the permanence ("This would remain") here in question concerns context, not content (114), as brief explanation will clarify. As an event, the supreme importance of the dinner party moment concerns not so much what happens as the context in which it occurs—the context, more precisely, that its occurrence creates. In reflecting on the dinner party moment as it unfolds, Mrs. Ramsay perceives it as encompassing its participants: "There it was, all round them" (114). Though the content of the moment is ephemeral, its coherence—its constitution of an encompassing wholeness and "common feeling" that bind the participants together in a felt unity—is eternal: "Of such moments, she thought, the thing is made that remains for ever after" (208, 114). But what is the nature of this "eternity"? Of what temporal properties does it consist? Since the moment, as a moment, must elapse, its permanence cannot concern continued presence. Nor can its permanence involve availability to memory after passing. If availability to memory were the criterion of permanence, then flux would never be a problem, for, in principle, anything that passes can be accessed later by memory. Moreover, as we have seen, mere memory provides no reassurance of permanence, since memory exacerbates the suffering of tragedy: recalling in the present that which elapsed or was lost in the past.

To understand the permanence of the moment, we must investigate the second pair of contraries: dispersion and coherence. Considered as incessant flux, the passage of time registered by awareness entails continuous dispersion of its parts. It displays continuity, but lacks coherence or wholeness. Though retentional consciousness binds together each new now-moment with the moment just past, and re-retains the moments preceding them, it cannot, as we have seen, prevent earlier moments from sinking beneath the horizon of conscious awareness. Husserl amplifies: "Consciousness is a perpetual Heraclitean flux. What has just been given sinks into the abyss" (1991, 360). In *To the Lighthouse*, this tendency toward dispersion provokes a countervailing need for and privileging of wholeness and coherence. There are several references in the novel to the cohering of elements or parts into a whole or unity: (a) "how life, from being made up of little separate incidents which one loved one by one, became curled and whole like a wave which bore one up with it and threw one down with it, there, with a dash on the beach" (53; (b) "like a fume rising upwards, holding them safe together" (114); (c) "the whole is held together" (116); (d) "struck everything into stability" (123); (e) "to assemble outwardly the scattered parts of the vision within" (144); (f) "Such were some of the parts but how bring them together?" (161); (g) "she brought together this and that and then this, and so made out of that miserable silliness and spite ... something ... which survived, after all these years, complete ... and it stayed in the mind almost like a work of art" (175); (h) "A steamer far out at sea had drawn in the air a great scroll of smoke which stayed there curving and circling decoratively, *as if the air were a fine gauze which held things and kept them softly in its mesh, only gently swaying them this way and that*" (198 [my emphasis]); (i) "some common feeling which held the whole together" (208).

In the world of *To the Lighthouse*, time does not merely pass. Its movement is a principle of dispersion. Nothing stays; all changes, as we have noted. But the fundamental change involves the disintegration, diffusion, scattering, or breaking up of prevailing pattern, order, unity, or configuration. *Time dissipates structure*. To retain or regain stability under these conditions—and to achieve an answer to the overwhelming question that loss of structure poses, "What is the meaning of life?"—human awareness requires a restorative principle: coherence (175). The ultimate function of this principle is to enable construction of a unifying perspective that grasps the passage of time in terms of what it brings together, not what it pulls apart—in terms, that is, of the deepening achievement of meaning in life that temporal continuity allows the individual, during a moment of "vision," to perceive (197, 226). In the novel, character is defined by point of view ("It was him—his point of view"), and the fundamental point of view concerns perspective on time (12). Indeed, on the first page, six-year-old James Ramsay is identified through temporal perspective: "Since he belonged, even at the age of six, to that great clan which cannot keep this feeling separate from that, but must let future prospects, with their joys and sorrows, cloud what is actually at hand" (7). Each of the primary characters—Mrs. Ramsay, Mr. Ramsay, and Lily Briscoe—emphasizes a different aspect of temporal dispersion. Mrs. Ramsay focuses on the evanescence of the present ("It will end"); Mr. Ramsay worries about the erosion of his fame in the future, and Lily plumbs the "anguish" caused by loss of the past (70, 196).

The urgent questions in *To the Lighthouse* regarding the meaning of life can be answered only through solving the problem of coherence: "Such were some of the parts but how bring them together?" (161). At bottom, these parts involve the tenses of time, and the task of reintegrating and interconnecting them defines the challenge of time management in the novel—a project entailing not how time is organized, but how its dispersive tendency is rectified. In the novel, the "annihilating character" of time (to transpose a phrase deployed by Paul Tillich) imposes the responsibility to view temporal passage appropriately—that is, in a way that enables the constitution of meaning, rather than facilitating its loss or forfeit (1963, 1.194). In this context, Mr. Ramsay epitomizes temporal irresponsibility: "He flicked his watch *carelessly* open" (74 [my emphasis]). Through "egotism," which construes the future as a perspective on the diminished lustre of his current fame, he increases his vulnerability to the passage of time—a condition culminating in his emotional helplessness after the unexpected onslaught of catastrophe: "His immense self-pity, his demand for sympathy poured and spread itself in pools at her feet" (167). In contrast, Mrs. Ramsay is linked with temporal responsibility, to the point where she is identified with the function of moving time forward. At the dinner party, she registers responsibility to foster social cohesion: "And the whole of the effort of merging and flowing and creating rested on her" (91). To discharge this responsibility, Mrs. Ramsay responds in a way that clearly associates her with the movement of time "giving herself the little shake that one gives a watch that has stopped, the old familiar pulse began beating, as the watch begins ticking—one, two, three, one, two, three" (91). Whereas Mr. Ramsay, in his temporal irresponsibility, "flicked his watch carelessly open," Mrs. Ramsay, in exercising her temporal responsibility, is compared to a watch whose function is not so much to measure time as to ensure that it keeps moving.

The watch-shaking metaphor is highly ironic, since the fundamental problem in *To the Lighthouse* is not that time stops, but that it relentlessly goes on, its passage entraining "darkness and desolation" (83). Yet the time administered by Mrs. Ramsay differs from that pertaining to actual temporality, for instead of engendering dispersion, it encourages cohesion. On the surface, this cohesion concerns bringing separate characters into "that community of feeling with other people which emotion gives," binding the participants into a whole that can be accessed later in memory, to provide a stable point of orientation and confirmation of meaning, in the midst of "this eternal passing and flowing" (123, 176) that every life endures, in its movement through time. Indeed, Mrs. Ramsay is so closely associated with this cohesive function that she almost becomes its incarnation or symbol, as especially evident when she appears to Lily as a ghost, flicking her knitting needles—implements that epitomize her combinatory prowess: "Mrs. Ramsay ... sat there quite simply, in the chair, flicked her needles to an and fro, knitted her reddish-brown stockings, cast her shadow on the step" (219). However, the most profound function of Mrs. Ramsay's cohesive faculty—the capability that "brought together this and that and then this, and so made ... something ... which stayed in the mind almost like a work of art"—pertains to uniting not separate people, but the parts of time (175). Just as, when perceiving the separate flashes of the Lighthouse beam continuously "stroking" the sea, Mrs. Ramsay combines fleeting instants into an extended or specious present, so, when reflecting on this experience of happiness, she combines it with predecessors to constitute a heightened sense of satisfaction in life. By bringing, through memory, past moments of "exquisite happiness, intense happiness" together with the current one, she deepens present pleasure, and constitutes the passage of time as an abiding source of fulfillment ("It is enough"), despite the condition of transience: "No happiness lasted" (72, 71). Indeed, transience becomes the necessary condition for fulfillment—not just because a present moment of happiness is enriched by the memory of prior ones, but also because the state of fulfillment itself is experienced as a transient bursting ("the ecstasy burst in her eyes") whose intensity, like an orgasm, builds inevitably to climax, and then subsides (72).

This is the supreme expression of Mrs. Ramsay's synthesizing (gathering or knitting together dispersed elements) mode of awareness. In their respective moments of vision, similarly involving the Lighthouse, both Lily and Mr. Ramsay achieve their own versions of temporal synthesis. Whereas Mrs. Ramsay reaches her vision by *affirming* the kinship of the present moment with past ones, Lily does so by first *negating* such connection, registering instead the alienation of the present from the past and therefore from everything familiar: "She had no attachment here, she felt, no relations with it" (160). Ironically, this sense of estrangement from the past facilitates creative synthesis of the past, enabling Lily to combine selected memories into a coherent whole the way Mrs. Ramsay, until her death, combines elements occurring in the present, "making of the moment something permanent" by bringing "together this and that and then this" (176, 175). Through this project to "re-fashion her memory," Lily constructs a perspective on the past, and through it, a new understanding of her position in the present: "Lily stepped back to get her canvas—so—into perspective" (187). Just as her painting expresses or represents her creative synthesis of the past ("She went on tunneling her way into her picture, into the past" (188), so her perspective on that synthesized past constitutes her outlook in the present—her "vision" (224) of the supreme meaning and purpose of the arduous passage through time that each human being undertakes.[11] Fundamentally, Lily's vision concerns seeing an answer to the question of continuity. What is the meaning of life when that which gave it meaning in the past has been lost? Nothing stays; all changes. In this predicament, how can the meaning of the past be reconstituted, so that loss of the past clarifies meaning in the present, instead of obscuring it? Through having "illuminated the darkness of the past" (187), Lily overcomes the problem of tragic aftermath—what might be termed post-traumatic temporal disorder: "How aimless it was, how chaotic" (160).[12]

Mr. Ramsay's voyage to the Lighthouse similarly entails resolution of post-traumatic temporal disorder. Just before embarkation, afflicted by "the immense pressure of his concentrated woe" regarding the past, Mr. Ramsay inundates Lily with his need for pity: "His immense self-pity, his demand for sympathy poured and spread itself in pools at her feet" (167). Yet on disembarkation, he appears marvelously rejuvenated and self-reliant, "as if he were leaping into space," boldly toward the future (224). The narration does not reveal Mr. Ramsay's private thoughts during the sailing voyage. His inward state is suggested by his outward demeanor: his few words, his gestures, activity (reading a book), and appearance. Basically, for him the journey constitutes a transit from one condition to another, as epitomized by Cam and James's perplexity regarding his thoughts just before the sailboat reaches the Lighthouse, while their father sits "in complete readiness to land": "We perished, each alone, or he might be thinking, I have reached it. I have found it, but he said nothing" (224).[13] "[S]taring at the frail blue shape which seemed like the vapour of something that had burnt itself away," Mr. Ramsay has gained perspective on the past, just as Lily has (224).[14] The spatial distance across which he gazes has earlier in the novel been associated with the temporal distance of the past from the present, as when Lily imagines the dead Mrs. Ramsay beckoning "at the end of the corridor of years" (190). In focusing on the island whence the sailing voyage began, Mr. Ramsay perceives his own ability to move beyond the past whose loss devastated him. Similarly, in leaping onto the rocks of the Lighthouse, like a leader, Mr. Ramsay shows his willingness to encounter the future. No longer lamenting the changes that transience brings ("You find us much changed"), he now displays "readiness" to face whatever occurs in the passage of time (162, 224). Thus, in their respective moments of vision associated with the Lighthouse, both Lily and Mr. Ramsay demonstrate the truth of T. S. Eliot's pronouncement in "Burnt Norton": "Only through time is time conquered" (1963, 192). In the novel, recession of the past from the present, though the source of tragic loss and dispersion, provides the means of overcoming chaos and reconstituting coherence, through encouraging—even demanding—the willingness to formulate oneself as a courageous and creative perspective on the fact and consequence of temporal passage.[15] The task is never completed. Since nothing stays and all changes, "the vision must be perpetually remade" (197).[16]

6

The Beckettian Mimesis of Post-Temporal Time

Any analysis of the Beckettian mimesis of time is challenged and thwarted by contradiction.[1] There is no consistency in the representation of time in the Beckettian opus, for fundamentally time is relegated to the status of illusion, as the driving aim of Beckettian texts is to express an abiding mentality or attitude toward experience that does not change ("The essential does not change" [1954, 14]) and remains impervious to local circumstance: "What vicissitudes within what changelessness" (1967a, 118). At bottom—and here I simply epitomize extended exegesis that I have provided elsewhere—the Beckettian attitude toward experience construes awareness in terms of the unremittingly uniform unpleasantness of suffering it—a predicament that Molloy terms "senseless, speechless, issueless misery" (1958b, 13, Levy 2007). In this context, references to time serve as a means of rendering the experience represented in Beckettian texts more susceptible to expression—and reception: *"These allusions to now, to before and after, and all such yet to come, that we may feel ourselves in time"* (1976c, 33 [my emphasis]). In Beckettian mimesis, "Time that old fornicator" spawns numerous representations (1957b, 114).

A convenient way to approach the Beckettian formulation of time is to contrast it with the Kantian construction. For Kant, time functions as an a priori condition of appearance—a "form of sensibility" that lies "at the basis of the empirical," prior to all experience and "antedating in my mind all the actual impressions through which I am affected by objects" (1950, 30, 31) Wilhelm Windelband explains: "the Forms of space and time ... present a universal and necessary mode in which things appear" in perception or experience (2.541). As an a priori condition of experience, time orders or configures the contents of perception such that they conform to the cognitive requirements of the perceiving mind. Turetzky elaborates: "Whatever things may be like in themselves, for us to experience them or have knowledge of them empirical objects must conform to the structure of our capacities to experience and know them" (86). Thus time is the conditioning form through which the objects of perception acquire the temporal properties of coexistence and succession in terms of which we experience them. In contrast, in Beckettian mimesis, time is not a condition *preceding* experience, but a conclusion *drawn* from experience and a means of expressing that experience. Our task is now to consider this matter in some detail.

Life takes time. Whitehead elaborates: "Every expression of life takes time. Nothing that is characteristic of life can manifest itself at an instant" (1961b, 57). Yet Pozzo, in *Waiting for Godot*, when responding to the question of when he suddenly became blind, repudiates the very notion of temporal passage and contracts the span of human life to one vain second: "[O]ne day we were born, one day we shall die, the same day, the same second, is that not enough for you? They give birth astride of a grave, the light gleams an instant, then it's night once more" (1954, 57). Whereas for Whitehead, "Nothing that is characteristic of life can manifest itself at an instant," for Pozzo, in virtue of whatever wisdom he gained through experience, life itself is the manifestation of an instant. This nullification of the time allotted to human life does not concern temporal brevity, as in Hamlet's mot regarding the importunity of mortality: "And a man's life's no more than to say 'one'" (1982, 5.2.74). Instead, the collapsing of an entire lifetime into one instant expresses the conviction—or discovery—that that nothing significant happens in human life, no fundamental change of intrinsic condition or perspective. Precisely this predicament is lamented by Vladimir in the same play: "*Nothing happens*, nobody comes, nobody goes, it's awful!" (Beckett 1954, 27 [my emphasis]). According to Aristotle, time is the measure of change: "Time is not change, therefore, but that in respect of which change is numerable" (1936, 4.219^{b}2). It follows from this proposition that, if there is no change, there is no time. Hence Vladimir's pronouncement: "Time has stopped" (Beckett 1954, 24). A variant formulation occurs in Beckett's *Endgame*, where time, deprived of passage, remains always at the same point. In response to Hamm's question, "What time is it?" Clov responds, "The same as usual" (1958a, 4). The narrator of *How It Is* similarly propounds temporal arrest ("the same instant always everywhere" [1964, 112]), as does the narrator of "Texts for Nothing": "one enormous second" (1967a, 82).

Yet the temporal dispensation represented in certain Beckettian texts displays discrepancies. On the one hand, as just seen, there is no time or no movement of time because there are no significant events ("Nothing happens") and therefore no substantive change: "Never any change" (Beckett 1961, 45). On the other hand, in the absence of events there is "just time"—temporal passage with no content: "I have just time, if I make haste, in the trough of all this time, just time" (Beckett 1967a, 108). This equivocation in the Beckettian mimesis of time entrains a fundamental question in the philosophy of time. Is time something on its own, apart from the things that happen in time, or is time dependent on what happens in it? That is, is time *substantive* (subsisting independently of the events occurring in it) or *relationist* (constructed from the series of events that happen)? The first theory is termed *substantivalism*, because it treats time as something real and autonomous in its own right. Newton provides an example: "Absolute, true, and mathematical time, of itself, and from its own name, flows equably without relation to anything external" (qtd. in Whitehead 1929, 70). The second theory is termed *relationism*, because it construes time in relation to events that occur. Leibnitz provides an example: "[I]nstants, consider'd without the things [or events], are nothing at all; and that they consist only in the successive order of things" (1956, 152). In this context, time is simply the sequence of events or happenings. Whitehead explains: "There is time because there are happenings, and apart from happenings there is nothing" (1961b, 83).

Beckettian mimesis conflates both views of time. In the Beckettian dispensation, time flows, instant to instant, as in substantivalism, without relation to anything external. But in virtue of the obsessive attention directed toward it, this autonomous continuity becomes the primary occurrence registered by experience. In that regard, time has stopped, because its passage leads to no change— no happening, that is, more significant or worthy of notice than the invariable occurrence of temporal succession: "I finally have the watch to my ear the hand the fist it's preferable I drink deep of the seconds delicious moments and vistas" (Beckett 1964, 59). The great paradox in the Beckettian mimesis of time is that temporal passage betokens temporal fixity; the more time passes, the more stagnation it accumulates: "the question may be asked ... why time doesn't pass ... why it piles up all about you, instant on instant, on all sides, deeper and deeper ... why it buries you grain by grain neither dead nor alive, with no memory of anything, no hope of anything, no knowledge of anything, no history and no prospects, *buried under the seconds*, saying any old thing, your mouth full of sand" (Beckett 1958d, 389 [my emphasis]). In this context, the invariable succession of identical units of time constitutes a single sustained interval during which nothing happens but perpetuation of the same predicament: "another instant of my old instant" (Beckett 1958d, 400). Here temporal continuity simply reiterates sameness. Hence, time is the measure not of change, as with Aristotle, but of constancy: "I say I used to say, Winnie, you are changeless, there is never any difference between one fraction of a second and the next" (Beckett 1961, 60).

In these circumstances, time retains its nature as what Whitehead terms "an unending uniform succession" (1961b, 91). But the dynamics of this succession differ radically from those in the conventional paradigm. To investigate that difference and clarify its implications, it is appropriate first to recapitulate the paradigm. Here our concern is not with philosophical theories regarding the nature of time in itself, but with the nature of time as given universally in experience and analyzed as such by phenomenology. In phenomenological terms, as Turetzky indicates, "time, as experienced, appears as an ordered flow, regardless of how it objectively exists in nature" (1998, 156). According to this paradigm, the serial continuity of time assures, as Turetzky notes, that all moments "belong to a single flow, always sharing the form of transience from not-yet to no-longer now" (170). That is, as registered in experience, time entails a sequence, where each new moment displaces its predecessor and then yields position to its successor. What happens to this paradigm in Beckettian mimesis? It is reconfigured, such that succession becomes addition. Moments do not pass in the sense of elapsing once their momentary duration expires. Instead, they accumulate and cumulatively encumber experience with their aggregation. Again, we can quote "The Unnamable": "time doesn't pass ... it piles up all about you, instant on instant, on all sides, deeper and deeper" (Beckett 1958d, 389). In the phenomenological paradigm, the passage of time presupposes elapse or expiry. If a given moment did not elapse, there would be no temporal position for the next moment to occupy. In these circumstances, time would stop, because the lack of expiration would prevent it from advancing. In contrast, Beckettian mimesis construes temporal passage in the absence of elapse. Time goes on yet does not pass. That is, its continuity remains uninterrupted, but the expiration of the moments constituting and enabling that continuity has been compromised. Moments pass or expire but, having passed or expired, they remain where they are, and are thus compounded with those that preceded them and those that follow. In this context, consciousness of the ordered flow of time becomes consciousness of the disordered redundancy of time: "buried under the seconds" (Beckett 1958d, 400).

In this predicament, awareness in the present is deprived of what Husserl, in his seminal phenomenological study, *Ideas*, terms "temporal horizon, infinite in both directions"—a term that refers to the versatile perspective that present awareness enjoys with respect to the attention it can direct toward the other tenses: "I can shift my standpoint in space and time, look this way and that, turn temporally forwards and backwards; I can provide for myself constantly new and more or less clear and meaningful perceptions and representations, and images also more or less clear, in which I make intuitable to myself whatever can possibly exist really or supposedly in the steadfast order of space and time". (Husserl 1931, 92). Instead of temporal horizon, Beckettian awareness displays temporal isolation or enclosure: "I am down in the hole the centuries have dug" (1967a, 76). Here present awareness is no longer a vantage point on past and future, real or imagined, but a point of view on the lack of connection with the other tenses: "with no memory of anything, no hope of anything, no knowledge of anything, no history and no prospects" (1958d, 400). The present no longer functions as the link between past and future, as with Aristotle, but instead merely occupies a position in an undifferentiated temporal agglomeration, without means of orientation: "I'm getting mixed, I must be getting mixed, confusing here and there, now and then" (1967a, 120).

Beckettian mimesis deploys a spectacularly original device for depicting awareness deprived of temporal horizon beyond the moving present. That device entails the "bold metaphor" (1958d, 333) of voice and auditor, wherein an auditor repeats words just uttered while hearing those that follow: "A second later, I'm a second behind them, I remember a second, for the space of a second, that is to say long enough to blurt it out, as received, while receiving the next, which is none of my business either" (1958d, 368). Here, the words heard a second earlier are all that remains of awareness of the past, while the words to come next are all that remain of awareness of the future. With local variations, the metaphor presides over such works as "The Unnamable" ("A parrot, that's what they're up against, a parrot" [1958d, 335]), *How It Is* ("I say it as I hear it" [1964, 7]), "Texts for Nothing" ("I'm the clerk and the scribe, not understanding what I hear, not knowing what I write" [1967a, 98]), and *Not I* ("words were coming ... a voice she did not recognize" [1973, 5]). This "matter of voices" (1958d, 325) is glossed over in "From an Abandoned Work" ("a voice dreaming and droning on all around, that is something, the voice that was once in your mouth" [1974c, 49]), and adumbrated in "Molloy" where both Molloy and Moran respond to the promptings of an inner voice: "And perhaps I was understanding it all wrong" (1958b, 59); "I understood it, all wrong perhaps" (176).

According to "The Unnamable," as we have just seen, temporal horizon in the voice-auditor predicament occupies "the space of a second," and that second concerns the second just passed: "I remember a second, for the space of a second, that is to say long enough to blurt it out" (368). The second actually elapsing in the present is "none of [his] business," until it enters the past and becomes the content of his current utterance, for one second. Thus time is experienced as a flow of instants whose sequential presence is registered only during the instant after each has passed. The present is present to awareness only after it has expired. Ultimately, nothing happens in the present moment but registration of yet another past one. This dispensation reconfigures temporal transience. In conventional formulation, transience pertains to the perpetually perishing present—the tendency of whatever has come into presence to vanish into the past. As such, the present is the site of transition from the not-yet to the no-longer. But in the Beckettian context under examination, transience pertains to the perpetually perishing *past*, not the present. The same idea appears explicitly in *How It Is*: "the space of a moment the passing moment that's all my past little rat at my heels the rest false" (1964, 16). In this way, transience is neutralized. For it pertains only to that which has *already* vanished, not to that which is still present. Hence, the temporal loss occasioned by transience applies only to that which no longer remains.

Paradoxically, this minute attention to the fleeting past ("for the space of a second") liberates temporal awareness from the past. In the conventional paradigm, the past extends indefinitely backward from the present, in a cumulative unfolding of that which has expired. But in certain texts, the Beckettian past, being momentaneous, extends no farther than "the space of a second," and thus is continually vanishing. When the present expires, it becomes the past. But when the past expires, as it does in some examples of Beckettian mimesis, it just disappears: "I'll never have a past never had" (Beckett 1964, 54). Focus on the present is preempted by focus on the past. But the past thus registered lasts for the space of a second, and then is no more. This is the apotheosis of regret celebrated by "The Unnamable": "Regretting, that's what helps you on ... regretting what is, regretting what was ... that's what transports you, towards the end of regretting" (1958d, 371). The ultimate aim of Beckettian regret or fixation on the past is paradoxically to deprive the past of any claim on the present: "or so long ago as to amount to never" ("He Is Barehead" 29). The present is encumbered with expiration of the past: "buried under the seconds" (Beckett 1976b, 400). The seconds that have accumulated are expired seconds. But they do not add up to a continuous past. Instead, they remain a heap of undifferentiated seconds that do not constitute a continuously ordered temporal extension prior to the present. The passage of time does not unfold a coherent past construed as a consecutive series of moments leading to and orienting experience in the present. Instead, the passage of time simply burdens the present with the detritus or remains of expiration: "Moment upon moment, pattering down, like the millet grains of... that old Greek, and all life long you wait for that to mount up to a life" (Beckett 1958a, 70). In contravention of the conventional paradigm, the present does not *succeed* the past (in the sense of occurring after it); instead, the present *secedes from* the past, and repudiates connection with it: "Yes, my past has thrown me out, its gates have slammed behind me, or I burrowed my way out alone, to linger a moment free in a dream of days and nights, dreaming of me moving, season after season, towards the last, like the living, till suddenly I was here, *all memory gone*" (Beckett 1967a, 112 [my emphasis]).

The last two quotations show the remarkable ambivalence toward the past evident in the Beckettian mimesis of time. On the one hand (as in the quotation from *Endgame*), there is dependence on the accumulation of the past—the addition of expired moments—to confer meaning or direction on the present: "all life long you wait for that to mount up to a life." On the other hand (as in the quotation from "Texts for Nothing"), there is repudiation of the relevance of the past to the present: "all memory gone." But the two positions are easily reconciled, as one is the obverse of the other. Memory is gone, because memory is disabled by its own content. Memory cannot function, because the sequence of expired moments whose accumulation is expected eventually "to mount up to a life" constitutes nothing but a mass of undifferentiated moments, without consecutivity. In this context, the past becomes a *static conglomeration* of moments, not an *ordered succession* of moments, cumulatively unfolding the life they concern. In the conventional paradigm, past moments are ordered serially, with each occupying an unvarying position in the sequence of moments constituting the flow of time. But in the Beckettian dispensation, past moments lose seriality. Instead of maintaining their respective positions in the flow of time, such that each moment sustains fixed relations with the one before and the one after it, all past moments are mixed together in an indiscriminate heap or indefinite expanse. There is no past, properly speaking, in this dispensation, just a zone of expiration.

The origin of this dispensation is clearly formulated in "The Expelled," where the narrator enunciates the paradoxical method of obliterating memory through obsessive rememoration. Retention of painful memories is eliminated by recurrently thinking of them: "Memories are killing. So you must not think of certain things, of those that are dear to you, or rather you must think of them, for if you don't there is the danger of finding them, in your mind, little by little. That is to say, you must think of them for a while, a good while, every day several times a day, *until they sink in the mud*" (1967c, 9 [my emphasis]). The passage serves as a superb gloss on the later Beckettian text, *How It Is*, whose narrator crawls, "ten yards fifteen yards right leg right arm push pull" (1964, 62), across a interminable landscape of mud that he repeatedly refers to as "vast tracts of time" or "vast stretch of time" (104): "the various times mixed up in my head all the various times before during after vast tracts of time" (107). Here, the expanse of mud is a reification of the undifferentiated past ("flop back into the past" [91])—a past whose contents have been rendered not only irretrievable but also nonexistent by the uniform indiscrimination to which they have been reduced: "all lost never was" (70). In an alternate formulation, the past is no more than the "[p]lace of remains" (Beckett 1976a, 11). But the remains have lost all particularizing notes indicating what is preserved in them or what they used to be—a circumstance opposite to that indicated in "First Love," where reverence for historical events is satirized: "Wherever nauseated time has dropped a nice fat turd you will find our patriots, sniffing it up on all fours, their faces on fire" (1974b, 21).

Ordinarily, the passage of time entails the transition of the passing moment from the present to the past. But in the Beckettian dispensation, such transience removes not only the present but also the past: "there are moments when it's like that, then they pass and it's not like that any more, never was like that" (1967a, 117–18). Conventionally, time is the devourer—consuming the present with its passage. But in the Beckettian dispensation, time devours both present and past: "time devours on" (127). What remains in the wake of time is temporal expanse with no parts by which to distinguish one moment from another. But time without parts is not really time at all. For time involves or measures change (even if only the change of the position of its own moving moments), and change involves distinctions (by which change is discernible). Without distinctions, there is nothing in time by which time can move or have moved: "Time has turned into space and there will be no more time till I get out of here" (1967a, 112). In a more technical formulation, if all moments were identical, with no principle of distinction among them, then their plurality would collapse into singularity: the many would become one, and time would remain forever at that moment. Roger Teichmann elaborates:

> [I]n a period of changeless time, there will be nothing to distinguish one moment from any other, since nothing is happening. But if every moment during the period is exactly similar to every other in all respects, then, by Leibnitz's principle of the Identity of Indiscernibles, they will not after all be numerically distinct: there will be at most one moment, and this an instantaneous one. Hence there could never be a *period* of changeless time. (1995, 153)

Hence, in Le Poidevin's formulation, "[a]ny statement to the effect that a period of time without change has occurred would have no meaning" (2003, 18).

Beckettian mimesis boldly violates the principle of discernibility in the moments of time and, in certain texts, formulates an impossible time with, to retrieve Teichmann's phrase above, "at most one moment." But instead of being instantaneous, the Beckettian moment is perpetual: "*an instant without bounds, where the light never changes and the wrecks look all alike*" (1958c, 233 [my emphasis]). The consequence is a *detemporalizing* of time, wherein time paradoxically continues but without the distinctions that enable its own movement. Again, we can quote from other texts: "one enormous second" (1967a, 82); "the same instant always everywhere" (1964, 112). However, as noted earlier, there is no logical consistency in the Beckettian mimesis of time. The reduction of time to one continuous moment alternates with its contrary—the reduction of time to the succession of identical moments (as we have observed before): "the seconds must all be alike and each one is infernal" (1958d, 395). "Malone Dies" expands the notion of the relentless continuity of changelessness to include the idea of time continuing beyond the possibility of movement proper to temporality: "And the ticking of an invisible alarm-clock was as the voice of that silence which, like the dark, would one day triumph too. And then all would be still and dark and all things at rest for ever at last" (1958c, 203). Here time itself becomes timeless, as if, to invoke Vladimir's mot in *Waiting for Godot*, "Time has stopped" (1954, 24). For there can be no more change in it, only endless immobility. In his reference to "the indestructible chaos of timeless things," Molloy posits a kinetic version of the same condition of perpetual changelessness or invariable sameness (1958b, 39).

Perhaps the most succinctly penetrating description of Beckettian time is formulated by Molloy (referring to his life): "at the same time it is over and it goes on, and is there any tense for that?" (1958b, 36). Nothing more can happen in time but repetition of what has already occurred: "the same things recur, they drive one another out, they draw one another back" (*Texts for Nothing*, 117). The future becomes an extension of the past. But the past is an extension of moments that cannot be distinguished from one another. Hence, "[a]ll mingles, times and tenses" (1967a, 78). A psychological version of this mingling is enunciated in *Mercier and Camier*: "They were perhaps not so much reflections as a dark torrent of brooding where past and future merged in a single flood and closed, over a present for ever absent" (1974e, 32).

Further investigation of the notion of futurity in the Beckettian mimesis of time will clarify this mingling of tenses. Ordinarily, futurity enables the present not to perpetuate or replicate the past. That is, to interpolate Turetzky's phrases (in a discussion of Heidegger), futurity enables the transition, in the present, "towards what is not-yet-now, and from ... what is no-longer-now" (1998, 187). But Beckettian mimesis displays a tendency to formulate the future as a revisiting of the past—not in the sense of regret or nostalgia, but in the sense of removing the possibility of change: "*the metamorphosis is accomplished, of unchanging future into unchangeable past*" (1958d, 367 [my emphasis]). The purpose of this tactic is to obviate hope; for hope is to be avoided: "This would keep hope alive, would it not, hellish hope" (1958b, 133). Hope is the source of moral suffering, deplored by the narrator of *How It Is*: "I have suffered must have suffered morally hoped more than once despaired to match your heart bleeds you lose your heart drop by drop" (1964, 23). A passage from my *Trapped in Thought: A Study of the Beckettian Mentality* will clarify:

> moral suffering arises from the conflict not between vice and virtue, but hope and despair. That is, the suffering results from the thwarting of personal goals or ends, occasioning disappointed hopes and the eventual abandonment of hope which constitutes the state of despair. Such suffering is properly termed, "moral," because, as Etienne Gilson indicates, morality concerns ends or purposes and the means of achieving them: "Morality consists in ordering all human acts in view of the true good, which is the true end" (1955, 715, n. 118). In the Beckettian universe, ends or purposes are abandoned, so that moral suffering can never rend: "What can it matter to me, that I succeed or fail?" (*The Unnamable* 347). In their place is conviction in futility—a state which recurs with variations throughout the Beckettian canon. Futility becomes purpose, because it protects from the moral suffering of botched purpose: "I have never been disappointed, and I often was in the early days, without feeling at the same time, or a moment later, an undeniable relief" ("The Expelled" 13). (2007, 4–5)

The prime project of Beckettian mimesis is to protect experience from the risk of hope and hence from the moral suffering of disappointment, discouragement, and despair that hope threatens. The most fundamental way to avoid such moral suffering is to formulate the future as recapitulation of the past, and thus to deprive expectation of any outcome other than more of the same: "And there is nothing for it but to wait for the end, nothing but for the end to come, and at the end all will be the same, at the end at last perhaps all the same as before" (Beckett 1958d, 370). In this context, the monotony of repetition guards against the threat of construing the future in terms of anything other than reiteration of the past: "Whereas to see yourself doing the same thing endlessly over and over again fills you with satisfaction" (1958b, 133). Repetition assures that the only purpose is reiteration of the irrelevance of purpose, in order to avoid the moral suffering of thwarted purpose. Tomorrow can offer no more than renewal of yesterday: "how will he manage tomorrow, to endure tomorrow, the dawning, then the day, the same as he managed yesterday, to endure yesterday" (1967a, 133).

Paradoxically, in the Beckettian mimesis of time, the ultimate way to repeat the past is to forget it. The only thing to remember is the imperative to forget: "All that goes before forget" (1974a, 53). Here forgetting is the fundamental repetitive act. It occurs in the present, but recurs in the future as an ongoing task, because the passage of time entails ongoing acquisition of experience: "Endlessly, omit" (1974d, 63). Forgetting is essential because, as already noted, "Memories are killing" (1967c, 9). More profoundly, to focus, in the present, on forgetting the past is to free the present, for a moment, from servitude to time: "free at last, for an instant free, at last, nothing at last" (1959, 202). Freedom from time is the Beckettian goal: "Then it will not be as now, day after day, out, on, round, back, in, like leaves turning, or torn out and thrown crumpled away, but *a long unbroken time without before or after*, light or dark, from or towards or at, the old half knowledge of when and where gone, and of what, but kinds of things still, all at once, all going, until nothing, there never was anything, never can be, life and death all nothing, that kind of thing" (1974c, 48–49). Time involves sequence, before and after. An "unbroken time without before or after" is not time at all. It is instead, to revisit a crucial passage, "an instant without bounds, where the light never changes and the wrecks look all alike" (1958c, 233). In these circumstances, the experience of time would be freed from the importunities of temporality that always demands the succession of one thing after another: "But it is forbidden to give up and even to stop an instant" (1958b, 81). Temporality is a harsh taskmaster: "But from time to time. What tenderness in these little words, what savagery" (83). For its movement, as construed in Beckettian mimesis, always entails deterioration: "It's much worse than yesterday" (79). Within the realm of time, the only recourse is to turn deterioration into liberation—to turn, that is, the oppression of time into exemption from time.

In certain texts, involving the "matter of voices" (1958d, 325), where the narrator's awareness, as we have seen, concerns the audition of voices whose speech he forgets the moment after repeating it, a mode of animation removed from the impingement of time is constructed: "time devours on, but not me" (1967a, 127). This mode of animation is labeled "inexistence"—a term invoked, for example, in *Ill Seen Ill Said* (1981, 54), *Texts for Nothing* (1967a, 91, 131), and *How It*

Is (1964, 69), and epitomized in *The Unnamable*: "who could not be and gave up trying" (1958d, 347). The "metaphor" (325) of voices narrates an awareness immersed in "this murmur of memory and dream" (1967a, 133), where nothing happens but the reiteration of impossibility: "nothing ever but nothing and never nothing ever but lifeless words" (1967a, 135). In this context, time is irrelevant, for there is no distinct being in which any change could occur. "we're ended who never were" (139). Hence, the temporality of Beckettian inexistence requires careful precision to define. It is not temporal in a conventional sense, because it is not involved in the temporal process of coming to be and passing away: "end of dream, of being past, passing and to be, end of lie" (139). Nor is Beckettian inexistence *atemporal*, because awareness of time remains. It is therefore what might be termed *post-temporal*, because here, to retrieve Molloy's phrase, time "is over and yet it goes on." That is, time continues, but its continuation simply measures its own irrelevance: "the metamorphosis is accomplished, of unchanging future into unchangeable past" (1958d, 367). Thus as time goes on, the moments of time are "moments for nothing" (1958a, 83). The narrator of *Texts for Nothing* concurs: "to speak of instants, to speak of once, is to speak of nothing" (1967a, 138). For nothing occurs in the passage of time but endless repetition of the inability either to be or not to be: "begging in another dark, another silence, for another alm, that of being or ceasing, better still, before having been" (115). In this context, the experience of time is driven by the synthesis of two deficiencies: one "without the courage to end," the other without "the strength to go on" (1967d, 72).

The notion of Beckettian post-temporal time can be clarified through analysis of the status of the present moment. In the conventional paradigm, with regard to the transition of tenses, everything that happens, happens *now*. Turetzky elaborates: "Everything that is happening happens in the living present" (1998, 218). But the present is not isolated from the other tenses, past and future. Instead, it is informed by its relation to what immediately precedes and succeeds it. Each present moment is not merely positioned between the ones respectively immediately before and after it, but includes in its own content reference to them. Alfred North Whitehead clarifies: "Each moment of experience confesses itself to be a transition between two worlds, the immediate past and the immediate future" (1961a, 192). Otherwise, each moment would be a transit through nothingness, with no coordinates by which to orient itself, nothing that it continues or surpasses from the preceding moment, nothing that it transmits to the next moment. In these circumstances, time would begin and end with each moment. This is precisely the experience of "The Unnamable" for whom time is paradoxically construed as *the passage of moments that do not flow*, because each moment is a new arrival, without connection to those before or after: "the seconds pass, one after another, jerkily, no flow, they don't pass, they arrive, bang, bang, when you have nothing left to say you talk of time, seconds of time, there are some people add them together to make a life, I can't, each one is the first, no, the second, or the third" (1958d, 395). Here time passes, but as the recurrence of a present moment that paradoxically repeats other moments in the series ("another instant of my old instant") without sustaining any relations to them: "each one is the first, no, the second, or the third" (400, 395). Hence, the Beckettian experience of time, as depicted in certain texts, is *new at every moment yet always the same*: "all a going over and over and all once and never more" (1974c, 47). The most epigrammatic formulation of this condition occurs in "Texts for Nothing": "What vicissitudes within what changelessness" (1967a, 118).

In these texts involving "the matter of voices," the temporal horizon does not extend beyond the passing moment. Moreover, as we have seen, that passing moment is associated not just with the transient present, but also with the transient past—the moment elapsed just before the moment currently elapsing: the perpetually perishing past preceding the perpetually perishing present. Yet there are Beckettian texts where the temporal horizon encompasses—or at least implies—an entire lifetime, decades into the past. Consider "Krapp's Last Tape," a play founded on retrieval—one might accurately say reanimation—of the past. In its extraordinarily inventive treatment of time, the play offers a superb illustration of the Beckettian epigram "What vicissitudes within what changelessness." For here, despite vast differences in presentation, we find, just as in "The Unnamable," the paradoxical construction of time as the passage of moments that do not flow. Time passes in "Krapp's Last Tape." Its movement is foregrounded each time Krapp recedes into the background to pour a drink: "Ten seconds. Loud pop of cork. Fifteen seconds" (1957a, 12). The passage of time is further emphasized by Krapp's gesture of displaying his "[h]eavy silver watch" (9) just before each trip backstage to decant (10, 17, 23). But its passage toward the future leads to fixation on one moment, 30 years earlier, in the past, when Krapp, lying on top of the girl in the punt, confirmed his belief that it was "no good going on" (27). In its original context, this belief referred to the futility of continuing a romantic relationship that caused too much discord. But in the later context when Krapp, at age 69, listens repeatedly to the account of the punt experience recorded at age 39, the conviction, "no good going on," acquires a supplementary meaning pertaining ironically to Krapp's relationship with the passage of time, not the girl in the punt. On this level of signification, the mimesis of post-temporal time in the play becomes more accessible, for here we find Krapp's own version of that Beckettian post-temporality wherein, as we noted before, time is over and yet goes on. Brief explication will clarify.

Krapp defines his life in terms of a series of tapes recorded on each birthday. The original purpose this annual ritual was to facilitate movement toward the future through gaining perspective on experience in the past by first listening to selected portions of selected tapes recorded on previous birthdays and then recording a new entry concerning the year just completed on the current birthday. Yet, by the time Krapp reaches his sixty-ninth birthday, this annual ritual appears to have backfired. Instead of encouraging movement into the future through enabling understanding of the past, the ritual leads to repudiation of the future in favor of fixation on one moment in the past—the punt moment, recorded at age 39, to which Krapp reverts again and again, until sinking into regretful reverie after the tape in question has been wound off the playing spool, leaving him oblivious to the fact that he is listening to silence: "The tape runs on in silence" (28). Here the tape is over and yet goes on, just as life for Krapp is over and yet goes on: "What's a year now? The sour cud and the iron stool" (25). From a conventional perspective, Krapp's predicament epitomizes failure. He failed in love, failed in the project for literary recognition, and wastes his declining years in abject reversion to the past. But from a Beckettian perspective, when slumped beside the silently running tape recorder at the end of the play, Krapp temporarily achieves his own apotheosis. That is, he momentarily fulfills the Beckettian project to become him whom the words recall: "Will they succeed in slipping me into him, the memory and dream of me, into him still living" (1967a, 134). In that prolonged trance, Krapp's immersion in silence simulates the supreme Beckettian consummation: "it will be the silence ... the lasting one" (1958d, 414). But, of course, for Krapp this slipping into silence cannot last. As time moves on, "ten seconds ... fifteen seconds," he will eventually have to rise from his seat and continue with the rhythm of his life, however depleted it has become. The passage of time will again reiterate the futility of continuation. He has given up going on, and can only wish vainly to go back. In these circumstances, Krapp's existence approximates the "inexistence" enunciated by the "Texts" narrator: "I'll have gone on giving up, having had nothing, not being there" (1967a, 125). Krapp's future will only recapitulate the futile compulsion to relive the past.

Krapp in his "den," listening to recorded voices to which he sometimes responds, lapsing into silence from which he must inevitably emerge, constitutes a liminal character in the Beckettian canon, poised on the threshold between two kinds of mimesis or representation. On one side of that threshold is conventional mimesis, representing character in terms of the familiar notions of body, mind, and at least vestigial relation to an external world and a continuously unfolding life through time. On the other side of the threshold is a radically unconventional mimesis, dissolving character into "the matter of voices" discussed earlier, wherein an awareness bereft of identity, location, and history registers and repeats the words of voices whose relation to himself he repudiates. The first mimetic mode is characterized by clarification or at least elaboration of self; the second, by "flight from self" (1958d, 367). In listening to voices, "The Unnamable" engages in continuous repudiation of identity: "it's not I, it's not I" (1958d, 399). His present is occupied with echoing words heard in the immediate past whose connection to himself he repeatedly denies. Krapp pursues a version of the same enterprise. When listening to the tapes, he occupies his present with the audition of words recorded on prior birthdays by past versions of himself whose relation to himself in the present he repeatedly disclaims: "Well out of that, Jesus yes!" (1957a, 17); "Just been listening to that stupid bastard I took myself for thirty years ago, hard to believe I was ever as bad as that. Thank God that's all done with anyway" (24). To interpolate phrases from Beckett's "Proust," through the ritual of recording annual retrospects, Krapp configures himself as a "succession of individuals," with each year extending the succession by one more term (1965, 19). But it is a succession from which he secedes, by repudiating relation to preceding formulations of himself, and ultimately, on this sixty-ninth birthday, repudiating the annual recording ritual that has continued to this point: "Leave it at that" (26). Thus, in Krapp's case, *succession becomes secession*. That is, the passage of time, year by year, is constituted as a flow from which Krapp withdraws or isolates himself. Paradoxically, he remembers the past in order to forget the passage of time. He discards everything except bananas, booze, and one obsessively rememorated moment in the past that he effectively cuts out of time. As such, in the present, Krapp occupies a moment in and out of time. As long as he is absorbed in the memory of that punt-moment 30 years earlier, he remains stationary in the flow of time. Indeed, the remembered moment itself foregrounds the tension between fixity and flux: "We lay there without moving. But under us all moved, and moved us, gently, up and down, and from side to side" (1957a, 27).

Krapp is not a failure. On the contrary, he approximates the Beckettian ideal proclaimed by The Unnamable: "No, one can spend one's life thus, unable to live, unable to bring to life, and die in vain, having done nothing, been nothing"

(1958d, 358)]. The reduction of awareness to futile longing for that which can never be achieved because it cannot exist is the quintessential Beckettian project, as formulated by The Unnamable in terms that constitute, as we shall see in a moment, a probing gloss on "Krapp's Last Tape": "[Y]ou come back from a far place, back to life, that's where you should be, where you are, far from here, far from everything, if only I could go there, if only I could describe it, I who am so good at topography, that's right, aspirations, when plans fail there are always aspirations, it's a knack, you must say it slowly, If only this, if only that, that gives you time, time for a cud of longing to rise up in the back of your gullet, nothing remains but to look as if you enjoyed chewing it" (1958d, 401). This is precisely the predicament of Krapp after the end of the play, when he will have concluded his immersion in the punt scene, which the compulsively replayed section of the thirty-ninth birthday tape concerns. At that time, to interpolate The Unnamable's words just quoted, Krapp will have "come back from a far place, back to life," filled with obsessive "longing" to be "far from here," his waking reality, and return to site of memory: "if only I could go there." This anguish to be "far from here, from everything," to be absent from his own life and live only in the life that never was, is exactly the preoccupation that The Unnamable describes: "If only this, if only that, that gives you time, time for a cud of longing to rise up in the back of your gullet" (1958d, 401). Here we find the perfect interpretation of "the sour cud" that Krapp chewed during the year concluded by his sixty-ninth birthday—an interpretation that corresponds closely to Krapp's own comment on his predilection for regretful reverie: "drowned in dreams and burning to be gone" (25).

Krapp is not The Unnamable, because he has a "here" distinct from "there." Krapp's need for absence is predicated on the intolerable necessity of presence. Unlike The Unnamable for whom "here is my only elsewhere" (1958d, 402), Krapp cannot at every instant delude himself that the only reality is the illusion that he can escape it. For Krapp, here is not also elsewhere—not always the site of absence from where he actually is. Yet, denying identification with voices that were once in his own mouth, seeking compulsively to "be again" (1957a, 26) in a moment severed from the flow of time, Krapp simulates the condition of The Unnamable whose interminable audition of voices turns the passage of time into the accumulation of immobile moments during which no change can occur. Change is anathema to The Unnamable: "all change to be feared, incomprehensible uneasiness" (1958d, 295). It is similarly eschewed by Krapp through a paradox that rewards analysis. On the one hand, his disowning of previous selves asserts his own change beyond identity or congruence with them. But on the other hand, this assertion of change through time enables fixation on one moment that can never change because it is immobilized in the past. *Succession enables regression.* What never changes in Krapp's moving present is his burning need to achieve absence from it through immersion in the immutable past. In this context, the reason for the breakup with his lover can be clarified. On the surface, it was due to incompatibility: "no good going on" (1957a, 22). But on a deeper level, severance from the lover ultimately serves Krapp's need to be severed from time—to overcome implication in the passage of time by succumbing to attachment to an earlier moment in time. That is, the deepest motive driving Krapp's decision not to go on with the girl in the punt was the unconscious wish not to go on in time—to precipitate, in the present, a means by which, in the future, he could remain attached to the past, and thus negate the anisotropy or one-way forward flow of time.

This claim gains corroboration through reference to the Beckettian notion of inevitability whose clearest formulation occurs in "Molloy": "The fact is, it seems, that the most you can hope is to be a little less, in the end, the creature you were in the beginning, and the middle" (1958b, 32). In this context, the course of life itself, in its passage through time, is "pre-established" or predetermined: "[w]atch wound and buried by the watchmaker" (62, 36). The factor determining this declension is the drive toward lessness—a process of continuous diminution or disintegration whose purpose is to wear out awareness ("hoping to wear out a voice, to wear out a head"), so that its contents will be less troubling: "as if to grow less could help, ever less and less and never quite be gone" (1967a, 112). "Krapp's Last Tape" constitutes a version of the inevitable decline toward lessness. Indeed the play is set in the future—a time that must inevitably becomes present: "A late evening in the future" (1957a, 9). That is, given Krapp's mentality, Krapp's predicament on his sixty-ninth birthday was always in store, always impending, until actually occurring. This is the Beckettian rendition of the Heracleitean dictum: "Character for man is destiny"—sometimes translated as "Character is man's fate" (Heracleitus 1966, 32). Moran formulates this dictum in Beckettian terms—in terms, that is, of the ineluctable disintegration of the conventional structures on which the coherence and intelligibility of character depend: "And what I saw was more like a crumbling, a frenzied collapsing of all that had always protected me from all I was always condemned to be" (1958b, 148). To be, as construed in Beckettian mimesis, is ultimately to devolve toward the condition of disintegration or repudiation of being—a process whose termination is presupposed by its very unfolding but never achieved: "finality without end" (1958b, 111). This is post-temporal time par excellence—time that is over and yet goes on, time in which nothing happens but the deferral of cessation ("towards an end it seems can never come") and reiteration of the wish to cease: "You must go on. I can't go on. I'll go on" (1958b, 40; 1958d, 414).

7

Postlapsarian Will and the Problem of Time in Ian McEwan's *Enduring Love*

According to Peter Childs, Ian McEwan (born in 1948) is "the foremost British novelist of his generation" (2006, 144). A highly thematic writer, McEwan instills his fiction with problems and preoccupations that are both topical and perennial, transitory and abiding. David Malcolm provides a serviceable summary: "a movement in and out of metafictional concerns, a complex interest in feminist issues, an interplay of moral relativism and moral judgment, and an enduring love of psychological fiction" (2002, 19). Perhaps the most fundamental topic—what might be termed the lowest common denominator of McEwan's fiction—concerns the intrusion of the psychologically deviant or disordered into the mimesis of character, a feature that Malcolm refers to as "the role of the irrational in his characters' lives" (2002, 14). In moral formulation, this intrusion entrains the notion of evil in the guise of psychopathology. Yet, with equal cogency but perhaps less resonance, such dysfunctional deportment can also be construed in sociologically pejorative terms as the depiction of a modern wasteland whose denizens are animated by what Jack Slay, Jr., labels "haunting desires and libidinal politics" (1996, 1). From either perspective—the ethical or the societal—McEwan's novels ground their behavioral dynamics in what J. B. Bury, in a different context, terms "the delinquencies of frail humanity" (1923, 2.416).

McEwan's fiction has undergone a signal evolution from the macabre and audaciously, even brazenly, repulsive to modulations of malfeasance that are at once less shocking and more sophisticated. The first four novels—*The Cement Garden* (1978), *The Comfort of Strangers* (1981), *The Child in Time* (1987), and *The Innocent* (1990)—respectively foreground such abhorrent events as incest, sadistic homicide, child abduction, and dismemberment. The fifth novel, *Black Dogs* (1992), deploys a countryside encounter with the two eponymous and savage canines as a device for opposing and interrogating two constructions of human life: the rational and the religious or mystical. Here, as Malcolm observes, McEwan eschews "the grisly horrors of his earlier fiction" (2002, 131). The subsequent novels—*Enduring Love* (1997), *Amsterdam* (1998), *Atonement* (2001), *Saturday* (2005), *Chesil Beach* (2007), *Solar* (2010), *Sweet Tooth* (2012), and *The Children Act* (2014)—similarly avoid graphic emphasis on abomination, and instead probe the interface between the rational and the irrational (to cite just one level of signification) in more subtle ways. Yet crime or deviance, in some instances, continues to influence the plot, though in more attenuated form. *Enduring Love*, as we shall see, hangs on the stalking of the protagonist by a victim of De Clérambault's syndrome—an affliction that obsesses him with a homosexual love of his own invention and illusion. *Amsterdam* turns on the ingenious stratagems of two men to kill a third who eventually achieves revenge. *Atonement* concerns guilt regarding the false accusation of rape. *Saturday* in part concerns the protagonist's extrication of himself and his family from mortal threat posed by an incensed man whom the protagonist, with the help of his son, throws downstairs and on whom he must, a few hours later, operate to repair the resultant brain injury. *Chesil Beach*, set in July 1962, narrates, by means of an elaborate flashback structure, the disastrous attempt of two virgin newlyweds to consummate a marriage that does not survive its wedding night. *Solar*, set in the first decade of the current millennium, concerns a Nobel-winning physicist, later specializing in synthetic photosynthesis, whose life eventually blows up, as it were, in his face, when his various problems converge disastrously. *Sweet Tooth*, set in the early 1970s, concerns a female Cambridge graduate, Serena Frome, who, after recruitment by MI5, the British counterintelligence and security agency, becomes involved with her assigned target, Thomas Haley, who, on learning of the program that hired her, decides to exploit the arrangement as fodder for a novel. In *The Children Act*, McEwan explores the conflict between rationality and irrationality through the interaction between a secularly minded High Court judge, Fiona Maye, and a 17-year-old adolescent, Adam Henry, whose parents, as Jehovah's Witnesses, refuse him recourse to the blood transfusion that could reverse his leukemia. A secondary conflict between rationality and irrationality concerns the intention of Fiona's 60-year old husband to copulate with a younger woman before his opportunity for a licentious liaison expires.

But let us turn now to the analysis of time in *Enduring Love*. The novel begins with a reluctance to start: "What idiocy to be racing into this story and its labyrinths, sprinting away from our happiness among the fresh spring grasses by the oak" (1).¹ The event that the beginning concerns concludes a cherished period in the life of the first person narrator, Joe Rose: "At that moment a chapter, no, a whole stage of my life closed" (8). The pivotal event or watershed moment involves Joe's desperately futile attempt—and that of four other men who have viewed the same predicament from adjacent places—to rescue a terrified boy accidentally stranded in a touring balloon that has just broken free of its moorings, due to the incompetence of the pilot, the boy's grandfather. Once converged at the site of distress, the men try to help the grandfather hold down the balloon by clinging to ropes dangling from its sides. Yet a sudden series of gusts lifts the balloon off the ground. One by one, the men release their respective grips and fall earthward, leaving only one potential rescuer, John Logan, still hanging on, as the balloon continues to rise. Eventually, he too lets go—from exhaustion, not choice—and falls to his death, as Clarissa, Joe's common law wife—with whom he had, until rushing to the rescue, been picnicking—watches in "horrified helplessness" (80).

This inaugural event foregrounds and conflates two concerns central to the text: the notion of the Fall (whether of Lucifer or Adam) and the notion of time. With respect to the Fall, Clarissa quotes Milton's description of the fall of Satan: "Hurl'd headlong flaming from th'Ethereal Sky" (29), while Joe, in a passage already quoted, subtly links (a) his running from the picnic toward the balloon with (b) the decision provoking the expulsion of Adam and Eve from the Garden of Eden: "sprinting away from our happiness among the fresh spring grasses by the oak" (1). Later, he explicitly invokes the notion of the Biblical Fall and consequent expulsion, when thinking about the estrangement of Man from "natural dependency" or complete participation in the cycles of nature: "We were no longer in the great chain. It was our own complexity that had expelled us from the Garden. We were in a mess of our own unmaking" (207). The notion of time is similarly central to the balloon passage and its aftermath. During the attempted rescue, the passage of time, moment to moment, becomes the vital focus of attention: "Every fraction of a second that passed increased the drop, and the point must come when to let go would be impossible or fatal" (14). But in narrating the "quick succession" (17) constituting this implacably progressive passage, Joe repeatedly invokes his reluctance to let it continue, and foregrounds his nostalgia for the period before his heightened awareness of temporal passage began: "I'm lingering in the prior moment because it was a time when other outcomes were still possible" (2). Thus, in narrating one time series in the past, he superimposes a second time series in the present: "Best to slow down. Let's give the half minute after John Logan's fall careful consideration" (17). The second series involves retrospective examination of the first series. Whereas, with respect to the prior series, the headlong pace of time preempted the prerogative of personal choice, in the second series the will is free to determine or choose the pace of events—in this context, the steps of "careful consideration." But it is an illusory freedom. Though he can control the *pace* of rememoration, by lingering over moments of his choosing, he cannot control the *compulsion* to remember. Moreover, that which he remembers concerns the occasion when the irreversible movement of time, proceeding at its own unalterable pace, forced him to let go and abandon the rescue attempt, before the balloon rose too high for his safety. As a result of this decision due to temporal duress, Joe is thereafter preoccupied with guilt regarding the past and foreboding regarding the future: "As guilt was to the past, so, what was it that stood in the same relation to the future? Intention? No, not influence over the future. Foreboding. Anxiety about, distaste for the future" (43).

Thus the balloon "catastrophe" eventually distorts awareness of time, such that the present is beset by past and future: "Guilt and foreboding, bound by a line from the past to the future, pivoting in the present—the only moment it could be experienced" (3, 43). In these circumstances, the will, whose choices are sometimes made for the sake of consequences in the future and whose motives are sometimes derived from influences in the past, surrenders its initiative to the importunity of time. Our task now is to analyze the effect of temporal awareness on the efficacy of the will in the world of the novel. The investigation will first clarify the predicament of the will in the novel, and then relate that dispensation to the alternative constructions of time operant in the text. Our goal is to clarify how the unique contribution made by *Enduring Love* to understanding the problem of free will concerns the linking of choice with the construction of time. Conversely, altering the construction of time liberates the will to act more freely.[2]

Prelapsarian and postlapsarian man

The first step toward clarifying the predicament of the will concerns explication of the notion of the Fall—a central thematic principle or topos in the novel, as noted earlier. The key to the doctrine concerns the opposition between the state of human nature *before* (prelapsarian) and *after* (postlapsarian) the event. Prelapsarian man (Adam before the Fall) enjoyed what J. N. D. Kelly terms "supernatural blessedness"—a condition characterized by faultless functioning of the two faculties of the rational soul: reason and will (1978, 253). According to St. Augustine, the Church Father who most embellished the doctrine of prelapsarian perfection, human nature in Adam, the first man, transcended all limitations, such as physical disease, mental error or perplexity, and moral culpability, which have afflicted it ever since the Fall. Kelly elaborates: "Adam, he holds, was immune from physical ills and had surpassing intellectual gifts; he was in a state of justification, illumination and beatitude (1978, 362). In contrast, as Kelly indicates, postlapsarian man languishes in a state of guilt, confusion, and misery, epitomized by "enslavement to ignorance, concupiscence and death" (1978, 364). The Fall disordered the human soul such that its two constituent faculties, reason and will, are in conflict, entailing, as Louis Duchesne indicates, "perpetual strife within us [between] the consciousness of the Law and the promptings of concupiscence (1924, 3.143). Etienne Gilson expands, with reference to the pronouncement of St. Thomas Aquinas: "His [Man's] will has been wounded by Original Sin with a consequent disordering of his concupiscence which no longer allows him to act always as his reason prescribes" (1988, 339).

Further investigation of the term "Original Sin," denoting the act by which Adam precipitated the Fall, will enhance our understanding of the doctrine concerned. Two points merit special emphasis. The first involves the *consequence* of the sinful act provoking the Fall; the second concerns the *cause* of the act itself. According to Christian doctrine, the Fall of Adam is simultaneously the Fall of Man or human nature; for the fault that the sin entailed is inherited and congenital. Kelly elaborates: "[A]s a consequence of Adam's rebellion which, as we have seen, is ours too, human nature has been terribly scarred and vitiated" (1978, 364). The degradation and disruption of human nature entrained by the Fall, through the misuse of free will in choosing inappropriately, is often termed the loss of innocence. In this context, loss of innocence entrains disruption of intrinsic nature or mode of operation through a misuse of free will that chooses inappropriately. Kelly elaborates, with reference to Athanasius: "It was through the fault committed by their free volition that the disintegrating forces in any case latent in our nature were released" (1978, 347). Thus, the doctrine of the Fall is both biographical and anthropological. That is, it both concerns an event in the life of one man (Adam) and one woman (Eve) and stipulates the cause of disorder in human nature, whenever and wherever that nature is instantiated in actual human beings. The disastrous consequence of the Fall flows immediately from its cause: pride, construed theologically as a transgression of boundaries whereby Adam sought, according to St. Ambrose, "equality with his Creator" (Kelly 1978, 353). Hence, the pride engendering Original Sin entails disobedience—in this instance, a turning away from subservience to divine precept in order to privilege personal will instead. Kelly clarifies, with reference to the teaching of St. Augustine: "[T]he latent ground of the act was pride, the desire to break away from his natural master, God, and be his own master" (1978, 362).

The moral site of the Fall is the will—the faculty by which the soul or inner principle of rational awareness inclines toward what is deemed desirable or appropriate and avoids what is undesirable or inappropriate. Kelly elaborates: "Any blame must lie exclusively with his own will, which, though inclined towards goodness, had the possibility, being free, of choosing wrongfully" (1978, 362). Here the imagery of spatial falling, invoked by the term, "the Fall," emerges most strongly. For what is entailed is a lapsing of the will, a releasing of its grip on righteous principle in favor of attachment to baser preferences. Gilson expands, with reference to Augustine: "This fall—for that is what it was—was not the natural and necessary fall of a falling stone, but rather the free fall of a will letting itself go [and forsaking its proper attachment to divine commandment]" (1960, 148). The implications of Augustine's image of the falling stone emerge more clearly once the definition of the will is clarified. For Augustine, as Gilson indicates, "willing means making use of free choice, for in Augustine the definition of free choice is always identical with that of the will" (1960, 157). Hershel Baker corroborates: "Adam sinned when he was free to choose either good (obedience) or evil (disobedience)" (1947, 173). As the faculty of free choice, the will can elect or choose according to its own motives. If it chooses wrongfully, as a result of allowing an inappropriate motive to reduce it to act, then the will declines from its proper operation. With respect to the Original Sin, the will chose that which vitiated its own functioning, for it renounced attachment to righteous motive for choice. In proper configuration, the will responds to the promptings of reason, as Gilson explains (with reference to Thomistic dictum): "[W]ithout Original Sin our will would be naturally capable of complying with the orders issued by our reason" (1988, 339). But after the Fall, and the loss of innocence that it entailed, the will turned away from the transcendent and immutable good disclosed by reason, and succumbed to concupiscence, which entails desire for gratification through that which is transient and mutable. Kelly explains: "In Augustine's vocabulary concupiscence stands, in a general way, for every inclination making man turn from God to find satisfaction in material things which are intrinsically evanescent" (1978, 364–65).

The problematizing of free will

In invoking the motif of the Fall, *Enduring Love* inverts its terms of reference. Whereas the Fall, as we have seen, hinges on the role of free will in the exercise of choice, the fall depicted in the novel systematically removes the relevance of choice, even as the issue of moral choice is emphasized. Initially, the attempt to rescue the boy stranded in the balloon is framed as a moral struggle between "selfishness" (14) and "altruism" (15): "Our mammalian conflict—what to give to others and what to keep for yourself" (14). Yet that construction is immediately deconstructed. For as the balloon continues to rise despite the ballast provided by his body, Joe perceives the futility of hanging on: "Being good made no sense. I let go and fell, I reckon, about twelve feet" (15). Hence, at bottom, his decision to let go and fall to the earth is predicated on the absence of a viable alternative and not on a choice between compellingly competing alternatives: "Suddenly the sensible choice was to look out for yourself" (15). This deconstruction of the relevance of choice continues in the case of the last man to fall—John Logan. His falling was involuntary. It was not his will that lapsed, but the muscles of his body. He did not choose to let go; he just could no longer hold on. But holding on was also not a choice, in the sense of deciding between alternatives. For once the other men had let go, enabling the balloon to soar ever higher, Logan's original purpose in holding on no longer applied. Thus his fall remains outside considerations of morality, because it was not determined by a free will exercising its power to choose. Whereas, as we have seen, the prelapsarian state entails adhesion of the will to proper principles by which to choose, Logan's fatal fall foregrounds the irrelevance of choosing. Paradoxically, his fall is exempt from the moral factors applying to the Biblical Fall.

The balloon episode problematizes the notion of choice in other ways. The obverse of *irrelevance of choice* (associated with Logan) is *inability to choose* (associated with Harry Gadd, the child whom he tries to rescue). Just as Logan is reduced to a state where choice is irrelevant, so Harry, overcome with fear and confusion, succumbs to "paralysis of will, a state known as learned helplessness, often noted in laboratory animals subjected to unusual stress" (11). In that terrified state, Harry loses the conative power to choose. Paralysis of will analogously affects Clarissa while watching Logan plunge to the ground, for she is reduced to "horrified helplessness," where the power of the will to choose—or, more precisely, to incline the self toward action through the exercise of choice—is nullified by traumatic circumstance (80).

The problematizing of free will in the exercise of choice ramifies throughout the novel, on various levels of signification. The first of these levels concerns, as we have already begun to see, key events or moments in the plot. Brief recapitulation will position us to excavate the deeper strata. As a direct consequence of Logan's fall, Joe involuntarily becomes the object of Jed Parry's equally involuntary obsession. Like Joe, Parry was one of the men who coincidentally happened to be near the balloon and tried to bring it back to the ground by hanging on to its dependent ropes. Following the "catastrophe," Joe and Parry, by separate routes, converge near Logan's broken body (3). There, as their gazes momentarily meet, Parry falls in love with Joe—a reaction determined not by choice, but by latent neurosis, termed De Clérambault's syndrome, which predisposes him to displace loneliness by "the inception of a delusional relationship" founded on the fantasy that its amatory object reciprocates a love that, in fact, he abhors and rejects—and desperately tries to understand in order to protect himself from it: "Parry caught my glance and became stricken with a love whose morbidity I was now impatient to research" (239, 127). Thus, to the extent that Parry is motivated by psychopathology beyond his control, he approximates the status of "an automaton," driven by factors that preempt the faculty of choice (41).

Ironically, through this unwilled relationship with Parry, Joe is rendered similarly vulnerable to impulses that compromise free will. The next day, following an unexpected telephone call from Parry in the middle of the night, Joe is overcome by the need to tell "the full story" to "a radio talks producer" who has no interest in the tale: "I pressed on because I could not stop" (40). During the ensuing days, Joe succumbs increasingly to both obsession and compulsion. Regarding obsession, Joe several times refers to his helpless susceptibility to the uncontrollable momentum of his own thought: "*Don't leave me here with my mind*, I thought. *Get them to let me out*" (58 [original italics]); "And driven, obsessed, undersexed? Who wouldn't be? Here was a diseased consciousness clamouring to batten itself to mine" (222). Regarding compulsion, Joe repeatedly acts without self-control—without, that is, the initiative of choice. A short list of references will illustrate: (a) arguing with Clarissa about his own preoccupation with Parry: "But now they seem cast in a play they cannot stop, and a terrible freedom is in the air"—here "freedom" paradoxically concerns the compulsion to express whatever hostility each is feeling (86); (b) losing sense of direction or purpose, while succumbing to the impulse to move: "I had no idea where I was going" (89), "As I crossed the kitchen, I could honestly have said that I had no idea where I was going" (104), "My motives in coming were no longer clear" (106); (c) halting to observe Parry, while wanting to avoid him: "But his rage was compelling and I was forced to look on" (91); (d) reacting instinctively to presumed threat (Parry's unseen presence) before being able consciously to choose response: "It's a system so ancient, developed so far back along the branchings of our mammalian and pre-mammalian past that its operations never penetrate into higher consciousness" (51).

As the last example indicates, the problem of compromised or preempted free will extends beyond the manifestation of obsession and compulsion, where thought and action are respectively prompted by internal factors resistant to conscious control, and reaches into other contexts, deepening its implications. One such context, already implicit in Joe's reference, cited above, to "our mammalian and pre-mammalian past," involves the notion of intrinsic nature, construed here as congenital constitution predisposing each member of the human species to develop in predetermined ways: "We come into this world with limitations and capacities, all of them genetically prescribed. Many of our features, our foot shape, our eye colour, are fixed, and others, like our social and sexual behaviour, and our language learning, await the life we live to take their course. But the course is not infinitely variable. We have a nature" (69–70).

Another context entrained by the problem of preempted free will concerns not intrinsic nature but extrinsic event or, more precisely, the special pattern of events that involves coincidence. The issue of coincidence centers on Joe's connection to Parry—the character who suffers from De Clérambault's syndrome. Meeting Parry in circumstances perfectly suited to activate his amatory neurosis is an obvious coincidence: "On a country walk he [Parry] was initiated into a makeshift community of passers-by struggling to tether a balloon caught in strong winds. Such a transformation, from a 'socially empty' life to intense teamwork may have been the dominating factor in precipitating the syndrome" (239). The coincidences multiply. A spectacular one concerns Parry's botched attempt to have Joe murdered by a hired assassin who erroneously shoots the wrong man (Colin Tapp) in a crowded restaurant. Yet Colin Tapp, by coincidence, survived an assassination attempt 18 months earlier in Addis Ababa (180), with the result that the police at first ignore Joe's insistence that he himself was the intended target: "All I needed at a time like this was a meaningless coincidence" (180). Several hours later, Parry invades Joe's apartment, and holds Clarissa hostage, forcing her to telephone Joe with instructions to return home. Having obtained a gun earlier that day in order to protect himself from Parry, Joe is fortuitously armed when entering his flat and finding Clarissa held at knifepoint. Joe shoots Parry, wounding him, with the result that Joe must go to the police station for the third time in 24 hours: "My third visit to a police station in twenty-four hours, the third in my life. More *random clustering*" (214 [my emphasis]). The preceding two visits respectively concerned attempts to interest the police in (a) a harassment complaint and then (b) an attempted murder accusation, both concerning Parry. Joe first invokes the term, "random clustering," when referring to his second visit to the police station: "Statisticians call this kind of thing random clustering, a useful way of denying it significance" (174). Here, in using the term, he simultaneously debunks it, replacing the notion of "meaningless coincidence" (180), which he invoked earlier, with that of significant conjunction—a notion ultimately associated with "fate" (83, 86, 136, 177) or at least with the purveying of hidden meaning.

Recourse to hypothetical alternatives

Joe's ambivalence regarding the meaningfulness of events rewards further investigation. As we shall see, coincidence or "random clustering" does have a meaning—one that concerns neither of the two alternatives already suggested: sheer fortuitousness or fateful predetermination. Instead, the meaning of coincidence pertains to its heuristic function in emphasizing the reality of occurrence—the fact that events actually happen. That is, coincidences underscore the happening of the events constituting them. This point can be better understood once Joe's difficulty accepting the reality or actual occurrence of events in his life is clarified. He has a tendency to construct alternative versions of the actual situation that his own freely chosen actions and decisions have constructed for him. The primary example of this tendency to contemplate a different result of his own exercise of free will concerns his career—a science writer revisited by his prior ambition to be a physicist: "[M]y thoughts returned to how I came to be what I was, and *how it might have been different* and, ridiculously, how I might find my way back to original research and achieve something new before I was fifty" (78 [my emphasis]). Joe is not comfortable with the consequences or "outcomes" of his choices (2, 43), and prefers to replace them mentally with more favorable ones. This tendency can be explicated through reference to what Whitehead in *Process and Reality: An Essay in Cosmology* terms "hypothetical alternatives" or "abstract notions, expressing the possibilities of another course of history" (1978, 185). Joe's own recourse to hypothetical alternatives involves recasting the choices made at some time in the past in order to imagine alternative consequences that would have flowed from them: "he wants to set about altering his fate" (83). In Joe's case, this enterprise is a recurrent practice—indeed a cyclic syndrome: "In fact, the last time round, a real crisis two years ago, he ended by concluding that he was reconciled to his life, and that it wasn't a bad one after all" (81).

The conflict between addressing reality as it is and reconstructing it mentally according to preferred variants is epitomized by Joe's reaction to Logan's fall: "I'm lingering in the prior moment because it was *a time when other outcomes were still possible*" (2 [my emphasis]). This is a highly ironic statement, since the "aftermath" of the balloon event is, for Joe, precisely the time when other outcomes are possible—but only as hypothetical alternatives, desperately formulated in his mind (2). Indeed among the consequences generated by the "explosion of consequences" (17) resulting from the event are those entertained in the hypothetical alternatives that Joe constructs, as when imagining himself propelled into the future in order to warn fellow customers in the restaurant of the attempted murder about to occur in their midst: "It was a mistake, it doesn't have to happen. *We could choose another outcome*" (169 [my emphasis]).

This very clear linking of hypothetical alternatives with the exercise of free will or the faculty of choice has important implications. As noted earlier, the Biblical Fall vitiated the intrinsic nature or mode of operation of the will such that, in its postlapsarian state, the will is apt to incline toward inappropriate choice. A similar degradation of function pertains to Joe's faculty of choice after Logan's fall, though with some overlap of before and after. That is, after Logan's fall, Joe tends to engage more urgently in the conative (i.e., involving the will) exercise to which he resorted earlier: namely, choosing hypothetical alternatives to the actual course of his own life. But frequency or intensity of recourse is not the main issue. Something has changed with respect to Joe's use of hypothetical alternatives or "abstract notions, expressing the possibilities of another course of history" (to retrieve Whitehead's phrasing). He has become consciously apprehensive of the future: "A fear of outcomes" (43). Consequently, he seeks not alternative outcomes so much as protection *from* outcomes. Fear of outcomes entails fear of the future—the tense in which outcomes of present circumstance will occur or be made manifest: "Anxiety about, distaste for the future" (43). Thus protection from outcomes requires protection from the future. For this security, he will have to inhabit or construct a temporal dispensation that wards off the future. He does this through obsession with the past: "the time of obsessive re-examination that followed: the aftermath, an appropriate term for what happened in a field waiting for its early summer mowing" (2).

In "the time of obsessive re-examination," the examining present becomes a perspective on the reexamined past that concerns a series of events whose occurrence is interrogated in terms of why they had to happen and how they might not have happened—or, having happened, not have generated such devastating consequences. In essence, the purpose of reexamining the past is not to clarify the present that results from the past, but to keep temporal focus on the past so that the future recedes from attention. Joe does this, for example, through his sense of guilt, which perpetuates in the present preoccupation with the past. Clarissa does it through accusation, blaming Joe in the present for his response to the problem of Parry in the past: "I can't quite get rid of the idea that *there might have been a less frightening outcome if you had behaved differently*" (216 [my emphasis]). Here blame—the attribution of fault to another person—serves as the means of replacing the past with a hypothetical alternative expressing the possibility of another course of history. Moral judgment becomes the means of altering the content of the passage of time toward the future. This is very clear in Clarissa's reaction when Joe suddenly draws a gun to shoot Parry, who is preparing to cut his own throat: "She was on her feet and staring at the gun in my hand with an expression of such repulsion and surprise that *I thought we would never get past this moment*" (214–15 [my emphasis]). Here Clarissa's intense and involuntary censure of Joe is associated with a stopping of time or, more precisely, a halting of the temporal movement into the future. Joe, of course, is aware that something—perhaps a clandestine affair—is skewing Clarissa's moral judgment of him with respect to his reaction to Parry: "It occurred to me that Clarissa was using Parry as a front" (103). Clarissa, as Joe confirms by rifling her desk for compromising correspondence, is not being unfaithful. Yet there is indeed a hidden (though unconscious) motive for her negative judgment of Joe's behavior with respect to Parry. Blame sustains notions of what Joe should and should not have done: it enables the proliferation of hypothetical alternatives whose purpose is to avoid the reality of what actually occurred. This unwitting project to undo the past, to replace the past with an alternative version, serves the need to gain control over the unfolding of the future. For, as we have seen, the most traumatic result of Logan's catastrophic fall is the "explosion of consequences" it produced (17).

Intention and conception of the future

Deeper probing of this matter will tighten our grasp of the postlapsarian will and the problem of time in *Enduring Love*. Joe conspicuously construes the operation of the will in terms of the project to control the future: "*intentionality, intention, tries to assert control over the future* (43 [original emphasis]). In the Aristotelian-Thomist tradition from which the notion of intentionality is derived, intention pertains to the tending of the will toward its end or purpose. Gilson confirms: "[t]his movement of the will which moves itself ... toward its object is called *intention*" (1988, 252). But in Joe's assessment, as we have just seen, the meta-motive moving the will—the motive, that is, underlying all particular instances of intentionality—is the project to influence the movement of time or, more precisely, "to assert control over the future." Indeed, we found the same to be true of guilt and blame. Yet the will to control the future presupposes a conception of the future. As a tense, how is the future understood? What distinguishes it from the other tenses? Brief recapitulation of relevant aspects of the philosophy of time will give us access to some answers that, in turn, will facilitate our study of the novel. The effort to grasp basic distinctions enunciated in the philosophical analysis of time will be rewarded by the precision that they accord to examination of time in the novel. For the convenience of readers who, before reading my study, were not already familiar with the temporal formulations of John McTaggart, I shall review, in condensed form, the relevant points earlier explicated in Chapter I, in the analysis of *Hamlet*.

In *The Nature of Existence*, John McTaggart undertook a celebrated analysis of the concept of time, identifying the dual ways in which "positions in time" are conceived (1927, 2.10). The first way orders temporal positions from the distant future to the present to the distant past. McTaggart labels this series of positions the *A*-series: "I shall give the name of the *A* series to that series of positions which runs from the far past through the near past to the present, and then from the present through the near future to the far future or conversely" (1927, 2.10). In this schema, any event or moment in time successively passes through the positions in the series, proceeding from the remote future toward the present and thence toward the remote past. The second way construes positions in time in terms not of changing tense (as with the *A*-series), but of what Turetzky labels "a permanent order of succession," characterized by the relations of earlier than, simultaneous with, and later than (1998, 151). McTaggart elaborates: "The series of positions which runs from earlier to later, or conversely, I shall call the *B* series" (1927, 2.10). Whereas changing tense is the hallmark of the *A*-series, unchanging order of sequence characterizes the *B*-series, as Oaklander explains: "if one event is ever earlier (later) than another event, then it is always earlier (later) than the other event; events do not change their positions in the B-series which runs from earlier to later" (1994b, 158).

The balloon episode in *Enduring Love* provides a spectacular example of the distinction between the *A*-series and the *B*-series. Let's begin with its relation to the *A*-series, and then proceed to the *B*-time correlation after our investigation has reached the appropriate point. In McTaggart's formulation, movement along the *A*-series occurs from future to present to past. But transition along the *A*-series can also be construed from the perspective of an ever-moving present, continually advancing toward what has not yet occurred (the future) and continually moving away from what has already happened (the past). The balloon episode is presented in these terms, as the transit, that is, of the present moment toward a future event whose pull it cannot resist: "The encounter that would unhinge us was minutes away, its enormity disguised from us not only by the barrier of time but by the colossus in the centre of the field that *drew us in* with the power of a terrible ratio that set fabulous magnitude against the puny human distress at its base" (2 [my emphasis]). As experienced event, the balloon episode constitutes a superb example of what Donald C. Williams describes as "the whoosh of process, the felt flow of one moment into the next" (1978, 108–9). This is *A*-time (time experienced as an *A*-series) par excellence, characterized by the impression of relentless impulsion beyond the status quo of the present. Clifford Williams elaborates: "One feature of our experience of time that *A*-theorists of time appeal to is the inexorability of the movement of time" (1994, 364). A superb description of the whoosh of passage concerns the act of hanging onto a runaway balloon that gains altitude each moment. Here the passage of time is depicted from instant to instant, even from "neuronal pulse" to neuronal pulse (13). In this context, the passage of time, as the continuous transition from present to future, has drastic import. One instant to the next can mean life or death—or loss of the ability to choose between life and death: "A delay of one second would have been enough to close his options" (15).

In the balloon scene, the future is fearsome because of the catastrophe it threatens. But, as we have seen, in the aftermath of this experience Joe fears the future itself: "Anxiety about, distaste for the future" (43). To understand the implications of this aversion, we must first deconstruct the notion of the future implicit in the doctrine of the *A*-series. Brief analysis will position us to grasp the link between time and free will in *Enduring Love* more firmly.

In McTaggart's construction, the future has, in one sense, already happened, even as it approaches the present. That is, events are construed as already constituted and occupying their respective positions in the *A*-series. The only change that occurs to events in the course of moving along the series concerns the dropping and acquisition of temporal properties (futurity, presentness, and pastness). George Schlesinger explains: "A typical event, on this view, is in the distant future to begin with; then it becomes situated in the less distant future; it keeps approaching until it becomes an event occurring in the present. As soon as this happens, the event loses its presentness and acquires the property of being in the near past. The degree of its pastness continually increases" (1994, 214). Yet, by construing the future in terms of the implacable continuity of movement of that which already subsists, McTaggart's schema of the A-series does not capture the utter novelty of the future. Moreover, it puts the future on par with the present and past, with respect to ontological status or degree of reality. The only distinction between the future and the past is that the events subsisting in the future have not happened yet. But they are no less real as a result.

C. D. Broad, the first and still one of the most illuminating critics of McTaggart's temporal philosophy, attacked the assumption of the preexistence of the future. In his view, the future has no reality: "the future is simply nothing at all" (1952, 66). It is not the repository or zone harboring events that have not yet occurred. According to Broad, the occurrence of new events is explained not by the procession of future events toward the present, but by the process of absolute becoming whereby events that had never before been suddenly occur: "But, when an event becomes, it *comes into existence*; and it was not anything at all until it had become" (1952, 68 [original emphasis]). Le Poidevin clarifies: "We should not think of there being events located in the future and destined, as it were, to become present. Rather, we should think of the future as being unreal. As events come into being, the sum total of reality—i.e. the past and present—increases" (1991, 19).

The distinct notion of the future unfolded in *Enduring Love* can be brought into focus through reference to the discrepant constructions respectively expounded by McTaggart and Broad. Insofar as Joe's awareness of the future is, as we have seen, animated by "foreboding," it suggests the approach of a future event already constituted, as in McTaggart's formulation (43). Yet insofar as Joe's account of the balloon catastrophe suggests the eruption in the present of an event that only the accidental convergence of diverse factors—"coincidences of time and place"—enables, the notion of the future entailed seems to approximate that propounded by Broad (10). Actually, as we shall now consider, Joe's notion of the future entrains a third option—one linking the future with the exercise of will. Here the future is construed as the zone of consequences of present choices. The consequences do not exist until after the choice is made. They come into being later. But present choice prepares them, though choice itself is conditioned or limited by antecedent and contemporaneous factors. The balloon rescue attempt foregrounds these considerations.

It begins as a contest of wills and confusion of purposes: "No one was in charge—or everyone was, and we were in a shouting match" (11). The boy whom everyone is trying to save is incapacitated, as we have seen, by "paralysis of will," induced by conditions that overwhelm his humanity and reduce him to the passivity typical of "laboratory animals subjected to unusual stress" (11). The incompetent pilot, who attempts to reenter the balloon when all the other men are trying to keep it on the ground, is characterized by intention that no one at the time understands: "What he was doing seemed ridiculous, but *his intentions, it turned out, were completely sensible. He wanted to deflate the balloon by pulling a cord that was tangled in the basket*" (11 [my emphasis]). The overwhelming of individual will by factors depriving it of efficacy culminates in the plight of Logan whose original choice to hold onto the ropes of the balloon eventually deprives him, as noted earlier, of the choice to let go until exhaustion fatally compels him to release his grip, while Clarissa watches in "horrified helplessness" (80).

But human will, in the novel, is not as thwarted, constrained, programmed, or helpless as it seems. Its choices—though hampered and influenced by conflict, conditioning, and circumstance—nevertheless lead to results. Except in circumstances of paralysis (as with the child in the balloon), extremity (as with Logan clinging to the rope), impotence (as with Clarissa powerlessly witnessing the fall), or compulsion (as with Parry in his madness), the will is free to choose, but it cannot choose the situation in which it makes choices or the factors influencing its own exercise of choice. Of course, the notion of the will choosing within a restricted field of choice, conditioned by factors that constrain it, whether the willing agent is aware of them or not, is not unique to this novel. An existentialist philosopher, for example, would say that the will is "situated"—engaged, that is, with the resistance and impulsions of the given, in all their ramifications. Paul Tillich provides a representative example: "But freedom is the possibility of a total and centered act of the personality, an act in which all the drives and influences which constitute the destiny of man are brought into the centered unity of a decision" (1963, 2.42–3). Here the human individual achieves authenticity through accepting what H. J. Blackham terms "the necessity of freedom"—the responsibility, that is, to determine the meaning of personal existence through constructing and enacting projects and choices that at once acknowledge and transcend the sheer "facticity and historicity of the embodied self in a situation" (1952, 162). Yet, at bottom, the Existential situation with which the human individual must deal concerns not the constraints constituted and imposed by concrete circumstance, but what Robert G. Olson terms "the anguish of being," which recognizes that the individual must, through decisions, become "the source of value and intelligibility" with regard to "the radical contingency and ultimate meaninglessness of both man and the world" (1962, 37). While *Enduring Love* is not an existential work, as it does not, to invoke I. M. Bochenski's criterion, treat "existence as the supreme object of inquiry," nevertheless the novel does isolate and probe the relation between situation and free will, especially insofar as the ultimate factor determining situation concerns involvement with time (1965, 159).

The crisis or turning point in Joe's relation to his own free will or faculty of choice occurs after Parry's botched attempt to have Joe shot to death in a restaurant. The event shows Joe that he is alone with the problem of survival, regarding both his own life and the future of his "enduring love" with Clarissa: "Clarissa thought I was mad, the police thought I was a fool, and one thing was clear: the task of getting us back to where we were was going to be mine alone" (161). Recognizing his "isolation and vulnerability" (177), Joe resolves to obtain a gun, acutely aware that the choice he has made will generate consequences beyond the reaches of his own will to control them: "Back in my study I sat with the phone in my lap, considering the moment, *this turning-point. I was about to step outside the illuminated envelope of fear and meticulous daydreaming into a hard-edged world of consequences. I knew that one action, one event, would entail another, until the train was beyond my control,* and that if I had doubts this was the moment to withdraw" (188 [my emphasis]). Here Joe moves from "fear of outcomes" to the decision to unleash them (43). Yet his efforts to obtain the gun, by visiting some seedy characters on the outskirts of London, foreground his own confinement within physiological and emotional compulsions that he cannot control, but only defer with extreme difficulty. During negotiations with the sellers of the gun, Joe's nervousness causes him to laugh involuntarily, forcing him to mask the sound "behind a yodeling shouting sneeze" (196). Later, while standing in a copse to practice shooting the gun with Johnny, his gun-purchasing assistant, Joe succumbs to an urge to defecate, which he forestalls temporarily only with "constant and conscious effort" (206).

Then, while squatting to release his bowels, he contemplates the "inhabitants of the microscopic realm" under the earth: "The blind compulsion of these organisms to consume and excrete made possible the richness of the soil" (207). Here Joe invokes the notion of the Biblical Fall, interpreting it in evolutionary terms as the exclusion of man from "the great chain" by which all organisms are linked to the irresistible promptings of reflex and instinct (207). This is the moment of supreme irony in the novel. On the one hand, according to Joe, "[i]t was our own complexity that had expelled us from the Garden" (207). But on the other hand, this complexity—this transcending of the innocence of biological compulsion through the morally complicated faculty of will—enables and constitutes a felix culpa—a fortunate fall. For it liberates the will to make its own choices, not always in thrall to that which nature and circumstance dictate.[3] Ironically, the character who forces Joe to act on his own and make the decision to buy a gun, accepting the consequences that might follow, is Parry—the figure who almost incarnates susceptibility to compulsion. Parry remains trapped in compulsion, manifested not just through the psychopathology of De Clérambault's syndrome, but also through uncontrollable movements, as when holding Clarissa hostage inside the apartment she shares with Joe: "He tossed his head from side to side. It was an *involuntary spasm*" (211 [my emphasis]).

A further irony follows. Though the mind separates the human species from what Joe terms "the great chain" connecting other life forms to modes of compulsion, the mind is itself a site of compulsion: in this case, concerning obsessive thoughts that confine the thinker within their own importunity—a state that Parry, "crouched in a cell of his own devising," virtually incarnates and to which Joe and Clarissa, in a less extreme way, respectively succumb: "the high-walled infinite prison of directed thought" (143, 48). The essence of the prison—that which makes thought a "little cage of reason"—is the need to interpret experience by means of prior concepts or logic that enable a "framing of reality" (133), so that the facts of experience might be rendered intelligible. Parry's neurosis, of course, constitutes a grossly "distorted" framing of reality (91). But, similarly, the police are unable to understand Joe's grievance regarding Parry unless it is "poured into the available bureaucratic mould"—that is, unless it is construed in terms of a framing of reality: "Parry's behaviour had to be generalized into a crime" (73).

Yet the "framing of reality" most profoundly linked with "the prison of directed thought" and the "little cage" constructed by reason concerns the concept of time. Brief recapitulation will position us to take one more step. As discussed earlier, the balloon incident precipitates in Joe—and to some extent, in Clarissa—a "distaste for the future," stemming from "[a] fear of outcomes" (43) and resulting in a need to wall off the future or to keep it at bay. Modes of warding off the future include blame, guilt, and recourse to hypothetical alternatives—all of them ways of displacing awareness of the future with what Joe terms "the time of obsessive re-examination" (2). Events eventually force Joe to overcome his "fear of outcomes" and accept the necessity of acting, even though action will provoke consequences that can be neither foreseen nor forestalled: "I was about to step outside the illuminated envelope of fear and meticulous daydreaming into a hard-edged world of consequences" (43, 188). Here, very clearly, Joe prepares to leave the prison or "illuminated envelope" that his mind has constructed to protect him from the future. That is, the fundamental function of his "prison of directed thought" is to defend against the unknown consequences of the movement of time away from the present moment.

The transition from *A*-time to *B*-time

There is, however, a more profound and subtle means by which Joe overcomes fear of the future—one that can be clarified by juxtaposing the end and the beginning of the novel. At the end of the novel proper, Joe and Clarissa are preparing to separate as a result of differences and grievances that arose during the period when Joe was pursued by Parry. Yet though the story constituting the novel ends at that point, the novel itself includes as one of its two appendices a case history ostensibly published in the *British Review of Psychiatry* (233). Here the sequence of events constituting Joe's episode with Parry is rendered in the dry prose of a clinical record, concluding with the information that Joe and Clarissa (identified respectively as R and M) were eventually "reconciled and later successfully adopted a child" (242). What are the implications of this ex post facto extension of the event-series constituting the plot of the novel? A preliminary answer is that sufficient time elapsed between the ending of Joe's narration and the writing of the case history in the appendix for the case history to include reference to the marital reconciliation and child adoption that, in Joe's narration, had not yet occurred. But a deeper answer emerges if we turn our attention from the appendix following the end of Joe's narration to the very *beginning* of that narration.

There Joe refers to time as a map: "*This was the moment, this was the pinprick on the time map*: I was stretching out my hand, and as the cool neck and the black foil touched my palm, we heard a man's shout" (1 [my emphasis]). He reinforces this spatialized conception of time—time, that is, construed as spread out like the locations or positions on a two-dimensional map—by also referring to "the buzzard's perspective" from which movement of time toward the balloon event can be halted or detained: "I'm lingering in the prior moment because it was a time when other outcomes were still possible; the convergence of six figures in a flat green space has a comforting geometry from the buzzard's perspective, the knowable, limited plane of the snooker table" (2). Thus the opening of the novel entails a remarkable opposition of two different schemas of time, corresponding respectively to the A-series and B-series formulated by McTaggart. In the first schema, time is construed as an inexorable temporal flow whose constituent moments continually move from future to present to past. But in the second schema, time is construed as a static manifold whose moments are arrayed in unchanging order, like points on the longitudinal-latitudinal grid of a map.

The image of a time map that Joe invokes corresponds precisely to the figure frequently used by philosophers of time to describe the B-series. Just as, to interpolate the phrasing of D. H. Mellor, "the space of maps [identifies] places without reference to spatial present (*here*)," so the B-series identifies temporal place or position without reference to a temporal present (*now*) or to the other two tenses, past and future (1993, 48). Moreover, just as on a map all points are displayed simultaneously at different locations on the same extended space, regardless of when or from what point of view the map is looked at, so in the B-series, as Delmas Kiernan-Lewis observes, "all temporal items are stretched out in a tenseless array," a continuity of succession whose elements are ordered according to the unchanging relations of prior to, simultaneous with, or subsequent to each other (1994, 322). That is, instead of locating moments in terms of ever-changing position in tensed time, the B-series construes moments, as Oaklander indicates, as arranged "tenselessly in the network of earlier than, later than, and simultaneity temporal relations" that never change (1994d, 345). This term, "tenselessly," is crucial to the construction of time pertinent to the B-series, for, in this context, time is not formulated as a movement in which the relation of a given moment to the transient properties of futurity, presentness, and pastness inevitably changes. Instead, in the construction of time pertinent to the B-series, as Oaklander notes, "the world is intrinsically tenseless, in that events and things are not in themselves past, present, or future," anymore than any given point on a map is intrinsically "here" or "there" when no one is looking at it (1994a, 58). Clifford Williams clarifies: "We do not think of hereness as a mind-independent property of objects in addition to their being in the proximity of the places we occupy or in addition to their locations" (1994, 363). In this dispensation, as Quentin Smith indicates, "events are not really future, present, or past; they merely sustain unchanging relations to each other of simultaneity, earlier than, or later than, such that the obtaining of these relations is describable in a tenseless language" (1994, 38). Most crucially, the future does not exist in its own right, as a tense with its own special properties. Instead, as Adolf Grunbaum explains, "To be future at time t_0 just means to be later than t_0, which is a tenseless relation" (1971, 206).

The novel opposes contrary constructions of time. In one, temporal awareness is threatened by futurity—the inexorable approach of consequences that cannot be forestalled: "fear of outcomes" (43). In the other, temporal awareness achieves the bird's-eye perspective from which, properly speaking, there are no tenses—no present, future, or past. Instead, there is simply a permanent sequence or succession of moments and events comprising "the time map" (1). These contrary constructions of time are linked with the image of the river that Joe, in the company of Logan's two children, contemplates at the end of the novel—the end, more precisely, of his narration that, in turn, is followed by the Appendix. Here, Joe invites the children first to think of the river as comprising an indefinite number of water molecules ("Two atoms of hydrogen, one of oxygen atoms") and then to think of the river as constituting an elongated container along which those innumerable water molecules flow toward the sea: "think of the river bed as a long shallow slide, like a winding muddy chute, that's a hundred miles long stretching to the sea" (225). The river image combines both A- and B-time. If we construe the river in terms of the continuous flux of water it contains, we retrieve an archetypal symbol of A-time—time, that is, construed as the continuous passage, from some perspective in the present, of events or moments (corresponding to water molecules) from the future to the to the past. Stephen Dedalus in James Joyce's *Ulysses* epitomizes this construction: "Hold to the now, the here, through which all future plunges to the past" (1992, 238). Scott Fitzgerald's *The Great Gatsby* (1925) offers a variant: "So we beat on, boats against the current, borne ceaselessly back into the past" (2012, 147). But if, following Joe's suggestion, we construe the river as an elongated, sloped container or "chute," whose topographical contours can be rendered as fixed points on a map, we reach a symbol of B-time—time, that is, formulated as a static order of succession whose terms or moments remain in fixed relation to each other, with respect to precedence and simultaneity. Mellor clarifies: "[T]enseless facts, unlike tensed ones, are facts at all dates" (1993, 56).

The opposition of A-time and B-time—or time as continuous transition of tense versus time as unalterable succession of moments, ordered according to the permanent relations of before and after—is central to *Enduring Love*. At the core of this opposition is the relation of the will to time. As we have seen, Joe's vivid sense of the passage of time hampers his will by making him reluctant to exercise choice, lest that election unleash consequences rendering the future even more ominous than it seems. But the bird's-eye perspective that perceives "the time map" is disengaged from the passage of time, if by passage we mean awareness of time in terms of transition of tenses or, more intimately, in terms of what

Clifford Williams, in a description of *A*-time, calls "the sense of being swept along against our wills," the feeling "of being taken to later times, and when we get to them, [feeling] ourselves taken to still later ones" (1994, 364). The bird's-eye perspective of "the time map" corresponds to the view of time constructed or formulated by philosophers of *B*-time (known professionally as *B*-theorists). From this viewpoint, no tense is real, in the sense of being mind-independent or unrelated to the point of view considering it. In this formulation, time is neither a flow nor a force, but simply a *B*-series whose direction, as Oaklander indicates, "is based on the unanalysable [or irreducible] temporal relation of succession" (1994c, 196).

As we have seen, this notion of a *B*-series based on the temporal relation of succession and not on transition of tenses emerges prominently in the novel in connection with "the time map" on the first page of Joe's narration and the riverbed on the last page. The third and culminating representation of *B*-time concerns the case history in the Appendix, which both reduces Joe's narration to a mere sequence or succession of events *and* extends that sequence beyond events included in Joe's own account. In the context of the first two representations of time as a *B*-series, the ultimate implication of the case history is perhaps that the perspective on time that Joe expressed in his narration (the perspective, that is, construing time in terms of the fearful progression of the present into the future) has been superceded by another that accepts inevitable succession and no longer either dreads or attempts to forestall it. Ultimately, this acceptance of inevitable succession constitutes the tragic perspective—or gives us a new way of understanding the tragic perspective. Catastrophe occurs. It is a fact of life. Its consequence can be either deepened immersion in the sense of *A*-time, with emphasis on dread of the future and regret or guilt concerning the past, or emancipation from preoccupation with tense, and heightened engagement with the inevitable succession by which events follow one another. This engagement with succession overcomes negative "intentionality" whereby, according to Joe, the will "tries to assert control over the future," and fosters positive intentionality whereby the goal or end of the will is to facilitate adaptation to emergent circumstance, not to resist the arrival of that which cannot be controlled (43). Ironically, after internment in an insane asylum, Parry parodies the liberation of the will enabled by positive intentionality: "I feel more purpose than I've ever known in my life. I've never felt so free" (245). But this is a bogus freedom. The first principle of genuine freedom is determination of purpose or end. But Parry's purpose—reunion with Joe—is the product of his "well-encapsulated delusional system" (238). Hence, it is not purpose but delusion. Thus Parry's freedom is freedom from freedom—exemption, that is, from the task of determining purpose and choosing the means to achieve or fulfill it. In Parry's predicament, the passage of time serves only to perpetuate the same delusion—in this case, the fantasy that Parry's reunion with Joe will be synchronized with Joe's own religious conversion: "Now you know that every day I spend here brings you one tiny step closer to that glorious light" (344–45). Ironically, of course, the conversion that Joe undergoes concerns not religion, but self-determination: recognition, that is, of the responsibility to exercise the will in the task of enacting choices in life and accepting the consequences as the ground and foundation of new decisions that will be enabled or required successively, as time unfolds.

8

Further Perspectives: Explication of Gilles Deleuze's Temporal Theory

The preceding chapters have probed the confrontations with time respectively represented in the texts treated, isolating in each case both the prevailing construction of temporality and the means, when available, of either transcending or achieving accommodation to it. Yet just as time comprises multiple moments, so the ways of investigating resistance to time are numerous and diverse. For this reason, as noted in the Introduction, I adopt a tomographic method of analysis, focusing on selected texts from different angles and at varying depths, in order to achieve a more complete and penetrating understanding of them. Having examined, through close reading, the texts from within—that is, in terms of the unfolding of their own intrinsic content, sometimes in conjunction with various philosophies of time—I shift now to an external perspective, and examine the texts from the point of view of principles enunciated in the philosophy of Gilles Deleuze (1925–1995). The Deleuzian construction of time, borrowing conspicuously from Kant, Husserl, and Bergson, offers a challenging, illuminating, and bracingly controversial account of how temporal awareness is constituted. Readers not interested in the intricacies of philosophical theory might omit this chapter and the next. Yet for those intrigued by innovative philosophical inquiry into the constitution of time and favorably disposed to its application to literary texts, as a supplement to the independent and detailed analysis earlier presented, the section on Deleuze affords an opportunity to gain fresh insights into the subject under examination.

In the common-sense view, time subsists apart from experience. That is, experience and time are parallel but separate versions of continuity. Experience unfolds, and its unfolding occupies a certain interval in the movement of time. Hence, the continuity of time is the means by which the duration of an experience can be measured and by which its location in the past, present, or future can be determined. Even when experience concerns temporality—that is, even when the focus of experiential awareness concerns temporal passage—the same assumption regarding the distinctness of time from experience applies. For here experience is on one side and its object, in this case the movement of time, is on the other. In contrast, the Kantian view of time, briefly summarized at the outset of the chapter on the Beckettian mimesis of time, construes time not as subsistent apart from experience, but as a *sine qua non* of experience—a structuring form necessary to the very possibility of experience. To understand this function of time and the transcendental construction of experience to which it pertains, further discussion of Kant's philosophy will be indispensable, and will also prepare the foundation for fruitful application of the temporal philosophy of Gilles Deleuze.

At the root of Kant's philosophy is what he terms a Copernican Revolution, reversing the relation between knowing subject and known object. In classical or "pre-Copernican" philosophy, the site of reality is in the object outside the mind contemplating it. In knowing, the mind is, in Germain Grisez's phrase, "a recipient of objective reality" (1969, 350). Sir Francis Bacon epitomizes this doctrine of classical epistemology: "[T]he truth of being, and the truth of knowing are one, differing no more than the direct beame, and the beame reflected" (1951, 65). Michael Delanda concurs: "[I]n some realist approaches the world is thought to be composed of fully formed objects whose identity is guaranteed by the possession of an *essence*, a core set of properties that defines what these objects are" (2002, 2–3 [original emphasis]). Yet, whereas in the classical schema the mind, in knowing, conforms to its object (by achieving in itself the concept of what the object actually is), in the Kantian system the object, to be known, must conform to the mind or, more precisely, to its mode of cognition. That is, in order to be knowable, the object must be adapted to what Sebastian Gardner terms "the cognitive constitution of the subject" (1999, 45). Things-in-themselves, as they are apart from our efforts at cognition, cannot become objects of experience. Thus, in Kantian epistemology, Andrew's advice to his mother in *To the Lighthouse* does not apply: "'Think of a kitchen table then,' he told her, 'when you're not there'" (Woolf 1927, 28). Instead, that which we actually experience or, more formally, admit to cognitive awareness must first be conditioned by the mind to constitute a systematic unity appropriate to our way of cognition. The structuring operations by which the mind imposes order and coherence on the manifold of empirical awareness—awareness, that is, of sensory contact with the external world—are a priori. For they *precede* actual experience, and provide the conditions under which experience or cognitive apprehension is possible. Kant employs the term, "transcendental," to indicate the means by which the mind conditions objects into intelligibility, and hence renders them accessible to experience or cognitive apprehension: "the word 'transcendental' ... does not signify something passing beyond all experience but something that indeed precedes it *a priori*, but that is intended simply to make knowledge of experience possible" (1950, 122, n. 2). Without such transcendental structuring, experience itself would be impossible, for awareness would confront what Keith Faulkner terms an "indefinite diversity" whose manifold disorder would not enable awareness to "form impressions" (2006, 15). Ernst Cassirer confirms: "The structureless could not only not be thought, it could not even become objectively seen, or an object of awareness" (1961, 65). If experience were purely empirical—if it were, that is, entirely the result and registration of disordered sensations pouring into awareness—there could be no experience at all, no coherent apprehension. In the Kantian schema, as Levi R. Bryant indicates, "Experience contains the imperative of organization" (2008, 163). Experience is not simply an indeterminate flow of awareness—"[a] mere stream, so to speak, of unconnected representations" (Copleston 1966, 6.2.47) or "a rhapsody of perceptions" (Cassirer 1981, 169). It is a cognitive activity—what Kant terms a "mode of knowing things"— and as such presupposes a priori rules of order and coherence that interrelate and combine disparate elements (1950, 99). Hence, as Father Copleston notes, "Without connection there is no experience" (1966, 6.2.49).

In the Kantian model, the production of experience involves several stages. The first step concerns the impingement of the unknowable thing in itself on the sensibility of the subject. Kant clarifies: "The effect of an object upon the faculty of representation, so far as we are affected by an object, is sensation (*Empfindung*)" (*Critique of Pure Reason*, qtd. by Copleston 1966, 6.2.31). The capacity to have sensations or, more formally, to receive representations of objects, is termed sensibility, and its defining function is sense intuition or sensuous perception. According to Kant, the external things that provoke or stimulate these representations remain unknowable in themselves, and are cognized only through "their appearances, which are mere representations of the sensibility" (1950, 36). Thus the representations provided by sensibility or "sensuous perception" pertain to "things not at all as they are, but only the mode in which they affect our senses" (1950, 38). As we have seen, if human awareness contained only the unstructured representations of sensibility—what Bryant terms "the interminable discourse of the senses"—there could be no experience, no cognitive registration of the external world, just the "rhapsody of irrational flux" (2008, 36). Experience requires coherence—something that mere sensibility cannot supply.

We reach here the core of Kant's transcendental epistemology: the notion that experience presupposes a priori principles of structure, ordering the data of sensibility into intelligibility. Content requires form, and that form must be supplied by the mind before it can achieve cognition of its own content. Without form, experience would remain an incoherent chaos to which the cognitive awareness of the subject could have no access. Sebastian Gardner provides a superb gloss on this paradox: "Kant's striking idea is that experience cannot be 'all content': however minimal and atomised it may be, it must have form, because a subject can only be cognitively conscious of its experience *as* something if it is organized in some way. Experience that had no form would be a mere buzzing confusion, and a subject of such experience would be cognitively unconscious of it; form is the unifying structure that allows the content of experience to show itself as such" (1999, 72). The requirement that experiential content has form brings us to the second step in the Kantian model of experience: the Forms of Sensibility or sensuous perception—namely, space and time. According to Kant, sensation itself, as the empirical matter or data of awareness, is subjected by the mind to a priori structuring that determines, in Gardner's phrasing, "the shape that sensation has in so far as it provides a content for thought" (1999, 72). This shape or form organizes the content of sensuous perception into what Gardner terms a "structure of relations" (1999, 72), *before* the mind becomes aware of that content. Copleston elaborates: "The ordering is a condition of awareness or consciousness, not a consequence of it" (1966, 6.2.33). As Forms of Sensibility, space and time respectively order the components of the sense experience in terms of juxtaposition (beside-one-another) and succession (after-or-before-one-another). Thus space and time have *transcendental*, but not *transcendent* reality. That is, though there can be no empirical reality (no reality registered through sensory perception) without them, they themselves have no reality except as "framework" principles by which "the manifold of sensation is ordered and arranged" (Copleston 1966, 6.2.33).

Whereas the sensory stage in the production of experience is *passive*, with the mind receiving impressions ordered a priori by the Forms of Sensibility, the next stage—understanding—is *active*. As Joe W. Hughes indicates, Kant calls the understanding an " 'active faculty', even though its only activity consists in representing reality as a unity" (2008, 21). Here, as Gardner has stated, the mind "produces concepts and applies them to objects" (1999, 67). According to Kant, these "concepts ... have their origin wholly *a priori* in the pure understanding, and ... every perception must first of all be subsumed [under them] and then by their means *changed into experience* (1950, 45 [my emphasis]). Experience is thus the "product of the sense and of the understanding" (Kant 1950, 47). At stake here is the production of *objective* experience—the experience of objects. But, as Gardner notes, "Experience of objects is possible only through the *concept of an object*" (1999, 151 [original emphasis]), and this concept is precisely that which (among others) the understanding provides, through orderly synthesis of the incoherent data of sense intuition. Without such synthesis or unification, the content of sensory perception would remain an inconstant flux of flickering and unstable intensities, increasing and diminishing according to no intelligible pattern or principle. Cognitively speaking, the function of objects is to be known. But nothing can be known as an object apart from the operation of the understanding, which imposes its organizing concepts a priori on the data of sensory perception. Copleston clarifies: "[O]bjects, to be objects (that is, to be known), must be subjected to the *a priori* concepts or categories of the human understanding, of which causality is one" (1966, 6.2.23). This stricture concerns what Frederick Beiser terms the "Kantian insistence that it is not possible to separate what appears in perception from the conditions of its appearance" (2005, 171). As Robert C. Solomon explains, these "conditions that make our experience possible ... *precede* every particular experience and so, in Kant's terms, are *a priori*—literally, 'before'" (1983, 73). Consider this example: the wind blows the leaves of a tree, causing them to flutter. This experience is not given by the data of sense intuition or perception. On the level of sensibility, it simply does not occur. However, once the understanding has organized the data of sense intuition according to such categories as substance, causality and dependence (cause and effect), community (reciprocity between agent and patient), and inherence and subsistence (part and whole), then and only then can the experience of the wind-blown tree be constituted.

A further example will clarify the requirement, just quoted, that "objects, to be objects (that is, to be known), must be subjected to the *a priori* concepts or categories of the human understanding." At one point in Flann O'Brien's *The Third Policeman*, the anonymous narrator perceives unintelligible objects in an underground chamber, and remains utterly baffled by them, because "[t]hey lacked an essential property of all known objects" (1967, 136). After considerable difficulty identifying the missing property, he finally determines that it concerns dimensionality: "I can only say that these objects, not one of which resembled the other, were of no known dimensions" (1967, 136). This situation is precisely that which could never occur in the Kantian dispensation. In this case, the Kantian concept missing appears to concern *magnitude*. All objects, to be known as objects, must have magnitude or, more precisely, be cognizable in terms of it. Unlike O'Brien's narrator, the Kantian mind cannot, in principle, be confronted with an object that does not conform to the mind's way of knowing or conceiving objects, because the object owes its very existence as object (that is, as an appearance structured by the cognitive function of the understanding) to the transcendental activity of the mind confronting it—an activity that, as Ivan Soll emphasizes, functions uniformly in each individual: "*every* human consciousness must experience according to the same basic conceptual scheme" (1969, 91 [original emphasis]). Thus, as Klaus Brinkmann indicates, in the Kantian system, "[s]ubjectivity becomes the source of objectivity within the immanence of experience, because it provides a universal and normative interpretive framework from within itself" (2005, 39). Our awareness of objects relies on our concepts of them. It follows, therefore, as Robert B. Pippin indicates, that "since the phenomenal world was 'conditioned' by our conceptual scheme, had we a different scheme, there would be a different (phenomenal) world; hence the thing-in-itself problem" (1989, 277, n. 1).

To grasp the Kantian theory of transcendental structuring of the content of experience, it is crucial to recognize that the knowing subject does not undertake this activity "deliberately, consciously, and of set purpose" (Copleston 1966, 6.2.21). Instead, as Wilhelm Windelband observes, "the consciousness of the individual knows nothing of this co-operation of the categories in experience," for the organizing of sensory content into conceptual form "does not go on in the individual consciousness, but lies already at the basis of this consciousness" and entails a principle of awareness that Kant terms the *transcendental unity of apperception* (1958, 2.545). According to Rex Welshon, "Kant's argument for the necessity of transcendental unity of apperception is one of the most famous passages in philosophy" (2004, 86). Let us briefly review what issues are at stake. In the Kantian system, the very possibility of experience presupposes relation to a subject aware of that experience, as Raymond Martin and John Barresi indicate: "There can be no experience which is not the experience of a subject" (2003, 61). Hence, the situation adduced by Mrs. Gradgrind in *Hard Times*, where a sensation exists without connection to its own subject, could not obtain: "I think there's a pain somewhere in the room ... but I couldn't positively say that I have got it" (Dickens 1969, 224). The term, "apperception," refers to the reflexive act by which the mind registers its own activity. James van Cleve clarifies: "[A]pperception is an act of consciousness that apprehends one or more of the subject's own perceptive states" (1999, 80). For example, if, when thinking, I direct my attention to the fact that I am thinking, I am thereby engaged in an act of apperception. Apperception is a second-order act of perception whose object is a first-order act of perception (such as thinking or feeling something). As Pippin indicates, "consciousness of objects is implicitly reflexive because, according to Kant, whenever I am conscious of any object, I can also be said to 'apperceive' implicitly my being *thus* conscious" (1989, 21). Mrs. Gradgrind is incapable of such apperception, since, when she feels something, she cannot relate herself to that feeling through awareness of her awareness of it. The most spectacular example in literature regarding lack of apperception occurs in Samuel Beckett's oeuvre, where a narrator suffers estrangement from his own words, which he hears and repeats as if reciting those of another: "I say it as I hear it" (1967a, 97); "only a voice dreaming and droning on all round, that is something, the voice that was once in your mouth" (1974c, 49).

Kant distinguishes between two kinds of apperception: empirical and transcendental. In empirical apperception, the mind attends to its own states (thinking, feeling, etc.), as each occurs, but without any means of establishing its own consistency across these serial acts of attention: "[T]he empirical consciousness, which accompanies different representations, is in itself diverse and without relation to the identity of the subject" (1933, A133). Each representation or, more loosely, experiential event of which empirical apperception is aware of being aware is different, with the result that "No fixed and abiding self can present itself in this flux of inner appearances" (Kant 1933, A107). Copleston elaborates: "The empirical consciousness, like the representations which it accompanies, is disunited" (1966, 6.2.49). Perhaps the most famous example in literature of the diversity and disunity of the empirical consciousness concerns Hamlet's fluctuation between normalcy and (concocted) madness or, in alternate formulation, between rage and remorse for outrageous behavior: "If Hamlet from himself be ta'en away, / And when he's not himself does wrong Laertes, / Then Hamlet does it not, Hamlet denies it. / Who does it then? His madness" (5.2.226–33).

Experience, as we have seen, requires a subject whose experience it is—a subject who knows, as William H. Bossart indicates, "that the representations in question are [his or her] representations" (1994, 13). But experience changes continuously. Hence, if there is to be experience, it must be continuously related to a subject that remains unchanging throughout all the changes of that which is experienced. Copleston elaborates: "No objective experience, no knowledge of objects, is possible unless the manifold of intuition is connected in one self-consciousness" (1966, 6.2.49). The empirical subject—the subject that I am aware of when I am experiencing—cannot satisfy this condition because, as Gardner explicates, it is "as many-coloured and diverse a self as I have representations of which I am conscious" (Gardner 1999, 147, quoting Kant 1933, B 134). To be possible, experience requires an "invariant" a priori subject that, through apperception, "can *represent itself as identical* in relation to all the representations comprising its experience" (Gardiner 1999, 147 [original emphasis]), and thereby sustain, as van Cleve indicates, their "cognitive togetherness" (1999, 81). This invariant subject is the transcendental unity of apperception—what Welshon describes as "that in virtue of which a continuous sequence of conscious psychological events is unified as *my* sequence of psychological events" (2004, 87). As Welshon further notes, without this transcendental unity of apperception, "nobody would have unified experience of anything" (2004, 87). Moreover, without such apperception, no subject could distinguish itself from its representations, with the result that, according to Kant, "all relation of knowledge to objects would fall away" (1933, A111). What remained would not be experience properly speaking (which requires separation of knowing subject from known object), but a kind of phantasmagoric trance, for, as Gardner observes, "A subject merged into its representations would be unable to think of itself as having representations, and for that reason, though it might be said to have consciousness of some sort, could not be self-conscious" (1999, 158).

Such, of course, is the predicament of Beckett's Unnamable, who is merged with the words he hears, unable to distinguish his own subjectivity (or intactness as a subject) from the representations (in this case, sounds) of which he is aware: "I'm in words, made of words" (1958d, 386). Lacking transcendental apperception, his only means of separating himself from his representations is to construe himself as a reified consciousness, forever aware of its own lack of self-awareness and thus forever seeking its own identity: "I'm something quite different, a quite different thing, *a wordless thing in an empty place*, a hard shut dry cold black place, where nothing stirs, nothing speaks, and that I listen, and that I seek" (1958d, 386 [my emphasis]). Yet this is precisely the opposite of the transcendental unity of apperception, which is not a thing-in-itself, a simple substance, but only the means by which the contents of awareness are related to each other and to the subject to which they commonly pertain. As Gardner indicates, the transcendental unity of apperception "consists in a merely *formal* unity that does not amount to knowledge of any object"—a unity or, in Cassirer's phrasing, "identical functions of unification" through which all my representations are related both to me as their subject and to each other in the manifold of my cognitive awareness (Gardner 1999, 147 [original emphasis]; Cassirer 1991, 195). In other words, to invoke Cassirer again, the transcendental unity of apperception is construed as a principle of relation, not as thing-in-itself independent of relations: "The 'I,' the 'transcendental apperception,' is permanent and unchangeable, but it is only an invariable relation *between* the contents of consciousness, not the unvarying substratum *from* which they arise. It is simple and undivided, but this is only so relative to the synthetic act of unification of the manifold, which as such can either be thought only totally and completely or else not thought at all" (1991, 201).

As the unvarying activity that relates all the contents of consciousness to the same center of awareness, transcendental unity of apperception is the fundamental self-consciousness, underpinning all that of which the subject is conscious. As such, it constitutes what Gardner (quoting Kant) terms "a 'pure original unchangeable consciousness' of self" (Gardner 1999, 147, quoting Kant 1933, A107). But according to Kant, this "consciousness of self is ... very far from being a knowledge of the self" (1933, B158). For, as Gardner explains, all it concerns is "awareness of myself as the source of the synthetic unity of objects" (1999, 158). In the Kantian system, to know the self in itself—the self in terms of its spontaneity or as the principle of its own activity—is impossible. The explanation for this impossibility lies in the Kantian epistemology, summarized earlier: "The understanding ... does not *find* some sort of combination of the manifold already in inner sense, but *produces* it, by *affecting* inner sense" (Kant 1933, B155). By attempting to know my self through awareness of its activity, I necessarily subject the contents of my inner sense to the categories of the understanding, and thereby produce an *appearance*, with the result that the I or self thus known is not my self "in accordance with what it is in itself," but only I "as I appear to myself" (Kant 1933, B156). Bryant elaborates: "The Kantian self, in and of itself, does not present itself as an object to be cognized, but instead must be 'produced' or results from synthesis" (2008, 180). Thus, through empirical apperception—awareness of my states or my activity—I know myself not as a spontaneous being, but only as a what Faulkner terms a "self-representation"—a product, that is, of the mind's cognitive process that orders the content of the inner sense into appearances (2006, 169). Kant epitomizes this predicament: "I cannot determine my existence as that of a self-active being; all that I can do is to represent to myself the spontaneity of my thought, that is, of the determination: and my existence is still only determinable sensibly, that is, as the existence of an appearance" (1933, footnote (a) to B158). The Kantian self is estranged from its own spontaneity by the very act of apperceiving it, in the course of experience. Bryant clarifies: "Rather than being immediate to itself, rather than being its own *spontaneity*, the self can only *represent* itself as spontaneous or as the origin of its own thoughts" (2008, 179 [original emphasis]).

This intractable discrepancy between the transcendental and empirical selves—between the self as the self-active and spontaneous "origin of its own thoughts" and the self as what Bryant terms "a representation to itself," that which "is mediated with respect to itself" (2008, 190)—is described by Deleuze, in a famous passage, as an irremediable "fissure or a crack in the pure Self of the 'I think,' an alienation in principle, insurmountable in principle: the subject can henceforth represent its own spontaneity only as that of an Other" (1994, 58). Deleuze labels this fissured or cracked self the "fractured I" (1994, 87). According to Deleuze, the notorious split in the Kantian self is based on time: "It is as though the I were fractured from one end to the other: fractured by the pure and empty form of time" (1994, 86). The empirical self—the self of which I become aware by reflecting on myself—is implicated in time, because, as we have seen, it is an appearance in the inner sense, and the organizing Form of the inner sense, as we have also seen, is time. Bryant confirms: "Just as all appearances must occur in time, so too must the self's appearance to itself transpire or unfold in time" (2008, 179). Kant formulates the matter with concise thoroughness: "Hence we must order the determinations of inner sense as appearances in time in just the same way as we order those of outer sense in space; hence if we admit that by the latter [outer sense] we cognize objects by means only insofar as we are externally affected, then we must also concede that through the inner sense we intuit ourselves only as we are internally affected *by our selves*, i.e. as far as inner intuition is concerned we cognize our own subject only as appearance but not in accordance with what it is in itself" (1933, B155–56).

This epistemological dispensation whereby, to requote Kant, "we cognize our own subject only as appearance but not in accordance with what it is in itself," leads Deleuze to transpose the site of identity from the transcendental self to the empirical one, which is the only self accessible to self-knowledge. But unlike the transcendental self whose inaccessible identity precedes experience and functions as the unifying condition making experience possible, the empirical self, in Deleuze's construction, continually undergoes elaboration of its identity. As a result of the crack in Kantian selfhood, separating the self as it is from the self as it appears, the subject knows itself only through its unfolding in time. For time is the Form through which appearances appear. Bryant clarifies: "Where the subject is fissured by time, where it can only experience its thoughts *within* time, the subject discovers itself as something undergoing actualization and individuation in time" (2008, 219 [original emphasis]). Perhaps the most vivid expression in literature of "the subject fissured by time" occurs in *Ulysses*, when Stephen Dedalus beholds his reflection in Buck Mulligan's "cracked looking-glass": "Stephen bent forward and peered at the mirror held out to him, cleft by a crooked crack, hair on end" (Joyce 1960, 6, 5). Yet here the fissured self signifies not the intractable dichotomy between the transcendental and empirical selves, but the "convulsions of metamorphosis" that, for both Stephen and Bloom, separate the present self from its past instantiations: "I am another now and yet the same"; "I was happier then. Or was that I? Or am I now I?" (Joyce 1960, 817, 12, 213). As we shall see later, Deleuze's construction of time does include one feature called the caesura that in some ways corresponds to the fissure in the self caused in *Ulysses* by metempsychosis. But Deleuze's notion of the "fractured I," just summarized, concerns not radical metamorphoses suffered in the course of the temporal development of selfhood, but radical discrepancy between antithetical constructions of selfhood—empirical and transcendental—such that one (empirical) undergoes what Bryant terms "the perpetual unfolding of itself" in time, while the other (transcendental) exists extra-temporally (2008, 219). Thus the halves of the fractured Kantian self are respectively in and out of time.

The philosophy of time propounded by Deleuze can offer an additional perspective from which to pursue our investigation of the literary representation of time. Whereas Kant construes time as an a priori Form of Sensibility, which conditions the data of sense such that they are registered in terms of permanence, succession, and simultaneity, Deleuze seeks to account for the procedure by which temporality is constituted a priori. That is, instead of construing time, with Kant, as a ready-made transcendental framework that conditions all that can be sensed *before* it passes into sensory awareness, Deleuze undertakes to clarify what Bryant terms "the actual production of the given"—to show, in other words, the transcendental steps by which the sensory manifold is conditioned into temporality by the awareness that confronts it (2008, 41).

In addition to connection with Kant, Deleuze's philosophy of time is also heavily dependent on the temporal theories of Edmund Husserl and Henri Bergson. Deleuze begins his analysis with the living present—a concept formulated by Husserl to designate the "standing, streaming" nature of "now" consciousness, through which, as Dermot Moran indicates, "one experience melds or comes into concordance with the next" (2005, 219). Florence M. Hetzler and Austin H. Kutscher elaborate: "This 'being here,' this 'presence' which is both perduring and flowing is the origin of the stream of lived mental experience *and* that stream" (1978, 119). According to Deleuze, "It is in this present that time is deployed" (1994, 70). Joe Hughes clarifies: "This living present is not time as such, but the general element in which time itself will unfold or spread out across" its other temporal dimensions. (2008, 131).

The first step in understanding the Deleuzian construction of the living present is to recognize that it does not construe time as the mere succession of instants. Instants are abstract, not empirical, entities; that is, they have their being as non-extensive temporal elements devised by the mind, not as data given in sense experience. Moreover, the function of each instant is to elapse in an instant. Thus, according to Deleuze, if time were constituted by instants, it would begin and end with each instant: "A succession of instants does not constitute time any more than it causes it to disappear; it indicates only its constantly aborted moment of birth" (1994, 70). Turetzky elaborates: "Were that [i.e., the succession of instants] the case, time would begin to arise at each instant only to fail to continue one instant into another" (1998, 212). (As we shall discuss later, this exactly the kind of time measured by Mr. Gradgrind's clock in *Hard Times*). The attempt to construct time as a series of instants encounters a further problem. As uniform temporal elements, instants lack differences from each other, with the result that transition from one instant to the next remains imperceptible, thus obviating the passage of time. Bryant clarifies: "So long as we conceive time as a passing of instants, then we are condemned to an eternal present in which no instant is different from any other" (2008, 109). Yet another problem confronts the notion of time as a series of instants. In order for time to pass from one instant to the next, there must be some principle of connection between successive instants. Otherwise, as soon as a current moment is displaced by the next, that new moment is cut off from its predecessor, and time is reduced to just that current moment. In this situation, time cannot move, but remains always at one instant or another. For Bergson, the principle of connection is memory—not conscious memory, but what Hughes terms "an impersonal or non-'anthropomorphic' consciousness [inserted] between the successive instants" (2008, 131). Bergson elaborates: "Without an elementary memory that connects the two moments, there will only be the one or the other, consequently a single instant, no before, no after, no succession, no time. We can bestow on this memory just what is needed to make the connection; it will be, if we like, this very connection, a mere continuing of the before into the immediate after with a perpetually renewed forgetfulness of what is not the immediately prior moment" (1965, 48).

Thus, the conventional construction of time as a succession of instants is challenged by three factors: instantaneous elapse of each instant, lack of differentiation between instants, and lack of continuity between instants. To overcome these difficulties, Deleuze founds the construction of the living present on what is termed the first passive synthesis ("first" because, as we shall see, his construction of the living present involves three passive syntheses and one active one). The first step in understanding the first passive synthesis is to clarify the meaning of "passive" and "synthesis." By "passive," Deleuze refers to a transcendental structuring operation that "is not carried out by the mind, but occurs *in* the mind which contemplates, prior to all memory and all reflection" (1994, 71). Bryant elaborates: "As such, the first passive synthesis is not an activity of intentional consciousness, but precedes any intentionality and renders intentionality possible in the first place" (2008, 89). By "synthesis," Deleuze signifies the gathering together or *contracting* of diverse elements into a unity of awareness. In this case, the diverse elements concern repeated instants—instants, that is, not as units of time (for time is not yet constituted), but as "excitations" (1994, 96) or "intensities" (1994, 50), at the most basic stratum of sensibility, before awareness has developed into self-awareness or even into subjectivity as such—indeed before it is anything more than rudimentary sensory registration that senses stimuli in terms of what Adrian Parr labels "affective magnitudes" (2008, 154). According to Hughes, these affective magnitudes or intensities refer to "the degree to which a body is affected in the instant" (2008, 145), for, as Bryant points out, "the defining feature of intensity is its property of increase and diminution" (2008, 246).

At this level of sensibility, sensory perception is no more than the registration of instants of affective magnitude. Deleuze terms such centers of sensory perception "contemplative souls" or minds, and populates each organism with myriads of them: "Underneath the self which acts are little selves which contemplate and which render possible both the action and the active subject. We speak of our 'self' only in virtue of these thousands of little witnesses which contemplate within us: it is always a third party who says 'me'. These contemplative souls must be assigned even to the rat in the labyrinth and to each muscle of the rat" (1994, 75).[1] The sole function of these "contemplative souls" or centers of rudimentary awareness is to contract or gather together instants, uniting them in what Deleuze terms a passive synthesis. Hughes elaborates: "These contemplative souls, like Bergson's nonanthropomorphic memory, are nothing more than the connection they bring about or the instants they contract" (2008, 131). According to Deleuze, the contraction or connection of repeated instants constitutes "the *fusion* of that repetition in the contemplating mind" (1994, 74). Each contemplative soul is limited by what Deleuze terms its "natural contractile range," determining the number of repetitions it can connect or gather together, before succumbing to fatigue (1994, 77). That which is grasped within this contractile range constitutes the living present of the contemplative soul concerned. Since an organism comprises numerous contemplative souls, pertaining respectively, for example to "the heart, to the muscles, nerves and cells," as well as to the primary or supervenient mind, "[t]he duration of an organism's present, or of its various presents, will vary according to the natural contractile range of its contemplative souls" (1994, 74, 77).

To illustrate this idea of passive synthesis, whereby disconnected instants are contracted or fused into a living present, which then constitutes the foundation of the experience of time, Deleuze provides the example of a ticking clock. Though the example is perhaps unfortunate in presuming the very notion of time whose process of constitution it seeks to illustrate, the paradigm of the ticking clock has the advantages of simplicity and familiarity. To understand it, we must first note that any passage of instants is governed by what Deleuze terms "[t]he rule of discontinuity or instantaneity in repetition," such that no instant can arise before its predecessor has expired" (1994, 70). If there were no contraction or gathering together of ticks and tocks in the sentient mind, there would be no connection between the different instants they concern. To hear one tock or tick would be to be oblivious to any earlier tock or tick and without expectation of any impending ones. In other words, without contraction, there can be no continuity of instants, only perpetual location in one instant, whichever it is. Bryant expands: "[T]ime would appear like a mass of unconnected instants in which no instant would ever seem to pass at all because I would always find myself in just this instant" (2008, 108). But with the contraction proper to the first passive synthesis, instants are no longer *un*connected, but *inter*connected according to what Bryant terms "relations of before and after," as a result of a nexus of retentions and expectations (2008, 87). That is, preceding moments are retained in the present moment as its past, and succeeding moments are expected in the present moment as its future. With respect to the ticking clock, for example, the first passive synthesis operates on the repetition of instants such that the present "tick" is connected through retention with the past "tock" and with the future "tick" through expectation. Thus the living present contains what Jay Lampert terms "temporally different parts; it 'retains' past instants, and 'anticipates' future instants. Past and future instants have status as backward and forward referents of the present" (2006, 15). In the context of the living present, past and future are dimensions of an extended present, not independent tenses on their own. Deleuze clarifies: "The past and the future do not designate instants distinct from a supposed present instant, but rather the dimensions of the present itself in so far as it is a contraction of instants" (1994, 70). Turetzky elaborates: "These past and future moments combine as dimensions of an extended or living present constituted by the contraction of moments which connects them" (2004, 145).

Though the first passive synthesis orders instants according to relations of before and after, the succession that this constitutes does not go beyond the boundaries of the living present—what Turetzky refers to as "a limited present, variable in extent" (1998, 213). As formulated in the first passive synthesis, the living present has no means of passing into the past and joining the succession of former presents preceding it—that is, the living present constituted by the first passive synthesis is not yet the present that passes. The living present *expands*, by retention and protention of instants, from a central "now" instant toward temporal boundaries, before and after, but it does not *pass* and become a former present. Such passage requires another synthesis—what Deleuze terms the active synthesis of memory. Whereas the first passive synthesis is a priori, precedes conscious awareness, and, as Deleuze indicates, "constitutes the general possibility of any present" (1994, 81), the active synthesis of memory occurs in consciousness, not on the level of transcendental process, and represents, according to Turetzky, "[o]ur experience of time [as] a passing succession of presents" (1998, 217). Through the active synthesis of memory, the living present both remembers the present prior to itself (that is, the former present) and reflects on itself. According to Deleuze, the living present cannot remember a present prior to itself without at the same time reflecting itself; for without such combination there would be no way to constitute the distinction between the present present and the former present that it recalls. Deleuze clarifies: "The former present cannot be represented in the present without the present one being represented in that representation" (1994, 80). Bryant elaborates: "If the present, when viewed from the perspective of the active synthesis of recognition, must represent both itself and the former present, this is because it cannot represent its difference from the former present without representing itself at the same time that it represents that former present" (2008, 114–15).

As constituted by the first passive synthesis, the living present contracts instants that comprise what Turetzky terms a "line of succession," all of whose instants occupy the extended present, with some designated past (as retained particulars) and others designated future (as expected repetitions, extrapolated from the preceding series) (1998, 214). The active synthesis of memory then distinguishes the *present* living present from its predecessor (the *former* present), by referring to or recalling the former present at the same time that it reflects itself. Unlike the first passive synthesis, this active synthesis constitutes time not as the succession of instants under the condition of the present, but as the succession of former presents nested in the present or current present. Deleuze clarifies: "The passive synthesis of habit constituted time as a contraction of instants with respect to a present, but the active synthesis of memory constitutes it as the *embedding* of presents in themselves" (1994, 81). Yet though the active synthesis construes the present in terms of its relation to (and distinction from) former presents, and though, to quote Deleuze, it represents former presents "in so far as forgetting is empirically overcome," it cannot account for the passage of the present—the temporal movement, that is, in virtue of which a present or current present becomes a former or past present, conserved in memory. In Lampert's phrasing, "nothing about the present explains how it 'passes'" (2006, 33). We reach here what Bryant terms "one of the signature marks of Deleuze's concept of time" (2008, 114). In Deleuze's analysis of the passing present, as we shall see, the active synthesis of memory, which distinguishes the present present from the former present, itself presupposes a prior passive or transcendental synthesis, because the sense of pastness on which the concept of the passing present depends can be established in no other way. That is, cognition of pastness cannot be achieved empirically, but requires an a priori, transcendental synthesis (termed the second passive synthesis) that gives, as Turetzky indicates, "the active synthesis [of memory] a dimension from which it can represent this passage" of the present into the past (1998, 217). As Deleuze's notion of the second passive synthesis bristles with paradox, explication will be facilitated by beginning with an account of the conventional construction of the past that the notion both critiques and displaces.

In the conventional formulation, which Deleuze attacks, the present simply elapses, and becomes the past, yielding its position in the present to the new moment that displaces it. Lampert clarifies: "The commonsense view is that a present moment is all there is at that moment, and that time passes when a second moment comes along and takes its place, causing it to move into the past" (2006, 33). Deleuze punctures this presupposition at two crucial points. The first concerns the notion of displacement of the present moment by the new one arriving from the future. The second concerns the notion of transformation of the present moment into a past one. Regarding displacement, Deleuze problematizes the notion that the retreat of a present moment into the past is caused by the advance of a future moment into the present. Lampert provides an excellent commentary:

> Now take the hypothesis that the present is forced to pass when another present comes along and takes its place. *How* is another present supposed to

come along? If the original does not pass on first, where will the new present arrive? Is the new present supposed to push the old one out of the way? Why does a new present not add on to what is present without displacing the old? And where does the new present come from: is there a store of new presents arranged serially that click into the present position one after another, dislodging their predecessors? Neither hypothesis is plausible. A present is not going to get out of the way, and if it does not, the next will not arrive. (2006, 45)

Coincidentally, Lampert's question, "Why does a new present not add on to what is present without displacing the old?" echoes the query of Beckett's Unnamable: "the question may be asked ... why time doesn't pass ... why it piles up all about you, instant on instant, on all sides, deeper and deeper" (1958d, 389). Similarly, Lampert's remark, in a slightly later passage, concerning the theoretical "absurdities of a temporal instant that refuses to get out of the way" provides an apt gloss on the plight of the Unnamable, doomed to watch the passage of Beckettian time: "the seconds pass, one after another, jerkily, no flow, they don't pass, they arrive, bang, bang, when you have nothing left to say you talk of time, seconds of time" (Lampert 2006, 45; Beckett 1958d, 395). We shall investigate the implications of these striking correspondences later, but our concern right now is with the Deleuzian critique of the common sense view of the passage of time. As Lampert states, the key to this critique is the point that "we cannot start a theory of time with the present and expect to explain the past" (2006, 45).

Just as the notion of displacement of the old present by the arrival of the new one is thus problematized, so the notion that the present is transformed into the past encounters challenges. In the Deleuzian analysis, the past cannot be constituted *after* the present through the transformation of a present moment into a former one, because once something is no longer present nothing further can happen to it. Lampert elaborates: "The only time when a present can become past is while it exists. It cannot become past after it no longer exists; for when something does not exist, it obviously cannot do anything" (2006, 45–46). Yet Deleuze uncovers a deeper reason why the past cannot be constituted *after* the present and instead must paradoxically be *contemporaneous* with the present. It concerns the notion of self-recognition as present. From the viewpoint of empirical memory, as Bryant notes, "the past is constituted after the present in that something must first be present if it is to later be remembered" (2008, 117). But this begs the question of how the present recognizes itself as present. As Bryant notes, regarding the active synthesis of memory, "the becoming of the present only discloses itself in differentiating itself from the past" (2008, 105). In this context, the past cannot come after the present, for the present, to be aware of itself as present, needs or requires the past. Thus, the past, in relation to which the present affirms its own identity, must coexist with the present, in a temporal mode separate from that of the present. Conversely, the current present could never give way to the next present and become a former present if it were not already past when present. Deleuze expounds:

> How would a new present come about if the old present did not pass at the same time that it *is* present? How would any present whatsoever pass, if it were not past *at the same time* as present? The past would never be constituted if it *had not been* constituted first of all, at the same time that it was present. (1991, 58 [original emphasis])

The essence of the passing present is passage into the past. But, for Deleuze, this passage does not entail a transformation of the present into the past, as presumed, for example, in *To the Lighthouse* when Mrs. Ramsay, standing on the threshold of the dining room, looks back at the prandial moment just concluded: "it had become, she knew, giving one last look at it over her shoulder, already the past" (Woolf 1927, 121). As Deleuze observes, "[e]very present passes, in favour of a new present" (1994, 81). Yet this passage occurs not because every present becomes a past or former present, but because "the past is contemporaneous with the present that it was" (1994, 81). Explanation of this paradox hangs on the notion of the double aspect of the present: each present is both present and past contemporaneously. Pearson concurs: "The past is never simply 'it was' but enjoys a virtual co-existence with the present" (1999, 101). Lampert amplifies: "His theory ... is that a temporal moment does exist in the present, and that that moment is, at a certain point, past, but that it is not the fact that it was once present that explains how it becomes past. A given temporal moment is a present, and that same moment is also a past" (2006, 33). According to Deleuze, the past cannot be precipitated by the passing of the present, for the passing of the present presupposes the past as its enabling condition. More precisely, the passing of the present presupposes the possibility of distinguishing between current and former presents (through the active synthesis of empirical memory), and that possibility, as we have seen, itself presupposes the coexistence of the past with the present, otherwise the present, which contains only that which is present, would have no means of achieving conception of that which is past and hence no means of reproducing, through memory, the former present in the present present. Deleuze expounds: "The present exists, but the past alone insists and provides the element in which the present passes and successive presents are telescoped" (1994, 85). Lampert glosses: "But Deleuze's point is that it is not qua former *present* that the moment is past. The past grounds the very possibility that something could become former" (2006, 39 [original emphasis]). Without coexistence with the past, the present would always remain present, reducing temporality to an accumulation of instants, each of which, when present, would constitute the entire scope of time. Bryant elaborates: "If the past were not contemporaneous with the present, then the present would be unable to pass. As such, time would deteriorate into a collection of disconnected instants forming nothing but an eternal present" (2008, 115).

This notion of the contemporaneity or coexistence of past and present makes more sense when we clarify what kind of past Deleuze is talking about. The past providing "the element in which the present passes and successive presents are telescoped" (to retrieve Deleuze's phrase) is the past contained in *transcendental* memory, not empirical memory. As Bryant explains, it is the past construed as a transcendental condition "under which it is possible for the present to pass," and therefore possible for any former present to be retained in empirical memory (2008, 122). Deleuze refers to the transcendental memory constituting this past as the second passive synthesis or the passive synthesis of memory (as distinct from the active synthesis of memory discussed earlier). Empirical memory remembers what was experienced, bound by the limits of its own recall. Transcendental memory recalls not that which was experienced in the past, but what Deleuze variously labels "the pure past," "the a priori past," "the past in general," or "the past as such"— terms that, as Bryant indicates, denote "an ontological dimension of experience itself and ... not the memory of once lived, but now past, empirical experiences" (2008, 111). At stake here is a notion that Deleuze borrows from Bergson: the idea of time as duration—a cumulative and accumulating totality. In this context, as Turetzky indicates, transcendental memory or "[t]he second [passive] synthesis constitutes the whole of the past coexisting with each present by going beyond the empirical present to the a priori past" (1998, 216). The present does not emerge into actuality ex nihilo. The present is present only through gathering together and extending all time before it. Lampert elucidates: "The present becomes present only once it is experienced as the particular moment that sums up, in a contracted way, the entire past at once" (2006, 48). Bryant elaborates: "each present expresses the totality of the past in a contracted state" (2008, 124). Thus, in the Deleuzian paradigm, the present functions as a contractile tense, according to the context under consideration. With reference to the first passive synthesis, the present contracts or gathers together sequential instants into a living present that they collectively comprise. With reference to the second passive synthesis, the present contracts what Lampert terms, "[t]he past as a whole, all that has happened" (2006, 50). Deleuze provides a lapidary formulation: "In one case, the present is the most contracted state of successive elements or instants which are themselves independent of one another. In the other case, the present designates the most contracted degree of an entire past, which is itself like a coexisting totality" (1994, 82).

Thus, in the Deleuzian schema, the present is bipartite, containing both the past and present. The present is actual reality, but the past, coexisting with it, is virtual reality, "preserving itself as something without actual existence," to adopt Turetzky's phrase (1998, 215). Though the second passive synthesis enables, as a necessary condition, the present to pass, by constituting the pure past as a virtual reality, the past cannot be the sufficient reason or motivating agent of passage, which requires a further operation—the third passive synthesis—that, as Turetzky notes, "constitutes the future, producing something new by splitting virtual from actual and making the present pass" (1998, 218). In its passage, therefore, time is bi-directional (moving continuously toward future and past), not linear (moving from present instant to present instant). Turetzky clarifies: "The living present continuously divides along these two directions, that of actuality, directed toward the future, that of virtuality directed toward the past" (1998, 204). In explication, Bryant applies the image of "a river dividing its flow as a fork between two streams (2008, 114). As a transcendental synthesis that conditions the content of sensibility so that knowledge of experience is possible, the third passive synthesis orders temporal awareness according to what Deleuze terms "the empty form of time (1994, 88)—or "the immutable form of change" (1984, viii). As Hughes indicates, "this third synthesis does not produce a determinate future, but the transcendental element of the future in general" (2008, 152). Deleuze construes this future in general as the eternal return not of the same, but of the new: "The eternal return is a force of affirmation, but it affirms everything of the multiple, everything of the different, everything of chance" (1994, 115). As such, the future constitutes what Bryant terms "the perpetual openness of time" (2008, 207).

9

Further Perspectives: Application of Gilles Deleuze's Temporal Theory

The Deleuzian construction of time, examined in the preceding chapter, offers a valuable lens through which the confrontation with time, represented in the literary texts that we earlier analyzed, can be further inspected. A signal candidate for investigation is the Beckettian mimesis of time—a topic already explored in Chapter 6. To begin with, Deleuze can answer The Unnamable's query:

> the question may be asked ... why time doesn't pass ... why it piles up all about you, instant on instant, on all sides, deeper and deeper, thicker and thicker, your time, others' time, the time of the ancient dead and the dead yet unborn, why it buries you grain by grain neither dead nor alive, with no memory of anything, no hope of anything, no knowledge of anything, no history and no prospects, buried under the seconds, saying any old thing, your mouth full of sand. (Beckett 1958d, 389)

In Deleuzian terms, time does not pass for The Unnamable, and expired instants "pile up" in the present instead of joining the past, because his awareness lacks the second passive synthesis that, as we have seen, makes the present pass, by linking it with the coexisting past, thereby allowing it to pass into the continuous and cumulative series of past instants. Without such transcendental and a priori structuring, The Unnamable's awareness cannot properly distinguish present from past. More precisely, in his awareness the past is no more than an agglomeration of unconnected former presents that encumber the present present with their irrelevance and redundancy: "buried under the seconds, saying any old thing, your mouth full of sand" (Beckett 1958d, 389). There is no awareness of the past as such in this dispensation ("no memory of anything"), for here the past is no more than the *densification* of the present: "on all sides, deeper and deeper, thicker and thicker" (Beckett 1958d, 389). Here, instead of a *passing* of the present, there is only the *massing* of the present—only the ceaseless accumulation of instants ("it piles up all about you, instant on instant") that never leave the present. Instead of *duration*, the Beckettian present, as enunciated by The Unnamable, concerns awareness of *stagnation*. Duration (as defined by Bergson and appropriated by Deleuze in the concept of the second passive synthesis) constructs the present as "the particular moment that sums up, in a contracted way, the entire past at once" (to retrieve Lampert's phrasing). In contrast, stagnation (as expressed by The Unnamable) constructs the present as the most recent addition to a sum of disordered instants that collectively constitute not cumulative advance, but monotonous reiteration of the same unchanging state: "the seconds must all be alike and each one is infernal" (Beckett 1958d, 395). Hence, passage is reduced to recapitulation: "it will pass on and something else will be there, another instant of my old instant" (Beckett 1958d, 400).

Without access to the second passive synthesis, The Unnamable is transcendentally challenged. Yet though his awareness lacks the a priori structuring afforded by the second passive synthesis, it displays robust recourse to the first passive synthesis. As earlier explained, the first passive synthesis contracts instants into an extensive unity, gathering together retained instants and expected ones. Through this transcendental structuring, it constitutes the living present. In this context, as we have seen, past and future do not designate distinct tenses or temporal dimensions, as they do respectively in the second and third passive syntheses. Instead, in relation to the first passive synthesis, past and future respectively denote the scope or breadth, anterior and posterior, of the present itself. Deleuze, as we have already noted, clarifies: "The past and the future do not designate instants distinct from a supposed present instant, but rather the dimensions of the present itself in so far as it is a contraction of instants" (1994, 71). As such, the first passive synthesis constructs the living present in terms of established pattern: what has happened in the past (that is, in the instants that contraction *retains*) is expected to occur in the future (that is, in the instants that contraction *anticipates*). For this reason, Deleuze refers to the first passive synthesis as *habitus*, since it involves, as Bryant notes, "expecting not this or that particular thing, but rather that things will continue in their resemblance to the past, as they generally have already. *Habitus* thus pre-delineates the set of possibilities to be realized in the unfolding of time" (2008, 89). The first passive synthesis or habitus applies conspicuously to The Unnamable's own construction of time. He experiences the present in terms of regular repetition and "the most perfect order": "Malone appears and disappears with the punctuality of clockwork, always at the same remove, the same velocity, in the same direction, the same attitude" (Beckett 1958d, 293, 294). Even his act of awareness, indicated by his eyes, operates according to habitus or established pattern: "they open and shut by the force of habit, fifteen minutes exposure, fifteen minutes shutter, like the owl cooped up in the grotto of Battersea Park" (Beckett 1958d, 392–93). For The Unnamable, retention determines protention: "I have passed by there, this has passed by me, thousands of times, its turn has come gain, it will pass on and something else will be there, another instant of my old instant" (Beckett 1958d, 400). This is the Deleuzian living present par excellence. But, as we have seen, it is a living present without reference to temporal dimensions, past and future, *outside* the instants bound together by its contraction. Moreover, The Unnamable eventually shrinks the contents of that contraction to just two seconds: the second when the words to be repeated were heard and the second immediately after when he repeats them: "I remember a second, for the space of a second, that is to say long enough to blur it out, as received, while receiving the next, which is none of my business either" (Beckett 1958d, 368).

As a text, "The Unnamable" constitutes perhaps the most astonishing example in literature of an awareness or consciousness conditioned transcendentally. But in this case, the transcendental conditioning *prevents* knowledge of experience, instead of enabling it: "I don't know, I'll never know, in the silence you don't know" (Beckett 1958d, 414). On the surface, it might appear that The Unnamable's predicament is empirical, not transcendental. That is, it might seem that the predicament is due to factors challenging or hampering cognitive conception and sensory perception—what The Unnamable refers to as "the intelligence and sensibility"—including (a) total amnesia ("Where now? Who now? When now?"); (b) environmental circumstances, such as inadequate illumination ("there is no light here"); (c) perspectival limitation and distortion, stemming, for example, from the inability to move or to see more than "what appears immediately in front of [him]"; and (d) deficient intellect ("he understands nothing, can't take thought" [Beckett 1958d, 320, 291, 304, 297, 360]). But the problem afflicting The Unnamable concerns not his *registering* of experience, but his a priori *structuring* of experience. His deconstruction of the distinction between subjective and objective points of view is a case in point: "I sometimes wonder if the two retinae are not facing each other" (Beckett 1958d, 301). The inability to distinguish definitively between that which is "in a head" and that which is outside it (between the psychical and the material) suggests that the ultimate object of The Unnamable's experience, which he is at such pains to record, concerns his mode of conditioning experience (Beckett 1958d, 350). That is, his experience fundamentally concerns the transcendental operations supplying or failing to supply the conditions under which his experience—and, more generally, Beckettian experience—is possible. Indeed, with Deleuze's help, we have already seen how, at bottom, his experience of time concerns his defective way of conditioning temporal experience.

The ordinary function of transcendental operations is to condition disordered sensory input into intelligibility. But in Beckettian mimesis, the function of such operations is to assure *un*intelligibility: "no means of knowing" (Beckett 1958d, 369). Further inquiry into this matter will deepen the implications of The Unnamable's representation of time. In the context of individual existence, the most vital temporal context is life: the temporal passage from birth to death. In Bergsonian terms, life is a cumulative process entailing, as indicated in *Creative Evolution*, "continuous progress" such that "the whole of the past goes into making the living being's present moment" (Bergson 1944, 32, 25). But The Unnamable is incapable of conducting life thus construed: "how to live, with their kind of life, for a single second" (Beckett 1958d, 334). The proximate reason, of course, is revealed by his way of formulating the enterprise: "for a single second." Instead of construing life in durational terms as the prolongation of the past into the present, he pulverizes time into micro-temporal units that lead nowhere but to their own elapse. For The Unnamable, moments or instants are consecutive but discontinuous, that is, they arrive one after the other, but without constituting a unified flux during which the consistent advance of life can unfold: "the seconds pass, one after another, jerkily, no flow, they don't pass, they arrive, bang, bang, when you have nothing left to say you talk of time, seconds of time, there are some people add them together to make a life, I can't, each one is the first, no, the second, or the third" (Beckett 1958d, 395). Such is the consequence of lacking the second passive synthesis. Time disintegrates into units that never constitute an emergent whole: "but an instant, an hour, and so on, how can they be represented, a life, how could that be made clear to me, here, in the dark" (Beckett 1958d, 407). Yet this temporal predicament suits The Unnamable admirably. Though he asks, "will I never stop wanting a life for myself?" (Beckett 1958d, 393), he would not want to be caught dead leading a life conventionally construed—"their kind of life." For life, thus understood, entails, to interpolate Bergson's phrasing, "continuous progress indefinitely pursued, and invisible progress, on which each visible organism rides during the short interval of time given it to live" (1944, 32). But the notion of life as the continuous unfolding of that which will eventually be complete appalls The Unnamable. For it engenders the striving to fulfill purpose, and purpose provokes hope, which in turn, as we noted in Chapter 6, risks the moral suffering of disappointment and despair: "Where there's life, there's hope" (Beckett 1958d, 333). It is preferable to live without a life, by inhabiting a discontinuous temporality that prevents the representation of a life, because nothing can happen but the registration of instants that lead only to their own disordered redundancy: "nothing has befallen me, nothing will befall me, nothing good, nothing bad, *nothing to be the death of me, nothing to be the life of me*" (Beckett 1958d, 363 [my emphasis]).

The Deleuzian analysis of time can also provide a new perspective on *To the Lighthouse*—a text whose construction of time in terms of unremitting transience ("nothing stays; all changes" [Woolf 1927, 195]) is the contrary of temporal construction in terms of unremitting stagnation in "The Unnamable": "Nothing changes" (Beckett 1958d, 370). The experience of time in *To the Lighthouse* foregrounds the need for synthesis, in a way that can be illumined by reference to Deleuze's emphasis on temporal synthesis. In the novel, time is construed as the element of mutability ("this eternal passing and flowing"), threatening human life with "strife, ruin, chaos" (Woolf 1927, 176, 164). Under these conditions, temporal experience is vulnerable to fragmentation ("the littered pieces") and dispersion: "the link that usually bound things together had been cut, and they floated up here, down there, off any how" (Woolf 1927, 140, 160). Without a principle of coherence, temporal experience loses its grasp on succession or consecutivity, with the result that the passage of time constitutes not ordered progress, but agglomerated confusion: "night and day, month and year ran shapelessly together" (Woolf 1927, 147). Conversely, the relentless continuity of succession requires a principle of discrimination by which to be rendered intelligible: "He began to search among the infinite series of impressions which time had lain down, leaf upon leaf, fold upon fold, incessantly upon his brain" (Woolf 1927, 184). Whereas for Deleuze synthesis is automatic, either as transcendental or empirical operation, in *To the Lighthouse* synthesis becomes an arduous but necessary task. For without it, clarification of the agonizing "perplexity of life" cannot be achieved (Woolf 1927, 55). With Deleuze, synthesis is the means of constituting the experience of time; with Woolf, in *To the Lighthouse*, synthesis is the means of conferring meaning on the experience of time: "What is the meaning of life?" (1927, 175). For the time concerned is a lifetime, and each lifetime is finite: "why was it so short, why was it so inexplicable" (Woolf 1927, 183).

Woolfian synthesis in *To the Lighthouse* centers on construction of the moment—an operation symbolized by Mrs. Ramsay's knitting needles, stitching together a whole from diverse parts: "she brought together this and that and then this, and so made out of that miserable silliness and spite ... something ... which survived, after all these years, complete ... and it stayed in the mind almost like a work of art" (175). Unlike Deleuzian synthesis, Woolfian synthesis does not constitute the flow of time as a splitting of actual from virtual that "keeps the past open, making the present pass in the production of something new" (Turetzky 1998, 217). Instead of *constituting* the flow of time, Woolfian synthesis *redeems* the flow of time from the consequences of its own fluency: "there is a coherence in things, a stability; something, she meant, is immune from change, and shines out ... in the face of the flowing, the fleeting, the spectral, like a ruby" (Woolf 1927, 114). In the world of *To the Lighthouse*, time imposes the condition of flowing and fleeting on human experience: "nothing stays; all changes" (Woolf 1927, 195). The result is vulnerability to tragic rupture: the "vanishing" into the past of that which sustains meaning and equilibrium in the present (Woolf 1927, 121). In this context, the function of synthesis is not to restore the past (an impossible task), but instead, through contemplation and selectivity, to contract or gather together diverse memories in order to stabilize the present, imbuing "the fluidity of life" with a "feeling of completeness" (Woolf 1927, 173, 208): "There might be lovers whose gift it was to choose out the elements of things and place them together and so, giving them a wholeness not theirs in life, make of some scene, or meeting of people (all now gone and separate) one of those globed compacted things over which thought lingers, and love plays" (Woolf 1927, 208–9). In the world of *To the Lighthouse*, only through time is time conquered. Only through the synthesis or contraction of past moments can the present be redeemed from the destructive influence of time. Through this synthesis, the experience of time, comprising "little separate incidents," coheres into a unity of abiding significance, enabling awareness of "a perfect whole," in the midst of temporal passage that tends inevitably to foster fission and futility: "How aimless it was, how chaotic" (Woolf 1927, 53, 140, 161). For Plato, in the *Timaeus*, time is the moving image of eternity. For Woolf, in *To the Lighthouse*, the synthetic moment, contracting elements experienced in the passage of time, is the static image of "eternity": "Of such moments, she thought, the thing is made that remains for ever after" (1927, 114).

Unlike *To the Lighthouse*, which foregrounds the need for synthesis in conferring meaning on the experience of time, *Hard Times* presents a world that deliberately denies synthesis, reducing time to a sequence of moments without connection to each other. The quintessential formulation of this temporality concerns the description of the "deadly statistical clock" in Mr. Gradgrind's Observatory, which "measured every second and with a beat like a rap upon a coffin-lid" (Dickens 1969, 132). Here, to invoke again Deleuze's account of time without synthesis, the passage of time is reduced to a "succession of instants" that indicate "only its constantly aborted moment of birth" (1994, 70). In this context, Mr. Gradgrind's clock does not so much *measure* time as recurrently *terminate* it, since each second, when measured, is instantly disposed of, "with a beat like a rap upon a coffin-lid." Here, to interpolate Turetzky's remark cited earlier, time begins "to arise at each instant only to fail to continue one instant into another" (1998, 212). Here, time the destroyer is made to destroy its own continuity. As we have seen in Chapter 2, the source of this temporal administration is the project to negate the anisotropy of time in order thereby to gain protection from the greatest threat of temporality: aging. Succession is reduced to recurrence. The present never gets farther than where it already is: "every day was the same as yesterday and tomorrow, and every year the counterpart of the last and the next" (Dickens 1969, 65). Lack of synthesis turns the present into a dead end: it leads nowhere but back to where it already was.

The temporal dispensation in Coketown entails a salient paradox, permissible because *Hard Times* is a literary, not a philosophical, text. On the one hand, as just noted, there is no synthesis of instants, and hence, to interpolate Turetzky's phrasing, no "succession of former presents *connected* to the present present," by which to constitute the living present (1998, 213 [my emphasis]). Instead, each instant enters the present without connection to before or after, rendering the present instantaneous, not continuous and extended. But, on the other hand, there is nevertheless a living present or habitus in Coketown, characterized by retention and protection. That is, in Coketown, to invoke again Turetzky's explication of Deleuze, "[t]he living present retains particular former presents," and expects the future to continue prior pattern (1998, 214): "Time went on in Coketown like its own machinery: so much material wrought up, so much fuel consumed" (Dickens 1969, 126). From this perspective, Coketown is a hell of habitus, where "the piston of the steam-engine worked monotonously up and down, like the head of an elephant in a state of melancholy madness" (Dickens 1969, 65). Yet the paradoxical combination of disconnected instants with habitus—of denial of synthesis with the result of synthesis—can be resolved. In Coketown, time propagates the continuity of discontinuity, where the tick-tock of chronological measurement is reconfigured such that the "tick" signifies the emergence of a new instant, and the "tock" indicates its annihilation by the next one. Each day is the same as those before and after, yet none can be connected with any other to constitute a sense of development or self-realization. Hence Louisa's despair: "It made me think, after all, how short my life would be, and how little I could hope to do in it" (Dickens 1969, 94).

An astonishing *peripeteia* or reversal in the administration of time occurs near the end of the novel, during the rescue of Stephen Blackpool, the Hand who fell into an abandoned mining shaft. Suddenly the movement of time signifies more than the same as usual. Temporal passage at last achieves urgent continuity, with each moment advancing the cumulative movement preceding it, instead of reiterating the impossibility of progression, as in the case of Mr. Gradgrind's deadly statistical clock. The symbol of this new temporal dispensation is the surgeon's watch, carefully consulted in the course of Stephen Blackpool's rescue. Here at last the future will be different from the past, for now the passage of time is the measure of expected change, when each passing moment brings the present closer to knowing what will happen: "Apparently so long an interval ensured with the men at the windlass standing idle, that some women shrieked that another accident had happened. But the surgeon who held the watch, declared five minutes not to have elapsed yet, and sternly admonished them to keep silence" (Dickens 1969, 287). In this context, the rope by which the basket containing Stephen is hauled up symbolizes, indeed almost reifies, the perpetual movement of time toward the future—a movement whereby each moment connects to its predecessor, constituting time as a cumulative progress toward the new: "But ring after ring was coiled upon the barrel of the windless safely, and the connecting chains appeared, and finally the bucket with the two men holding on at the sides—a sight to make the head swim, and oppress the heart—and tenderly supporting between them, slung and tied within, the figure of a poor, crushed, human creature" (Dickens 1969, 289).

In *Hard Times*, time is construed as continuous operation. In the primary temporality, dominant before Stephen's rescue, continuous operation is represented by the pistons, mechanically moving up and down, ceaselessly returning to where they already were. Here the operation of time cannot produce anything new. In the secondary temporality, initiated during the rescue, continuous operation is represented by the rope pulled by the windlass, progressively bringing into presence that which has not been there before. Whereas the primary temporality prioritizes habitus and sustains the status quo ante, the secondary temporality construes time as perpetual openness to the future, and continually advances disclosure of the new. Whereas the first temporality entails recurrent return of the same, the secondary temporality entails recurrent return of the different. In the first temporality, each new moment *terminates* its predecessor, "with a beat like a rap upon a coffin-lid," in the same instant that it *duplicates* its predecessor. In these circumstances, a terminated moment cannot join a preexisting past, because nothing distinguishes a prior moment from a current one.

Hence, each terminated moment is *obliterated* by its common identity with the present one. In the secondary temporality, each new moment *preserves* its predecessor, because each new moment *extends* the continuity constituted by its predecessors. All moments participate in and collectively constitute the continuous unfolding of time. This dispensation is vividly symbolized by the rings of rope either accumulating or diminishing around the windlass, according to whether the rescue basket is raised out of or lowered into the mining shaft. Unlike the isolated instants measured by Mr. Gradgrind's clock, which have no connection to their respective predecessors or successors, each ring of rope around the windlass occupies its position only through relation to its predecessors, just as its successors occupy or relinquish their respective positions only through relation to their predecessors. This is a vivid demonstration of the condition enabled by Deleuze's second passive synthesis, wherein the past coexists with the present, and is the factor enabling it to pass.

Perhaps no novel treats the coexistence of the past with the present more vividly than *Ulysses*, where the primary characters, Stephen Dedalus, Leopold Bloom, and Molly Bloom, inhabit a present rife with memory of the past, to the extent that the present risks inundation by it: "Memories beset his brooding brain" (Joyce 1960, 10). Of course, the activity of empirical memory does not entail what Deleuze, with Bergson, construes as coexistence of the past, since such coexistence involves transcendental, not empirical memory. That is, as we have seen, it involves that which empirical memory could never recall—namely, to cite Turetzky again, "the whole of the past co-existing with each present by going beyond the empirical past to the a priori past" (1998, 216). This pure, continuously extending past is presupposed by the passing present, for without it the present would have no orientation in time, no location in which to be *this* present, distinct from former presents. In *Ulysses*, the primary context of the pure, continuously extending past pertains to the notion of life, construed as "the field of individual development and experience" that retains earlier phases while advancing toward new ones: "the fact of vital growth, through convulsions of metamorphosis from infancy through maturity to decay" (Joyce 1960, 817). But, as this formulation shows, it is continuity "cloven" by discontinuity, not the seamless prolongation posited by Bergson and Deleuze (Joyce 1960, 633). The factor cleaving continuity concerns the Joycean version of "metempsychosis" (Joyce 1960, 77, 542) or "convulsions of metamorphosis" (817)—a process entailing agonizing and destabilizing separation of the present from a past whose "accepted order" (226) can never be reconstituted or retrieved. At the core of this disruptive discontinuity is the urge to reverse the direction of "irreversible time"

(858)—a need that, for both Stephen and Bloom, reaches the intensity of hallucination as when Stephen's dead mother "raises her blackened withered right arm slowly towards Stephen's breast with outstretched fingers" (682), or when Bloom's dead son, Rudy, suddenly appears to him at the age Rudy would have been, had he not died in infancy: "a fairy-boy of eleven, a changeling" (702).

Of course, the status of these apparitions remains ambiguous. Are they actual hallucinations or mere fantasies perpetrated by the text, consistent with the oneiric or dream-like style of the chapter ("Circe") concerned? Yet, regardless of their mode of being, the apparitions suggest a transcending of attachment to the past, even as they reify it. In Stephen's case, his assault on the maternal apparition terminates an entire temporal dispensation: "Time's livid final flame leaps and, in the following darkness, ruin of all space, shattered glass and toppling masonry" (Joyce 1960, 683). Time itself has not ended, since succession still continues, as shown by the darkness that follows the extinction of light. But something temporal, by implication, has ended nevertheless—namely, Stephen's involvement in a temporality susceptible to the irresistible pull of the past. Indeed, he had warned himself of this susceptibility earlier that day: "Hold to the now, the here, through which all future plunges to the past" (Joyce 1960, 238). Bloom's subsequent observation, in the kitchen of his home at number 7 Eccles Street, seems to corroborate Stephen's progress from a temporal attitude that prioritizes the past to one that prioritizes the future: "He saw in a quick young male familiar form the predestination of a future" (Joyce 1960, 808). Like Stephen, Bloom too appears to move from a temporal attitude oriented toward the past to one oriented toward the future, when confronting an apparition—in this case, the vision of Rudy as a boy of eleven. Here, Rudy has posthumously grown beyond the infancy in which he died, suggesting that, at a deep level, Bloom has let go of or at least loosened attachment to the past in favor of recognizing and accepting the continuity of "vital growth" (Joyce 1960, 817).

Deleuze's notion of contraction can help us to bring into focus a central aspect of the "convulsions of metamorphosis" that the novel narrates, and which lie at the core of its "epitome of the course of life" (Joyce 1960, 817, 546). As we have seen, Deleuze deploys the term "contraction" to signify the act of synthesis that, in Turetzky's phrasing, "binds independent elements together into a single time" (1998, 312). If we combine this philosophical sense of contraction with the more familiar physiological one of tightening a muscle, we arrive at a new way of construing the "convulsions of metamorphosis" in *Ulysses*. Let us begin with the notion of contraction as a physiological metaphor for the psychological "convulsions" provoked by ending one stage of life and beginning the next. The text links these contractions with the convulsions of the womb in the act of parturition or giving birth, when the old way of life is superseded by the new one: "The childman weary, the manchild in the womb" (Joyce 1960, 870). The defensive reaction to these parturitional convulsions is spasmodic clenching of the past in the present—the refusal or inability to let go of memory regarding a prior period of life and accept "the fact of vital growth" beyond the reaches of the past (Joyce 1960, 817). For, to interpolate Peter Brown's phrase from a different context, metempsychosis is not a sudden event, but a protracted and fluctuating process characterized by the intermingling of acceptance and resistance, and therefore imbued with "the dynamic quality of the relations of change and continuity" (1972, 51). The hidden implications of obsessive rememoration emerge when we apply Deleuze's philosophical notion of contraction, as it pertains to the active synthesis of memory, earlier described. Here the present present is said to *contract* the former present: to include or gather together, within awareness of its own content, awareness also of the content of the former present. This double content is necessary, for, to requote Bryant, the present "cannot represent its difference from the former present without representing itself at the same time that it represents that former present" (2008, 114–15). According to Deleuze, the passing of the present is founded on this synthesis of the present present and the former present. For through it, the present present recognizes its distinction from the former present, and thereby affirms the passage of the present. In *Ulysses*, where Stephen and Bloom writhe in the convulsions of metamorphosis, this dispensation is reversed. Instead of *enabling* the passage of the present, the contraction of the past by the present, whereby the present represents its difference from a former present, *impedes* acceptance of passage. Yet before we proceed to explicate this matter, it should be noted, for the sake of clarity, that whereas with Deleuze the contraction entailed in the active synthesis concerns the present present and the *immediately preceding* former present, in *Ulysses* the contraction concerns not the immediately preceding present, but a much earlier former present, located on the other side of the divide between prior and emergent phases of life.

Bloom's nostalgia provides a superb example of the active synthesis of memory gone awry. Here, in representing its difference from the past, the present seeks return to the past, instead of confirming its own passage toward the future: "Me. And me now" (Joyce 1960, 224). In this example, Bloom opposes two temporal versions of himself—the past one (me) and the current one (me now). The past identity precedes the current one not just temporally, but also ontologically. That is, in representing the difference between his present and past selves, Bloom accords primary identity to his past self (me), and derivative or secondary identity to his current self (me now). The latter is construed as a debased or vitiated version of the former. This construction is the opposite of the Bergsonian one in which the subject, through enduring in time, continually advances toward fuller evolution and development of its identity, for until Bloom identifies more positively with the possibilities open to his present self ("Too late now. Or if not? If not? If still?"), the unfolding of time offers not development, but pining: "Happy. Happier then" (Joyce 1960, 367, 196). Stephen displays a different relation to "the past and its phantoms" (543). Instead of "looking for something lost in a past life" (57) through nostalgic yearning ("Far away now past") like Bloom, Stephen feels haunted by a guilt-laden "memory of the past" that he can neither forget nor expel: "No mother. Let me be and let me live" (Joyce 1960, 57, 81, 466, 11). In this predicament, the active synthesis of memory, whereby the present present represents its difference from a former present, destabilizes the present whose distinct identity it is designed to maintain, for in this case, difference from the past signifies failure to fulfill obligations in the past: "the piteous vesture of the past, silent, remote, reproachful." (Joyce 1960, 552). Yet Stephen is able to surmount the problem, and contemplate a properly operating active synthesis in which the present reflects its own identity while representing its difference from the past: "So in the future, the sister of the past, I may see myself as I sit here now but by reflection from that which then I shall be" (Joyce 1960, 249).

The great problem in *Ulysses* concerns "their each his remembered lives" (Joyce 1960, 353). More precisely, the "convulsions of metempsychosis," occasioned when one stage of life yields to the next, entail compulsive clinging to the former stage as entry into the next one begins. Striking—but very different—emphasis on the dichotomy between past and present also informs *Enduring Love*. Let us see how application of Deleuze's philosophy of time can suggest a new way of approaching it. To begin with, the novel opens on the recollection of an astonishingly compressed metempsychosis: "At that moment a chapter, no, a whole stage of my life closed" (McEwan 1997, 8). Unlike *Ulysses*, which concerns the convulsive unfolding of metempsychosis, *Enduring Love* focuses on the aftershocks of metempsychosis. The actual transition occasioned by metempsychosis is compressed into a few minutes in the course of the failed attempt to rescue the child aloft in the gondola of the wayward balloon. This compression entails the division of time into the succession of its smallest units: "Every fraction of a second that passed increased the drop, and the point must come when to let go would be impossible or fatal" (McEwan 1997, 14). Deleuze can help us isolate an important element here. In his schema, contracting or gathering together a succession of moments into a living present is the function of the first passive synthesis. By means of retention and protention, it enables awareness of an extended present, stretching before and after a central instant. Ironically, in the passage under consideration from *Enduring Love*, this living present threatens to become a dying present, if the decision to let go is not taken immediately. In this context, the span of the living present contracts or is abbreviated, until it encompasses mere fractions of seconds. But though those fractions follow each other with unvarying regularity, this dispensation where each new moment might be the last is the opposite of habitus—the pattern of regularity prompting, to retrieve Bryant's phrasing, the expectation "that things will continue in their resemblance to the past, as they generally have already" (2008, 89)—a dispensation that Joe himself invokes: "the separate assumptions of recent pasts and what they would be doing next, the growing tottering frame they carried of where they were in the story of their lives" (McEwan 1997, 170). Yet for Joe, instead of constituting the basis of continuity, the living present now becomes the site of discontinuity and interruption. Thus the balloon "catastrophe" shatters Joe's complacency regarding temporal passage (McEwan 1997, 3). He projects the dread experienced regarding the living present—the passage of "[e]very fraction of a second"—onto his conception of the future: "Anxiety about, distaste for the future, pivoting in the present—the only moment it could be experienced" (McEwan 1997, 3, 43). The only security in time resides in the past, where nothing more can happen. But the past offers no comfort either, for in it resides Joe's guilt concerning what he has done or, more precisely, failed to do—namely, hold onto the dangling rope in order to save the boy carried aloft by the balloon: "But even as I felt the nausea of guilt return, I was trying to convince myself I was right to let go" (McEwan 1997, 32).

Further reference to Deleuze's construction of time can clarify Joe's temporal predicament. As already discussed, Deleuze distinguishes two constructions of the future: one concerns the living present proper, the other involves the future as such—a tense or temporal dimension distinct from the living present. In the living present, the future is simply the impending sequence of instants expected to follow those that have already just occurred. In this context, the future defines the horizon of the living present, in the direction of what is about to come. During the botched balloon-rescue attempt, Joe obviously defines the future in terms of the living present—in terms, that is, of expectation of continuation of the immediate sequence of moments: "And perhaps my impulse to hang on was nothing more than a continuation of what I had been attempting moments before, simply a failure to adjust quickly." But, as we have seen, that pattern of expectation is suddenly broken: "And again, less than one adrenally incensed heartbeat later, another variable was added to the equation: someone let go, and the balloon and its hangers-on lurched upwards another several feet" (McEwan 1997, 14). Hence, for Joe, the future encompassed by the living present is no longer construed in terms of continuity, but rupture. Yet, after the balloon incident, Joe persists in inhabiting a living present whose posterior boundary encloses and determines the meaning of the future for him, with the result that he resembles "a creature doomed to inhabit a perpetual present" (McEwan 1997, 41). This tendency to define the future as a distension of the present appears vividly in Joe's description of moving toward a door while seeming still to sit in a chair: "It may have been an illusion caused by visual persistence, or a neurally tripped delay of perception, but it seemed to me that I was still slumped in my smooth leather chair staring at that door even while I was moving towards it" (McEwan 1997, 44). In these circumstances, Joe's task—his challenge—is to rehabilitate his sense of the future, through freeing it from contamination by his sense of the living present, which underwent distortion as a result of his traumatic experience during the rescue attempt. We grasp now a deeper implication of Joe's observation, "Time had folded in on itself" (McEwan 1997, 177), for his skewed perception of the living present causes him to construe the future in terms of events that should not happen ("It was a mistake, it doesn't have to happen. We could choose another outcome"), thus stranding him in the present when all that he wants to happen is "obsessive re-examination" of events that have already occurred" (McEwan 1997, 170, 2).

Jed Parry, the figure who stalks Joe, ultimately homicidally, as a result of an infatuation caused by De Clérambault's syndrome, comes to symbolize the future that Joe dreads: "Then he represented the unknown into which I projected all kinds of inarticulate terrors" (McEwan 1997, 69). Thus, to deal effectively with Parry is to overcome resistance to the future. This connection emerges very clearly when Joe, goaded by the fear that Parry will again threaten his life, decides to buy a gun illegally, fully aware that this decision constitutes a "turning-point," plunging him into "a hard-edged world of consequences," where "one action, one event, would entail another, until the train was beyond [his] control" (McEwan 1997, 188). By coincidence, on returning home with the gun that he has just purchased, Joe finds Parry holding Clarissa hostage at knifepoint. Joe then shoots Parry, causing the shocked Clarissa to glare at him "with an expression of such repulsion and surprise that *I thought we would never get past this moment*" (McEwan 1997, 214–15 [my emphasis]). This crisis both epitomizes and resolves Joe's resistance to the passage of time, precipitated by the balloon trauma. From this point, he accepts the movement of time beyond the present, for only then can reconciliation—"mutual forgiveness, or at least tolerance"—with Clarissa be achieved (McEwan 1997, 230).

Enduring Love hinges on a catastrophic event that explodes Joe's habitual relation to the passage of time, and forces him to forge a new one. In his analysis of *Hamlet*, Deleuze construes the eponymous protagonist in terms of the "caesura" or the "unique and tremendous event" that alters the structure of time, and "constitutes the fracture in the I" persisting in it (1994, 89). By requiring radical change in the subject's mode of operation and radical reformulation of purpose and capability, intrusion of the caesura into lived experience stamps a "triadic structure" on time, entailing "the before, the caesura and the after" (1994, 92). According to Deleuze, the suddenly received imperative to avenge his father's murder constitutes a caesura that imposes a task too big for Hamlet, as he has been up to this point, to fulfill. Who he has been up to this point yields to who he must become in order to accomplish his goal. Thus receipt of the revenge imperative initiates a "metamorphosis," entailing "the becoming-equal to the act [of revenge] and a doubling of the self," through "the projection of an ideal self in the image of the act" (1994, 89). Deleuze opposes the new temporality, introduced by the caesura, to the old temporality preceding it. For Deleuze, the old temporality is a chronology of periodicity, based on the regular repetition of distinctive events. Tamsin Lorraine elaborates: "Chronological time is measured against events that repeat at regular intervals: the sun rises and sets, the king takes a queen, they have a son, the king dies, the prince becomes king" (2003, 37). The implicit foundation of this dependence on regular repetition is habitus—the pattern of retention and corresponding expectation that constitutes what Bryant terms "the conservative structure of the living present" (2008, 92). As Bryant indicates, the encounter with caesura "introduces a gap, explosion, event, or discontinuity which calls into question the smooth functioning of the living present," such that the future can no longer be construed in terms of "patterns that have been inferred from the past" (2008, 102, 90). Instead, the future opens on to the perpetually new, because time itself is construed in terms of its own intrinsic movement, not in terms of the things that move in time and assume their respective positions in it. Deleuze clarifies: "Time itself unfolds ... instead of things unfolding within it .... It ceases to be cardinal and becomes ordinal, a pure *order* of time" (1994, 88 [original emphasis]). Deleuze terms this empty form of time *Aion*, and treats it, in Turetzky's phrase, as "the a priori unchanging form of all change" (1998, 219). In view of this linkage of Hamlet with transition from a temporality based on the regular recurrence of events to a temporality based on the movement of time toward change, Lorraine cites Hamlet as "Deleuze's example of someone forced by circumstances to experience the third synthesis of time" (2003, 36), for the third passive synthesis, as we have seen, is the transcendental operation that constitutes the future as the eternal return of the new.

Unfortunately, Deleuze's prowess as a philosopher does not extend into literary criticism. Deleuze detaches Hamlet the character from *Hamlet* the play, with the result that the encounter with caesura concerns presumed flaw or limitation in the character only (the commanded act is too big for him), not flaw or limitation in his environment—the world of the play. To address this matter, let us begin with Deleuze's interpretation of Hamlet's complaint, immediately after receiving the Ghost's revenge imperative: "The time is out of joint. O cursed spite, / That ever I was born to set it right" (1.5.196–97). According to Deleuze, Hamlet here refers to the caesura he has just encountered. Time is out of joint, because it no longer unfolds as it did prior to his being tasked with revenge. Deleuze argues that Hamlet cannot act in time, until reconfiguring time by achieving openness to the future, instead of counting on regular recurrence of patterns established in the past. Lorraine elaborates: "Hamlet must reestablish the meaning of his world by establishing a new chronology despite his glimpse of a time without the repetition of events that happen at regular intervals" (2003, 37). But this interpretation misconstrues the temporal function of revenge in the world of the play. Far from enabling the removal or displacement of a temporality founded on recurrence, the revenge morality demands perpetuation of recurrence. One murder must be avenged by another, which in turn risks provoking another. As Roland Barthes has observed in another context, revenge installs the rule of "[r]eiterative time," thereby prompting the need for "a new administration of time, which will no longer be based on the immutable cycle of vengeances" (1964, 50, 79). Moreover, as I have demonstrated in Chapter 8 of *"Hamlet" and the Rethinking of Man*, the prolonged interval between receipt of the revenge imperative and execution of the required deed concerns not delay due to character inadequacy (as Deleuze and many others claim), but conceptual development through which Hamlet constructs a new temporality—one based not on reiteration, but teleological process:

> In the context of reiterative time, morality demands conformity through repetition. In the context of teleological time, morality encourages rehabilitation (as regarding the Ghost's eschatological purgation) or self-development through maturation: "The inward service of the mind and soul / Grows wide

> withal" (1.3.13-14). But the play also emphasizes negative examples of processes unfolding in teleological time, such as those involving "corruption" which "mining all within / Infects unseen" (3.4.150-51) or "foul disease" that "feed[s] / Even on the pith of life" (4.1.21, 22-23). Ironically ... the primary cause of this negative version of teleological time is dependent on the recurrence characteristic of reiterative time and encouraged by the revenge morality. (Levy 2008, 192-93)

I shall not revisit my detailed investigation of reiterative and teleological time here. but we can note that Chapter 1 ("The Mimesis of Time in *Hamlet*") of the present study approaches from a different angle the need for Hamlet to construct, *before* achieving revenge, an alternate temporality overcoming the defects of the dominant temporality in the world of the play. There we found that, in a world beset by expiration anxiety, the fundamental motive of the revenge morality concerns not vengeance, but reversal of the anisotropy of time. The ultimate injury that the revenge morality seeks to redress concerns the inevitable passage of the present into the past, as the future reaches the present. It achieves this redress by demanding that the future, when the vengeance will be accomplished, be formulated in terms of the past, when the outrage to be avenged occurred. The fearsome forward movement of time is thus turned awry and forced to flow backward, for movement toward the future simply confirms the primacy of the past. In this context, Hamlet's presumed delay signifies not character deficiency, but the struggle to rehabilitate the construction of time underpinning the revenge morality, even as he seeks to obey that morality. Central to this rehabilitation is (a) recognition of "happy time," whose passage from the present to eventual expiration in the future is administered by providence, and (b) reconstitution of the past, such that it denotes the zone not of expiration, but continuous transformation. Deleuze contends that Hamlet can avenge only after achieving "a doubling of the self" through which he becomes big enough to do what must be done (1994, 89). Yet this interpretation obscures the crucial link, for Hamlet, between thought and revenge. From its inception, Hamlet associates the revenge project with the movement of thought: "Haste me to know't /That I with wings as swift as meditation or the thoughts of love / May sweep to my revenge" (1.5.29-31). One result of this thinking concerns construction of a new basis for engagement with time (as examined in Chapter 1).

According to Lorraine, explicating Deleuze, "The symbolic act of murdering his uncle is the act by which [Hamlet] will attempt to reorder chronology" (2003, 37). But this interpretation of the play puts the cart before the horse. On its own, the act of revenge can only reinforce the chronology of repetition and vindictive recurrence. Yet through the movement of thought that Hamlet, from the outset, associates with the revenge imperative, he is able to reconfigure the conceptual context in which the act eventually occurs. What he conceives, through this thinking and thoughtful reaction to changing circumstance, does not concern acceptance of the Deleuzian notion of the empty form of time in which "[t]ime itself unfolds ... instead of things unfolding within it" (Deleuze 1994, 88). Unlike Deleuze, Hamlet is a tragic character whose identity and perspective are developed by and expressed through the situations in which he is engaged. Experience is always contextual, and the ultimate context in the world of the play is "the single, and peculiar life," limited by mortality (3.3.11). Here time is not formal, but *dramatic*. It is encountered and registered in terms not of its "empty form," but of the events that recede from, advance toward, and actually occur in the present. This is the inescapable condition of "our circumstance and course of thought" (3.3.83), as dramatized by the play.

Epilogue: Time and Agency

Experience is temporal. Time configures experience as a flow of awareness, articulated by succession. But what happens when awareness focuses on its own structuring of time and on the effect of this structuring on conception of the meaning and purpose of life? This is the question framing the preceding inquiry into literary confrontations with time—an inquiry entailing detailed examination of complex texts formulating the need for reconciliation with time—or for refuge from it—as an urgent issue. There, relation to time is initially adversarial, and means of protection against temporal threat are elaborately devised and tenaciously retained, until (except in the Beckettian case) temporal awareness achieves accommodation with the object of its attention. In this Epilogue, let us consider the matter of relation to time and the texts linked with it from a different perspective in order to expand the implications of our topic.

According to Charles Taylor, self-awareness or "self-understanding" entails one's sense of identity as "a being who is growing and becoming" (1989, 50). As such, self-awareness presupposes "temporal depth" and therefore needs some device, like a personal "narrative," by which to confirm and express cohesion or "meaningful unity" through time (Taylor 1989, 50, 51). Yet the need thus to achieve cohesion through time presupposes a construction of time. Hence the most fundamental ground of self-awareness is not narrative, which binds together the moments or phases of personal unfolding, but the sense of time itself.

Characterization of time is perhaps one of the most intimate expressions of the meaning of life—the meaning, that is, of living a life, moving through the temporal interval extending between birth and death. The matter can be clarified by opposing Pozzo to Kierkegaard. To Pozzo, in *Waiting for Godot*, the time between birth and death is insignificant. There is not enough time in life to do anything but die: "one day we were born, one day we shall die, the same day, the same second, is that not enough for you?" (Beckett 1954, 57). Time is characterized as "accursed," because its duration offers nothing but extinction (Beckett 1954, 57). Here the agent is time, and its passive victim is human life. Time forces the human agent to suffer inconsequentiality—the inability, through action, to propagate consequences: "Nothing to be done" (Beckett 1954, 7). A similar loss of agency, due to characterization of time, pertains to Louisa Gradgrind in *Hard Times*: "It made me think, after all, how short my life would be, and how little I could hope to do in it" (Dickens 1969, 94).

A diametrically opposed characterization of the relation between time and human agency (which, like Pozzo's, relies on reference to the transit of human life) obtains in the philosophy of Søren Kierkegaard:

> To have been young, and then to grow older, and finally to die, is a very mediocre form of human existence: this merit belongs to every animal. But the unification of the different stages of life in simultaneity is the task set for human beings. (1941, 311)

Here the temporal trajectory from birth to death presents the human agent with the task of unifying "the different stages of life in simultaneity." For Kierkegaard, the factor charged with effecting this unification is the will in its existential act of choosing according to what H. J. Blackham terms "total inward commitment (decision, for example, as to vocation, marriage, faith)" (1952, 9). Through such exertion of the will, the individual constitutes "a stable ethical reality" that confers continuity of meaning on his or her existence (Blackham 1959, 9). Here, unlike with Beckett, time is not "accursed," but *redemptive*, in that it offers the human agent the opportunity to affirm and sustain, through what Blackham labels "reflective willing and authentic choice," the ultimate and essential significance of human existence (1959, 21). This characterization of time as redemptive in relation to human agency contrasts also with Claudius's pronouncement in *Hamlet* regarding the tendency of time to *weaken* the will, and not, as with Kierkegaard, to afford it scope for exercise: "That we would do, / We should do when we would: for this 'would' changes / And hath abatements and delays" (4.7.117–19)—a sentiment shared by the Player King: "But what we determine, oft we break" (3.2.182).

The opposition between the Beckettian and Kierkegaardian characterizations of time (in one, accursed; in the other, redemptive) rests on another opposition: that between agency and passivity. The human agent lives in time. But the relation of that agent to time is variable and ambiguous. In one characterization, time *preserves* agency, by giving it scope—and indeed, incentive—for operation.

In the other, time *undermines* agency by subjecting the will to depletion (as in Claudius's example) or futility (as in Pozzo's and Louisa's examples). Ordinarily, analyses of agency take time for granted. But, in the literary texts that we have examined, characterization of time is crucial to agency. To clarify this matter and probe its implications, let us first clarify the notion of agency.

As Terry Pinkard indicates, agency entails "the idea of a self-determining subject" (1996, 289).[1] He further notes that such self-determination engages the agent in the task of determining ends, and then implementing the means to achieve them: "The most general way in which an agent can be said to be determining for himself what he is doing is to consider that his actions are component parts of his adopting certain plans or projects in terms of which he carries out his actions" (1996, 283). But the responsibility of the self-determining agent does not stop here, for, again as Pinkard observes, actions undertaken to achieve ends or goals have effects or consequences, which, in turn, impinge upon the moral quality of the agent provoking them: "But in carrying out the plan, I act, and any action produces consequences. The issue therefore is whether and to what extent the consequences of my action can be said to be part of my plan" (1996, 283). The transit from determining ends to provoking consequences occurs in time. Regarding the "crucial feature of human agency," Charles Taylor emphasizes the notion of occupying "a moral space, a space in which questions arise about what is good or bad, what is worth doing and what not, what has meaning and importance for you and what is trivial and secondary" (1989, 33, 28). However, agency occupies not just moral space, but temporal interval or duration as well. In literature, characterization of time can infiltrate moral space, and influence—or even usurp—judgment concerning "what is good or bad, what is worth doing and what not." In the wake of Michel Foucault's *Surveiller et Punir: Naissance de la Prison* (1975) and other contributions to poststructuralism, it has become fashionable to refer to the displacement of agency by *discourses*, which Roland Bleiker defines as "subtle mechanisms that frame our thinking process" (2000, 135).[2] Yet various literary texts, in investigating agency, highlight instead the centrality of time in its constitution.

To be genuinely self-determining, agency requires a criterion by which to order itself—what Charles Taylor terms a "truth which is criterial for it, i.e., a standard on which it regulates itself" (1989, 132). Otherwise, the actions undertaken by the agent are no more than random or spontaneous responses to heterogeneous promptings and impulses. In the classical schema, action is determined by ends and means that, in turn, are determined by the principles of reason.[3] In *Hard Times*, Bitzer is explicitly described in terms of regulation: "His mind was so exactly regulated, that he had no affections or passions" (Dickens 1969, 150). He is further described in terms of regulation by reason (though here that faculty has been debased to self-interested calculation). When asked whether his heart is "accessible ... to any compassionate influence," Bitzer replies: "It is accessible to Reason, sir ... [a]nd to nothing else" (277). But the fundamental principle responsible for Bitzer's self-regulation is time, with the result that he is virtually an incarnated clock: "I have heard him on such occasions produce sounds of a nature similar to what may be sometimes heard in Dutch clocks" (Dickens 1969, 209). When we recall how a clock functions, the implications of Bitzer's assimilation to one emerge vividly. Regular recurrence is the principle by which clocks operate. Roger Teichmann elaborates: "*a clock is a system of repeated events*, such as the revolutions round the sun, or the falling of water-droplets. A true clock is one whose repeated events are all of the same duration" (1995, 108–9 [my emphasis]). Similarly, Bitzer's mind is "a system of repeated events," for it functions as Mr. Gradgrind's pedagogy trained it to: always responding to circumstances in terms of "self-interest" (Dickens 1969, 277), calculating his advantage in the same "business-like and logical manner" (277)—a conditioning intended, as we saw in Chapter 2, to circumvent the anistropic movement of time by emphasizing recurrence and repetition: "deaf to the call of time" (12). To the extent that Bitzer is a product of this conditioning, he is not so much an agent as a patient—a recipient of action originating elsewhere, a subject acted upon by formative influences, and thereafter acting according to their design or instruction: "We are so constituted. I was brought up in that catechism when I was very young, sir, as you are aware" (277). As such, he is not a genuinely *self-determining* agent, since his ends are *pre-determined* by his conditioning.

The ultimate end or purpose in Coketown is to convert time into static repetition, as clearly seen with regard to Mr. Gradgrind's clock, "which measured every second and with a beat like a rap upon a coffin-lid" (Dickens 1969, 132). Bitzer is indeed like such a clock, for which time is the measure of reiteration, not continuity. Similarly, Mr. Bounderby, who appears as the dominant agent in Coketown, operates according to a deliberative process configured as a "system of repeated events" (to retrieve Teichmann's phrase) reiterating instantaneity: "I always come to a decision ... and whatever I do, I do at once" (Dickens 1969, 265). He is an instantaneous decision-making machine, just as Mr. Gradgrind's clock is a second-measuring machine. In describing himself as "a determined character," Mr. Bounderby misses the irony of his words. As an agent, he is ultimately determined not by his own unfettered will, but by the temporal administration he epitomizes and conserves (Dickens 1969, 22).

Literal loss of agency is a recurrent motif in *Hard Times*: (a) Mr. Jupe feeling "himself to be a poor, weak, ignorant, helpless man" (Dickens 1969, 99); (b) the invalid Mrs. Gradgrind lying feebly in bed, without even enough agency to claim her own sensations; (c) Louisa, after fleeing to her father, "lying, an insensible heap, at his feet" (212); and (d) Stephen Blackpool supine at the bottom of the Old Hell Shaft, "with one arm doubled under him" (261). As we saw in detail in Chapter 2, the plight of Mr. Jupe (the first example in the list just cited) epitomizes the problem of human vulnerability to time (in the mode of susceptibility to senescence or the process of deterioration with age). The temporal administration of Coketown is designed to overcome this problem, by configuring time in terms of instantaneity, not anisotropy (one-way forward movement beyond prior moments). This dispensation is obvious in the plight of the Hands or workers, bent over their looms in the factory, as the "piston of the steam engine worked monotonously up and down" (27). But it applies equally to those whose social position is based on employment of the laborers. The relentless pursuit of self-interest, the construal of everything as objective "facts" to facilitate the calculations of self-interest, and the ruthless suppression of compassion, which would encumber self-interest, similarly enforce a temporality of invariant reiteration. Thus time is made to mimic the piston of the steam engine, rendering each moment the same as its predecessor and successor: "Time went on in Coketown like its own machinery" (126). In these circumstances, agency can do nothing but more of the same, regardless of social level. Agency cannot achieve true self-determination, because agency is estranged from awareness of its own feelings, as surely as Mrs. Gradgrind is estranged from hers. Hence, even the captains of Coketown, Messrs. Bounderby and Gradgrind, remain unsatisfied: "they were restless... *they never knew what they wanted*" (Dickens 1969, 29 [my emphasis]). At bottom, their agency is powerless to know its own purpose.

In Coketown, the only way to fulfill agency—to enable agency to know and achieve its own authentically satisfying purpose—is to replace self-interest with communal concern for another's welfare. But this shift in focus entails a change in awareness of time. Such change, as we have seen, occurs in the course of the rescue of Stephen Blackpool from the bottom of the Old Hell Shaft into which he had fallen. During his challenging rescue, the passage of time is measured in terms of continuity and interconnection, not repetitive instantaneity that isolates each new second from its predecessor. Here, time is measured by the gradual declension of the sun as day progresses toward night and by the successive links of the rope winched up from the depths, not by the second-bashing chronometry of Mr. Gradgrind's clock. In this context, each new moment does not merely expire, to be replaced by another identical to it. Instead, each new moment participates in and enables sequential advance toward a future with potential to differ radically from the past. Despite eventual rescue, Stephen dies a few minutes later. Yet his death is not in vain. His plunge toward utter helplessness—the extinction of agency—at the bottom of the shaft provokes movement toward the redemption of agency from the time scheme and corresponding mentality constraining and perverting it.

Among the texts we have investigated, perhaps the most vivid depiction of agency's surrender of self-determination to time occurs in *Mrs. Dalloway*, when the eponymous protagonist observes the old lady in the house opposite, at the moment that Big Ben booms:

> Big Ben struck the half-hour. How extraordinary it was, strange, yes touching to see the old lady (they had been neighbours ever so many years) move away from the window, *as if she were attached to that sound, that string*. Gigantic as it was, it had something to do with her. Down, down, into the midst of ordinary things, the finger fell making the moment solemn. *She was forced, so Clarissa imagined, by that sound, to move, to go*—but where? (Woolf 1992, 139 [my emphasis])

Here time, as promulgated by Big Ben, appears to compel agency to obey its command. But what compliance does time require? The "leaden circles" propagated by Big Ben's booms provide the answer. Here the movement of time is configured not linearly or anistropically, but cyclically, and the cycle itself is construed in terms of the hands revolving regularly around the face of the clock, dividing time into recurrent phases, so that the ongoing, cumulative advance is not noticed, only the duties ("She was forced") and activities appropriate to a properly scheduled routine. Thus time is formulated as cyclical imperatives, enclosing agency within predetermined bonds that regularize life and render it placidly predictable. Such is the Big Ben approach to achieving "unification of the different stages of life in simultaneity" (to retrieve Kierkegaard's phrase), reducing the awesome transit from birth to death to a matter of punctuality.

It is not Mrs. Dalloway's approach. She is acutely aware of the task of living "a whole life, a complete life," and acutely aware of the difficulty of doing so: "there was the terror; the overwhelming incapacity, one's parents giving it into one's hands, this life, to be lived to the end, to be walked with serenely; there was in the depths of her heart an awful fear" (Woolf 1992, 202). Here the supreme goal of agency is to master "the art of living" (60). The cardinal challenge in this regard is the threat of time: the exposure of life to the temporality of living, where it is "very, very dangerous to live even one day" (9), because awareness is invaded by other instants, past and future, that might either remind of happiness lost or terminate happiness present: "as if she had known all along that something would interrupt, would embitter her moment of happiness" (39). Moreover, even if these hazards are successfully negotiated or endured, there is no security in time ("She feared time itself"); for its passage imposes "the dwindling of life"—the same process of aging that posed such a problem in *Hard Times*: "they would grow old" (Woolf 1992, 32, 33, 202).

Both *Hard Times* and *Mrs. Dalloway* depict an official temporality (symbolized in the former by Mr. Gradgrind's clock and in the latter by Big Ben) designed to protect against the threat of time. Remarkably, in both novels. the official temporality is overcome by the catastrophic fall of one character: Stephen Blackpool's fall into the Old Hell Shaft and Septimus Warren Smith's suicidal plunge from a balcony. Each fall entails total loss of agency. With Stephen, this loss leads to gain, because through the effort to rescue him a new construction to time is communally achieved, in which temporal continuity is affirmed and embraced. With Septimus Warren Smith, surrender of agency leads to fulfillment of agency, through Mrs. Dalloway's intense meditation on his fate. By means of that astonishingly intuitive communion, Mrs. Dalloway is enabled to reaffirm the movement of time—to overcome her own prior conviction that the need to preserve a moment or memory from eventual elapse into the past or from the intrusion of the future justifies the sacrifice of life: "had he plunged holding his treasure?" (Woolf 1992, 202).

Yet she achieves much more than this, as further analysis will disclose. As we have seen, agency entails self-determination. In the novel, the ultimate self-determination concerns determining, from one's own perspective, the meaning and value of experience, through appreciative understanding of experience: "the power which adds the supreme flavour to existence,—the power of taking hold of experience, of turning it round, slowly, in the light" (Woolf 1992, 86). In his trauma-induced madness, Septimus occupies the opposite pole, unable to confront experience: "But he would not go mad. He would shut his eyes; he would see no more" (24). Thus, in the context of this Woolfian sense of agency, Septimus loses agency before his plunge to literal death. The deeper implications of this loss emerge when we note the correspondence between Septimus's plight as a victim of "shell shock" and Clarissa and Peter's suffering of analogous concussion (201). We recall, from discussion in Chapter 4, that loss of intimacy in the present (Clarissa when Peter interrupts her closeness with Sally, and Peter when Clarissa tells him of her love for Richard) is consistently described in terms of violent collision with a hard, unyielding surface: in other words, with concussion. Thus, Septimus is not the only victim of concussion in the novel. He cannot accept the loss of the past (the intimate friendship with Evans), and so hallucinates it as terrifyingly present. His madness is a denial of the passage of time. He requires simultaneity of tenses, but in a mode horrifyingly different from the one Kierkegaard had in mind. In the world of the novel, the plight of Septimus, with respect to vulnerability to the passage of time or, more precisely, to the elapse of a present moment or state and its replacement by its successor, is not anomalous, though it is, of course, extreme.

In *Mrs. Dalloway*, the passage of time brings many occasions when life seems "hollowed out," and subject to "emptiness" or "worthlessness" (53, 33, 124). In such circumstance, agency cannot operate successfully. For instead of determining the value of life, it determines the nullity of life. Consequently, agency is susceptible to suffering awareness of its own deterioration: "she frittered her time away, lunching, dining, giving these incessant parties of hers, talking nonsense, sayings things she didn't mean, *blunting the edge of her mind, losing her discrimination*" (86 [my emphasis]). In the novel, the plight of agency is a function of its constitution. For here agency, like the intellect in Aristotelian-Thomist epistemology, must be passive before it can be active. Before it can act (by determining the meaning and value of experience), it must passively receive impressions: "the drip, drip, of one impression after another" (166). Yet "[t]his susceptibility to impressions" can compromise the ability of agency to give value to what it absorbs or registers. For the quality of experience can distort the way of evaluating experience: "there were experiences, again experiences, such as change a face in two years from a pink innocent oval to a face lean, contracted, hostile" (78, 92). Such defective operation is obvious in the case of Septimus, who is so overwhelmed by experience that he feels "like a drowned sailor on a rock" (75). But it threatens every character vulnerable to "the uttermost depths of misery" (200). Doris Kilman, "[b]itter and burning," provides an apt example: "the hot and painful feelings boiled within her, this hatred of Mrs. Dalloway, this grudge against the world" (136). Though both Peter and Clarissa succumb repeatedly to negative impressions, both recover and rebound. This resilience and recuperative power preserves Clarissa's agency and that of her admirer, Peter: "it was this; it was middle age; it was mediocrity; then forced herself with her indomitable vitality to put all that aside, there being in her a thread of life which for toughness, endurance, power to overcome obstacles, and carry her triumphantly through he had never known the like of" (170). What sustains them is conviction in the "process of living"—"absorbing, mysterious, of infinite richness, this life," unfolding in time (203, 179).

This magnificent tribute to Clarissa applies equally to Mrs. Ramsay, Lily Brisco, and ultimately Mr. Ramsay in *To the Lighthouse*. In that novel, the notion of agency as self-determination through reconstruction of time achieves perhaps its most powerful expression in literature. Here awareness, to achieve its own salvation from temporal fragmentation, is charged with the exhausting task of reconstituting temporal wholeness—the sense that, after shattering tragedy, life can again sustain cohesive shape "[i]n the midst of chaos" (Woolf 1927, 176). Though the enterprise is mental, the intensity of the effort it entails approximates supreme physical exertion: "Yes, she thought, laying down her brush in extreme fatigue, I have had my vision" (226). Without such temporal reconstruction, agency—understood as self-determination in movement through life—lapses into impotence. Mr. Ramsay's helplessness is a case in point. All he can do in the tragic aftermath is beg for pity, until he too achieves temporal perspective by a contemplative process analogous to Lily's strenuous act of painting. Before her own temporal reconstitution, Lily flounders in "the waters of annihilation" (196)—a metaphorical version of the waters over which Mr. Ramsay sails, where "[w]e perished, each alone" (224). Just as the kitchen table, in Andrew's example, exists "when you're not there" (28), so too temporal passage, in which "night … succeeds to night," exists, whether or not anyone is around to experience it (139). But in *To the Lighthouse* the problem of time concerns not *passage*, but *presence*. Think again of the kitchen table. In the epistemology of the novel, it is there whether or not anyone sees it. But temporal presence—the sense of being in this moment of time *now*—presupposes awareness, and that awareness, in turn, is burdened in the novel with the task of constituting the cohesion of the present with other moments, such that the "little strip of time" allocated to a given life is infused with "a wholeness" of "compacted" meaning (209). The supreme function of agency in the novel is to synthesize or gather together "little separate incidents" into a unity whose contemplation engenders an exalted perspective on the "eternal passing and flowing" that the transit of life through time must endure (176). But that perspective is itself unstable, "so that the vision must be perpetually remade" (197).

Ultimately, what the vision or perspective reveals is meaning: "What was the value, the meaning of things?" (133); "What is the meaning of life? (175). This confrontation between the urgent need for meaning and the devastating loss of meaning entails the same "anxiety of meaninglessness" (Paul Tillich's term) that informs Existentialism—a philosophical movement whose concerns the novel to some extent shares, as many critics have noted. According to Tillich, "The anxiety of meaninglessness is anxiety about the loss of an ultimate concern, of a meaning which gives meaning to all meanings" (1952, 47). In the novel, temporal passage, epitomized by the transience of life and therefore of the personal relationships that sustain meaning in life, is the factor that destroys meaning and requires its reconstitution. In this circumstance, human existence suffers the encounter with nonbeing, and inhabits, to invoke Tillich's account of the Existential perspective, "a world in which the categories, the structures of reality, have lost their validity" (1952, 147). Lily's bewilderment exactly expresses this predicament: "How aimless it was, how chaotic, how *unreal* it was, she thought, looking at her empty coffee cup. Mrs. Ramsay dead; Andrew killed; Prue dead too" (Woolf 1927, 160 [my emphasis]). Here the encounter with nonbeing, resulting from awareness of temporal passage and the loss of that which was, corresponds closely to Tillich's account: "It stands behind the experience that we are driven, together with everything else, from the past toward the future without a moment of time which does not vanish immediately" (43). In this context, the dynamics of Woolfian agency emerge clearly. Whereas in Existentialism, according to Tillich, the threat of nonbeing is met by a robust "vitality that can stand the abyss of meaninglessness" (1952, 177), and achieve "self-affirmation 'in-spite-of,' that is in spite of that which tends to prevent the self from affirming the self" (32), the mastery of meaninglessness in *To the Lighthouse* requires more than the courage to be. For, in addition, it requires dauntless concentration and creativity, focused by the resolve to bring "together this and that and then this" into a meaningful temporal unity, despite "decrepitude and exhaustion and sorrow" (181), and despite the relentless tendency of time to reduce temporal order to chaos.

Time is the vehicle of nonbeing in *To the Lighthouse*. But as such, it invites a heroically creative response—"the one dependable thing in a world of strife, ruin, chaos" (Woolf 1927, 164). Through such response, instilled with "the determination not to be put off, not to be bamboozled" (218), agency can acknowledge "the truth about things" (219)—the instability and frailty of human structures and attachments—and become the means whereby "the whole is held together" (116), after "the unity of the whole [has been] broken" (60). In this respect, the novel presents an intensely moving and profound confirmation of Tillich's existential pronouncement: "But nonbeing drives being out of its seclusion, it forces it to affirm itself dynamically" (179).

The distinction between the role of agency respectively in *Mrs. Dalloway* and *To the Lighthouse* can now be epitomized, in order to highlight some of the major points just discussed. In *Mrs. Dalloway*, the simultaneity of isochronic and durational time (time artificially divided into equal parts and time construed as the continuous unfolding of an emergent whole) entails discrepant formulations of agency, such that, in one, action is in accord with the time allotted to it, while in the other action expresses and invokes awareness of a simultaneity of moments (as when Mrs. Dalloway, on the first page, opens the French windows and suddenly plunges into a memory of a similar moment long ago). In this circumstance, the great risk that agency confronts is that simultaneity of awareness will be shattered by *discontinuity*, when awareness in the present, through some intrusive event or circumstance, suddenly suffers excruciating severance from what it has come to treasure, and loses the ability—or the will—to regain equilibrium in the present through maintaining connection with the past. In *To the Lighthouse*, agency is stymied, indeed for long periods overwhelmed, by the shattering impact of temporal passage—what Lucio P. Ruotolo terms "the shock of time passing" (1986, 131). In this context, action—most profoundly, the activity of thought—must be formulated as reconstitution of dispersed fragments into a new unity, so that meaning and purpose can be restored to the sense of life, otherwise devastated by awareness of "strife, ruin, chaos" (1927, 170). Here, unlike in *Mrs. Dalloway*, the task of agency is not just to restore—and accept—continuity, but to achieve a deeper affirmation of life through constructing a more penetrating—a more appropriate word in this context is "cohesive"—perspective on it.

In moving from *To the Lighthouse* to *Ulysses*, we find the relation of agency to time reversed. Instead of provoking agency to act (by restoring meaning to life through creatively recombining the moments constituting it), in *Ulysses* time tends to sap agency of motivation, for the focus of attention is shifted from the present to the past: "Memories beset his brooding brain"—a predicament applying equally to both Stephen and Bloom (Joyce 1960, 10). Each character, to appropriate Stephen's phrase about the dog digging on Sandymount Strand, is "looking for something lost in a past life"—in a phase of life, that is, before the present (57). Stephen is obsessed with filial guilt and Bloom with paternal grief. As a result of attachment to the past, each character is both "agent and reagent" or agent and "reactor" (Joyce 1960, 864, 866). For here, agency is conditioned by reaction to past circumstance. In this predicament, the scope and vitality of agency is restricted by the need to counteract the pull of the past ("Hold to the now, the here, through which all future plunges to the past") or to adjust to loss of the past: "Can't bring back time. Like holding water in your hand" (238, 213). In *Ulysses*, the cause of this difficulty with the movement of "irreversible time" is the nature of (human) time itself (858). For according to the "view of life" unfolded in the novel, the transit from birth to death is marked by "convulsions of metamorphosis" (181, 817). The movement of time is thus punctuated by shocks and rebounds, destabilizing and disorienting to the subjects enduring in it. Whereas the Kierkegaardian ethics, as we have seen, enjoin "the unification of the different stages of life in simultaneity," Joycean morality demands not *unification in simultaneity*, but *negotiation in consecutivity* of the stages that the passage through life comprises.

Until ready fully to inhabit the new stage of life, character tends to cling to or perseverate the past one. In their different ways, both Stephen and Bloom achieve distraction and protection from the present by "chewing the cud of reminiscence" (540). In this context, Nosey Flynn's story about the woman who "who hid herself in a clock" gains ironic import (226). Preoccupation with time or with a past phase of time becomes the means of hiding from time or, more precisely, from the addressing and mastering the jarring changes that its movement entails. Yet the novel remains positive. Characters, at least by implication, are ultimately redeemed through "the wonderfully unequal faculty of metempsychosis possessed by them" (534). As a result, "tomorrow will be a new day," even as it is just another day (529-30). That is, awareness of change, instead of perpetuating pain or paralysis, will progressively foster development, and inspire self-determination with "[s]omething new to hope for" (128). Released from resistance, character is no longer "debarred from seeing more of the world," from opening up to more of life as to "a new world" (724, 899). Through depicting the struggle with metempsychosis, *Ulysses* contributes magnificently to "the eternal affirmation of the spirit of man in literature" (777).

The novel ends, of course, with Molly's impassioned affirmation: "yes I said yes I will Yes" (933). In the immediate context, she is remembering the initial consummation of her love for Bloom—the man she married and from whom she became estranged. More deeply—indeed deeper than her conscious awareness—she is saying yes to love in the past in order to renew it in the immediate future: the next morning, in fact, when she will likely change a longstanding routine, and bring Bloom breakfast in bed. These changes and developments, of course, remain ambiguous and unconfirmed. Yet their possibility is enough to suggest that, on a level deeper still, Molly is doing what Bloom and Stephen must also do: affirming the past in order to pass from it, "wholly, slowly" (73), into the present. What does this mean? Here, to affirm the past means to affirm that it *is* past, and hence beyond access, except through memory. *As* past (or, in technical diction, qua past), the past has something positive to give to the present.

But it can do so only if the pastness of the past is accepted. In contrast, Stephen and Bloom have *denied* the pastness of the past. In this predicament, agency is directed toward impossible projects: for Stephen, undoing the past; for Bloom, remaining in it. Consequently, each is vulnerable to the horrifying fantasy of the return of the past or what is already dead: "No mother. Let me be and let me live"; "No, no: he is dead, of course" (11, 140).

The liberation of agency from attachment to the past is at once the most crucial and ambiguous aspect of Joycean metempsychosis. Unlike the onset of the thunderstorm described in "Oxen of the Sun," the "transformation" entailed in metempsychosis is not "violent and instantaneous" (553). Instead, it proceeds undetected and cumulatively, like "a darkness shining in brightness which brightness could not comprehend" (34). Once passage through a stage has been completed, the subject is able to look back at it, with detached understanding, as when Stephen sees the image of his own childhood vulnerability in his student, Cyril Sargent: "My childhood bends before me" (34). When, however, a character is still immersed in transformation—especially a transformation that is resisted or refused—he or she cannot yet grasp, on the emotional level, that change must be accepted in order for further growth to follow. More precisely, since growth is part of life and cannot be prevented as long as life continues, acceptance of change facilitates the transit through the metamorphoses "from infancy through maturity to decay" (817), and frees, through the "disintegration of obsession" (815), agency from the nets of denial and resistance in which it might otherwise be ensnared. Yet the concussive movement of time in *Ulysses* ensures that the agency of character remains split between the two modes cited earlier: "agent and reagent" (864). To the extent that the movement of time in life is ineluctably punctuated by "convulsions of metamorphosis" (817), agency must react before it can act. That is, self-determination is shaped by and must adapt to life-transforming circumstance.

A similar split between agent and reagent obtains in *Hamlet*, but for different reasons whose explication will clarify the matter of Hamlet's celebrated delay. In his initial registration of the revenge imperative, Hamlet construes himself not as an agent, in the sense of a self-determining subject proposing its own ends, but as a mere instrument through which a purpose outside himself is fulfilled or achieved. In other words, he is not so much an agent as a reagent: one who must react with appropriate promptitude to the instruction received. Indeed, he associates the will to obey with loss of the will to think of anything but the commandment that he must heed. To obey is to wipe his mental slate clean, to have neither thought nor motive but those pertaining to the swift execution of his task, his duty: "And thy commandment all alone shall live / Within the book and volume of my brain" (1.5.102–3). Yet he does not remain inside the nutshell of this dispensation. By the time Hamlet achieves revenge, the meaning of his act and of his agency in performing it have completely changed.

In this context, the vexed question of Hamlet's delay attains more profound meaning. Conventionally, Hamlet's delay is construed in terms of inordinate temporal elapse: taking too long to do what should be done. Hamlet himself endorses this interpretation: "Do you not come your tardy son to chide?" (3.4.107). As such, temporal interval becomes a criterion of character evaluation, just as (though for different reasons) with respect to Gertrude's "o'er-hasty marriage" (2.2.57). That is, time here functions as a measure of moral quality or worth. Ironically however, through delay Hamlet achieves a different construction of time—one in which temporal passage no longer determines the appropriate time line or schedule of agency (dictating, i.e., when something should or should not be done), but instead enables agency, through progressive understanding of the movement of time, to deepen the implications and widen the scope of its own ends.

The concern of the revenge morality with when things are to be done is, of course, especially ironic, for the time period most important to that morality is neither the present nor the future, but the past. As we saw in detail in Chapter 1, the revenge morality is driven by the need to reverse the one-way forward movement of time. Hence, it installs the past as the primary tense, by requiring that movement toward the future seek redress for what happened in the past. Hamlet's task is to redeem agency from servitude to the past. Agency must determine not just to avenge the past, but to secure the "readiness" regarding temporal passage that the past denied (5.2.218). The play unfolds the steps of this development. In Ophelia's closet, soon after receiving the revenge imperative, Hamlet is a ghost, not a man; for he looks "As if he had been loosed from hell / To speak of horrors" (2.1.83–4). He has temporarily subordinated his agency to service to the past. He cannot even see where he is going, only where he was, "with his head over his shoulder turn'd" (2.1.97). Yet with the arrival of the Players at Elsinore, Hamlet displays heightened awareness of the changes accompanying the passage of time, as with respect, for example, to transient theatrical "fashion" and the fleeting fusion of factors that give "the very age and body of the time his form and pressure" (2.2.339; 3.2.23–24). Here the movement of the present away from the past is not baleful ("It is not, nor it cannot come to good"), but benign (1.2.158). Later, when observing Claudius "a-praying" after the truncated performance of *The Murder of Gonzago*, Hamlet breaks decisively with the view of time associated with the revenge morality (3.3.73). That is, he moves from preoccupation with the *causes* or reasons for action, which reside in the past, to concern with the *consequences* of action, which will emerge in the future. Self-determining agency involves choice—what Beiser defines as "the power to do otherwise" (2005, 73). At this crucial juncture, Hamlet's agency is poised between two choices: to act "now" and kill Claudius for the sake of what was done in the past or to defer action for the sake of optimizing consequences in the future, when death would lead Claudius to damnation, not salvation (3.3.73).

Of course, this choice entails a new relation to the movement of time. Temporal passage is no longer resisted, but accepted—indeed harnessed. This new attitude toward time develops further during the scene in Gertrude's closet, where another progression from prioritizing the past to prioritizing the future unfolds. Until the entrance of the Ghost distracts him, Hamlet violently excoriates his mother for transferring her "ardour" from husband past to husband present (3.4.86). But after the Ghost indicates Gertrude's psychological distress, Hamlet pivots from (a) flaying her for what she did and continues to do to (b) encouraging her to begin the process of exchanging "habits evil" for those "fair and good" (3.4.164, 165). Here movement toward the future enables supersession of the past. The faults of the past can be modified in the future. The die is not cast, but continually undergoing revision, refashioning. Just before leaving Gertrude's closet, Hamlet extends this newly acquired valorization of temporal passage to his conflict with Claudius. Now the passage of time, instead of entraining the stigma of delay, will provide opportunities to exploit emergent circumstance in the battle against "knavery": "For 'tis the sport to have the enginer / Hoist with his own petard" (3.4.207, 208–9).

At this point, a vital paradox emerges. One the one hand, we (the observers outside the play) can see the tremendous advance, articulated in stages, that Hamlet has made so far regarding temporal awareness. But on the other hand, Hamlet himself still lacks understanding of his own awareness. In other words, Hamlet knows—more precisely, his knowing grows—but only we, through analysis, know what he knows, until he himself eventually begins to share that registration. The incandescent intensity of his thinking (and of his thinking on his thinking, in various soliloquies) entails the excruciating process of thought going beyond the reaches of its own limitations, while still limited by them: a circumstance ironically expressed by Hamlet's reference to the Ghost's ability "So horridly to shake our disposition / With thoughts beyond the reaches of our souls" (1.4.55–56). Ironically, Hamlet's delay—a measure of temporal passage—provides the time needed for Hamlet to pass through stages of enlightenment regarding the relation between time and agency.

Perhaps nowhere in the play is the tension between (a) what progressively unfolds in Hamlet's awareness and (b) what he nevertheless does not yet recognize more dramatic than in the soliloquy just before his forced embarkation on the ship bound for England. In a passage included in the Second Quarto text of the play (1604–5) but not in the First Folio version (1623), Hamlet contrasts his own inaction to the examples of action around him: "How all occasions do inform against me" (4.4.32). Here he addresses the problem of agency ("this thing's to do") in terms of conformity to the revenge morality, where action, heedless of consequence ("Makes mouths at the invisible event") or intrinsic value ("for a fantasy and a trick of fame") is demanded, "[w]hen honour's at the stake" (4.4.44, 50, 61, 56). Though lines such as these have fueled the arguments of critics (such as René Girard) who maintain that Hamlet delays because of reluctance to kill Claudius, such interpretation, in my opinion, distorts the character it concerns. Hamlet does not lack motivation to avenge: "Sith I have cause, and will, and strength, and means / To do't" (4.4.45–46). Moreover, on achieving revenge, he regrets not the deed, but only the fact that his own death prevents him from explaining why he did it: "Report me and my cause aright" (5.2.343). Yet motivation, capability, and opportunity are not enough for Hamlet. He needs something more and, until he has it, the time for revenge remains "out of joint" (1.5.196).

To be an avenging agent—to do what must be done—Hamlet needs a more adequate model of agency than that provided by the revenge morality. In his terse epitome of the revenge morality, Hamlet emphasizes the role of action and reaction. Provocation that compromises honor should immediately trigger appropriate response, regardless of the intrinsic significance of the injury concerned: "even for an eggshell" (4.4.53). There is no self-determining agency here, just rhetorically embellished stimulus-response behavior. However, as we saw in Chapter 1, the fundamental stimulus provoking reaction is the movement of time. To reverse that movement, the revenge morality installs the past as the primary tense, and demands that past injury provoke prompt future response, thus construing what will be in terms of retaliation for what was. Before finally achieving revenge, Hamlet will arrive at a construction of agency that, instead of attempting to reverse the movement of time, takes full account of it. Yet his progress toward such understanding is not an intellectual exercise. Instead, it involves productive encounter of thought with the emergent series of events that the movement of time entails. This synergy of thought and the sequence of happenings through time constitutes the extraordinary dynamic of Hamlet's deepening insight into the relation between agency and time.

Further development of Hamlet's enlightenment in this regard occurs aboard the ship bound for England. Though at first Hamlet feels helplessly captive ("Methought I lay / Worse than the mutines in the bilboes"), he suddenly constitutes himself as a free agent, groping "in the dark" from his cabin to the one occupied by Rosencrantz and Guildenstern, removing their diplomatic "packet" as they sleep, then rewriting it so that they, not Hamlet, will be executed on arrival at their destination (5.2.5–6, 13, 15). Here Hamlet acts not for the sake of the past, as enjoined by the revenge morality, but to ensure his survival in the future—at least longer than the time allotted to him by Claudius. Moreover, in this episode Hamlet's relation to the past changes. Whereas, according to the revenge morality, the function of the past is to *determine* the future through coercion ("this thing's to do"), on the ship Hamlet finds that the function of the past is to *liberate* the present through enabling or empowering it to fulfill its ends. For, on discovering the instructions from Claudius to the English King, Hamlet draws on calligraphic training acquired when he was younger (and which he tried—fortunately without success—to "forget" later): "It did me yeoman's service" (5.2.35, 36). Here the past serves Hamlet's agency, whereas in the revenge morality agents serve the past.

The next great advance Hamlet makes regarding construction of the past occurs in the Graveyard scene. Here, amid the bones and skulls of the dead, Hamlet achieves detachment from the past—an attitude opposite to that required by the revenge morality. Here he views the past not as directly influencing the present, but as undergoing its own process of modification, as when the corpse of Alexander the Great ends up, through stages of decomposition and recombination, as loam employed to "stop a beer-barrel"—a conception informing his earlier mot regarding "how a king may go a progress through the guts of a beggar" (5.1.205; 4.3.30–31). In the Graveyard version of this concern with decomposition, Hamlet adds a crucial notion—instrumentality: "To what base uses we may return, Horatio!" (5.1.196). Here the past is *used*, not obeyed. That is, it *serves* the purposes of agency, instead of determining them.

Hamlet's eventual detachment from the past is soon matched by his detachment from the future: "If it be now, 'tis not to / come; if it be not to come, it will be now; if it be not / now, yet it will come. The readiness is all. (5.2.216–18). Hamlet is referring to death—an event imminent every moment until it actually occurs. In the context of "providence," death can be neither too late nor too soon, for it occurs at its appointed time: "There is special providence in the fall of a sparrow" (5.2.215–16). The time is no longer out of joint. It does not entail the inopportune arrival of events, because occurrences are ordered in time according to the purposes of divinity. Hamlet's notion of readiness entails an extraordinary fusion of time and providence. Readiness is enabled by acceptance of mortality and conviction that providence determines the appropriate moment for death to occur, "[n]ow or whensoever" (5.2.199). In Hamlet's formulation, this acceptance of fatal inevitability entails and requires acceptance of temporal passage—something that Hamlet, as we have seen, has been moving toward in the course of the play, independently of his notion of providence. His notion of providence and his notion of readiness regarding the determinations of providence depend on and culminate his emergent acceptance of temporal passage. Such acceptance is the sine qua non of readiness and conviction in providence.

Let us examine the implications of this dispensation more closely. In Hamlet's ultimate view, the operation of providence involves reciprocity between divine and human agency: "There's a divinity that shapes our ends, / Rough-hew them how we will" (5.2.10–11). Divine agency works through human agency, whose purposes or ends, though determined by human agents, ultimately serve the ends determined by divine agency. In this formulation, Hamlet conflates two constructions of character: character construed as determined by destiny and character construed as self-determining. Historically, the former precedes the latter, and Hamlet himself can be understood as a character at the point where destiny begins to yield to self-determination. Conception of time is the means by which he advances from one to the other. In the first (character as destiny), the unfolding or development of character is predetermined by factors beyond the reaches of individual control or self-determination. In the play, that factor concerns the tragic flaw—"the stamp of one defect" or *hamartia* (1.4.31). In the second (character as self-determination), explicitly formulated in Gertrude's closet, character can "almost change the stamp of nature" through sustained self-discipline whereby "habits evil" are progressively annulled: "Repent what's past, avoid what is to come" (3.4.170, 164, 152). Whereas in the revenge morality the past determines the future, here movement toward the future is driven by self-determination to achieve freedom from the past.

The urgent and relentless concern in *Hamlet* with the moral imperative and the time allocated to its fulfilment finds its opposite in the Beckettian oeuvre, which spurns the "moral plane" (1964, 57). Here "what the fuck" (131) replaces "What should we do?" (1.4.57). More elegantly, here the repeated disclaimer, "Nothing to be done," rampant in *Waiting for Godot* but recurrent elsewhere, displaces "this thing's to do" (4.4.44). There is nothing to be done, because nothing can be accomplished but conviction in futility: "No, one can spend one's life thus, unable to live, unable to bring to life, and die in vain, having done nothing, been nothing" (Beckett 1958d, 358). There is nothing to achieve, because nothing abides but loss: "all is lost" (Beckett 1964, 46), "Loss of spirits ... lack of keenness ... want of appetite" (Beckett 1961, 13 [original ellipsis]). In these circumstances, time is an irrelevance that simply continues the wish for its absence: "a little less of to be present past future and conditional of to be and not to be" (Beckett 1964, 38). The paradoxical plight of Beckettian awareness concerns the suffering of *endurance without duration*. To adopt Hamm's phrasing, "something is taking its course," and for that process time is required. But all that happens or unfolds is awareness of the void or nothingness: terms that resound throughout the Beckettian oeuvre. Hence, as The Unnamable notes, "time doesn't pass" (1958d, 389), and instead merely perpetuates, according to the narrator of *How It Is*, "the same instant always everywhere" (1964, 112), since all it comprises are what Hamm terms "moments for nothing" (1958a, 83).

We cannot speak of agency in this context, because the function of agency is to act, and here, as already noted, there is nothing to be done. Moreover, instead of the project of self-determination, Beckettian awareness pursues self-divestiture, as in the ubiquitous refrain, "It's not I." The only act that Beckettian agency seeks to perform is disappearance into nothingness: "Ah if only this voice could stop, this meaningless voice which prevents you from being nothing" (1958d, 370). Nothingness, as Findlay points out in another context, is "the absolute absence of anything" (1958, 156). The absence that Beckettian awareness strives to achieve is itself: "Absent, always. It all happened without me" (1958a, 74). Hence, in some texts all that is accorded to agency is the bare awareness of thoughts whose ownership it denies.

The project of "flight from self" (Beckett 1958d, 367) is coordinated with a flight from time. For summary purposes, two tactics by which this is attempted can be noted. The first concerns the de-temporalizing of time—the removal from time, that is, of the temporal distinctions or properties by which time is measured: "the various times mixed up in my head all the various times before during after vast tracts of time" (1964, 107). To interpolate a phrase from *How It Is*, all things "with time shall pass away" (15). But in certain Beckettian texts, time itself passes away, as a result of its interminable and indeterminate elapsing. All that remains of temporality is amorphous and boundless duration ("vast tracts of time"), deprived even of continuity, since it is constituted not by serial order, one thing after another, but indiscriminate agglomeration: "buried under the seconds" (1958d, 398). Agency as self-determination cannot operate in such an environment, because agency presupposes temporal distinctions between intention, act, and consequence. In T. S. Eliot's "The Hollow Men," agency is thwarted by the Shadow: "Between the motion / And the act / Falls the Shadow" (1963, 92). In the Beckettian dispensation prevailing in certain texts, the Shadow that falls upon agency is time. Though actions occur and movements are made, they do not effect change. Agency is denied efficacy and hence its defining function. The same "enormous second" abides unaltered and unalterable (1967a, 82). The second tactic for flight from time concerns rememoration. Here the past becomes the zone of absence: the place affording escape from the present. "It is then I shall have lived or never" (1974a, 57). In this context, agency means no more than the project not to be present to the present, but instead to be in a past that never was or that could not continue as it was, and to identify with the self that might have been: "Will they succeed in slipping me into him, the memory and dream of me, into him still living" (1967a, 134).

Perhaps no literary text more spectacularly opposes the Beckettian disposal of time than Ian McEwan's *Enduring Love*, where the narrator, Joe Rose, clings precariously to a rope dangling from the basket of an errant touring balloon, as the interval between life and death swiftly elapses: "Every fraction of a second that passed increased the drop, and the point must come when to let go would be impossible or fatal" (14). We are at the opposite pole from Pozzo's abbreviation of the transit of an entire lifetime from birth to death to "the same second." Time loses significance in *Waiting for Godot*, because there is nothing to be done during it. In contrast, time gains significance in the balloon episode in *Enduring Love*, because miscalculation at just one instant will suddenly truncate the transit from birth to death. In this predicament, agency must act promptly or never have the chance to act again: "A delay of one second would have been enough to close his options" (15). Though conspicuous in *Hamlet*, delay in the balloon scene is not a viable alternative, and Joe's traumatic encounter with the imperative of survival launches him, just as prolonged delay regarding the revenge imperative propels Hamlet, on an extended and urgent reconceptualization of the relation of agency to time.

The primary problem that agency confronts in the aftermath of the balloon catastrophe concerns reluctance to act, because action propagates consequences, and consequences occur in the yet unknown future: "Anxiety about, distaste for the future" (McEwan 1997, 43). As a result, agency seeks through action to achieve not self-determination, but future-determination—to determine, that is, the future, so that nothing threatening can happen: "*intentionality, intention, tries to assert control over the future*" (43 [original emphasis]). Eventually, following a series of events that predispose him to exercise self-determination, lest Parry's insanity close his options as surely as did involuntary ascent with the balloon earlier, Joe decides to act (by purchasing a gun for defence against Parry), despite the risk that action might precipitate uncontrollable effects: "I knew that one action, one event, would entail another, until the train was beyond my control, and that if I had doubts this was the moment to withdraw" (188). He might well have added, with Hamlet, "The readiness is all." Indeed, both Hamlet and Joe ultimately construe agency in terms of readiness, and both achieve their respective notions of readiness through extended reflection on and experience with the relation between agency and time. For Hamlet, readiness results from awareness of the synergy between human and divine agency, wherein the ends of human agency, though freely devised (once the primacy of the past is superseded by openness to the future), nevertheless have their ultimate purposes shaped and designed by providence, beyond the reaches of human agency to foresee or even conceive. For Joe, readiness results from awareness of the need to brave or hazard the consequences of action, even though untoward consequences cannot be completely forestalled. After the balloon catastrophe, when he suffered temporal trauma, shocked by the experience of finding present action (the attempt to rescue the balloon boy) precipitating consequences that threatened his own survival in the immediate future, Joe at first distrusts action and repudiates agency, lest they populate the future with menacing possibilities. Later, after subsequent events show Joe that inaction might render him hostage to a future utterly beyond his control because it will be controlled by a madman, Joe acts, with full awareness of his predicament in doing so.

Essentially, the madness of Parry—the man who, due to mental disease, falls in love with Joe—foregrounds Joe's central problem with time: not merely the unpredictability and imprevisibility of the future, but more importantly the vulnerability of any phase of life to disruption, truncation, and termination. That which is treasured might not last. Conversely, that which is abhorred might last instead. This is the basic irony of the title: *Enduring Love*. Regarding Clarissa, his common-law wife, Joe wants love to last, though his preoccupation with Parry eventually leads to marital separation: "It had always seemed to me that our love was just the kind to endure" (158). Ironically, in his delusion, Parry conceives his relation to Joe in terms of the promise of perpetual exemption from temporal change—or, more precisely, from the struggle with events that intrude inevitably upon the present, compelling agency to deal with them: "No more rocky uphill! *Peace, and time stretching out before us* (McEwan 1997, 137 [my emphasis]). Joe's temporary suspension or abdication of agency serves a similar project: to denature time by eliminating from it the possibility of "a tainted future" that will undermine or destroy the security of the present (169).

According to Joe, "time protects us from our worst mistakes," because the swiftness of events now and then prevents too much reflection on what to do before their occurrence (171). This is his version of Hamlet's caveat regarding "thinking too precisely on th'event" (4.4. 41). Conversely, as the texts under examination show, time can precipitate our worst mistakes, by tempting us to try to detain time or to obliterate the significance of its passage. *Everyman*, a late-fifteenth-century English morality play, refers famously to the relentless advance of time in terms of a tidal metaphor: "For, wit thou well, the tide abideth no man" (1996, 9). In the texts we have investigated, Canute-like projects to halt, retard, reverse, or ignore the advance of time proliferate. In all cases except the Beckettian, those projects to alter or deter temporal movement yield eventually to readiness to accept and clarify the implications of being in time, to dismantle structures intended to oppose or dispose of them, and, as a result, to free agency from a crucial factor undermining its own power of self-determination.

Notes

Introduction

1 A celebrated contrary of this dream is the vision of the Carmelite nun St. Teresa (1515–1582), in which an angel stabbed her heart repeatedly with a spear, provoking intense spiritual ecstasy. Such spiritual wounding of the heart is termed transverberation. St. Teresa's written account of the vision inspired the great Baroque sculptor Gian Lorenzo Bernini (1598–1680) to carve a superb statue of the event for placement above the altar of the Cornaro Chapel in the church of Santa Maria della Victoria in Rome.

2 Writers on time often cite Augustine's perplexity when launching their respective investigations: "What then is time? I know well enough what it is, provided that nobody asks me; but if I am asked what it is, and try to explain, I am baffled" (Augustine 1961, XI:14). See, for example, Ridderbos 2002, 1; Strauss 2010, 167; and Lloyd 1993, 14.

3 Hence Eva Brann describes philosophy as the language of "the inquiring intellect" (1999, xii).

4 In Mark Currie's formulation, "Time is a universal feature of narrative, but it is the topic of only a few" (2007, 2).

5 Pozzo's metaphor of life as no longer than a flash of light perhaps derives from Miguel de Unamuno's *The Tragic Sense of Life in Men and Nations* (first published in Spanish in 1913): "If consciousness is no more—as some inhuman thinker said—than a flash of lightening between two eternities of darkness, then there is nothing more execrable than existence" (1972, 17). In this regard, one can note that both Beckett and Unamuno contributed to the third issue of *New Review*, edited and published by Sam Putnam in Paris in August 1931.

6 Compare Hegel: "It is rather the very being of finite things, that they contain the seeds of perishing as their own being-in-self: *the hour of their birth is the hour of their death*" (1929, 1.142, my emphasis).

7 Ironically, Pirenne himself is associated with a famous theory, the Pirenne Thesis, which asserts that the Middle Ages stemmed not from the fall of the Western Roman Empire, but from the rise of Islam during the seventh and eighth centuries: a circumstance that closed the Mediterranean Sea to Christian trade, thereby forcing European civilization to become more insular.

8 Sylviane Agacinski also links modernity with irreversible time: "modern temporality is the endless interlacing of the irreversible and the repetitive" (2003, 12).

9 One year earlier, an exhortatory reference to irreversible time animated Richard Baxter's *The Saint's Everlasting Rest* (1650): "The time we have lost cannot be recalled; should we not then redeem and improve the little which remains?" (1831, 196). Baxter here epitomizes the Puritan stricture regarding time—a concern ably explained by Wallace Notestein: "The Puritan believed in the careful use of time. At his back he heard always time's winged chariot. Much time ought to be reserved to the use of God and the remainder should be devoted to one's calling" (1954, 153).

10 Less technical, though nevertheless explicit, British linkings of time with irreversible succession also abound, as in the following examples, drawn from the fourteenth, seventeenth, and eighteenth centuries. A Late Medieval linkage of temporal passage with succession appears in William of Occam's *Dialogue on the Power of the Pope and the Emperor* (Part III, Tract I, dated 1334–1347): "What has been believed from the time of the Apostles until our own time by prelates and doctors of the Church *succeeding one another in a continuous series* and by the peoples subject to them should be held firmly by all Catholics" (1995, 227, my emphasis). A devotional yet enchanting seventeenth-century characterization of temporal succession, blending the Aristotelian notion of time as the measure of motion with the Christian notion of "self-entity" or aseity, occurs in Sir Thomas Browne's *Religio Medici* (1642), where "the essence of time" is construed as sequential movement, which God in principle could reverse to a prior point, like a film wound back upon the spool, we might anachronistically say today, and then allowed to "travel on again by the same motions, and upon the same wheels it rolled upon before" (1835, 128–29). An eighteenth-century linking of time with irreversible succession informs a passage in Edmund Burke's *Reflections on the Revolution in France* (1790): "This mixed system of opinion and sentiment had its origin in the ancient chivalry; and the principle, though varied in its appearance by the varying state of human affairs, subsisted and influenced *through a long succession of generations, even to the time we live in*" (1959, 92, my emphasis).

11 Cf. Plato, *Parmenides*: "Whatever occupies time must always be becoming older than itself, and 'older' always means older than something younger" (1963, 141a).

12 In Fritz Chenderlin's phrasing, chronos "always emphasizes chronology, while [kairos] tends to emphasize content" (1982, 50).

13 For further discussion of Xenophon's *Anabasis*, see Levy 2003.

14 To these I can add Gene A. Brucker, who notes "the development of a sense of time in history" in Renaissance Florence (1983, 251).

15 Another counterexample pertains to St. Hilary of Poitiers, who, in 365, as Coulton indicates, "deplored the gradual revolution which had brought an Apostolic brotherhood of sufferers into a newer institution of persecutors for the Faith: 'The

Church terrifieth with threats of exile and dungeons; and she, who of old gained men's faith in spite of exile and prison, now brings them to believe in her by compulsion'" (1938, 16).

16 The same chronological self-consciousness informs the letter (not mentioned by Moorhead) sent in 547 by Belisarius, a general of the Eastern emperor Justinian, to Totila, the penultimate Ostrogothic king, at that time poised to demolish Rome as his occupying troops were preparing to leave the city. Belisarius, in the course of undertaking Justinian's project to recover the western provinces, had earlier recaptured Rome from the Ostrogoths, but lost it to Totila in 546. In his letter to Totila, Belisarius warns the Ostrogothic king of the ignominy that will stain his name in the future should he destroy a city built "in the course of a long history": "Her monuments belong to posterity, and an outrage committed upon them will rightly be regarded as a great injustice to all future generations as well as to the memory of those who created them" (quoted in Bury 1923, 2. 244). Here, very clearly, Belisarius places an impending event (the destruction of Rome) in the context of temporal passage and historical transition.

17 Cf. Otto Von Simpson: "[W]hat constituted reality for medieval man was not the palpable fact, but its transcendental meaning: in the light of ideas and beliefs every phenomenon appeared romantically transformed" (1988, 88). According to Emile Mâle, history itself, during that era, was construed not as an open-ended progression through time but as a fixed series of acts in a drama designed by God: "The Old Testament shows humanity awaiting the Law, the New Testament shows the Law incarnate, and the Acts of the Saints shows man's endeavour to conform to the Law" (1958, 131).

18 Compare Ramsay Macmullen: "There are certain irreducibles in human history deriving from neither culture nor events but rather from the species itself" (1988, 75).

19 On Second Temple nostalgia, see, for example, Cohen 2007, 131, and Davies 2003, 165.

20 As Anna-Theresa Tymieniecka, in the Introduction to *Temporality in Life as Seen Through Literature: Contributions to Phenomenology of Life*, indicates: "Always operative, whatever the perspectives within which the writer seeks to situate his inquiry, is the cultural climate of a given period" (2007, 14).

21 Ralph M. Rosen expands: "Although each human being presumably experiences time in a personal, idiosyncratic way, the phenomenon itself has a distinctly universal quality about it that aligns it with the other imperatives—birth, death, hunger—that all humans at all times must confront" (2004, 2).

22 Hegel provides another formulation of relationist time: "It is therefore the processes of actual things which constitutes time" (qtd. in Taylor 1975, 356). Einstein (according to Heidegger's characterization of him in *The Concept of Time*)

concurs: "Time is nothing. It persists merely as a consequence of the events taking place in it" (qtd in Scott 2006, 205, n. 56).

23 Referring to the contention of William James, Charles M. Sherover straddles these alternatives: "time is somehow the meeting ground of human consciousness and the world that it is conscious of" (1975, 7).

Chapter 1

1 Shakespeare 1982. All quotations from this play are indicated parenthetically in my text.
2 For the first two phrases, see Turetzky 1998, 198, 151. For the third phrase, see Kiernan-Lewis 1994, 322.
3 Compare with Northrop Frye: "The basis of the tragic vision is being in time, the sense of the one-directional quality of life, where everything happens once and for all, where every act brings unavoidable and fateful consequences, and where all experience vanishes, not simply into the past, but into nothingness, annihilation" (1967, 3).
4 According to Marjorie Garber, "Ophelia herself is constantly associated with the need to remember" (1994, 311). To Kent Cartwright, "Ophelia stands for memory—and forgetting" (1991, 125).
5 See note for 4.4.50 in Shakespeare 1982, 345.
6 Aristotle 1941, 48.

Chapter 2

1 For critics applauding the social accuracy of the novel, see Schwartzbach 1979, 145; Johnson 1989; Smith 1990, 169; Sicher 1993; Friedman 1990. For a discussion of Victorian modes of feminine discourse in the novel, see Carr 1989. For comparisons of the Gradgrind school to contemporary education, see Collins 1963, 148; Alton 1992; Gold 1972; Gilmour 1967. For critics who find the novel socially inaccurate, see Lucas 1979, 254; Holloway 1962, 166; Cowles 1991, 84.
2 Dickens 1969, 47. All further references pertain to this edition and will be cited parenthetically in the text.
3 Critics have variously interpreted the Horse-riding: J. Hillis Miller views the circus as "an image of the good society" (1965, 332); to Myron Magnet, it embodies "art" (1985, 43); Mildred Newcomb relates the horses to Plato's image of the soul in *Phaedrus* (1989, 126); to Raymond Williams, the circus represents "[t]he instinctive,

unintellectual, unorganized life ... of genuine feeling, and of all good relationships" (1963, 106); to Claire Tomlin, the Horse-riding communicates "Dickens' message ... that if people are not amused, they will become not merely dull and desiccated but brutal and evil" (1990, 92).

4 Whereas in *Hard Times* repetition compulsion seeks to negate the movement of time, according to Freud it seeks *regression* in time in order "to restore an earlier state of things" (1961, 51). In the context of political organization and control in Coketown, one should not overlook the assertion of Elias Canetti: "the regulation of time is the primary attribute of all government" (1962, 462).

5 Josiah Tucker, in *Instructions for Travellers* (1758), when treating the relation of the master to his journeymen in mid-eighteenth century cloth manufacturing in Yorkshire, describes what might be termed the Primal Sire of Mr. Bounderby: "The master ... however well disposed himself is continually tempted by his situation to be proud and overbearing, to consider his people as the scum of the earth, whom he has a right to squeeze whenever he can; because they ought to be kept low and not to rise up in competition with their superiors" (1758, 38).

6 For an excellent study of Dickens's use of the erection motif, see Lougy 1992, 44–48; 53–55.

7 Yet, according to Cynthia Northcutt Malone, the gaze "induces conformity to bourgeois codes of sexual behaviour" (1989, 16).

8 It is hoped that the foregoing analysis of time in *Hard Times* rescues Dickens from the criticism of Gwen Watkins: "Perhaps there were too many themes in one short book for him to examine any profoundly" (1987, 78).

Chapter 3

1 Joyce 1960, 40. All page references to this edition appear parenthetically in my text.
2 See, for example, Shechner 1974; Brivic 1980; and Gose, Jr., 1980.

Chapter 4

1 Woolf 1992. All further references pertain to this edition and will be cited parenthetically in the text.
2 For a Derridean deconstruction of time in *Mrs. Dalloway*, see Fay Chen and Chung-Hsiung Lai (2007). For a Cubist interpretation of time, see Jennie-Rebecca Falcetta (2007).
3 See Tzonis and Lefaivre (1986, 88); Chatham (1985, 113).

Chapter 5

1. Woolf 1927. All further references pertain to this edition and will be cited parenthetically in the text.
2. Critics have subjected *To the Lighthouse* to diverse temporal analyses. For readings emphasizing Einstein's notion of relativity, see Brown (2009), Beer (2000), and Stockton (1998); for Derrida (with most of the attention devoted to *Mrs. Dalloway*), see Chen and Lai (2007); for Proust, see Mares (1989); for Heidegger, see Storl (2008); for the status of the future, see Banfield (2000). Harper posits a dialectic in *To the Lighthouse* founded on the "two states of consciousness described by Bergson, in which time is experienced as either durational and leading to freedom or as immutable and leading to necessity" (1982, 139). For an earlier formulation of this dichotomy, see Hafley 1963, 43–44. For other discussions of Bergson and *To the Lighthouse*, see Kendoza 1978, 255–56, n.16; Roberts 1934; Troy 1970, 85–89; Kumar 1963, Richter 1970, and Vieira 1990; For an introductory application of Husserl, see Strehle 2006. For a presumed correspondence between Woolf's notion of self and that of John McTaggart (with a fragmentary review of McTaggart's notion of time), see Fleishman (1969).
3. For an application of concepts formulated by Lacan and Kristeva to a discussion of the subject-object relation in terms of the damage caused by love to both the lover and the beloved, see Brivic 1994. In contrast, William Handley reads the novel as a critique or deconstruction of the "[s]ubject-object philosophy [that] positions subjects toward each other as objects to be dominated [by the interpretive frame in which the judging subject places them]" (1993, 314).
4. Cf. Guiguet: "The passing of time is ... a metaphor ... there is only the futility and insensibility of nature, its life where, as in our own, *before* and *after* have no meaning" (1965, 393).
5. Compare Matthiessen: "For if it is part of the function of every great artist to transform his age, the tragic writer does not do so by delivering an abstract idealization of life, but by giving to the people who live in the age a full reading of its weakness and horror; yet, concurrently, by revealing some enduring potentiality of good to be embraced with courage and with an ecstatic sense of its transfiguring glory" (1958, 107).
6. For a discussion of Mrs Ramsay's communion with the Lighthouse in terms of Indian mysticism, see Stewart 1977, 380. In contrast, Su Reid interprets Mrs. Ramsay's communion as "a non-signifying delight in the lighthouse beam on the sea, an image that might well be compared with Kristeva's idea of the semiotic, the store within consciousness of non-figurative experience" (1991, 88).
7. Yet Poresky identifies the Lighthouse with God (1981, 128); and Thakur views the Lighthouse as a "symbol of the Eternal and the Immutable" (1965, 79).

8 For the use, in dreams, of spatial distance as a symbol of temporal distance, see Freud 1964, 1973–86.
9 For a related view of the indefinitely vast content of the past, see David Lowenthal: "No historical account can recover the totality of past events, because their content is virtually infinite" (1985, 214–15).
10 For detailed discussion of this scene, see Levy, 2008, 162–63, 200–3.
11 In contrast, several critics interpret the act of creativity in the novel as a symbol of the act of creativity represented by the novel itself. See Miller 1983; Caughie 1991, 33–39; and Richter 1985, 203.
12 Many critics emphasize the influence of Roger Fry on Lily's aesthetics. See Mepham 1992, 41; Dowling 1985, 96–98. For a contrary opinion, see Matro 1984. According to Richter, emphasis on perspective "is what separates [Woolf] most clearly from the Post-Impressionists" (1970, 75).
13 For Oedipal interpretations of James' relation to Mr Ramsay, see Bowlby 1988, 68–69; Abel 1989, 46–58; and Diabattista 1980. Perhaps the most extreme Freudian interpretation of the novel is that of Minow-Pinkney, who explicates Mrs Ramsay's celebrated knitted stocking as "a counter-phallus" (1987, 87). See also Jacobus 1988. Other critics emphasize James's developmental shift in emphasis from paternal to institutional and political tyranny. See Batchelor 1991, 107; and Zwerdling 1986, 195.
14 According to Haring-Smith, characters "define themselves" by their perceptions (1983, 156).
15 The polar opposite of this interpretation emphasizing the fulfillment of self through the achievement of tragic vision is that which stresses the *loss* of self. See Daiches: "To reach the Lighthouse is ... to surrender the uniqueness of one's ego to an impersonal reality" (1942, 86). See also Naremore, who emphasizes "the intense desire to lose the self through love or union" (1973, 150).
16 For a companion study of *To the Lighthouse*—one that explores the reconstitution of order and meaning not through the phenomenology of post-traumatic temporal disorder, but through inquiry into the Woolfian metaphysics of tragic vision that recasts the Aristotelian notions of form and matter in temporal terms—see Levy 1996.

Chapter 6

1 The present study is the first to examine the Beckettian representation of time in relation to the conceptual complexity of time itself—the cluster of concepts informing the idea of time, philosophically construed. Many critics, in treating the Beckettian representation of time, refer to the temporal analysis enunciated in Beckett's *Proust*, where the passage of time, from future to past, is considered

in relation to the succession of individuals, along with the destabilizing intervals of transition between them, which, in Beckett's interpretation of Proust's art, characterize the individual lifetime. See, for example, Torrance 1967; Collins 1974; Postlewait 1978; and Brinkley 1988. For detailed explication of Beckett's bursting of the Proustian paradigm in *Krapp's Last Tape*, see Levy 2007 (180-94). For an analysis of Beckettian representations of time according to various geometric shapes, such as the line (*Act Without Words*), concentric circles (*Krapp's Last Tape*), circle (*Play*), mobius strip (*Embers*), and spiral (*Waiting for Godot*), see Morse 1990. For discussion of the violation, in Beckett's late theatre, of "dramatic timespace—the constructed, coherent, organized, sequence of thoughts, actions, and events that provides the basic structure of the self in conventional drama"—see Pattie 2000 (402, 393-403).

Chapter 7

1 McEwan 1997. All quotations from this novel are indicated parenthetically in my text.
2 *Enduring Love* has not yet elicited extensive critical comment, and only one prior critic, Jago Morrison, has addressed the notion of time in the novel. However, his study treats time only tangentially, in connection with what he terms Joe's "sense of temporal dislocation" or awareness of the exclusion of his personal life from the historical continuity of "medical-scientific discourse"—an enterprise in which he formerly participated as a student of physics (2001, 260, 259).
3 Joe's notion of the exclusion of man from "the great chain" constitutes a modern version of the argument of Pico della Mirandola (1463-1494) in his 1498 *Oration on the Dignity of Man*. There, Pico ascribes to man the choice of any link on the chain, according to the moral quality of his will. Eugene F. Rice, Jr., explains: "Man is an autonomous moral agent, containing in his own nature the possibility of the most varied development, who can by free choice become akin to any being, become like a rock or plant or beast if he turn toward evil, like the angels or like a mortal god if he turn toward good" (1970, 78).

Chapter 8

1 Deleuze's populating of the body with "contemplative souls" entrains a venerable philosophical notion, construing the body as the site of numerous spirits or souls, defined as local functions or forces of motion or perception. The notion was already fully developed in Stoicism, as Windelband indicates: "The individual soul, also,

the vital force of the body, which holds together and rules the flesh, is fiery breath, pneuma; but all the individual forces which are active in the members and control their purposive functions, are also such vital minds or spirits (*spiritus animales*)" (1958, 1.187). See also Zeller, 1879/1962, 214–215.

Epilogue

1 Compare E. J. Lowe: "A paradigm example of an agent would be a human being or other conscious creature capable of performing intentional actions" (2002, 195).
2 The project of post-structuralist theory to evacuate selfhood and treat it as a zone of competing discourses has antecedents in nineteenth-century idealism and naturalism. Paul Tillich expands: "In both cases the individual self is an empty space and the bearer of something which is not himself, something strange by which the self is estranged from itself. Idealism and naturalism are alike in their attitude to the existing person; both of them eliminate his infinite significance and make him *a space through which something else passes*" (1952, 137–38 [my emphasis]).
3 For a compact account of the classical schema of rational action, see Levy 2008, 75–77.

Works Cited

Abel, Elizabeth. 1989. *Virginia Woolf and the Fictions of Psychoanalysis*. Chicago: University of Chicago Press.
Ackerman, James S. 1986. *The Architecture of Michelangelo*. 2nd ed. Harmondsworth: Penguin.
Agacinski, Sylviane. 2003. *Time Passing: Modernity and Nostalgia*. New York: Columbia University Press.
Allingham, Philip V. 1991. "Theme, Form, and the Naming of Names in *Hard Times for These Times*." *The Dickensian* 87.1: 17–31.
Alton, Anne Hiebert. 1992. "Education in Victorian Fact and Fiction: Kay-Shuttleworth and Dickens's *Hard Times*." *Dickens Quarterly* 9.2: 67–80.
Amis, Kinglsey. 1953. *Lucky Jim*. New York: Compass Books.
Andreau, Jean. 2002. "Twenty Years After Moses I. Finley's *The Ancient Economy*." In *The Ancient Economy*, edited by Walter Schiedel and Sitta Von Reden, translated by Antonia Nevill, 35–52. New York: Routledge.
Aquinas, St. Thomas. 1952. *The Summa Theologica*, translated by Fathers of the English Dominican Province. New York: Benziger Brothers.
Aristotle. 1936. *Physics*, translated by W. D. Ross. *Aristotle's Physics: A Revised Text with Introduction and Commentary by W. D. Ross*. Oxford: Clarendon.
Aristotle. 1936. 1941a. *De Interpretatione*, translated by E. M. Edghill. In *The Basic Works of Aristotle*, edited by Richard McKeon. New York: Random House.
Aristotle. 1936. 1941b. "Physics," translated by R. P. Hardie and R. K. Gaye. In *The Basic Works of Aristotle*, edited by Richard McKeon. New York: Random House.
Aristotle. 1936. *Metaphysics*. 1941c. "Metaphysics," translated by W. D. Ross. In *The Basic Works of Aristotle*, edited by Richard McKeon. New York: Random House.
Ascham, Roger. 1864. *The Schoolmaster: The Whole Works of Roger Ascham*. Volume 3. Edited by John A.Giles, 88–276. London: John Russell Smith.
Auerbach, Erich. 1953. *Mimesis: The Representation of Reality in Western Literature*, translated by Willard Trask. Princeton: Princeton University Press.
Augustine, A. 1961. *Confessions*, translated by R. S. Pine-Coffin. London: Penguin Books.
Augustine, Saint. 1951. *The Confessions of Saint Augustine*, translated by Edward B. Pusey. New York: Washington Square Press.
Aurelius, Marcus. 1961. *The Communings With Himself of Marcus Aurelius, Emperor of Rome, Together With his Speeches and Sayings*. Translated by C. R. Haines. Cambridge: Harvard University Press; London: William Heinemann.

Bacon, Sir Francis. 1951. *The First Book of the Proficience and Advancement of Learning, Divine and Human.* In *Seventeenth-Century Verse and Prose.* 2 vols. Edited by Helen C. White, Ruth C. Wallerstein, and Ricardo Quintana, 60–70. New York: Macmillan.

Baker, Hershel. 1947. *The Image of Man: A Study of the Idea of Human Dignity in Classical Antiquity, the Middle Ages, and the Renaissance.* New York: Harper & Row.

Banfield, Ann. 2000. "Tragic Time: The Problem of the Future in Cambridge Philosophy and *To the Lighthouse*." *Modernism/modernity* 7.1: 43–75.

Barthes, Roland. 1964. *On Racine*, translated by Richard Howard. New York: Hill & Wang.

Batchelor, James. 1991. *Virginia Woolf: The Major Novels.* Cambridge: Cambridge University Press.

Baumlin, James S. 2002. "*Chronos, Kairos, Aion*: Failures of Decorum, Right-Timing, and Revenge in Shakespeare's *Hamlet*." In *Rhetoric and Kairos: Essays in History, Theory, and Praxis*, edited by Phillip Sipiora, 165–86. Albany, NY: State University of New York Press.

Baxter, Richard. 1831. *The Saints' Everlasting Rest.* Sixth Edition. Abridged by Benjamin Fawcett. Introductory essay by Thomas Erskine. Glasgow: William Collins.

Beauchamp, Gorman. 1989. "Mechanomorphism in *Hard Times*." *Studies in the Literary Imagination* 22: 61–77.

Beckett, Samuel. 1954. *Waiting for Godot*, translated by Samuel Beckett. New York: Grove Press.

Beckett, Samuel. 1957a. "Krapp's Last Tape." In *Krapp's Last Tape and Other Dramatic Pieces.* New York: Grove Press.

Beckett, Samuel. 1957b. *Murphy.* New York: Grove Press.

Beckett, Samuel. 1958a. *Endgame*, translated by Samuel Beckett. New York: Grove Press.

Beckett, Samuel. 1958b. "Molloy." In *Three Novels: Molloy, Malone Dies, The Unnamable*, translated by Samuel Beckett with Patrick Bowles assisting with the translation of *Molloy.* New York: Grove Press.

Beckett, Samuel. 1958c. "Malone Dies." In *Three Novels: Molloy, Malone Dies, The Unnamable*, translated by Samuel Beckett with Patrick Bowles assisting with the translation of *Molloy.* New York: Grove Press.

Beckett, Samuel. 1958d. "The Unnamable." In *Three Novels: Molloy, Malone Dies, The Unnamable*, translated by Samuel Beckett with Patrick Bowles assisting with the translation of *Molloy.* New York: Grove Press.

Beckett, Samuel. 1959. *Watt.* 1953. Reprint. New York: Grove Press.

Beckett, Samuel. 1961. *Happy Days.* New York: Grove Press.

Beckett, Samuel. 1964. *How It Is*, translated by Samuel Beckett. New York: Grove Press.

Beckett, Samuel. 1965. "Proust." In *Proust, and Three Dialogues with Georges Duthuit.* London: John Calder.

Beckett, Samuel. 1967a. "Texts for Nothing." In *Stories and Texts for Nothing*, translated by Samuel Beckett. New York: Grove Press.

Beckett, Samuel. 1967b. "The Calmative." In *Stories and Texts for Nothing*, translated by Samuel Beckett. New York: Grove Press.

Beckett, Samuel. 1967c. "The Expelled." In *Stories and Texts for Nothing*, translated by Samuel Beckett. New York: Grove Press.

Beckett, Samuel. 1967d. "The End." In *Stories and Texts for Nothing*, translated by Samuel Beckett. New York: Grove Press.

Beckett, Samuel. 1973. *Not I*. London: Faber and Faber.

Beckett, Samuel. 1974a. "Enough." In *First Love, and Other Shorts*, translated by Samuel Beckett. New York: Grove Press.

Beckett, Samuel. 1974b. "First Love." In *First Love, and Other Shorts*, translated by Samuel Beckett. New York: Grove Press.

Beckett, Samuel. 1974c. "From an Abandoned Work." In *First Love, and Other Shorts*, translated by Samuel Beckett. New York: Grove Press.

Beckett, Samuel. 1974d. "Imagination Dead Imagine." In *First Love, and Other Shorts*, translated by Samuel Beckett. New York: Grove Press.

Beckett, Samuel. 1974e. *Mercier and Camier*, translated by Samuel Beckett. London: Calder.

Beckett, Samuel. 1976a. "For to End Yet Again." In *For to End Yet Again, and Other Fizzles*, translated by Samuel Beckett. London: John Calder.

Beckett, Samuel. 1976b. "He Is Barehead." In *For To End Yet Again, and Other Fizzles*, translated by Samuel Beckett. London: John Calder.

Beckett, Samuel. 1976c. "Horn Came Always." In *For to End Yet Again, and Other Fizzles*, translated by Samuel Beckett. London: John Calder.

Beckett, Samuel. 1981. *Ill Seen Ill Said*, translated by Samuel Beckett. New York: Grove Press.

Beer, Gillian. 2000. *Wave, Atom, Dinosaur: Woolf's Science*. London: Virginia Woolf Society of Great Britain.

Beiser, Frederick. 2005. *Hegel*. New York: Routledge.

Bergson, Henri. 1910. *Time and Free Will: An Essay on the Immediate Data of Consciousness*, translated by F. L Pogson. London: George Allen and Unwin.

Bergson, Henri. 1944. *Creative Evolution*, translated by Arthur Mitchell. New York: Modern Library.

Bergson, Henri. 1965. *Duration and Simultaneity (with Reference to Einstein's Theory)*, translated by L. Jacobson. Indianapolis: Bobbs-Merrill.

Bernet, Rudolf, Iso Kern, and Eduard Marbach. 1993. *An Introduction to Husserlian Phenomenology*. Foreword by Lester Embree. Evanston: Northwestern University Press.

Bevan, Edwyn. 1923. "Hellenistic Popular Philosophy." In *The Hellenistic Age: Aspects of Hellenistic Civilization*, edited by J. B. Bury, E. A. Barber, Edwyn Bevan, and W. W. Tarn. New York: Norton. 79–107.

Blackham, H. J. 1952. *Six Existentialist Thinkers*. New York: Harper & Row, 1959.
Bleiker, Roland. 2000. *Popular Dissent: Human Agency and Global Politics*. Cambridge: Cambridge University Press.
Blunt, Anthony. 1953. *Art and Architecture in France 1500–1700*. Melbourne, London, Baltimore: Penguin.
Bochenski, I. M. 1965. *Contemporary European Philosophy*, translated by Donald Nicholl and Karl Aschenbrenner. Berkeley and Los Angeles: University of California Press.
Bony, Jean. 1983. *French Gothic Architecture of the 12th & 13th Centuries*. Berkeley; Los Angeles; London: University of California Press.
Bossart, William H. 1994. *Apperception, Knowledge, and Experience*. Ottawa: University of Ottawa Press.
Bowlby, Rachel. 1988. *Virginia Woolf: Feminist Destinations*. Oxford: Basil Blackwell.
Bramble, J. C. 1982. "Martial and Juvenal." In *The Cambridge History of Classical Literature: Latin Literature*, edited by E. J. Kenney, 597–623. Cambridge: Cambridge University Press.
Brann, Eva. 1999. *What, Then, Is Time?* Lanham, Maryland: Rowman and Littlefield.
Brinkmann, Klaus. 2005. *Idealism Without Limits: Hegel and the Problem of Objectivity* London and New York: Springer.
Brivic, Sheldon. 1994. "Love as Destruction in Woolf's *To the Lighthouse*." *Mosaic* 27.3: 65–85.
Broad, C. D. 1933. *Examination of McTaggart's Philosophy*. 2 vols. Cambridge: Cambridge University Press.
Broad, C. D. 1952. *Scientific Thought*. New York: Humanities Press.
Brooks, Peter. 1984. *Reading for the Plot: Design and Intention in Narrative*. New York: Alfred A. Knopf.
Brown, Paul Tulliver. 2009. "Relativity, Quantum Physics, and Consciousness in Virginia Woolf's *To the Lighthouse*." *Journal of Modern Literature* 32.3: 39–62.
Brown, Peter. 1972. *Religion and Society in the Age of Saint Augustine*. London: Faber and Faber.
Browne, Sir Thomas. 1835. *Religio Medici. Sir Thomas Browne's Works*. Volume 2. Edited by Simon Wilkin. London: William Pickering. 1–158.
Brucker, Gene A. 1983. *Renaissance Florence*. Berkeley: University of California Press.
Bryant, Levi R. 2008. *Difference and Givenness: Deleuze's Transcendental Empiricism and the Ontology of Immanence*. Evanston: Northwestern University Press.
Burke, Edmond. 1959. *Reflections on the Revolution in France*. Edited by William B. Todd. New York: Rinehart.
Burton, Robert. 1838. *The Anatomy of Melancholy*. London: B. Blake.
Bury, J. B. 1923. *History of the Later Roman Empire from the Death of Theodosius I to the Death of Justinian*. 2 vols. New York: Dover, 1958.
Butler, Samuel. 1966. *The Way of All Flesh*. Introduction by Richard Hoggart. London: Penguin.

Calderwood, James. 1983. *To Be and Not To Be: Negation and Metadrama in* Hamlet. New York: Columbia University Press.
Calendar, Craig. 2008. "The Common Now," *Philosophical Issues* 18: 339–61.
Calinescu, Matei. 1987. *Five Faces of Modernity: Modernism, Avant-Garde, Decadence, Kitsch, Postmodernism*. Durham, NC: Duke University Press.
Canetti, Elias. 1962. *Crowds and Power*, translated by Carol Stewart. Harmondsworth: Penguin, 1973.
Carr, Jean Ferguson. 1989. "Writing as a Woman: Dickens, *Hard Times*, and Feminine Discourses." *Dickens Studies Annual* 18: 161–78.
Cartwright, Kent. 1991. *Shakespearean Tragedy and Its Double: The Rhythms of Audience Response*. University Park: Pennsylvania State University Press.
Cassirer, Ernst. 1957. *The Philosophy of Symbolic Forms*. 3 vols., translated by Ralph Mannheim. New Haven; London: Yale University Press.
Cassirer, Ernst. 1961. *The Logic of the Humanities*, translated by Clarence Smith Howe. New Haven: Yale University Press.
Cassirer, Ernst. 1963. *The Individual and the Cosmos in Renaissance Philosophy*, translated by Mario Domandi. Philadelphia: University of Philadelphia Press.
Cassirer, Ernst. 1981. *Kant's Life and Thought*, translated by James Haden. Introduction by Stephan Korner. New Haven; London: Yale University Press.
Castoriadis, Cornelius. 1991. "Time and Creation." In *Chronotypes: The Construction of Time*, edited by John Bender and David Wellbery, 38–64. Stanford: Stanford University Press.
Caughie, Pamela L. 1991. *Virginia Woolf & Postmodernism: Literature in Quest and Question of Itself*. Urbana and Chicago: University of Illinois Press.
Chandler, James. 1998. *England in 1819: The Politics of Literary Culture and the Case of Romantic Historicism*. Chicago: University of Chicago Press.
Chatham, Robert. 1985. *The Classical Orders of Architecture*. New York: Rizzoli.
Chen, Fay and Chung-Hsiung Lai. 2007. "'The Time Is Out of Joint': A Derridean Reading of Virginia Woolf's *Mrs. Dalloway*." *EurAmerica: A Journal of European and American Studies* 37.2: 227–54.
Chenderlin, Fritz. 1982. *Do This As My Memorial*. Rome: Biblical Institute Press.
Childs, Peter, ed. 2006. *The Fiction of Ian McEwan*. Basingstoke: Palgrave Macmillan.
Clausen, W. V. 1982. "Theocritus and Virgil." *The Cambridge History of Classical Literature: Latin Literature*. Edited by E. J. Kenney, 301–19. Cambridge: Cambridge University Press.
Cleve, James van. 1999. *Problems from Kant*. New York and Oxford: Oxford University Press.
Cohen, Shaye J. S. 2007. "The Judean Legal Tradition and the Halakhah of the Mishnah." In *The Cambridge Companion to The Talmud and Rabbinic Literature*, 121–43. Cambridge and New York: Cambridge University Press.
Coles, Nicholas. 1986. "The Politics of *Hard Times*." *Dickens Studies Annual* 15: 145–80.

Collins, P. H. 1974. "Proust, Time, and Beckett's Happy Days." *French Review: Journal of the American Association of Teachers of French* 47.6 (Supplement): 105–19.
Collins, Philip. 1963. *Dickens and Education*. London: Macmillan.
Copleston, Frederick. 1966. *A History of Philosophy*. 9 vols. Garden City: Image.
Coulton, G. G. 1938. *Inquisition and Liberty*. Boston: Beacon Hill.
Coulton, J. J. 1977. *Ancient Greek Architects at Work: Problems of Structure and Design*. Ithaca: Cornell University Press.
Cowles, David L. 1991. "Having It Both Ways: Gender and Paradox in Hard Times." *Dickens Quarterly* 8.2: 79–84.
Currie, Gregory. 1999. "Can There be a Literary Philosophy of Time?" In *The Arguments of Time*, edited by Jeremy Butterfield, 43–63. Oxford: Oxford University Press.
Currie, Mark. 2007. *About Time: Narrative, Fiction and the Philosophy of Time*. Edinburgh, Scotland: Edinburgh University Press.
Daiches, David. 1942. *Virginia Woolf*. Binghamton: New Directions, 1963.
Dainton, Barry. 2000. *Stream of Consciousness: Unity and Continuity in Conscious Experience*. Abingdon, Oxon.: Routledge.
Davies, John K. 2005. "Linear and Nonlinear Flow Models for Ancient Economies." In *The Ancient Economy: Evidence and Models*, edited by J. G. Manning and Ian Morris, 127–56. Stanford: Stanford University Press.
Davies, Philip R. 2003. "From Zion to Zion: Jerusalem in the Dead Sea Scrolls." In *Jerusalem in Ancient History and Tradition*, edited by Thomas L. Thompson, 164–70. London: T & T Clark International.
Da Vinci, Leonardo. 2008. *Notebooks*, edited by Thereza Wells, translated by Irma A. Richter, and Preface by Martin Kemp. Oxford: Oxford University Press.
Delanda, Michael. 2002. *Intensive Science and Virtual Philosophy*. London; New York: Continuum.
Deleuze, Gilles. 1984. *Kant's Critical Philosophy*, translated by Hugh Tomlison and Barbara Habberjam. Minneapolis: University of Minnesota Press.
Deleuze, Gilles. 1991. *Bergsonism*, translated by Hugh Tomlison and Barbara Habberjam. New York: Zone Books.
Deleuze, Gilles. 1994. *Difference and Repetition*, translated by Paul Patton. New York: Columbia University Press.
DeWeese, Garrett J. 2004. *God and the Nature of Time*. Aldershot: Ashgate.
Diabattista, Maria. 1980. "*To the Lighthouse*: Virginia Woolf's Winter's Tale." In *Virginia Woolf: Revaluation and Continuity*, edited by Ralph Freedman, 161–88. Berkeley: University of California Press.
Dickens, Charles. 1969. *Hard Times*, edited with an introduction by David Craig. London: Penguin.
Dohrn-van-Rossum, Gerhard. 1996. *History of the Hour: Clocks and Modern Temporal Orders*, translated by Thomas Dunlap. Chicago: University of Chicago Press.

Dowling, David. 1985. *Bloomsbury Aesthetics and the Novels of Forster and Woolf.* London: Macmillan.

Duchesne, Louis. 1924. *Early History of the Christian Church: From Its Foundation to the End of the Fifth Century.* 3 vols., translated by Claude Jenkins. London: John Murray.

Dummett, Michael. 1960. "A Defense of McTaggart's Proof of the Unreality of Time." *The Philosophical Review* 69.4: 497–504.

Eliot, George. 1979. *The Mill on the Floss*, edited with an introduction by A. S. Byatt. London: Penguin.

Eliot, T. S. 1963a. *Four Quartets. Collected Poems: 1909–1962*. London: Faber and Faber. 189–223.

Eliot, T. S. 1963b. "The Hollow Men." *Collected Poems: 1909–1962*. London: Faber and Faber. 89–92.

Everyman. 1996. London: Nick Hern Books.

Falcetta, Jennie-Rebecca. 2007. "Geometries of Space and Time: The Cubist London of Mrs. Dalloway." *Woolf Studies Annual* 13: 111–36.

Faulkner, Keith W. 2006. *Deleuze and the Three Syntheses of Time.* New York: Peter Lang.

Federman, Raymond. 2001. *Surfiction: Fiction Now ... and Tomorrow.* 2nd edition. Chicago: Swallow.

Ferguson, Wallace K. 1962. *Europe in Transition 1300–1520.* Boston: Houghton Mifflin.

Findlay, J. N. 1958. *Hegel: A Re-examination.* London and New York: Oxford University Press.

Fitzgerald, F. Scott. 2012. *The Great Gatsby.* London: Urban Romantics.

Fleishman, Avrom. 1969. "Woolf and McTaggart." *ELH* 36.4: 719–38.

Focillon, Henri. 1989. *The Life of Forms in Art*, translated by Charles B. Hogan and George Kubler. New York: Zone Books.

Forster, E. M. 1927. *Aspects of the Novel.* New York: Harcourt, Brace & World.

Foucault, Michel. 1975. *Surveiller et Punir: Naissance de la Prison.* Paris: Gallimard.

Fowler, Roger. 1989. "Polyphony in Hard Times." In *Language, Discourse and Literature: An Introductory Reader in Discourse Stylistics*, edited by Ronald Carter and Paul Simpson, 77–93. London: George Allen and Unwin.

Frankl, Paul. 1962. *Gothic Architecture.* Harmondsworth: Penguin.

Freud, Sigmund. 1961. *Beyond the Pleasure Principle*, translated by James Strachey. New York: Norton.

Freud, Sigmund. 1964. *New Introductory Lectures on Psychoanalysis*, edited and translated by James Strachey. Vol. 2 of *The Pelican Freud Library* (15 volumes). New York: Pelican, 1973.

Friedman, Stanley. 1990. "Sad Stephen and Troubled Louisa: Paired Protagonists in Hard Times." *Dickens Quarterly* 7.2: 254–62.

Frye, Northrop. 1967. *Fools of Time: Studies in Shakespearean Tragedy.* Toronto: University of Toronto Press.

Garber, Marjorie. 1994. "*Hamlet*: Giving Up the Ghost." In *William Shakespeare Hamlet*, edited by Suzanne L. Wofford, 297–331. Boston: Bedford Books.

Gardner, Sebastian. 1999. *Routledge Philosophy Guidebook to Kant and the Critique of Pure Reason*. London: Routledge.

Gibbon, Edward. 1910. *The Decline and Fall of the Roman Empire*. 3 volumes. Edited by Oliphant Smeaton. New York: Random House.

Gillies, Mary Ann. 1996. *Henri Bergson and British Modernism*. Montreal and Kingston: McGill-Queen's University Press.

Gilmour, Robin. 1967. "The Gradgrind School: Political Economy in the Classroom." *Victorian Studies* 11: 207–224.

Gilson, Etienne. 1955. *The History of Christian Philosophy in the Middle Ages*. New York: Random House.

Gilson, Etienne. 1960. *The Christian Philosophy of St. Augustine*, translated by L. E. M. Lynch. New York: Random House.

Gilson, Etienne. 1988. *The Christian Philosophy of St. Thomas Aquinas*, translated by L. K. Shook. New York: Octagon.

Gold, Joseph. 1972. *Charles Dickens: Radical Moralist*. Toronto: Copp Clark.

Goldberg, S. L. 1969. *The Classical Temper: A Study of James's Joyce's Ulysses*. London: Chatto and Windus.

Grebanier, Bernard. 1960. *The Heart of* Hamlet. New York: Crowell.

Grisez, Germain G. 1969. "The First Principle of Practical Reason: A Commentary on the *Summa Theologiae*, 1–2, Question 94, Article 2." In *Aquinas: A Collection of Critical Essays*, edited by Anthony Kenny, 340–82. Garden City: Doubleday.

Gruen, Erich S. 1984. *The Hellenistic Age and the Coming of Rome*. 2 volumes. Berkeley: University of California Press.

Grunbaum, Adolf. 1971. "The Meaning of Time." In *Basic Issues in the Philosophy of Time*, edited by Eugene Freeman and Wilfrid Sellars, 195–228. Lasalle, Illinois: Open Court.

Guiguet, Jean. 1965. *Virginia Woolf and Her Works*, translated by Jean Stewart. London: Hogarth.

Hafley, James. 1963. *The Glass Roof: Virginia Woolf as Novelist*. New York: Russell & Russell.

Handley, William R. 1993. "The Housemaid and the Kitchen Table: Judgment, Economy, and Representation in *To the Lighthouse*." In *Virginia Woolf: Themes and Variation, Selected Papers from the Second Annual Conference on Virginia Woolf*, edited by Vara Neverow-Turk and Mark Hussey, 309–20. New York: Pace University Press.

Haring-Smith, Tori. 1983. "Private and Public Consciousness in *Mrs. Dalloway* and *To the Lighthouse*." In *Virginia Woolf: Centennial Essays*, edited by Elaine K. Ginsberg and Laura Moss Gottlieb, 143–62. Troy, New York: Whitson.

Harper, Howard. 1982. *Between Language and Silence: The Novels of Virginia Woolf*. Baton Rouge: Louisiana State University Press.

Hayman, David. 1970. *Ulysses: The Mechanics of Meaning*. Englewood Cliffs, NJ: Prentice Hall.
Hegel, G. W. F. 1991. *Encyclopaedia of Philosophical Sciences*. Translated by T. F. Geraets, W. A. Suchting, and H. S. Harris. In *The Encyclopaedia Logic: Part I of the Encyclopaedia of Philosophical Sciences with the Zusatze*. Indianapolis: Hackett.
Hegel, G. W. F. 1929. *Hegel's Science of Logic*. 2 vols. Translated by W. H. Johnston and L. G. Struthers. Introductory Preface by Viscount Haldane of Cloan. New York: Macmillan.
Heise, Ursula K. 1997. *Chronoschisms: Time, Narrative, and Postmodernism*. Cambridge: Cambridge University Press.
Henke, Suzette A. 1978. *Joyce's Moraculous Sindbook*. Columbus: Ohio State University Press.
Heraclitus of Ephesus. 1966. *Ancilla to the Pre-Socratic Philosophers: A Complete Translation of the Fragments in Diels*. Fragmente der Vorokratiker, edited and translated by Kathleen Freeman. Cambridge: Harvard University Press.
Hetzler, Florence M. and Austin H. Kutscher. 1978. *Philosophical Aspects of Thanatology*. New York: MSS Information Corporation.
Hobbes, Thomas. 1958. *Leviathan Parts I and II*. Edited by Herbert W. Schneider. Indianapolis: Bobbs-Merrill.
Hollington, Michael. 1992. "Physiognomy in *Hard Times*." *Dickens Quarterly* 9.2: 58–66.
Holloway, John. 1962. "*Hard Times*: A History and a Criticism." In *Dickens and the Twentieth Century*, edited by John Gross and Gabriel Pearson, 159–74. London: Routledge.
Hooker, Richard. 1888. *The Laws of Ecclesiastical Polity: Books I–IV*. Introduction by Henry Morley. London: Routledge.
Hughes, Joe. 2008. *Deleuze and the Genesis of Representation*. London: Continuum International Publishing Group.
Huizinga, J. 1954. *The Waning of the Middle Ages*. Translated by F. Hopman. New York: Anchor Books.
Hume, David. 1887. *A Treatise of Human Nature* Edited by L. A. Selby-Bigge. Oxford: Clarendon Press.
Hunt, Maurice. 2004. "'Forward Backward' Time and the Apocalypse in *Hamlet*." *Comparative Literature* 38.4: 379–99.
Husserl, Edmund. 1931. *Ideas: General Introduction to Pure Phenomenology*, translated by W. R. Boyce Gibson. New York: Collier Books.
Husserl, Edmund. 1960. *Cartesian Meditations: An Introduction to Phenomenology*, translated by Dorian Cairns. The Hague: Martinus Nijhoff.
Husserl, Edmund. 1991. *On the Phenomenology of the Consciousness of Internal Time*, translated by John Barnett Brough. Dordrecht, The Netherlands: Kluwer Academic Publishers.

Huxley, Aldous. 1923. *Antic Hay*. Foreword by David Lodge. Biographical Introduction by David Bradshaw. London: Flamingo.

Jackson, T. G. 1915. *Gothic Architecture in France, Italy, and England*. 2 volumes. Cambridge: Cambridge University Press.

Jacobus, Mary. 1988. "'The Third Stroke': Reading Woolf with Freud." In *Grafts: Feminist Cultural Criticism*, edited by Susan Sheridan, 93–110. London: Verso.

Jenkins, Harold, ed. 1982. *Hamlet*, by William Shakespeare. London and New York: Methuen.

Johnson, Patricia E. 1989. "*Hard Times* and the Structure of Industrialism: The Novel as Factory." *Studies in the Novel* 21.2: 128–37.

Johnson, Samuel. 1883. *The History of Rasselas, Prince of Abyssinia*. London:Fisher Unwin.

Jordan, Robert. 1972. "Time and Contingency in St. Augustine." In *Augustine: A Collection of Critical Essays*, edited by R. A. Markus, 255–79. New York: Anchor.

Joyce, James. 1960. *Ulysses*. Introduction by Declan Kiberd. London: Penguin.

Joyce, James. 1992. *A Portrait of the Artist as a Young Man*, edited with an introduction by Seamus Deans. London: Penguin.

Kain, Richard M. 1966. "The Position of *Ulysses* Today." In *James Joyce Today: Essays on the Major Works*, edited by Thomas F. Staley, 83–95. Bloomington: Indiana University Press.

Kant, Immanuel. 1933. *Critique of Pure Reason*. 2nd ed., translated by N. Kemp Smith. London: Macmillan.

Kant, Immanuel. 1950. *Prolegomena to Any Future Metaphysics*, translated by Lewis White Beck. Indianapolis: Bobbs-Merrill.

Kant, Immanuel. 1959. *Foundations of the Metaphysics of Morals*, translated by Lewis White Beck. Indianapolis: Bobbs-Merrill.

Kastan, David Scott. 1982. *Shakespeare and the Shapes of Time*. Hanover, NH: University Press of New England.

Keats, John. 1951. "Ode on a Grecian Urn." In *John Keats: Selected Poetry and Letters*, edited and introduced by Richard Harter Fogle, 247–48. New York: Holt, Rinehart, and Winston.

Kelly, J. N. D. 1978. *Early Christian Doctrines*. Rev. ed. New York: Harper & Row.

Kendoza, Kathleen. 1978. "'Life Stand Still Here': The Frame Metaphor in *To the Lighthouse*." *Virginia Woolf Quarterly* 3.3–4: 254–67.

Kermode, Frank. 1967. *The Sense of an Ending: Studies in the Theory of Fiction*. New York: Oxford University Press.

Kern, Stephen. 2003. *The Culture of Time and Space: 1880–1918*. 2nd edition. Cambridge, MA: Harvard University Press.

Kierkegaard, Søren. 1941. *Concluding Unscientific Postscript*, translated by David F. Swenson and Walter Lowrie. Princeton: Princeton University Press.

Kiernan-Lewis, Delmas. 1994. "Not Over Yet: Prior's 'Thank Goodness' Argument." In *The New Theory of Time*, edited by L. Nathan Oaklander and Quentin Smith, 322–27. New Haven: Yale University Press.

Kockelmans, Joseph J. 1994. *Edmund Husserl's Phenomenology*. West Lafayette, IN: Purdue University Research Foundation.

Kojève, Alexandre. 1969. *Introduction to the Reading of Hegel: Lectures on the Phenomenology of Spirit*, edited by Allan Bloom, translated by James H. Nichols, Jr. Ithaca and London: Cornell University Press.

Koselleck, Reinhart. 1985. *Futures Past: On the Semantics of Historical Time*. Cambridge, MA: MIT Press.

Kumar, Shiv K. 1963. *Bergson and the Stream of Consciousness Novel*. New York: New York University Press.

Lacey, A. R. 1989. *Bergson*. London: Routledge.

Lampert, Jay. 2006. *Deleuze and Guattari's Philosophy of History*. London: Continuum.

Leavis, F. R. 1960. *The Great Tradition: George Eliot, Henry James, Joseph Conrad*. London: Chatto & Windus.

Leibnitz, Gottfried Wilhelm von. 1956. "Scholium to Definition VIII of Isaac Newton's *Principia*." In *The Leibniz-Clarke Correspondence*, edited by H. G. Alexander. Manchester: Manchester University Press.

Le Poidevin, Robin. 1991. "The Past, Present, and Future of the Debate About Tense." In *Questions of Time and Tense*, edited by Robin Le Poidevin, 13–42. Oxford: Clarendon.

Le Poidevin, Robin. 2003. *Travels in Four Dimensions: The Enigmas of Space and Time*. Oxford: Oxford University Press.

Levey, Michael. 1972. "Painting and Sculpture." In *Art and Architecture of the Eighteenth Century in France*, edited by Wend Graf Kalnein and Michael Levey, 3–197. Harmondsworth, Middlesex: Penguin.

Levy, Eric P. 1996. "Woolf's Metaphysics of Tragic Vision in *To the Lighthouse*." *Philological Quarterly* 75.1: 109–32.

Levy, Eric P. 1982. "'Company': The Mirror of Beckettian Mimesis." *Journal of Beckett Studies* 8: 95–104.

Levy, Eric P. 2003. "The Implications of Keats' Cortez." *Lamar Journal of the Humanities* 28.1: 5–18.

Levy, Eric P. 2007. *Trapped in Thought: A Study of the Beckettian Mentality*. Syracuse: Syracuse University Press.

Levy, Eric P. 2008. *"Hamlet" and the Rethinking of Man*. Madison: Fairleigh Dickinson University Press.

Lloyd, Genevieve. 1993. *Selves and Narrators in Philosophy and Literature*. London and New York: Routledge.

Locke, John. 1996. *An Essay Concerning Human Understanding*. Abridged and edited by Kenneth P. Winkler. Indianapolis: Hackett Publishing Company.

Lorraine, Tamsin. 2003. "Living a Time Out of Joint." In *Between Deleuze and Derrida*, edited by Paul Patton and John Protevi, 30–45. London and New York: Continuum.

Lorris, Guillaume de and Jean de Meun. 1962. *The Romance of the Rose*. Edited by Charles W. Dunn. Translated by Harry W. Robbins. New York: Dutton.

Lougy, Robert E. 1992. "Repressive and Expressive Forms: The Bodies of Comedy and Desire in *Martin Chuzzlewit*." *Dickens Studies Annual* 21: 37–61.

Loux, Michael J. 2006. *Metaphysics: A Contemporary Introduction*. 3rd edition. London and New York: Routledge.

Lowe, E. J. 1991. "Tense and Persistence." In *Questions of Time and Tense*, edited by Robin Le Poidevin. 13–42. Oxford: Clarendon.

Lowe, E. J. 2002. *A Survey of Metaphysics*. Oxford: Oxford University Press.

Lowenthal, David. 1985. *The Past Is a Foreign Country*. Cambridge: Cambridge University Press.

Lucas, John. 1979. *The Melancholy Man: A Study of Dickens' Novels*. London: Methuen.

Luck, Georg. 1982. "Love Elegy." *The Cambridge History of Classical Literature: Latin Literature*. Edited by E. J. Kenney, 405–19. Cambridge: Cambridge University Press.

Machiavelli, Niccolò. 1977. *The Prince*. Translated and edited by Robert M. Adams. New York: Norton.

Macmullen, Ramsay. 1988. *Corruption and the Decline of Rome*. New Haven: Yale University Press.

Magnet, Myron. 1985. *Dickens and the Social Order*. Philadelphia: University of Pennsylvania Press.

Malcolm, David. 2002. *Understanding Ian McEwan*. Columbia, SC: University of South Carolina Press.

Mâle, Emile. 1958. *The Gothic Image: Religious Art in France of the Thirteenth Century*. Translated by Dora Nussey. New York: Harper & Row.

Malone, Cynthia Northcutt. 1989. "The Fixed Eye and the Rolling Eye: Surveillance and Discipline in *Hard Times*." *Studies in the Novel* 21.1: 14–26.

Mares, C. J. 1989. "Reading Proust: Woolf and the Painter's Perspective." *Comparative Literature* 41.4: 327–59.

Maritain, Jacques. 1939. *A Preface to Metaphysics: Seven Lectures on Being*. Freeport: Books for Libraries Press.

Martin, Raymond and John Barresi. 2003. "Introduction: Personal Identity and What Matters in Survival: An Historical Overview." In *Personal Identity*, edited by Raymond Martin and John Barresi, 1–6. Malden, MA; Oxford; Victoria; Berlin: Blackwell Publishing.

Matro, Thomas G. 1984. "Only Relations: Vision and Achievement in *To the Lighthouse*." *Proceedings of the Modern Language Association* 99: 212–24.

Matthiessen, F. O. 1958. *The Achievement of T. S. Eliot*. 3rd ed. London: Oxford University Press.

McBride, Margaret. 2001. *Ulysses and the Metamorphosis of Stephen Dedalus*. Lewisburg: Bucknell University Press.

McEwan, Ian. 1997. *Enduring Love*. Toronto: Vintage Canada.
McTaggart, John. 1908. "The Unreality of Time." *Mind: A Quarterly Review of Psychology and Philosophy* 17: 456–73.
McTaggart, John. 1927. *The Nature of Existence*, edited by C. D. Broad. 2 vols. Cambridge: Cambridge University Press.
Meier, Christian. 1996. *Caesar*. Translated by David McLintock. London: Fontana.
Meister, Jan Christoph and Wilhelm Schernus, eds. 2011. *Time from Concept to Narrative Construct: A Reader*. Berlin: Walter De Gruyter.
Mellor, D. H. 1993. "The Unreality of Tense." In *The Philosophy of Time*, edited by Robin Le Poidevin and Murray MacBeath, 47–59. Oxford: Clarendon.
Melville, Herman. 1852. *Pierre: or, The Ambiguities*. New York: Harper & Brothers.
Mepham, John. 1992. *Criticism in Focus: Virginia Woolf*. New York: St Martin's Press.
Middleton, Peter and Tim Woods. 2000. *Literatures of Memory: History, Time and Space in Postwar Writing*. Manchester: Manchester University Press.
Miller, Henry. 1961. *Tropic of Cancer*. New York: Grove Press.
Miller, J. Hillis. 1965. *Charles Dickens: The World of his Novels*. Cambridge: Harvard University Press.
Miller, J. Hillis. 1983. "The Rhythm of Creativity in *To the Lighthouse*." In *Modernism Reconsidered*, edited by Robert Kiely, 167–90. Cambridge: Harvard University Press.
Mills, Alice. 1991. "Happy Endings in *Hard Times* and *Granny's Wonderful Chair*." In *The Victorian Fantasists: Essays on Culture, Society, and Belief in the Mythopoeic Fiction of the Victorian Age*, edited by Kath Filmer, 184–94. London: Macmillan.
Minow-Pinkney, Makiko. 1987. *Virginia Woolf & the Problem of the Subject*. Brighton: Harvester.
Moorhead, John. 2001. *The Roman Empire Divided: 400–700*. Harlow, Essex: Pearson Education.
Moran, Dermot. 2005. *Edmund Husserl: Founder of Phenomenology*. Cambridge, UK; Malden; Cambridge, MA: Polity Press.
Morrison, Jago. 2001. "Narration and Unease in Ian McEwan's Later Fiction." *Critique: Studies in Contemporary Fiction* 42.3 (Spring): 253–68.
Morse, Donald E. 1990. "'Moments for Nothing': Images of Time in Samuel Beckett's Plays." *Arbeiten aus Anglistik und Amerikanistik* 15.1: 27–38.
Murray, Peter. 1969. *The Architecture of the Italian Renaissance*. London: Thames and Hudson.
Najemy, John. 2008. *A History of Florence 1200–1575*. Oxford: Blackwell.
Naremore, James. 1973. *The World Without a Self: Virginia Woolf and the Novel*. New Haven: Yale University Press.
Nashe, Thomas. 1964. *The Unfortunate Traveller. Thomas Nashe: Pierce Penniless his Supplication to the Devil, Summer's Last Will and Testament, The Terrors of the*

Night, The Unfortunate Traveller, and Selected Writings, edited by Stanley Wells, 189–278. London: Edward Arnold.

Newcomb, Mildred. 1989. *The Imagined World of Charles Dickens.* Columbus: Ohio State University Press.

Newman, Karen, Jay Clayton, and Marianne Hirsch. 2002. *Time and the Literary.* London: Routledge.

Notestein, Wallace. 1954. *The English People on the Eve of Colonization: 1603–1630.* New York: Harper & Row.

O'Brien, Flann. 1967. *The Third Policeman.* London: Granada Publishing.

Oaklander, L. Nathan. 1994a. "A Defense of the New Tenseless Theory of Time." In *The New Theory of Time,* edited by L. Nathan Oaklander and Quentin Smith, 57–68. New Haven: Yale University Press.

Oaklander, L. Nathan. 1994b. "Introduction: McTaggart's Paradox and the Tensed Theory of Time." In *The New Theory of Time,* edited by L. Nathan Oaklander and Quentin Smith, 157–62. New Haven: Yale University Press.

Oaklander, L. Nathan. 1994c. "McTaggart's Paradox and the Infinite Regress of Temporal Attributions: A Reply to Smith." In *The New Theory of Time,* edited by L. Nathan Oaklander and Quentin Smith, 195–201. New Haven: Yale University Press.

Oaklander, L. Nathan. 1994d. "On the Experience of Tenseless Time." In *The New Theory of Time,* edited by L. Nathan Oaklander and Quentin Smith, 344–50. New Haven: Yale University Press.

Occam, William of. 1995. *William of Occam: A Letter to the Friars Minor and Other Writings.* Edited by Arthur Stephen McGrade and John Kilcullen. Translated by John Kilcullen. Cambridge: Cambridge University Press.

Olson, Robert G. 1962. *An Introduction to Existentialism.* New York: Dover.

Onians, John. 1988. *Bearers of Meaning: The Classical Orders in Antiquity, the Middle Ages, and the Renaissance.* Princeton: Princeton University Press.

Panofsky, Erwin. 1939. *Studies in Iconology: Humanistic Themes in the Art of the Renaissance.* Reprint. New York: Harper & Row, 1962.

Parr, Adrian. 2008. *Deleuze and Memorial Cuture: Desire, Singular Memory and the Politics of Trauma.* Edinburgh: Edinburgh University Press.

Patterson, Lee. 1991. *Chaucer and the Subject of History.* Madison: University of Wisconsin Press.

Pattie, David. 2000. "Space, Time, and the Self in Beckett's Late Theatre." *Modern Drama* 43.3 (Fall): 393–403.

Pearson, Keith Ansell. 1999. *Germinal Life: The Difference and Repetition of Deleuze.* London and New York: Routledge.

Petrarch. 1898. "Francesco Petrarca to Posterity." In *Petrarch, the First Modern Scholar and Man of Letters.* Translated and edited by James Harvey Robinson and Henry Winchester Rolfe, 59–76. New York: Putnam.

Philip, Lotte Brand. 1971. *The Ghent Altarpiece and the Art of Jan van Eyck*. Princeton: Princeton University Press.

Pinkard, Terry. 1996. *Hegel's Phenomenology: The Sociality of Reason*. Cambridge: Cambridge University Press.

Pippin, Robert B. 1989. *Hegel's Idealism: The Satisfactions of Self-Consciousness*. Cambridge: Cambridge University Press.

Pirenne, Henri. 1936. *Economic and Social History of Medieval Europe*. Translated by I.E. Clegg. New York: Harcourt, Brace & World.

Plato. 1961a. "Timaeus." Translated by Benjamin Jowett. In *The Collected Dialogues of Plato Including the Letters*, edited by Edith Hamilton and Huntington Cairns. Bollingen Series LXXI, 1153–211. New York: Bollingen.

Plato. 1961b. "Parmenides." Translated by F.M Cornford. In *The Collected Dialogues of Plato Including the Letters*, edited by Edith Hamilton and Huntington Cairns. Bollingen Series LXXI, 921–956. New York: Bollingen.

Plumb, J. H. 1950. *England in the Eighteenth Century (1714–1815)*. Baltimore: Penguin.

Poresky, Louise A. 1981. *The Elusive Self: Psyche and Spirit in Virginia Woolf's Novels*. Newark: University of Delaware Press.

Postlewait, Thomas. 1978. "Self-Performing Voices: Mind, Memory, and Time in Beckett's Drama." *Twentieth Century Literature: A Scholarly and Critical Journal* 24.4 (Winter): 473–91.

Poulet, Geogers. 1956. *Studies in Human Time*, translated by Elliott Coleman. Baltimore: The Johns Hopkins Press. Reprint. Westport, CT: Greenwood, 1979.

Quillen, Carol. 2010. "The Uses of the Past in Quattrocento Florence: A Reading of Bruni's Dialogues." *Journal of the History of Ideas* 71.3: 363–85.

Quinones, Ricardo. 1972. *The Renaissance Discovery of Time*. Cambridge: Harvard University Press.

Quint, David. 1985. "Humanism and Modernity: A Reconsideration of Bruni's Dialogues." *Renaissance Quarterly* 38.3: 423–45.

Reid, Su. 1991. *The Critics Debate: To the Lighthouse*. London: Macmillan.

Rice, Eugene F., Jr. 1970. *The Foundations of Early Modern Europe, 1460–1559*. New York: Norton.

Richter, Harvena. 1970. *Virginia Woolf: The Inward Journey*. Princeton: Princeton University Press.

Richter, Harvena. 1985. "Hunting the Moth: Virginia Woolf and the Creative Imagination." In *Critical Essays on Virginia Woolf*, edited by Morris Beja, 13–28. Boston: Hall.

Ricoeur, Paul. 1984. *Time and Narrative*. 3 vols. Vol. 1, translated by Kathleen McLaughlin and David Pellauer. Chicago: University of Chicago Press.

Ricoeur, Paul. 1985. *Time and Narrative*. 3 vols. Vol. 2, translated by Kathleen McLaughlin and David Pellauer. Chicago: University of Chicago Press.

Ridderbos, Katinka. 2002. "Introduction." In *Time*, edited by Katinka Ridderbos, 1–5. Cambridge: Cambridge University Press.

Roberts, J. H. 1934. "Toward Virginia Woolf." *Virginia Quarterly Review* 10: 587–602.
Rodemeyer, Lanei. 2006. *Intersubjective Temporality: It's About Time*. Dordrecht, The Netherlands: Springer.
Rosen, Ralph M. 2004. "Ancient Time Across Time." *Time and Temporality in the Ancient World*. Edited by Ralph M. Rosen, 1–10. Philadelphia: University of Pennsylvania Museum of Archaeology and Anthropology.
Ross, Sir David. 1949. *Aristotle*. 5th ed. London: Methuen.
Rowse, A. L. 1950. *The England of Elizabeth: The Structure of Society*. New York: Macmillan.
Rudd, Niall. 1982. "Horace." *The Cambridge History of Classical Literature: Latin Literature*. Edited by E. J. Kenney, 370–404. Cambridge: Cambridge University Press.
Ruotolo, Lucio P. 1986. *The Interrupted Moment: A View Of Virginia Woolf's Novels*. Stanford: Stanford University Press.
Ryan, Lawrence V. 1963. *Roger Ascham*. Stanford: Stanford University Press.
Saunders, Corinne. 2010. "Introduction." *A Companion to Medieval Poetry*. Edited by Corinne Saunders, 1–10. Chichester: Wiley-Blackwell.
Schlesinger, George. 1994. "Temporal Becoming." In *The New Theory of Time*, edited by L. Nathan Oaklander and Quentin Smith, 214–20. New Haven: Yale University Press.
Schwartzbach, F. S. 1979. *Dickens and the City*. London: Athlone.
Scott, David. 2006. "The 'Concept of Time' and the 'Being of the Clock': Bergson, Einstein, Heigegger and the Interrogation of the Temporality of Modernism." *Continental Philosophy Review* 39.2: 183–213.
Shakespeare, William. 1942a. *Macbeth*. *The Complete Plays and Poems of William Shakespeare*, edited with introduction and notes by William Allan Neilson and Charles Jarvis Hill. 1180–212. Cambridge, MA: Houghton Mifflin.
Shakespeare, William. 1942b. *Sonnets*. In *The Complete Plays and Poems of William Shakespeare*, edited and introduced by William Allan Neilson and Charles Jarvis Hill, 1369–396. Cambridge, MA: Houghton Mifflin.
Shakespeare, William. 1982. *Hamlet*, edited by Harold Jenkins. London: Methuen.
Sherover, Charles M., ed. 1975. *The Human Experience of Time: The Development of Its Philosophic Meaning*. New York: New York University Press.
Sicher, Efraim. 1993. "Acts of Enclosure: The Moral Landscape of Dickens' *Hard Times*." *Dickens Studies Annual* 22: 195–216.
Slay, Jack, Jr. 1996. *Ian McEwan*. New York: Twayne Publishers; London: Prentice Hall International.
Smith, Grahame. 1990. "'O reason not the need': *King Lear*, *Hard Times* and Utilitarian Values." *The Dickensian* 86.3: 164–70.
Smith, Quentin. 1994. "Problems with the New Tenseless Theory of Time." In *The New Theory of Time*, edited by L. Nathan Oaklander and Quentin Smith Edition, 38–56. New Haven: Yale University Press.

Soll, Ivan. 1969. *An Introduction to Hegel's Metaphysics*. Foreword by Walter Kaufmann. Chicago: University of Chicago Press.

Solomon, Robert C. 1983. *In the Spirit of Hegel: A Study of G. W. F. Hegel's Phenomenology of Spirit*. New York and Oxford: Oxford University Press.

Spiegelberg, Herbert. 1994. *The Phenomenological Movement: A Historical Introduction*. Dordrecht, The Netherlands: Kluwer Academic Publishers.

Starr, Chester G. 1965. *Civilization and the Caesars: The Intellectual Revolution in the Roman Empire*. New York: Norton.

Stewart, Jack. 1977. "Light in *To the Lighthouse*." *Twentieth Century Literature* 23.3: 377–89.

Stockton, Sharon. 1998. "Public Space and Private Time: Perspective in *To the Lighthouse* and in Einstein's Special Theory." *Essays in Arts and Sciences* 27: 95–115.

Storl, Heidi. 2008. "Heidegger in Woolf's Clothing." *Philosophy and Literature* 32.2: 303–14.

Strauss, D. F. M. 2010. "Do We Really Comprehend Time?" *South African Journal of Philosophy* 29.2: 167–77.

Strehle, Ralph. 2006. "A Risky Business: Internal Time and Objective Time in Husserl and Woolf." In *Literature and Philosophy: A Guide to Contemporary Debates*, edited by Davied Rudrum, 81–91. New York: Palgrave Macmillan.

Summerson, John. 1969, 1986. *The Architecture of the Eighteenth Century*. London and New York: Thames and Hudson.

Syme, Ronald. 1939. *The Roman Revolution*. Oxford: Oxford University Press.

Sypher, Wylie. 1976. *The Ethic of Time: Structures of Experience in Shakespeare*. New York: Seabury Press.

Tawney, R. H. 1926. *Religion and the Rise of Capitalism*. New York: Harcourt, Brace and Company.

Taylor, Charles. 1975. *Hegel*. Cambridge: Cambridge University Press.

Taylor, Charles. 1989. *Sources of the Self: The Making of the Modern Identity*. Cambridge, MA: Harvard University Press.

Taylor, Richard. 1978. "Fatalism." In *The Philosophy of Time*, edited by Richard M. Gale, 220–31. Atlantic Highlands: Humanities Press.

Teichmann, Roger. 1995. *The Concept of Time*. London: Macmillan.

Tennyson, Alfred Lord. 1959. "You Ask Me Why, Though Ill At Ease." In *Victorian Poetry and Poetics*, edited by Walter E. Houghton and G. Robert Stange. Boston: Houghton Mifflin.

Terdiman, Richard. 1993. *Present Past: Modernity and the Memory Crisis*. Ithaca: Cornell University Press.

Thakur, N. C. 1965. *The Symbolism of Virginia Woolf*. London: Oxford University Press.

Thucydides. 1972. *History of the Peloponnesian War*. Translated by Rex Warner. Introduction and Notes by M. I. Finley. London: Penguin.

Tillich, Paul. 1952. *The Courage To Be*. New Haven and London: Yale University Press.

Tillich, Paul. 1963. *Systematic Theology: Three Volumes in One*. Chicago: University of Chicago Press.

Tomlin, Claire. 1990. *The Invisible Woman: The Story of Nelly Ternan and Charles Dickens*. London: Viking.

Torrance, Robert M. 1967. "Modes of Being and Time in the World of Godot." *Modern Language Quarterly* 28: 77–95.

Troy, William. 1970. "Virginia Woolf and the Novel of Sensibility." In *Virginia Woolf: To the Lighthouse: A Casebook*, edited by M. Beja, 65–88. London: Macmillan.

Tucker, Josiah. 1758. *Instructions for Travellers*. Dublin: William Watson.

Turetzky, Philip. 1998. *Time*. London and New York: Routledge.

Turetzky, Philip. 2004. "Rhythm: Assemblage and Event." In *Deleuze and Music*, edited by Ian Buchanan and Marcel Swiboda, 140–58. Edinburgh: Edinburgh University Press.

Tymieniecka, Anna-Theresa. 2007. "Introduction: Timing Our Life." In *Temporality in Life as Seen Through Literature: Contributions to Phenomenology of Life*. edited by Anna-Theresa Tymieniecka, xiii–xix. Dordrecht, The Netherlands: Springer.

Tzonis, Alexander and Liane Lefaivre. 1986. *Classical Architecture: The Poetics of Order*. Cambridge, MA; London: MIT Press.

Unamuno, Miguel de. 1972. *The Tragic Sense of Life in Men and Nations*. Translated by Anthony Kerrigan. Princeton: Princeton University Press.

Vieira, Josalba Ramalho. 1990. "Henri Bergson's Idea of Duration and Virginia Woolf's Novels." *Ilha Do Destero: A Journal of Language and Literature* 24.2: 9–20.

Von Simpson, Otto. 1988. *The Gothic Cathedral: Origins of Gothic Architecture and the Medieval Concept of Order*. 3rd ed. Princeton: Princeton University Press.

Warren, Nicolas de. 2009. *Husserl and the Promise of Time: Subjectivity in Transcendental Phenomenology*. Cambridge: Cambridge University Press.

Watkins, Gwen. 1987. *Dickens in Search of Himself: Recurrent Themes and Characters in the World of Charles Dickens*. London: Macmillan.

Watt, Ian. 1965. *The Rise of the Novel: Studies in Defoe, Richardson and Fielding*. Berkeley and Los Angeles: University of California Press.

Watts, Isaac. 1806. *The Songs and Hymns of the Rev. Isaac Watts*. New Edition. Edited by Rev. G. Burder. London: Williams and Smith.

Weber, Jean Jacques. 1989. "Dickens's Social Semiotic: The Modal Analysis of Ideological Structure." In *Language, Discourse and Literature: An Introductory Reader in Discourse Statistics*, edited by Ronald Carter and Paul Simpson, 95–111. London: Unwin.

Welshon, Rex. 2004. *The Philosophy of Nietzsche*. Montreal and Kingston: McGill-Queen's University Press.

Whitehead, Alfred North. 1925. *Science and the Modern World*. New York: Mentor Books.

Whitehead, Alfred North. 1929. *Process and Reality: An Essay in Cosmology*, edited by David Ray Griffin and Donald W. Sherburne. New York: Free Press, 1978.
Whitehead, Alfred North. 1961a. *Adventures of Ideas*. 1933. Reprint. New York: Macmillan.
Whitehead, Alfred North. 1961b. *Interpretation of Science: Representative Selections*, edited by A. H. Johnson. Indianapolis: Bobbs-Merrill.
Whitrow, G. J. 1988. *Time in History: Views of Time from Prehistory to the Present Day*. Oxford: Oxford University Press.
Wickham, Chris. 2005. *Framing the Early Middle Ages: Europe and the Mediteranean, 400–800*. Oxford: Oxford University Press.
Williams, Clifford. 1994. "The Phenomenology of B-Time." In *The New Theory of Time*, edited by L. Nathan Oaklander and Quentin Smith, 360–72. New Haven: Yale University Press.
Williams, Donald C. 1978. "The Myth of Passage." In *The Philosophy of Time*, edited by Richard Gale, 100–16. Atlantic Highlands: Humanities Press.
Williams, Raymond. 1963. *Culture and Society 1780–1950*. Harmondsworth: Penguin.
Windelband, Wilhelm. 1958. *A History of Philosophy*. 2 vols., translated by James H. Tufts. Reprint. New York: Harper & Row, 1901.
Wittgenstein, Ludwig. 1967. *Tractatus Logico-Philosophicus*, quoted in G. E. M. Anscombe. "Aristotle and the Sea Battle: *De Interpretatione*, Chapter IX." In *Aristotle: A Collection of Critical Essays*, edited by J. M. E. Moravcsik, 15–33. Garden City, NY: Anchor Books.
Wittkower, Rudolf. 1971. *Architectural Principles in the Age of Humanism*. New York, London: Norton.
Woolf, Virginia. 1992a. *To the Lighthouse*. Harmondsworth: Penguin, 1964.
Woolf, Virginia. 1992b. *Mrs. Dalloway*. Introduction and notes by Elaine Showalter. London: Penguin, 1925.
Workman, Herbert B. 1960. *Persecution in the Early Church*. New York: Abingdon Press.
Xenophon. 1972. *The Persian Expedition*. Translated by Rex Warner. Introduction and Notes by George Cawkwell. London: Penguin.
Yachnin, Paul. 2002. "Millenarian Ghosts: Hamlet and Nationhood." In *Elizabethan Theatre 15*, edited by A. L. Magnusson and C. E. McGee, 241–59. Toronto: P. D. Meany.
Yasuo, Yuasa. 2008. *Overcoming Modernity: Synchronicity and Image-Thinking*. Translated by Shigenori Nagatomo and John W. M. Krummel. Albany: State University of New York Press.
Zahavi, Dan. 2003. *Husserl's Phenomenology*. Stanford: Stanford University Press.
Zeller, E. 1879, 1962. *The Stoics, Epicureans, and Sceptics*. Translated by Oswald J. Reichel. New York: Russell & Russell.

Zemka, Sue. 2012. *Time and the Moment in Victorian Literature and Society*. Cambridge: Cambridge University Press.

Zimmerman, Dean W. 2005. "The A-Theory of Time, The B-Theory of Time, and 'Taking Tense Seriously.'" *Dialectica* 59.4: 401–57.

Zwerdling, Alex. 1986. *Virginia Woolf and the Real World*. Berkeley: University of California Press.

Index

Abel, Elizabeth 87–90, 243n. 13
Ackerman, James S. 100
active synthesis (of memory) 191–5, 207–8
Adam (the first man) 155–8
adequation 5
affective magnitudes 189
agency and time *see* time and agency
Amis, Kinglsey 120
Anabasis 13, 238n. 13
The Anatomy of Melancholy 12
Andreau, Jean 38
anisotropy of time 8, 11
  and concussion 6
  control of 5
  as a disastrous force 7
  in *Hamlet* 33–4, 37–8, 40, 45, 47
  in *Mrs. Dalloway* 93–4, 110
  and pain 1–2
  resistance to 3, 7
  reversal or halting of 34–5
Antic Hay 1–2
anxiety 40, 111, 126
  about, distaste for the future 156, 163, 166, 209, 234
  due to passage of time 34–6, 46–7
  expiration 44–5, 213
  of meaninglessness 223–4
  temporal, about futurity 41–2, 45, 106
apperception 182–3
  empirical 183, 185, 186
  transcendental unity of 182, 184–6
Aquinas, St. Thomas 69, 157
Aristotle 3, 42, 43, 69, 98, 112, 113, 114, 118, 136, 137, 139, 240n. 6
A-series 29, 116, 165
  distinction from B-series 29–30, 31, 166
  dynamic time 29
  in *Enduring Love* 166–7
  in *Hamlet* 30–1, *see also* A-series time in *Hamlet*
  presupposition of change 29–30
  in *To the Lighthouse* 118

A-series time in *Hamlet*
  anisotropy of time in 33–4, 37–8, 40, 45, 47
  anxiety about the passage of time 34–6, 40–2, 46–7, *see also* expiration anxiety
  conceptualization of time 32, 35, 37–40
  construction of time 31–2
  death of Hamlet 44–5
  elapse of time 32, 36–7, 39, 44, 46
  expiration of time 32–6, 44–7, *see also* expiration anxiety
  Hamlet's voyage to the future 40–4
  "happy time" 37, 44, 213
  madness
    of Hamlet 35
    of Ophelia 36–7
  openness of the future 43–4
  Ophelia's vulnerability to the passage of time 35–6
  remoteness of the past 45–7
  revenge mortality 33–4, 36, 37, 46, 212–13, 228–32
  reversal or halting of anisotropy 34–5
  sea-fight 42–3
  "secure hour" (assassination time) 34
  The Murder of Gonzago 31, 34, 38–9
Auerbach, Eric 96
Aurelius, Marcus 12
"awareness of conditions of movement from one historical epoch to the next" 16–17, *see also* historical awareness

Baker, Hershel 158
Battle of Waterloo 16
Baumlin, James S. 29
Beckett, Samuel 1, 9, 23, 121, 124
  oeuvre 2, 4, 183, 232, 233
  see also Beckettian mimesis of time
Beckettian mimesis of time 8, 135
  ambivalence toward the past 140–1

as devourer of present and past 142, 145–6
Endgame 136, 141
"The Expelled" 141–2, 144
expiration 140–1
forgetting the past 145–6
freedom from time 145–6
futurity, notion of 143–5
How It Is 136, 139, 140, 141, 144, 233
indiscernible moments in 142–3, 146–7
vs Kantian construction of time 135–6
"Krapp's Last Tape" 147–52
"Molloy" 139, 143, 151
paradox in 137–8, 140, 141, 143, 145, 147
present moment, status of 146–7
relationism 23, 137
substantivalism 23, 137
temporal dispensation, discrepancies in 136–7
temporal horizon 122, 138–40, 147
temporal isolation 139
"Texts for Nothing" 8, 136, 139, 141, 147
transience 140, 142
"The Unnamable" 138, 139–40, 144, 146–7, 149–50, 197–201, 233
Beiser, Frederick 181, 229
Bergson, Henri 3, 24, 57, 91–4, 103, 177, 187–9, 195, 198, 200, 205, 208, 242n. 2
  Creative Evolution 91
  Duration and Simultaneity 91, 92
  Time and Free Will 91
  see also *duration* or *durée*
Bernet, Rudolf 121, 122, 124
Bevan, Edwyn 17
Big Ben (tower-clock) 87, 97–8, 100–6, 109, 220, 221, see also Big Ben's "leaden circles" of time
Big Ben Man 7, 98, 106
Big Ben's "leaden circles" of time 97–8
  step 1: theology of the circle 98–9
  step 2: proportion and Vitruvian Man inscribed in a circle 99–101
  step 3: reformulating proportion in *Mrs. Dalloway* 102–4
  step 4: interpenetration of isochronal and fluid time 104–8

step 5: reconciliation with temporal passage 108–10
Bitzer (*Hard Times*) 52, 62, 217–18
Blackpool, Stephen (*Hard Times*) 6, 21, 58, 59, 61, 63, 204, 219, 221
Bloom, Leopold (*Ulysses*) 6, 68, 70–2, 75–82, 187, 206–8, 225–7
  adolescent rebellion of 75
  clinging to the past 76, 78, 81–2
  coexistence of opposed tendencies in 75–6
  discomfort with the present 76–7, 81–2
  drowning man image 76, 77
  fear of aging 76, 77
  fear of the future 76–7
  joint self-perception of Stephen and 78–9
  Molly Bloom, see *Ulysses* (novel), Molly's adultery
  self-contained harmony of 80–1
  specular selfhood of 71–2
  voyeurism with Gerty 77–8, 82
Blunt, Anthony 20
Bochenski, I. M. 91, 121, 169
Bollery, Jérome 20
Bony, Jean 18
Bounderby, Mr. (*Hard Times*) 52, 54, 57–65, 218–19, 241n. 5
Boylan, Blazes (*Ulysses*) 77, 79, 81
Bradshaw, William Sir (psychiatrist in *Mrs. Dalloway*) 86, 101–3, 105–7
  imposition of clock-measured time 89, 98, 102
  insistence on conformity 89
Bramble, J. C. 19
Briscoe, Lily (*To the Lighthouse*) 112, 117, 118–19, 128, 131, 132–4, 223–4, 243n. 12
Broad, C. D. 3, 7, 116, 117, 119, 120, 167
Brooks, Peter 51
Brown, Peter 38, 43
Bruni, Leonardo 15
Bryant, Levi R. 92, 179, 185–93, 195–6, 198, 207, 209, 211
B-series 29, 116, 117, 165
  distinction from A-series 29–30, 31, 166
  in *Enduring Love* 166, 172–5
  exclusion of change 29

in *Hamlet* 30–1, *see also* B-series time in *Hamlet*
  static time 29
  in *To the Lighthouse* 118
B-series time in *Hamlet* 47–9
  recapitulative compulsion 48–9
Burton, Robert 12
Butler, Samuel 18, 19

Caffrey, Cissey 70
Calderwood, James 29
Calendar, Craig 24
Calinescu, Matei 11, 12, 13, 14
Cassirer, Ernst 55, 103, 179, 184
Castoriadis, Cornelius 23
Chandler, James 16, 17, 18
changelessness 8, 95, 135, 143, 147
Chaucer, Geoffrey 16, 18
chronos 14, 29, 238n. 12
Clarissa (*Enduring Love*) 155, 159, 160–1, 164, 168, 169, 170–1, 210–11, 235
Claudius (*Hamlet*) 33, 36, 39–40, 42, 44–6, 48, 216–17, 228–31
Clausen, W. V. 19
Clayton, Jay 21
clock(s)
  Big Ben's 87, 97–8, 100–6, 109, 220, 221
  Dutch 62, 218
  Gradgrind's/statistical 21, 24, 54, 56, 62, 64, 188, 202, 203, 204, 218, 219, 220, 221
  of Harley Street 89, 90, 98, 100, 107
  public 101, 102, 106–7
  signification of 107
  ticking 120, 143, 190
Coketown (*Hard Times*) 6, 59, 62, 63, 65, 241n. 4
  formative principle of 51, 54
  momentaneous time in 57
  monotony in 54–6
  residents of 54
  temporal dispensation in 203, 219–20
  thinking mentality in 51–3
  value and purpose of time in 54, 218
Coles, Nicholas 51
concussion 6, 221–2
Confessions 55
contemplative soul 189–90, 244n. 1

"convulsions of metamorphosis" 6, 67, 68, 69, 70, 71, 73, 75, 78, 81, 83, 187, 205, 206, 207, 226, 227
Copleston, Frederick 179–83
Coulton, G. G. 17
Coulton, J. J. 100
counterexamples 4, 10, 11, 13, 14, 16–17, 19, 21, 22, 238n. 15
Cratylus 19
Creative Evolution 91, 200
The Culture of Time and Space: 1880–1918 10
Currie, Gregory 3, 24

Dainton, Barry 119–20, 122, 126, 128, 129
Dalloway, Clarissa (*Mrs. Dalloway*) 85–6, 92, 104–6
  fear of time 109–10
  formulation of her own identity 90–1
  happiness of 88
  meditation on Septimus's death 87–8, 108, 110, 221
  references to darkness/blackness 86, 93, 103, 108–10
  rejection of Peter 93–4, 103, 110
  response to Septimus's suicide 86–7, 107
  sister's death 93
  on time and loss 95, 110
  view on individual difference as uniqueness 88
Davies, John K. 38
da Vinci, Leonardo 12, 100, 101
De Clérambault's syndrome 154, 160, 161, 170, 210
The Decline and Fall of the Roman Empire 16
Delanda, Michael 178
delay 5, 36–7, 39, 40, 58, 61, 117, 166, 210, 212, 213, 216, 227–30, 234
Deleuze, Gilles 4, 92, 177, 178, 186–90, *see also* Deleuze's temoral theory/ philosophy of time
Deleuze's temoral theory/philosophy of time
  active synthesis 191–5, 207–8
  contemplative souls 189–90
  in *Enduring Love* 208–11
  "fractured I" 186–7, 211
  in *Hamlet* 211–14

in *Hard Times* 202–5
living present 187–91, 196, 198–9, 203, 209–11
passive synthesis
 first 188–91, 196, 198, 209
 second 192, 195–8, 200, 205
time as instants 188–93, 195–201, 203, 205, 209
in *To the Lighthouse* 194–5, 201–2
in *Ulysses* 186–7, 205–8
and The Unnamable 197–203
de Lorris, Guillaume 12
de Meun, Jean 12
de Warren, Nicholas 123
DeWeese, Garrett J. 23, 24
Dialogues 15
Dickens, Charles 6, 51, see also *Hard Times* (novel)
Dohrn-van-Rossum, Gerhard 27
dream/dreams 1, 13, 14, 141, 148, 237n. 1
Duchesne, Louis 157
Dummett, Michael 112
durational time 7, 21–2, 24, 225, see also punctualist present
duration or *durée* 91–6, 102–4
 Bergsonian 91–3
 as "enduring becoming" 91, 94
 memory's role in constituting 92
 Woolfian 103, 104

elapse of time 25, 32, 36–7, 39, 46, 64, 81–2, 93, 102, 106, 123, 127, 129–30, 138, 147, 171, 188, 192, 200, 204, 221, 222, 228, 234, *see also* expiration
Eliot, George 21
Eliot, T. S.
 "Burnt Norton" 2, 134
 "The Hollow Men" 234
empirical memory 193–5, 205
Enduring Love (novel) 4, 8, 24
 "Anxiety about, distaste for the future" 156, 163, 166, 170, 209, 234
 A-series in 166–7
 balloon catastrophe 155–6, 159–60, 209, 235, 236
 Biblical Fall 155, 159, 163, 169–70
 B-series in 166, 172–5
 Deleuzian analysis of time in 208–11

distinction between the A-series and B-series in 166
hypothetical alternatives, Joe's recourse to 162–4
intention and conception of the future 164–71
notion of the fall 155, 156–8
notion of time 155
prelapsarian and postlapsarian man 156–8
predicament/problematizing of free will 155, 156, 159–62
"random clustering" 162
rescue attempt 155–6, 159, 167–8, 209–10
time and agency in 234–6
transition from A-time to B-time 171–5
see also Clarissa (*Enduring Love*); Gadd, Harry (*Enduring Love*); Logan, John (*Enduring Love*); Parry, Jed (*Enduring Love*); Rose, Joe (*Enduring Love*)
ensuing or emergent self 6, 74–5, 78, 79
An Essay Concerning Human Understanding 12–13
Eve 155, 157
expiration 32–6, 44–7, 81, 96, 109, 138, 140–1, *see also* expiration anxiety
expiration anxiety 44–5, 213

Faulkner, Keith 5, 179, 185
Federman, Raymond 72
Ferguson, Wallace K. 15
"figures of suddenness" 21
Findlay, J. N. 3
flux 12, 30, 32, 36, 104, 111, 122, 129–30, 149, 173, 179, 181, 183, 200, *see also* temporal flux; transience
Focillon, Henri 102, 107
Forster, E. M. 4
Fortinbras (*Hamlet*) 34, 40, 45
Freud, Sigmund 68, 241n. 4, 243n. 8
 developmental paradigm of *Mrs. Dalloway* (novel) 87–91

Gadd, Harry (*Enduring Love*) 159
Gardner, Sebastian 178, 180–1, 183–5
generalization 9–11, 20–1

abstractive 9
historical 10, 22
risk of 22–3
Gertrude (*Hamlet*) 23, 39, 44, 48, 228, 229, 232
Gibbon, Edward 16
Gillies, Mary Ann 94
Gilson, Etienne 69, 99, 144, 157, 158, 165
Glaber, Ralph 16
Goldberg, S. L. 68
Gradgrind, Mr. (*Hard Times*) 61–2, 64–5, 188, 202–5, 216, 218, 221, 240n. 1
  artificial barriers to subtle essences of humanity 52–3
  Observatory of 54
  pedagogy of thinking 52–3, 54, 61, 218
  statistical clock of 54, 56, 62, 64, 202, 204
  struggle to overcome barrier 53
Gradgrind, Mrs. (*Hard Times*) 58, 182–3, 219
Grebanier, Bernard 29
Gruen, Erich S. 20

habitus (first passive synthesis) 188–91, 196, 198–9, 203–4, 209, 211
Hamlet (*Hamlet*)
  celebrated delay of 5, 36–7, 39, 40, 227–30, 234
  conceptualization of time by 32, 35, 37–40
  death of 44–5
  madness of 35
  relation to the past 37–8, 45–8, 231–2
  voyage to the future 40–4
  see also A-series time in, *Hamlet*; B-series time in, *Hamlet*; *Hamlet* (play)
Hamlet (play) 2–3, 4, 20, 21, 23, 24
  approach to the problem of 28–9
  A-series in 30–1, *see also* A-series time in *Hamlet*
  B-series in 30–1, *see also* B-series time in *Hamlet*
  Deleuzian analysis of time in 211–14
  dual mimetic project in 30
  punctiform time 28
  reiterative time vs teleological time in 29

representation of time as binary oppositions 28–9
  revenge mortality in 33–4, 36, 37, 46, 212–13, 228–32
  temporal awareness in 5–6
  The Murder of Gonzago 21, 31, 34, 38–9, 228–9
  time and agency in 216–17, 227–34
  tragedy in 5–6, 38, 44–6, 49
Hard Times (novel) 4, 5, 6, 22, 24, 51
  adult independence and immaturity 62
  aging, shame of 54, 62–3
  artificial barriers to subtle essences of humanity 52–3, 59
  boredom 60–1
  of Bounderby 57–9, 63
  closure of 65
  Deleuzian analysis of time in 202–5
  escape from vulnerability to time 54
  fast and slow time 59–60
  formative principle of Coketown 51, 54
  Gradgrind's pedagogy of thinking 52–3, 54, 61
  of Harthouse 60–1
  impatience 60, 64
  intervening time 60–1
  languor 58, 60–1, 64
  of Louisa 56–7
  monotony in Coketown 54–6
  paradox of time 55
  parental desertion 54, 62–3
  parental discipline in Tom's childhood 61–2
  pathological nature vs philosophical counterpart of time 55, 57
  purpose of time in Coketown 54–5
  self-interest 51, 52, 53, 58–64
  self-suppression 52, 54, 61
  shame/shameful 58, 62–5
  of Stephen 59
  time and agency in 216, 217–20, 221
  victims in 58, 60, 63
  weakness and vulnerability 63–4
  see also Coketown (*Hard Times*); Gradgrind, Mr. (*Hard Times*); Gradgrind, Mrs. (*Hard Times*)
Harthouse, James, Mr. (*Hard Times*) 52, 60–1, 63

Hayman, David 72
Hegel, G. W. F. 3, 22, 237n. 6, 239n. 22
Heise, Ursula K. 22
Henke, Suzette 68
Hirsch, Marianne 21
historical awareness 15, 17
The History of Rasselas, Prince of Abyssinia 12
History of the Peloponnesian War 17
Hobbes, Thomas 13
Holmes, Dr. (*Mrs. Dalloway*) 86, 89, 105
Homer 19
Hooker, Richard 16
Horse-riding (circus) (*Hard Times*) 53–4
How It Is 136, 139, 140, 141, 144, 233
Hughes, Joe W. 180, 187, 188, 189, 196
Huizinga, J. 19
human time 9, 226
Hume, David 13
Hunt, Maurice 28
Husserl, Edmund 3, 8, 120–6, 128–30, 138–9, 177, 187, 242n. 2, *see also* phenomenology of time
Huxley, Aldous 1

immanence 99, 121, 182
impressional consciousness 122–7
inveterate self 6, 74–5, 78, 79
irreversible time 11–14, 75, 205, 238n. 8, 238n. 9, *see also* succession; unrepeatable time
isochronal time 7, 98, 102–7

Jackson, T. G. 18
Johnson, Samuel 12
Joyce, James 19, *see also* Joycean metempsychosis; *Ulysses* (novel)
Joycean metempsychosis 68–9, 78, 82–3, 227
  great pathos of 75
  hallmark of 6–7, 74–5
  see also convulsions of metamorphosis
Jupe, Mr. (*Hard Times*) 54–5, 62, 65, 219

Kain, Richard 67
kairos 13–14, 29, 238n. 12
Kant, Immanuel 3, 61
  apperception, *see* apperception
  Copernican Revolution 178
  model of experience 179–82
  time as an a priori form of sensibility 135, 178, 186–7
  and the "transcendental" 178–80, 182
Kastan, David Scott 28
Keats, John 67
Kelly, J. N. D. 156–8
Kermode, Frank 29
Kern, Stephen 10–11
Kierkegaard, Søren 215–16, 220, 222, 226
Kiernan-Lewis, Delmas 31
Kockelmans, Joseph J. 121, 122
Koselleck, Reinhart 14–15

Lacey, Alan Robert 91, 92
Lampert, Jay 91, 93, 190, 192, 193–6, 198
The Laws of Ecclesiastical Polity 16
"leaden circles" 7, 87, 97–8, 100, 103, 105, 220, *see also* Big Ben's "leaden circles" of time
Leavis, F. R. 51
Leibnitz, Gottfried Wilhelm von 137, 142
Leland, John 15
Le Poidevin, Robin 29, 143, 167
"Letter to Posterity" 15
Levey, Michael 20
Leviathan 13
"life in time" 4
literary texts
  analysis based on philosophical theories of time 3–4, 9–10
  relation between time and agency 4
  tomographic method 3
  approach to the study of 8–9, 11
  depiction vs examination of time in 4
  selection criteria for study of 4–5
living present 123, 146, 187–91, 196, 198–9, 203, 209–11
Locke, John 12
Logan, John (*Enduring Love*) 164
  fall and death of 155, 159–60, 168
  Joe's reaction to the fall 163
Lorraine, Tamsin 211–13
loss of the past 19–20, 75, 103, 131, 133, 222, 225–6
Louisa (Gradgrind's daughter) (*Hard Times*) 5, 52–3, 56–61, 63, 203, 216–17, 219
Loux, Michael J. 117

Lowe, E. J. 27
Luck, Georg 19
Lucky Jim 120
Luther, Martin 20

Macbeth (play) 11–12
MacDowell, Gerty (*Ulysses*) 77–8, 82
Machiavelli 15
Malcolm, David 153–4
Maritain, Jacques 57
Maxims of Theology 99
McBride, Margaret 72
McCarthy, Patrick 68
McEwan, Ian 23, 208–11, 234, 235, 244n. 1
  novels of 153–4
  see also *Enduring Love* (novel)
McTaggart, John 3, 6, 24, 25, 27–8, 29, 30, 31, 116, 118, 165–7, 172, 242n. 2, see also *A*-series; *B*-series
meaning of life, questions on 67, 111, 115, 131, 133, 201, 215, 223
Meditations 12
Meier, Christian 17
Meister, Jan Christoph 22
Mellor, D. H. 32, 172, 173
Melville, Herman 2
memory crisis 18–19
metempsychosis, 6–7, 67, 68, 78, 81, 82
  drowning man vs the drowned man 74, 76, 77
  effect on individual development and experience 71
  fissure between past and present 70–1
  specular selfhood, notion of 71–4, 79
  "vital growth" 68, 73, 82–3, 205, 206, 207
  see also Joycean metempsychosis; *Ulysses* (novel)
Middle Ages 20, 101, 237n. 7
  Early 10
  Gothic phase of 17–18
  Late 16
Middleton, Peter 22
The Mill on the Floss 21, 22
Miller, Henry 1
modernity/modernism 11, 14, 15, 18, 238n. 8
The Moonstone 18
Moorhead, John 17

Mrs. Dalloway (novel) 4, 7, 24
  Bergsonian prolongation of the past into the present 7, 91–5, 200, see also duration or*durée*
  Big Ben's "leaden circles" of time, implications of, see Big Ben's "leaden circles" of time
  Clarissa's response to Septimus's suicide 86–7, 107
  conversion and conformity 89
  darkness/blackness 86, 93, 103, 108–10
  division and subdivision of time 89, 91, 98, 100–2, 107
  emotions, oscillation of 85–6
  experience(s) 92, 94, 108, 110
    basis of 85
    human 96–7
    temporal 87, 102–6
  foreground and background time in 95–7
  formulations of redemption 87
  Freudian interpretation of 87–91
  motif of changelessness 95
  power of feeling 7, 86, 90, 110
  privacy of the soul 86, 105
  selfhood, notion of 88, 90–1
  time and agency in 220–3, 225
  time measured by clocks 89, 91, see also clock(s)
  youth vs maturity 90–1
  see also Bradshaw, William Sir (psychiatrist in *Mrs. Dalloway*); Dalloway, Clarissa (*Mrs. Dalloway*); Smith, Septimus Warren (*Mrs. Dalloway*); Walsh, Peter (*Mrs. Dalloway*)
Mulligan, Buck 70, 73
Murray, Peter 100

Najemy, John M. 86
Nashe, Thomas 9
Nattier, Jean Marc 20
The Nature of Existence 27, 165
Newman, Karen 21
Newton, Isaac Sir 12, 23, 51, 137
"Night Thoughts" 1
nostalgia 19–20, 144, 155, 207, 239n. 19
Notebooks 12
now-phase, see impressional consciousness

O'Brien, Flann 116, 181, 182
Oaklander, Nathan L. 27, 30, 165, 172, 174
objective experience 181–3
The Odyssey 19, 81
Olson, Robert G. 168–9
"one enormous second" 8, 136, 143
Onians, John 100
Ophelia (*Hamlet*) 23, 33, 35–8, 44, 48, 127, 228, 240n. 4

Panofsky, Erwin 15, 28
Parry, Jed (*Enduring Love*) 168, 171, 174–5, 235
   attempted murder of Joe 161–2, 164, 169–70
   De Clérambault's syndrome of 154, 160, 161, 170, 210
passive synthesis
   first (*habitus*) 188–91, 196, 198–9, 203–4, 209, 211
   second 192, 195–8, 200, 205
Patterson, Lee 16, 18
perceptive peculiarities 72–5, 79
Petrarch 15
The Phenomenology of Internal Time Consciousness 122, 124
phenomenology of time 120–6, 129
Philip, Lotte Brand 18
philosophical theories of time/temporal awareness 3–4, 9–10, *see also* generalization
philosophy 237n. 3
   and precision 3
   and theories of time 3–4, 9–10
Pierre: or, The Ambiguities 2
Pinkard, Terry 22, 217
Pippin, Robert B. 182, 183
Pirenne, Henri 9
Plato 19, 98, 101, 202, 238n. 11, 240n. 3
   Timaeus 98, 101, 202
Player King (*Hamlet*) 33–4, 36, 39, 216
Plotinus 19, 98, 101
Plumb, J. H. 11
Polonius 35, 38, 48
   construction of time 27, 32, 40
Pontifex, Ernest 18
Poulet, Georges 28
"power of feeling" 7, 86, 90, 110

Pozzo 9, 136, 215–17, 234, 237n. 5
primal impression 122–4, 126
The Prince 15
"the process of living" 7, 87, 88, 108
punctualist present 21–2, *see also* durational time
Pythagoras/Pythagorean system 101–2

Quillen, Carol 15
Quinones, Ricardo 28
Quint, David 15

Ramsay, Andrew (*To the Lighthouse*) 112, 119, 121, 178, 224
Ramsay, Mr. (*To the Lighthouse*) 112, 126, 128, 131
   agony of 114–15
   temporal responsibility of 131, 132
   voyage to the Lighthouse 133–4
Ramsay, Mrs. (*To the Lighthouse*) 112, 119, 120, 126–7, 128, 129, 134, 194, 201–2, 223, 242n. 6
   death of 114, 133, 224
   meditation 118
   social cohesion/cohesive faculty of 132–3
   temporal responsibility of 131–2
Ramsay, Prue 112, 119, 129, 224
recapitulative compulsion 48
relationism 23, 137
Renaissance 12, 15–16, 28, 99, 100, 101, 238n. 14
retentional consciousness 123–8, 130
revenge morality 2, 5, 33–4, 36, 37, 46, 212–13, 228–32
Ricoeur, Paul 4, 24, 96–7
Rodemeyer, Lanei 123, 124, 128
The Romance of the Rose 12, 18
Rose, Joe (*Enduring Love*)
   attempted murder by Parry 161–2, 164, 169–70
   control of the future 164–5, 167
   "fear of outcomes" 163, 169, 170–1, 173
   guilt and foreboding 156, 164, 165, 167
   and Logan's children 173
   reaction to Logan's fall 163
   recourse to hypothetical alternatives 162–4

re-examination of the past 163–4
vulnerability and compromised free will 160–1, 169, 235
Rowse, A. L. 10, 15, 16
Rudd, Niall 19
Russell, A. E. 67
Ryan, Lawrence V. 15

Sauders, Corinne 20
Schernus, Wilhelm 22
Schlesinger, George 31, 167
Scientific Thought 116
self-destruction 2, 6, 55
self-determination 4, 43, 175, 217, 219, 220, 221, 223, 226, 227, 229, 230, 232–6
self-reflection 7, 72, 80, *see also* specular selfhood
self-suppression 6, 52, 54, 61
series of time movement 6, 27, 29
  A-series, *see* A-series
  B-series, *see* B-series
Seton, Sally (*Mrs. Dalloway*) 85, 93, 103, 108, 109, 110
Shakespeare, William 1, 11, 39, 68, see also *Hamlet* (play)
"shocks of suffering" 7, 106
Sissy (*Hard Times*) 54, 59, 62–5
Smith, Quentin 25, 30, 172
Smith, Septimus Warren (*Mrs. Dalloway*) 85
  delusions regarding Evans 93–5, 103
  lack of distinction between past and present 93–5
  psychological disorder of 86
  salvation of soul 86
  suicidal death of 86–7, 89, 110, 221–2
Sonnet 12/twelfth sonnet 1, 39
soul 17, 47, 73, 74, 99, 101, 157–8, 212, 229
  Aristotelian-Thomist 69, 70
  contemplative 189–90, 244n. 1
  dark night of the 114–15
  privacy of the 86, 105
  salvation of the 86
  transmigration of the 68–70
Sparsit, Mrs. (*Hard Times*) 58, 60, 63
specious present 119–20, 132
specular selfhood 7, 71–4, 79–80

St. Augustine 55, 101, 157, 158, 237n. 2
stagnation 137, 198, 201
Starr, Chester G. 98
Stephen (*Hard Times*), *see* Blackpool, Stephen (*Hard Times*)
Stephen, Dedalus (*Ulysses*) 6, 68–82, 173, 186–7, 205, 206, 208, 225–7
  death agony of mother 73–4
  discomfort with the present 77, 81–2
  drowning man image 76, 77
  fear of the future 76
  guilt of 70, 73, 74, 75, 77, 208, 225
  hallucination of his mother 71, 76, 80, 206
  joint self-perception of Bloom and 78–9
  specular selfhood of 71–4
Stow, John 15
substantivalism 23, 137
succession 11, 12–13, 238n. 8, *see also* irreversible time
Summerson, John 16
Survey of London 16
Syme, Ronald 19
Sypher, Wylie 28

"tales about time" 4
"tales of time" 4
Tawney, R. H. 20
Taylor, Charles 215, 217
Taylor, Richard 113
Teichmann, Roger 142–3, 218
temporal awareness 3, 104, 129, 140, 156, 173, 177, 196, 215, 229
  distortion in *Hamlet* 36
  history of 11–25
  philosophical theories of 9, *see also* generalization
  in the Renaissance period 28
  and tragedy 5–6
temporal congruity 18
temporal continuity 6, 18–19, 21, 131, 137, 221
temporal difference (between present and past) 14–16, 18, 28
temporal discrimination 15, 18
temporal dislocation 27, 244n. 2
temporal elapse, *see* elapse of time
temporal fixity 49, 127, 137, 149

temporal flux 7, 8, 49
temporal horizon 122, 138–40, 147
temporal passage
  acceptance of 7
  dream as a reflex to obstruct 1
  as fluvial flow 11–12
  series of, see A-series; B-series
  struggle against 4–5
  as succession 11, 12–13, 238n. 8
  and suffering of loss and depletion 1–2
  see also time
temporal succession 36, 38, 116, 137, 238n. 10, see also A-series; B-series
temporal theory/theories 3, 4, 9, 25, 187, see also generalization
temporal tragedy 5–6
Ten books on Architecture (De architectura libri decem) 100
Terdiman, Richard 18, 19, 20
Tess of the D'Urbervilles 18
theory/theories
  of human time 9
  philosophical, see philosophical theories of time/temporal awareness
  temporal 3, 4, 9, 25, 187
  see also generalization
The Third Policeman 116, 181
Thucydides 17
Tillich, Paul 14, 55, 131, 168, 223–4, 245n. 2
time
  and agency, see time and agency
  anisotropy of, see anisotropy of time
  Beckettian mimesis of, see Beckettian mimesis of time
  bipartite structure of 6
  coherence of 118–20, 134
  consciousness 27
  control of 5
  cosmological and phenomenological 24
  cumulative 56, 91
  Deleuze's philosophy of, see Deleuze's temoral theory/philosophy of time
  destructive passage of 28, 37, 39, 67, 112–14, 202
  division and subdivision of 89, 91, 98, 100–2, 107
  durational 7, 21–2, 24, 225
  dynamic and tensed 24, 29
  elapse of, see elapse of time
  extensive aspect of 25
  fast and slow 59–62
  "flowing irresistibly onwards" 11–12, 14, see also anisotropy of time
  fluid 104–5
  Freudian construct of 90
  human 9, 226
  and human consciousness 24
  human response to 1, 2
  as instants 188–93, 195–201, 203, 205, 209
  irreversible 11–12, 13, 14, 75, 205, 238n. 8, 238n. 9
  isochronal 7, 98, 102–7
  Kantian construction of 135, 178, 186–7
  leaden circles of, see Big Ben's "leaden circles" of time
  literary representation of 1–3, 8–11, 237n. 2
  measured/clock, see chronos
  momentaneous 56
  one-way forward movement of, see anisotropy of time
  and pain 1–2, 5–6
  paradox of 55
  pathological nature vs philosophical counterpart of 55, 57
  phenomenology of 120–6, 129
  philosophical theories of 3–4, 9–10
  physical philosophy of 24
  physical to personal 24
  punctiform 28
  reconceptualization of 5–6
  reiterative vs teleological 29
  relationist 23, 137
  salvation from 87
  salvation through 87
  and selfhood 7, 88
  scientific and experiential 24
  spotlight model vs Lighthouse model of 118
  spotlight view of 116–18
  static and tenseless 24–5, 29, 30–1, 32, 48
  substantive 23, 137
  and tragedy 112
  transitory aspect of 25, see also transience

unreality/nonreality of 27–8
unrepeatable 11, 12, 13–14
Woolfian construct of 90
see also temporal passage
time and agency 4, 14
  in *Enduring Love* 234–6
  in *Hamlet* 216–17, 227–34
  in *Hard Times* 216, 217–20, 221
  in *Mrs. Dalloway* 220–3, 225
  in *To the Lighthouse* 223–5
  in *Ulysses* 225–7
Time and Narrative 24
Time and the Literary 21
Time from Concept to Narrative Construct: A Reader 22
Tom (Gradgrind's son) (*Hard Times*) 53, 61–2, 64
tomographic analysis 3, 177
To the Lighthouse (novel) 4, 7–8, 23, 111
  anxiety of meaninglessness 223–4
  A-series in 118
  in the Beckettian oeuvre 232–4
  B-series in 118
  coherence of time
    reconstitution of 119, 134
    severance of 118–19, 120
  dark night of the soul 114–15
  Deleuzian analysis of time in 194–5, 201–2
  dinner party 126, 129–30, 132
  dispersion vs coherence 129, 130
  expanded present, implications of 119
  Lighthouse beam 113, 114, 118–19, 132, 242n. 6
  meaning of life, questions regarding 111, 115, 131, 133, 201, 223
  now-phase/impressional consciousness 122–7
  objective inquiry 112–13
  phenomenology of time 120–6, 129
  post-traumatic temporal disorder 133, 243n. 16
  primal impression 122–4, 126
  problems in time analysis 112, 115
  retentional consciousness 123–8, 130
  retention vs recollection 128
  sedimentation (sinking process of experiences) 124–5
  specious present 119–20, 132

spotlight model vs Lighthouse model of time 118
spotlight view of time 116–18
time and agency in 223–5
time and tragedy 112
time as a destructive force 112–14
"Time Passes" section 112, 113–14, 118
transience vs permanence 129
Woolfian memory 128
Woolfian moment 119, 129
see also Briscoe, Lily (*To the Lighthouse*); Ramsey, Andrew (*To the Lighthouse*); Ramsay, Mr. (*To the Lighthouse*); Ramsay, Mrs. (*To the Lighthouse*)
transcendence 99, 121
transcendental memory 195
transience 28, 36, 39, 47, 49, 55, 82, 111, 112, 118–19, 126, 129, 132–4, 138, 140, 142, 201, 224, see also flux
transverberation 237n. 1
trauma 8, 93, 95, 103, 114, 159, 164, 210–11, 221, 234, 235
A Treatise of Human Nature 13
Turetzky, Philip 31, 36, 42–3, 47, 48, 49, 91, 94, 121–5, 129, 135, 138, 144, 146, 165, 188, 190–2, 195–6, 202–3, 205–6, 211, 240n. 2

Ulysses (novel) 4, 6–7, 19
  Aristotelian-Thomist soul 69, 70
  Bloom, Leopold, see Bloom, Leopold (*Ulysses*)
  "Circe" chapter 71, 77, 80, 206
  convulsions of metamorphosis, see "convulsions of metamorphosis"
  Deleuzian analysis of time in 186–7, 205–8
  drowning man vs the drowned man 74, 76, 77
  ensuing vs inveterate self 6, 74–5, 78, 79
  expression of "the subject fissured by time" 186–7
  formulation of time in 67
  "human mentality" in 68
  "Ithaca" chapter 67, 70, 74, 81
  joint self-perception of Stephen and Bloom 78–9

Joycean metempsychosis 68–9, 74–5, 78, 227, *see also* Joycean metempsychosis
metempsychosis, *see* metempsychosis
Molly's adultery 68, 75–8, 80–1, 205, 226
"Nausicaa" chapter 77–8, 82
perceptive peculiarities 72–5, 79
"Proteus" chapter 74, 81
"Scylla and Charybdis" chapter 67, 72, 74, 81
self-contained harmony 80–1
self-reflection 7, 72, 80
specular selfhood 7, 71, 72–3, 79
   of Bloom 71–2, 79–80
   of Stephen 71–4
Stephen, *see* Stephen, Dedalus (*Ulysses*)
"Telemachus" chapter 73
time and agency in 225–7
transmigration of the soul 68–70
The Unfortunate Traveller 9
"The Unnamable" 138, 139–40, 144, 146–7, 149–50, 197–201, 233
unrepeatable time 11, 12, 13–14, *see also* irreversible time

van-Rossum, Dohrn 28
Vitruvian Man 7, 99–100, 105–6
Vladimir 136, 143
von Simpson, Otto 101, 239n. 17

Waiting for Godot 1, 9, 23, 136, 143, 215, 232, 234, 244n. 1
Walsh, Peter (*Mrs. Dalloway*) 85–6, 90, 92, 95, 104–5, 108, 109, 221–2
   rejection by Clarissa 93–4, 103, 110
Watt 121, 124

Watt, Ian 17
Watts, Isaac 12
The Way of All Flesh 18
Weber 51
Whitehead, Alfred North 9, 23, 70, 72, 74, 75, 82, 85, 136–8, 146, 162, 163
Whitrow, G. J. 10
Wickham, Chris 10
Williams, Clifford 166, 172, 174
Williams, Donald C. 113, 166
Windelband, Wilhelm 135, 182, 244n. 1
Wittgenstein, Ludwig 43
Wittkower, Rudolf 99–101
Woods, Tim 22
Woolf, Virginia 5, 7, 24, see also *Mrs. Dalloway* (novel); *To the Lighthouse* (novel)
Woolfian memory (reconstructive rememoration) 128
Woolfian moment 119, 129, 201–2
Workman, Herbert B. 17
Works and Days 19
Wuthering Heights 18

Xenophon 13–14, 238n. 13

Yachnin, Paul 28
Yasuo, Yuasa 13
Young, Edward 1

Zahavi, Dan 123, 124
Zemka, Sue 20–2
Zimmerman, Dean W. 117